MW00715478

ELEMENTS OF ENVIRONMENTAL MANAGEMENT

As businesses face a growing array of environmental challenges, including climate change, air and water pollution, and solid waste management, environmental management has become an increasingly important area of expertise. *Elements of Environmental Management* is an interdisciplinary textbook for students and business professionals that integrates corporate environmental strategy with environmental economics, environmental law, and environmental engineering.

In *Elements of Environmental Management*, Werner Antweiler, an expert on international trade and environmental economics, considers a number of fundamental questions. How can businesses respond to public policies and regulatory requirements? How does emission permit trading work? What technological options are available to prevent or mitigate pollution? Using examples from a wide range of industries, Antweiler addresses these and other important questions, while providing the essential tools for examining and addressing environmental problems from a business perspective.

WERNER ANTWEILER is an associate professor in the Sauder School of Business at the University of British Columbia.

WERNER ANTWEILER

Elements of
Environmental
Management

UNIVERSITY OF TORONTO PRESS
Toronto Buffalo London

www.utppublishing.com

ISBN   978-1-4426-4835-7 (cloth)
ISBN   978-1-4426-2613-3 (paper)

Publication cataloguing information is available from Library and Archives Canada.

University of Toronto Press acknowledges the financial assistance to its publishing program of the Canada Council for the Arts and the Ontario Arts Council, an agency of the Government of Ontario.

University of Toronto Press acknowledges the financial support of the Government of Canada through the Canada Book Fund for its publishing activities.

Contents

List of Boxes x

List of Figures xi

List of Tables xiii

Preface xv

1   Sustainability and the Firm   1
    1.1   What is environmental management?   1
    1.2   The systems approach   3
    1.3   What is sustainability?   4
          1.3.1   Intergenerational trade-offs   5
          1.3.2   Exhaustible resources?   8
          1.3.3   Ecological footprint   9
          1.3.4   Macro measure: Adjusted net savings 12
          1.3.5   Micro measure: Entropy 13
    1.4   Which companies should care the most? 16
    1.5   Corporate social responsibility 18
          1.5.1   Characteristics of CSR 19
          1.5.2   Do stakeholders recognize CSR? 20
          1.5.3   The economics of CSR 22
          1.5.4   CSR strategy 27
    1.6   Summary 29
    1.7   Study questions and exercises 31

2   Environmental Issues 32
    2.1   Energy 32
    2.2   Fresh water 34
    2.3   Air pollution 38
    2.4   Waste management 39
    2.5   Transportation 41
    2.6   Noise 43
    2.7   Climate change 44
    2.8   Summary 52
    2.9   Study questions and exercises 53

3   Environmental Economics 55
    3.1   Basic economic concepts 56
          3.1.1   Pollutants and externalities 56
          3.1.2   Public goods and property rights 59
          3.1.3   Efficiency and fairness 61
    3.2   Policy instruments 63
          3.2.1   Instrument choice criteria 66

3.2.2   Technology and emission standards.............. 68
3.2.3   Environmental taxes 69
3.2.4   Tradeable emission permits 73
3.2.5   Hybrid regimes 77
3.2.6   Subsidies 79
3.2.7   Second-best approaches........................ 80
3.2.8   Static and dynamic efficiency 81
3.2.9   Dealing with uncertainty....................... 85
3.3   Environmental markets in action 85
3.4   Valuing the environment 88
3.4.1   Revealed-preference approaches................ 90
3.4.2   Stated-preference approaches 91
3.5   Cost-benefit analysis 94
3.6   International trade repercussions...................... 99
3.7   Summary 100
3.8   Study questions 101

4   Life Cycle Assessment....................................103
4.1   Concepts...104
4.2   Goal definition and scoping 106
4.3   Inventory analysis 106
4.4   Impact analysis 107
4.5   Improvement analysis...............................109
4.6   Environmental input-output analysis 110
4.7   Summary 113
4.8   Study questions and exercises........................114

5   Environmental Law 116
5.1   Pollution as a legal concept 116
5.2   Environmental law in Canada 118
5.2.1   Federal jurisdiction 120
5.2.2   Provincial jurisdiction 124
5.2.3   Municipal jurisdiction 125
5.2.4   Interjurisdictional cooperation..................126
5.2.5   Aboriginal rights 129
5.3   Environmental law in the United States 130
5.3.1   The Clean Air Act 133
5.3.2   The Clean Water Act...........................137
5.3.3   Hazardous pollutants and the superfund 139
5.4   Civil liability for environmental harm 141
5.5   Corporate and personal duties 142
5.5.1   The Canadian legal context.....................144
5.5.2   The US legal context 145
5.6   Damage, compensation, and remediation 146
5.7   International environmental treaties 148
5.7.1   International law 150
5.7.2   The GATT, the WTO, and NAFTA 153

      5.7.3 Environmental border adjustments 157
5.8 Summary 160
5.9 Study questions and exercises 161

6 Environmental Impact Assessment 163
6.1 Objectives and process overview 164
      6.1.1 The EIA process in the United States 164
      6.1.2 The EIA process in Canada 166
6.2 Screening 168
6.3 Scoping 169
6.4 Impact prediction 170
      6.4.1 Fixed-point scoring 174
      6.4.2 The analytic hierarchy process 175
6.5 Impact management 177
      6.5.1 Avoidance and mitigation 177
      6.5.2 Remediation techniques 178
6.6 Summary 179
6.7 Study questions and exercises 180

7 Environmental Management Systems 181
7.1 EMS components 181
7.2 Code of conduct 183
7.3 Environmental management plan 184
      7.3.1 Pollution prevention (P2) plan 186
      7.3.2 Environmental emergency (E2) plan 188
7.4 Environmental audit 190
7.5 ISO 14000 191
      7.5.1 The certification process 193
      7.5.2 The adoption decision 194
      7.5.3 Effectiveness 197
7.6 Summary 199
7.7 Study questions 199

8 Corporate Environmental Strategy 200
8.1 Strategy space 200
8.2 Green innovation and technology 202
      8.2.1 Process innovation 203
      8.2.2 Product innovation and differentiation 206
      8.2.3 Servicizing 208
8.3 Green sourcing 209
8.4 Green marketing 212
      8.4.1 Green branding 213
      8.4.2 Eco-labelling 214
      8.4.3 The greenwashing trap 217
      8.4.4 Green price premium 219
      8.4.5 The credibility gap 221
8.5 Stakeholders and the role of ENGOs 223

  8.6   Overcoming nimbyism 228
  8.7   Managing adversity 230
        8.7.1   Environmental risk management 230
        8.7.2   Crisis management 231
  8.8   Summary 234
  8.9   Study questions and exercises 235

9   Pollution Abatement Technology 237
  9.1   Air pollution 237
        9.1.1   Dispersion 238
        9.1.2   Control strategies 241
        9.1.3   Abatement devices: Particulates 242
        9.1.4   Abatement devices: Gases 252
        9.1.5   Specific pollutants 256
  9.2   Water pollution 260
        9.2.1   Types and sources 260
        9.2.2   Wastewater treatment 264
  9.3   Solid waste management 276
        9.3.1   Solid waste streams 279
        9.3.2   Landfills 280
        9.3.3   Incineration 284
        9.3.4   Hazardous waste 286
  9.4   Summary 287
  9.5   Study questions and exercises 288

10   Energy Systems 290
  10.1   Energy supply, energy demand, and Hubbert's peak 291
  10.2   Coal, oil and gas 294
  10.3   Nuclear power 296
  10.4   Levellized energy cost 301
  10.5   Renewable energy 304
  10.6   Smart power grids and super grids 313
  10.7   Energy conservation and energy efficiency 315
        10.7.1   Technology 317
        10.7.2   Conservation measures 319
  10.8   Summary 323
  10.9   Study questions and exercises 324

11   Resource Management 326
  11.1   Mining 327
        11.1.1   Economics of exhaustible resources 328
        11.1.2   Backstop technologies 334
        11.1.3   Recycling 335
        11.1.4   Environmental challenges 339
  11.2   Forestry 340
        11.2.1   Optimal forest rotation 342
        11.2.2   Management practices 346
        11.2.3   Pulp and paper mills 349

11.3 Fisheries 351
11.3.1 Fisheries economics 352
11.3.2 Fisheries management and public policy 354
11.4 Summary 361
11.5 Study questions and exercises........................ 362

12 Environmental Management for the Next Thousand
Centuries 363
12.1 The time horizon 364
12.2 Population growth 365
12.3 Survival challenges 368
12.4 Long-term power sources 370
12.5 Long-term mineral resources 372
12.6 The sustainability agenda 374
12.7 Study questions 379

Reference Tables 381

Bibliography 383

Index 387

List of Boxes

1.1 The Easter Island Mystery 9
1.2 CSR and RBC's Blue Water Project 30
2.1 Yemen's Water Crisis 35
2.2 Bisphenol-A 41
2.3 How do firms measure their carbon dioxide releases? 53
3.1 Water Rights in California 62
3.2 Carbon Offsets in British Columbia 89
3.3 The Glen Canyon Dam and Recreation 95
4.1 Fluorescent or Incandescent? 105
4.2 An LCA Battle: Disposable or Reusable Diapers? 110
5.1 The Genetically Modified Organism (GMO) Dispute 119
5.2 Directors' Responsibility 144
5.3 The Mexico-US Tuna-Dolphin Case 154
5.4 The Shrimp-Turtle Case 156
5.5 Green Protectionism? 158
6.1 Mackenzie Valley Gas Project EIA 167
7.1 A Tale of Two Mines 185
7.2 ISO 14001 and Parks Canada 196
8.1 Apple's Green Notebooks 204
8.2 Servicizing Cars: The Story of car2go 210
8.3 The Ten Signs of Greenwashing 218
8.4 The Oil Industry's Credibility Gap 224
8.5 Partnering with ENGOs 227
9.1 Victoria's Secret 266
9.2 Shell, Dawson Creek, and Water Recycling 275
9.3 Plastic Bag or Paper Bag? 278
10.1 Energy Efficiency and the Rebound Effect 316
10.2 Energy Efficiency in the Pulp and Paper Industry 318
11.1 The Green Paradox 336
11.2 Mining and Tailings 341
11.3 Logging and the Northern Spotted Owl 348
11.4 Mountain Pine Beetle Epidemic 350
11.5 The Canada-US Pacific Salmon Dispute 358
11.6 Chilean Sea Bass 360

List of Figures

1.1   An Input-Output View of the Environmental Impact of a
      Firm   3
1.2   Sustainable = bearable + equitable + viable?   4
1.3   Ecological Footprint and Economic Development 11
1.4   Ecological Footprint and Biocapacity 11
1.5   CSR Strategy 28

2.1   World Water Scarcity 36
2.2   Global Surface Temperature Anomalies 46
2.3   Global GHG Mitigation Cost Curve 51

3.1   Pollution Sources and Sinks 57
3.2   Cap-and-Trade versus Green Tax 70
3.3   Effect of Green Tax on Firm 71
3.4   Firm Heterogeneity and Marginal Abatement Cost 74
3.5   Hybrid Regimes 78
3.6   Feebate 79
3.7   Abatement Costs and Innovation 83
3.7   Abatement Cost and Innovation (continued) 84
3.8   Cost-Benefit Analysis and Uncertainty 97

4.1   Life Cycle Assessment 104

7.1   The Enviromental Management System Pyramid 182
7.2   Environmental Management Standards 192

8.1   The Corporate Environmental Strategy Space 202
8.2   Organic Eco-labels in the United States, Canada, and the
      European Union 215
8.3   Generic and Plastic Recycling Logos 216
8.4   Elements of Green Credibility 222
8.5   Corporate Environmental Stakeholders 225

9.1   A Decision Tree for Particulate Matter Abatement 244
9.2   Characteristics of Particles and Effective Range of
      Abatement Devices by Particle Diameter 244
9.3   Baghouse 245
9.4   Cyclone 245
9.5   Electrostatic Precipitator 247
9.6   Venturi Scrubber 251
9.7   Spray Chamber 251
9.8   Bubbler 252
9.9   Packed Tower 252

9.10 Regenerative Thermal Oxidizer 255
9.11 Parallel Plate Separator................................. 268
9.12 Circular Settling Tank with Sludge Scraper and Scum
     Skimmer 270
9.13 Trickling Filter.. 271
9.14 Effective Range of Water Filtration Methods 273
9.15 Waste Stream Composition 279
9.16 Diverted Materials by Type 279
9.17 Landfill Cross-Section 281
9.18 Landfill Top Cover 281
9.19 Bottom Liner 281

10.1 The Rising Price of Crude Oil 1988–2013 291
10.2 The Hubbert Curve: U.S. Oil Production 1900–2013 292
10.3 The North American Oil Price Gap 293
10.4 Nuclear Energy around the Globe 301
10.5 Levellized Energy Cost: Sample Calculation (cents per
     kWh) 303
10.6 Worldwide Net Electricity Generation from Renewable
     Sources, 1980–2011 305
10.7 Worldwide Net Electricy Generation from Wind Energy
     (left panel) and Solar, Tide, and Wave Energy (right
     panel), 2000–2011 309
10.8 Worldwide Production of Biofuels, 2000–2010 311

11.1 Resource Price Path 330
11.2 Recycling and Government Intervention 337
11.3 Forest Rotation Sequence 343
11.4 Optimal Forest Rotation 343
11.5 Collapse of the Atlantic Cod, 1950–2009 351
11.6 Efficient Yield and Maximum Sustainable Yield for a
     Fishery.. 353
11.7 Fisheries Policy under Uncertainty 355

12.1 Cartogram of World Population.......................... 366
12.2 Trends in Birth and Death Rates of Developing and
     Developed Countries 366
12.3 Fertility Drops as Affluence Rises 367

List of Tables

1.1   Adjusted Net Savings, including particulate emission damage, as a percentage of gross national income, 2006–2010 average 13

1.2   Shannon-Wiener Diversity Index for Canadian Forest Biomass [million tonnes] circa 2004 14

1.3   Principles and Subject Areas of ISO 26000 20

1.4   *Corporate Knights* S&P/TSX 60 Corporate Responsibility Ranking, 2010 21

1.5   CSR Typology 23

3.1   The Value of a Statistical Life (VSL) 92

3.2   Cost-Benefit Analysis and Discount Factors 98

5.1   Canadian Ambient Air Quality Standards 128

5.2   US National Ambient Air Quality Standards (2013) 134

6.1   Classification System for Environmental Impacts 171

6.2   Example of a Weighted Magnitude Matrix 175

6.3   The Analytic Hierarchy Process 176

7.1   The ISO 14000 Family 191

7.2   Reasons for obtaining ISO 14001 certification 198

9.1   Air Quality Health Index 240

9.2   Separation Process Matrix for Gasesous Output 242

9.3   Municipal Wastewater Plants in Metro Vancouver, 2009 . . . 262

9.4   Wastewater Treatment Stages 265

9.5   Municipal Wastewater Treatment in Canada 265

9.6   Wastewater Treatment Methods in Canada 267

9.7   Comparison of LFGTE and WTE 285

10.1   Fossil Fuels in Comparison 295

10.2   Current and Future Nuclear Reactor Designs 299

10.3   Estimated Levellized Energy Cost for 2017 Plants ($/MWh) 304

10.4   Ontario, Residential Weekday Time-of-Use Pricing, May 2012 314

12.1   Long-Term Potential for Energy Sources 371

12.2   Long-Term Resource Abundance and Scarcity 374

A.1   Orders of Magnitude 381

A.2   Metric System 381

A.3 Energy Units and Their Conversion 382
A.4 Common Metric and Imperial Units and Their Conversion 382

Preface

Environmental management is becoming increasingly important for businesses. Firms need to manage their direct and indirect impact on the environment, and they need to develop a corresponding corporate environmental strategy. At a managerial level, the interdisciplinary nature of environmental management poses a major challenge because decision-makers are often trained only in one subject area. Environmental managers need to develop competence in a broad range of subject areas, from law to economics to engineering. This book attempts to bridge the gap across these subject areas by making them accessible to a managerial audience. It provides a bird's-eye perspective on the "tools of the trade" of an environmental manager and develops an interdisciplinary framework for formulating corporate environmental strategy.

Many of the environmental management books currently on the market focus quite narrowly on management systems or quite broadly on incorporating sustainability themes into a business context. My book aims at a different audience. It is targeted at business students who wish to familiarize themselves with the role of an environmental manager in a business. This book originates in a course on Environmental Management that I have developed for the Sauder School of Business at the University of British Columbia. This course for senior undergraduate and first-year graduate students is less concerned with identifying environmental problems from a societal perspective and more concerned with identifying environmental solutions from a business perspective. Because of the interdisciplinary character of the book, the key building blocks (economics, law, engineering, and strategy) are covered at a level that is readily accessible to non-specialists.

I have tried to avoid mathematical notation and relied where necessary on diagrams and illustrative examples instead. The exception is the chapter on resource management, where dynamic optimization is used to develop the key principles of optimal resource extraction. I have also purposefully limited citations to those sources that the reader may find useful for further consultation, or where acknowledging the source of material that I have used is essential. At the beginning of each chapter I discuss relevant sources that the reader may wish to refer to for deepening the understanding of the subject matter of that chapter.

The books that I acknowledge at the beginning of each chapter were consulted extensively in the preparation of this book. I would like to acknowledge specifically Goodstein (2010) for environmental economics, Benidickson (2008) for environmental law, Esty and Winston (2006) for corporate environmental strategy, Davis and Cornwell (2008) for environmental engineering, and Bonnet and Woltjer (2008) for the concluding chapter on the time horizon of sustainability. The influence of these books is clearly visible in many places. I owe these authors a debt of gratitude and appreciation. As I am an economist by training, my domain expertise covers environmental economics. My business school experience influenced my thinking on corporate environmental strategy. Distilling the knowledge from other disciplines, especially law and engineering, has been a pleasant learning experience over the course of many years.

This textbook has been designed so that it can be used comfortably as a teaching tool for a one-semester course (about 36 teaching hours). This made it necessary to limit the scope of the book. The focus of this book is on industry and businesses. Environmental issues relating to private households and private transportation are not covered extensively. Along these lines, urban development and improving building designs are not covered here.

This book has been written from a North American perspective. Specifically, the chapter on environmental law has been written with a focus on the institutional context in Canada and the United States, highlighting both the similarities and differences of the regulatory approaches in both countries.

I would like to thank the many people who have contributed ideas and thoughts to this book. My co-authors on a number of research papers—Brian Copeland, Sumeet Gulati, Kathryn Harrison, and Scott Taylor—have all greatly influenced my understanding of environmental economics and environmental policy. They have all contributed to turning my attention towards this area of study. My divisional colleagues James Brander, Keith Head, Masao Nakamura, Peter Nemetz, and Ralph Winter have all engaged me in stimulating discussions about various subject matters related to this book. I would also like to acknowledge the feedback from the many students who have taken my Environmental Management course at UBC. The discussions I had with many of them have inspired me to explore new topics and issues. Last but not least, this book would not have been possible without the encouragement, support, and patience of my wife Melanie.

Finally, I would also like to thank Jennifer DiDomenico and her colleagues at University of Toronto Press for their advice, help, and expertise along the way towards publishing this book.

Vancouver, December 2013   *Werner Antweiler*

Chapter 1
Sustainability and the Firm

1.1 What is environmental management?

Environmental management is becoming increasingly important for businesses. Yet there are many misperceptions about what environmental management entails. Environmental management is sometimes confused with *management of the environment*—but it is not the environment that needs managing but the human interaction with it. Environmental management is also sometimes equated with sustainability. We will explore the notion of sustainability in greater detail in the next section, but in short, sustainability is a concept that captures the ecological capacity to endure. As such, sustainability is a much more general concept and an *objective* that focuses on outcomes. Environmental management focuses more narrowly on tools, methods, procedures, and *process*, and therefore its scope is much more limited. Most environmental improvements require economic trade-offs, and therefore environmental management is primarily a decision-making framework.

Environmental management should also not be confused with the setting of environmental policies for businesses. Defining environmental objectives is primarily up to society, represented by governments and regulators. Businesses are primarily concerned with compliance: doing what they are asked to do by society when it comes to environmental concerns. Some businesses go beyond compliance by voluntarily exceeding government-mandated standards. We will explore the motivations behind these voluntary actions in much greater detail in a later part of this book.

To understand the scope and purpose of environmental management it is also useful to know the managerial roles in a firm that deal with environmental concerns. At the top, many companies have created the role of a Chief Sustainability Officer (CSO). A CSO is charged with a company's overall environmental strategy just like a Chief Financial Officer (CFO), Chief Operations Officer (COO), or Chief Technical Offer (CTO) is charged with top-level corporate strategy in their respective domains. At mid-management levels, we may often find a genuine 'environmental manager' (with a business administration background) who oversees the implementation of environmental policies, develops plans for deploying pollution abatement equipment, and is responsible for keeping track of the company's environmental performance. Environmental managers often work in a team with environmental engineers (typically with a background in civil or chemical engineering), who are in charge of a company's water and air pollution control devices, and who manage recycling, waste disposal, or public health issues. Larger firms may also employ an environmental lawyer whose main area of responsibility is to deal with legal compliance issues, prepare legal documents for obtaining required environmental permits, or deal with issues of legal liability. Firms may also obtain third-party help from environmental auditors (for example, as part of their ISO-14000 certification) or environmental consultants (to deal with specific problems outside their own expertise).

> **Environmental management** is a system of administrative functions that are used to (i) develop; (ii) implement; and (iii) monitor the *environmental strategy* of a business.

There are two key ingredients in this definition. First is the reference to corporate environmental strategy. A firm's environmental strategy is the set of *environmental objectives* and the accompanying *techniques or procedures* to achieve them. In turn, environmental objectives aim to prevent, reduce, minimize, or remedy environmental damage caused by a firm's productive activities. Objectives can also involve presenting a particular corporate image or developing new technologies. Techniques or procedures focus on the implementation of these objectives and may include the choice of particular pollution prevention methods, the choice of particular pollution abatement equipment, or engaging a firm's stakeholders in a particular manner. Techniques tend to be very specific in nature, such as methods for reducing pollution, waste, consumption of natural resources, or energy.

The second key element in the definition is the reference to a systems approach. The systems approach ties together all functions, often through an explicit environmental management system (EMS). The ISO-14001 standard is aimed at providing a unified framework for adopting an EMS that can be audited by independent third parties. The systems approach considers environmental strategy as a closed-loop process. Developing objectives is followed by implementing these objectives through particular techniques. The implemented techniques then get monitored for achieving the objectives. Finally, the results from the monitoring process feed back into the design of the objectives, as they may inform which objectives are attainable and which are not, or they may inform which techniques need to be adjusted or modified in order to improve their performance.

Fig. 1.1 An Input-Output View of the Environmental Impact of a Firm

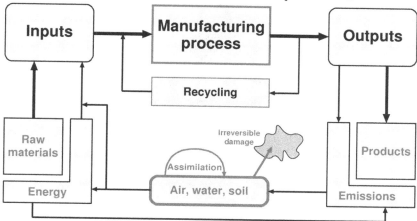

1.2 The systems approach

A system is a complex structure of interacting units. The ecosystem is a prime example, where natural elements such as air and water interact with living organisms of all kinds in interdependent ways. Systems thinking, or integrative thinking, is a way to understand such complex structures. In many areas of research we are used to focus on precisely identifiable individual components of the system, trying to understand the mechanisms in isolation. By comparison, when confronted with a complex system, one needs to take into account that small changes in one part of the system can have noticeable changes throughout the entire system. This is particularly true when systems exhibit tipping points or other forms of non-linear behaviour. An improvement in one part of the system can adversely affect another part of the system.

Businesses interact with the ecosystem in a myriad of ways. Figure 1.1 tries to capture some of these paths. It is useful to think of a business in terms of its inputs and outputs. On the input side there is a variety of raw materials (metals, minerals, plastics, etc.) and energy (oil, gas, electricity, etc.). Human labour could be thought of as a particular form of energy as well in this context. Manufacturing transforms inputs into outputs, both desirable outputs such as the goods a company wants to sell and undesirable outputs such as emissions and waste products that are by-products of the manufacturing process. Some undesirable outputs can be captured and transformed back into inputs. In the car industry, scrap metal or aluminum is collected and transformed back into usable materials. Emissions are released into the natural en-

Fig. 1.2 Sustainable = bearable + equitable + viable?

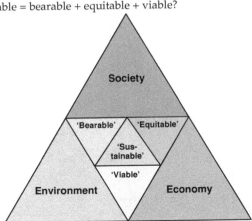

vironment, where they can be either assimilated or accumulated. As-similated emissions are rendered harmless through natural processes or through dilution. On the other hand, accumulated emissions persist and cause damage to the ecosystem, and this damage may at times be irreversible. To reduce emissions, energy is needed for end-of-pipe treatment or breaking harmful substances into harmless substances.

1.3 What is sustainability?

Sustainability is a notion that has been embraced widely in society. Many businesses are committed to sustainable development. Yet, it is difficult to agree on a precise definition of what is implied by sustainable development. Sustainability is aimed at balancing the needs of society with the need to preserve the natural environment. Many attempts have been made to define sustainability, but ultimately the problem comes down to finding a *quantitative measure* that describes whether a certain human activity, such as industrial or agricultural production, is sustainable or unsustainable.

A popular definition of sustainability describes it as the intersection of three areas that decompose sustainability into social sustainability, environmental sustainability, and economic sustainability. Figure 1.2 illustrates the concept. What is socially and environmentally sustainable is bearable to society and the environment. Activities that are both socially and economically sustainable are equitable, and activities that are environmentally and economically sustainable are viable. Therefore, sustainable activities must be bearable, viable, and equitable. This implies that there are trade-offs in each direction. It is immediately clear that it is immensely difficult to operationalize these concepts. What exactly is bearable, viable, and equitable? Different people will have very different notions about these concepts.

The sustainability triangle in figure 1.2 of environment, society, and economy is also referred to as the 3Ps of sustainability: **planet, people, profits**. Businesses frequently incorporate the 3Ps into their public reporting: environmental and social accounting are added to the conventional financial accounting and reporting.

1.3.1 Intergenerational trade-offs

In 1983 the United Nations convened a commission to study environment and development in the context of an accelerating deterioration of the human environment and natural resources. In 1987 the commission issued a report that was named after its chair, Gro Harlem Brundtland. The *Brundtland Report* provided one of the first widely accepted definitions of sustainability: 'Sustainable development is development that meets the needs of the present without compromising the ability of future generations to meet their own needs.'

There are two key concepts embedded in this definition: (i) the concept of 'needs,' and (ii) the concept of intergenerational responsibility. Unfortunately, both concepts suffer from critical flaws. First, what exactly is a 'need'? How is a need different from, say, consumption or utility (a concept widely used in economics)? What precisely are the needs of current and future generations? How do we even know the needs of future generations that have not even been born yet? The implicit assumption is that future generations wish to maintain a standard of living no less than our own, although it is not clear what the appropriate measure for a 'standard of living' might be. Is gross domestic product (GDP) per capita the appropriate measure, or energy consumption per person, or biomass per square kilometre?

Perhaps most problematic in the above definition is the lack of reference to a notion of ecological balance or ecological equilibrium, one that is based on the planet's ability to sustain a population of a given size indefinitely.

Eventually, a report by the United Nations Environment Programme (UNEP) developed a more useful definition that makes explicit reference to the concept of a *carrying capacity*:

Sustainable development means improving the quality of human life while living within the carrying capacity of supporting ecosystems.

(UNEP 1991, *'Caring for the Earth'*)

To economists this sounds a lot more meaningful. It entails a familiar concept: constrained optimization. We wish to increase (maximize) human welfare subject to the constraint of maintaining a viable (nondegrading) ecosystem that supports a population. The notion of a carrying capacity is closely linked to the idea of an ecological footprint that tries to measure a population's use of that capacity.

Before exploring the notion of an ecological footprint in greater detail, it is worthwhile returning to the notion of intergenerational equity that was raised in the Brundtland definition of sustainability. Implicit in this definition is that current generations care about the well-being of future generations. Economists have developed a method for quantifying how much we take future generations into account, and thus for quantifying the trade-off between current welfare and future welfare. This method involves a discount rate, or more precisely, a *social discount rate r*. This measure is widely used in cost-benefit analysis and has important implications for resource allocation. A high discount rate (say, 3-8% per annum) gives greater weight to current welfare by discounting future welfare. A low discount rate (say, 0.1-2.0% per annum) gives much greater weight to future welfare by discounting it less. Mathematically, for benefits b and costs c that occur indefinitely into the future, the discount rate r implies a net present value of $(b - c)/r$. As r gets smaller and smaller in the denominator, holding $b - c$ constant, the net present value becomes larger and larger. Consider a project where all the costs occur now and all the benefits accrue in the future (but at a constant rate). Then the net benefit of this project is $b/r - c$ because c is not discounted. It is immediately apparent that assuming different social discount rates will lead to big changes in the net present value, and thus influence whether the project is adopted or not.

Sustainability arguments tend to give greater weight to future generations than most economic applications do, where future gains and losses are discounted at commercial rates of 3-8% per annum that closely track interest rates. Which discount rate is most appropriate remains a matter of great controversy. Nowhere is this controversy more apparent than in the discussion about the appropriate policy towards climate change. The *Stern Review* on the economics of climate change (Stern, 2006, 2007) made the case for drastic action on climate change, suggesting that 1% of world GDP needed to be devoted to fighting climate change if the world was to avoid a 20% reduction in world GDP. Nordhaus (2007) and others criticized the *Stern Review* for using a very low discount rate of 1.4%, which is unusual for economic modelling. To be clear, there is no consensus among economists about what the 'right' discount rate is, but any study that employs social discount rates should probably provide sensitivity tests that identify how changes in the social discount rate effect the results.

The use of a constant discount rate to study long-lived environmental problems such as climate change has two disadvantages: (i) the prescribed policy is sensitive to the discount rate; and (ii) with moderate-to-high discount rates, large future damages have almost no effect on current decisions.

Nevertheless, there are possible solutions to the problem of using a simple discount rate. Economists have suggested discount rates that change over time, starting at a high level today and declining progressively in following years. Consider the following example: you may prefer $1 today to $2 tomorrow, but you may prefer to receive $2 in ten years plus one day to $1 in ten years. The elapse of a single day is relevant over a short period but not over a very long period. This notion is captured in what is known as quasi-hyperbolic discounting. This notion is based on the assumption that individuals' ability to make distinctions between valuations diminishes for more distant events and thus displays a present bias.

There is yet another caveat that impedes intergenerational trade-offs of any sort. Transacting between current and future generations is made difficult by the absence of an organized market for such transactions. This is a fundamental market inefficiency. Overcoming this intergenerational market inefficiency is proving hard. How can you make a contract with a party that has not been born yet? In the end, the current generation may bequeath their children and grandchildren with environmental burdens just as nations can pile up debt and more debt to leave to future taxpayers. The unborn generations can't complain and don't have a vote in elections.

The social discount rate plays an important role in economic growth models. Intertemporal choice problems can be summarized in the Ramsey equation of economic growth. In a welfare optimum of an economic growth model, the rate of return on capital—equivalent to the social discount rate—is determined by (i) the generational rate of time preference ϱ, (ii) policy aversion to intergenerational consumption inequality α, and (iii) the rate of growth of generational consumption g. Then the Ramsey equation stipulates that $r = \varrho + \alpha g$. A key point about the Ramsey equation is that the social discount rate is the return on capital as determined by the Ramsey model: private and social returns are the same.

In the context of climate change and the *Stern Review*, the appropriate social discount rate was, and is, hotly disputed. Arguably, it is the rate of return on capital that drives efficient current emissions reductions. The *Stern Review* assumes $\alpha = 1$ and $g = 1.3\%$ long-run growth, along with $\varrho = 0.1\%$. But $r = 1.4\%$ is well below the typical $r = 4\%$ observed empirically.

Which discount rate should one use in practice? The answer to this question is perhaps one of the most important in all of economics. The question is also contingent on the location and whether the discounting is within the same generation or across generations. In the context of Canada, Boardman et al. (2010b) recommend a discount rate of 3.5% for projects that are intra-generational (less than 50 years), while for issues involving inter-generational impacts—such as climate change— a schedule of time-declining social discount rates is most appropriate. Time-declining discount rates reflect greater uncertainty about the future. Moore et al. (2013) find similar numbers for the United States.

1.3.2 Exhaustible resources?

A common perception among environmentalists is that our global economy is outgrowing the capacity of the earth to support it, that we are consuming renewable resources faster than they can regenerate, and that we are consuming exhaustible resources at a precarious rate that will impede the economic opportunities of future generations.

One of the first to warn about the perils of rapid population growth was the Reverend Thomas R. Malthus (1798). He proposed a dynamic model that linked population growth to resource use. Specifically, Malthusian population dynamics maintains that increases in real income arising from productivity growth will lead to population growth, which in turn will dampen or even reverse the income gains. Population growth may also overshoot productivity gains at times, which would then lead to painful economic adjustments. The case of Easter Island, discussed in box 1.1 on page 9, is a revealing example of a society falling into the trap of excessive resource exploitation that ultimately led to its collapse.

Some renewable resources, such as forests, may depend on a particular state of the ecosystem to maintain their productivity. Excessive harvesting of forests can lead to soil erosion, and monocultures can impede forests' resilience with respect to infestations or natural fires.

Exhaustible resources pose a particular dilemma. What is the optimal path of resource extraction? How fast, and how much? What happens when the resource is depleted is another problem. Is there an alternative resource that can be used as a substitute? As resources become scarce, their price will rise. This will make alternatives (substitutes) more attractive economically. Such alternatives are known as backstop resources or backstop technologies.

Box 1.1: The Easter Island Mystery

Easter Island is a small Pacific island some 3,200 km off the coast of Chile with a population of just under 5,000 (in 2010). The island was discovered by the Dutch explorer Jacob Roggeveen on Easter Sunday 1722, hence the name. The Polynesian population at the time of discovery was estimated at about 3,000, which appeared to be significantly less than a few hundred years earlier. The island's history has been an archaeological mystery. It has been estimated that the island had been colonized by about 700 CE. Evidence of a high culture is found in the presence of large carved statues, some weighing as much as 80 tons. When the island was discovered in 1722, the island's population size and technical skills seemed incapable of having produced such monuments. The island was also effectively without any forests.

While many exotic theories have been advanced to explain the Easter Island Mystery, the theory that best explains the facts is an adaptation of a Ricardo-Malthus model described in Brander and Taylor (1998). After initial settlement, the island supported a great palm forest, as was shown through carbon-dated samples of pollen records. An important activity after settlement was using the available forests to make canoes and other tools, or as firewood. With rapid population growth—peaking at about 10,000 sometime around 1400—the forests declined rapidly. The prime period of sculpture carving took place between about 1100 and 1500. However, by about 1500 the palm forest was entirely gone. Loss of forest cover also impacted agricultural production negatively. By about 1500, the Polynesian high culture that was supported by ample forests had collapsed.

Easter Island is a story of a society that experienced a boom and a crash, one that is quite consistent with the Malthusian story of rapid population growth that starts depleting resources precipitously. Once the resources had depleted past the point of possible recovery (due to soil erosion), economic collapse was inevitable.

1.3.3 Ecological footprint

The idea of measuring sustainability through an index called the ecological footprint was pioneered by William Rees at the University of British Columbia together with his then doctoral student Mathis Wackernagel. As described in Rees and Wackernagel (1994), a person's ecological footprint represents the amount of biologically productive land and sea area needed to regenerate the resources consumed by that person, and to absorb and render harmless the corresponding waste, given prevailing technology and resource management practices. Originally this was captured in a measure of hectares of land per person. Thus it is possible to compare a country's land area with its ecological footprint, showing that some countries had a much larger footprint than territory.

As is shown in figure 1.3 with a double-logarithmic axis, there is a strong correlation between human development (as captured by per-capita GDP) and the size of the ecological footprint. Rich nations have a much larger per-capita footprint than poor ntations. The dotted line at a level of 1.8 global hectares per person marks the global average biocapacity. Whether the ecological footprint of consumption is above or below a country's total biocapacity is indicated by the colour of the bubble: green (dark grey) for an ecological reserve and red (light grey) for an ecological deficit.

> A country whose **ecological footprint** exceeds its **biocapacity** runs an ecological deficit, while a country whose **biocapacity** exceeds its **ecological footprint** maintains an ecological reserve.

Figure 1.4 compares each country's ecological footprint against its biocapacity. The diagonal line indicates equality. Countries above and to the left have an ecological deficit, and countries below and to the right have an ecological reserve. A country's total biocapacity is the sum of cropland, grazing land, forest, fishing ground, and built land. A country's ecological footprint of consumption is the sum of footprints on these five land categories, plus an additional carbon footprint. Countries such as the United States and Canada have large footprint: 7.0 and 8.0, respectively. This is considerably larger than the average 2.7 hectares per person on a global scale. However, Canada has a much larger biocapacity (14.9) than the United States (3.9), and as a result, Canada has a large ecological reserve while the United States has a large ecological deficit. What contributes most to Canada's large biocapacity are its vast forests and fishing grounds.

Despite being a milestone in quantifying sustainability and capturing the notion of carrying capacity or biocapacity, the concept of an ecological footprint suffers from a number of shortcomings. A popular criticism of the footprint analysis is the application of this analysis to small, densely populated areas such as cities (e.g., New York) or small countries (e.g., Singapore). The large footprints of these geographic entities seem to suggest that these cities are unsustainable. Yet, the footprint analysis confined to small spatial entities ignores these regions' hinterland. Economic specialization and international trade further complicate the footprint analysis. Some critics argue that the footprint concept makes sense only globally, as the Earth as a whole is a closed system. Viewed globally, the footprint measure of the Global Footprint Network indicates that the current ecological footprint of consumption (at 2.7 hectares per person) exceeds the earth's biocapacity (at 1.8 hectares per person) by 50%. Whatever the merits of this estimate, the trend in the footprint indices has been mostly upward, and that remains alarming.

Fig. 1.3 Ecological Footprint and Economic Development

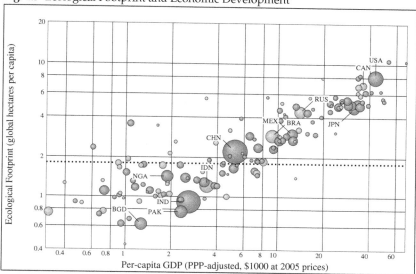

Fig. 1.4 Ecological Footprint and Biocapacity

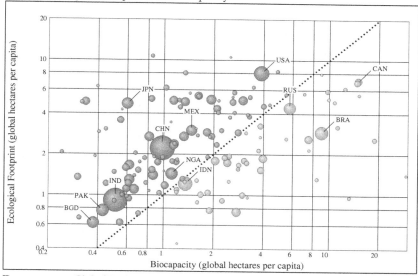

Data sources: Global Footprint Network, *National Footprint Accounts*, 2010 edition; World Bank, *World Development Indicators*. Bubble size: population.

1.3.4 Macro measure: Adjusted net savings

Sustainability comes in two varieties, weak and strong. Strong sustainability keeps animate natural capital intact, while weak sustainability maintains human living standards. Strong sustainability employs absolute standards. Weak sustainability allows future generations to achieve the same living standards as our own. This is essentially the notion expressed in the *Brundtland Report* definition of sustainability. Weak sustainability employs relative standards. Strong sustainability entails the concept of stewardship toward the natural world and other species on our planet. It thus relies heavily on measures of biocapacity, biodiversity, and other ecosystem variables. Weak sustainability allows for environmental-economic trade-offs. However, even capturing weak sustainability at the country level poses significant empirical challenges.

A nation's economic performance is captured by its GDP, often expressed in per-capita terms. However, it is widely recognized that GDP does not take a nation's environmental performance into account. Numerous alternatives have been suggested to express the notion of sustainability in a single figure for an individual country. For example, the United Nations Development Program (UNDP) uses the *Human Development Index* to capture health, education, and income as the three key dimensions of a country's wealth. The UNDP does not take environmental performance into account, however.

Head (2012) argues that the most useful macro measure is adjusted net savings (ANS), which starts off with a country's national accounts in a similar manner as GDP. ANS has three main elements. The first element is investment in plant and equipment net of depreciation. The second element is investment in human capital through education and investment in intellectual property through research and development. The third element, subtracted from the sum of the first two, is the degradation of natural capital, which includes depletion of natural resources and pollution damages. The World Bank has recently started publishing such numbers.

While there remain methodological difficulties calculating pollution damages and resource depletion, the insights gained from this approach nevertheless shed an interesting light on development. Table 1.1 shows the top and bottom twenty countries by adjusted net savings, expressed as a percentage of gross national income, over the five-year period 2006–2010. Remarkably, China is on top of this list despite major environmental problems. Its top spot on the sustainability ranking is due to to China's enormous investment in human and physical capital. Congo is the least sustainable country due to underinvestment in education and capital formation, as well as overexploitation of natural resources.

Table 1.1 Adjusted Net Savings, including particulate emission damage, as a percentage of gross national income, 2006–2010 average

Top 20 Countries			Bottom 20 Countries		
Rank	Country	ANS(%)	Rank	Country	ANS(%)
1	China	36.13	133	Congo	−66.67
2	Singapore	35.51	132	Burundi	−28.56
3	Nepal	25.91	131	Angola	−27.98
4	Namibia	25.66	130	Trinidad and Tobago	−20.08
5	Botswana	24.90	129	Guinea	−17.07
6	Morocco	24.65	128	Yemen	−14.71
7	Algeria	24.55	127	Liberia	−13.96
8	Bangladesh	24.03	126	St.Vincent	−8.57
9	India	21.63	125	Oman	−8.28
10	Panama	21.21	124	Solomon Islands	−6.59
11	Thailand	20.89	123	Kazakhstan	−6.59
12	South Korea	20.87	122	Sudan	−5.83
13	Switzerland	19.49	121	Greece	−2.89
14	Sweden	19.13	120	Iceland	−2.36
15	Belarus	18.53	119	Portugal	−1.35
16	Sri Lanka	17.96	118	Mozambique	−1.26
17	Malaysia	17.62	117	Brunei	−0.82
18	Kuwait	17.54	116	Syria	−0.71
19	Norway	16.67	115	Georgia	−0.47
20	Luxembourg	16.04	114	Saudi Arabia	−0.29

Source: World Bank, *World Development Indicators*, series NY.ADJ.SVNG.GN.ZS.

1.3.5 Micro measure: Entropy

In the attempt to quantify sustainability, some progress is being made to use concepts borrowed from physics, specifically thermodynamics. The fact that an ecosystem contains thousands of interacting species leads to the question of how to capture the system's dynamics and stability, and whether the system has a stable stationary state (a steady state in which all growth rates are zero). Entropy is a useful statistical measure to capture overall changes of a complex system and to determine if it is in a steady state. Entropy can also be usefully employed as a measure to capture diversity of an ecosystem, such as species biodiversity.

Biodiversity of an ecosystem can be captured through the Shannon-Wiener diversity index:

$$S = -\sum_{i=1}^{n} p_i \ln p_i \quad , \tag{1.1}$$

where p_i is the fraction of individuals belong to species i. If there are n species with equal occurrence so that $p_i = 1/n$, then $S = \ln(n)$ and

Table 1.2 Shannon-Wiener Diversity Index for Canadian Forest Biomass [million tonnes] circa 2004

Species	\multicolumn{12}{c}{Age Group (20 Years Each)}

Species	≤20	≤40	≤60	≤80	≤100	≤120	≤140	≤160	≤180	≤200	≥201	Total
Birch	14	80	305	325	263	48	20	3	1	<1	<1	1059
Cedar, conifer	142	79	39	29	38	23	11	11	10	19	550	951
Douglas-fir	2	36	82	157	167	192	166	86	64	36	202	1190
Fir	20	142	245	274	238	129	111	95	102	99	838	2291
Hardwoods	73	20	38	51	25	12	2	<1	<1			220
Hemlock	1	52	70	90	65	53	31	37	26	28	1239	1691
Larch	28	6	19	35	36	33	19	10	5	2	10	202
Maple	17	45	349	193	300	75	43	23	4	3	<1	1052
Pine	57	159	306	554	648	471	433	251	131	68	95	3173
Poplar	43	198	798	1323	882	287	98	24	8	2	5	3670
Spruce	51	310	805	1859	4851	3394	1535	424	244	158	635	14267
Total	449	1127	3055	4889	7512	4716	2469	964	596	417	3574	29768
Shannon Index	1.98	2.05	1.94	1.73	1.30	1.10	1.28	1.58	1.59	1.64	1.59	1.76
$\exp(S)$	7.2	7.8	6.9	5.7	3.7	3.0	3.6	4.9	4.9	5.2	4.9	5.8

Source: Canada's National Forest Inventory 2006.

the index is maximized. For any less equal distribution, the diversity index will be smaller. Furthermore, diversity increases logarithmically with the number of species n. Therefore, it is useful to think of $\exp(S)$ as the 'effective number of species.' When interpreting S, making comparisons in terms of $\exp(S)$ is more intuitive. Table 1.2 provides an illustration for Canada's forest cover. The table shows the composition in terms of millions of tonnes of biomass by major species and age group. Applying the Shannon-Wiener measure reveals that there are significant differences in biodiversity across age groups. Trees in the 100-120 age group are the least diverse: the effective number of species is only 3, and it is heavily dominated by spruce. It should be noted that young trees account for little total biomass because these trees are still small, while very old trees are rare either naturally (normal lifetime) or through harvesting. Furthermore, different species of trees have different expected lifetimes. Therefore, the variation of the diversity index across age groups is less interesting than tracking the changes of the diversity index over time.

Entropy can also be used to define sustainability in a manner that is more readily quantifiable than more abstract sociological definitions, as those advanced by the *Brundtland Report*.

Sustainability is linked to an ecosystem's robustness to human or natural perturbations. An ecosystem is more sustainable if it has a higher probability of remaining in the current regime (returning to the initial equilibrium or steady state) in the face of a perturbation, rather than moving toward a new and very different regime.

Consider the effects of climate change in this context. If emitting carbon dioxide leads to very gentle changes in climate and after ceasing emissions the ecosystem returns gradually to its original climate, this is sustainable. If the carbon dioxide emissions lead to a new climate equilibrium or regime without the possibility of returning to the original climate, this would be unsustainable. But how do we measure this notion of sustainability?

The Fisher information index has been suggested as a useful empirical tool to capture the notion of sustainability. This measure has been used successfully to study food web problems with multiple species. In simple terms, the Fisher information index captures the ratio of acceleration to the speed of a system, evaluated over a length of time along the system's trajectory. Consider a complex dynamic food system described by a vector $\mathbf{x}(t)$ of state variables (such as the biomass of each species) evolving over time t. Let $\dot{\mathbf{x}}(t)$ and $\ddot{\mathbf{x}}(t)$ denote speed and acceleration of these state variables. Standard Lotka-Volterra 'predator-prey' equations for the n state variables are used to describe the mass balances of species so that $\dot{x}_i(t) = x_i \sum_{j=1}^{n}(a_{ji} - b_{ji}x_j)$. Then the Fisher information index I is given by the equation

$$I = \frac{1}{\Delta t} \int \frac{\left[(\dot{\mathbf{x}}(t))^T \ddot{\mathbf{x}}(t)\right]^2}{||\dot{\mathbf{x}}(t)||^6} dt \quad , \qquad (1.2)$$

The index integrates the probability of finding an ecosystem in a particular state. Stable systems that remain in the same regime for a long time have a high I. By comparison, I drops when the system's variability increases. This indicates a loss of stability and predictability, and may even point to a possible catastrophic shift to a new regime. The Fisher information index can also be used to compare policies that are either increasing or decreasing the stability of the system.

Nevertheless, there are problems with such an index measure as well. For example, what is the appropriate integration time Δt? Some states of the ecosystem may be difficult to capture empirically, let alone their speed and acceleration. The Fisher information index does not tell us if a particular regime is sustainable or not; it is not a binary indicator. Instead it only tells us if a particular regime is likely to be more stable or not. While I is not relying on any particular weighting of indicators as other indices, the inclusion or exclusion of indicators (elements of the vector $\mathbf{x}$) influences the results.

While there are numerous possible indicators and indices of sustainability, they all have in common the desire to find an empirical way of identifying policies and regimes that are more or less sustainable, taking a 'general equilibrium' perspective of the entire ecosystem. If the concept of sustainability wants to be taken seriously in a scientific manner, it must embrace the notion of measurability, or quantifiability.

1.4 Which companies should care the most?

It seems that every company wants to be seen to be 'green' these days. However, some companies want to be 'greener' than others, for one reason or another. Perhaps another way to put this is to ask: which companies need to be 'green'? For which type of company will being 'green' make a difference?

1. **High brand exposure.** Companies with substantial goodwill and intangible values, such as those in the food and beverage sector, are strongly exposed to consumer reactions. Environmental problems, if not dealt with swiftly and decisively, can erode the brand quickly and leave reputational damage that will be difficult or impossible to repair.
2. **Big environmental impact.** Resource extraction and heavy manufacturing companies (e.g., oil companies, mining companies, metal smelters, cement manufacturers) operate under the potential threat of a major environmental disaster. Oil rigs can blow up, oil tankers can break up, pipelines can leak, and pollution abatement equipment can fail unexpectedly. This may happen even when many precautions have been taken. No safety system is infallible. In large organizations, warning signs may get overlooked, and safety precautions may sometimes be carried out haphazardly. When a disaster happens, the sheer size of the disaster may put the resources of the company to the test, and may even spell bankruptcy.
3. **Natural resource dependency.** Companies that sell food, fish, and forest products are exposed even if they do not have an exposed brand image or when they are further up the supply chain and thus do not face immediate exposure to consumer backlash. Nevertheless, in response to environmental or health concerns, consumer goods companies may switch suppliers if problems emerge. Concerns about a product's healthiness may affect consumers even stronger than concerns about a product's environmental damage, which tends to be much less immediate for the individual consumer.
4. **Current exposure to regulation.** Companies that are already subject to environmental monitoring and regulation (such as those handling toxic substances) face regulatory backlash in the case of noncompliance or spills and leaks. Such companies may experience a

tightening of regulatory requirements, and therefore higher costs, as a result of their environmental problems.

5. **Increasing potential for regulation.** Even if companies do not face regulatory interventions yet, emerging environmental issues may expose them to future regulation. An example are mandatory take-back programs that require producers of goods to plan for the eventual decommissioning of these goods. For example, a car maker or an electronics producer could be asked to take back their cars or computers, disassemble them, and return recovered materials to the production process.

6. **Competitive markets for talents.** The labour market may also play a role in channeling environmental concerns. Companies perceived to be 'dirty' may be unable to attract talented workers, who may be hesitant to work for such a company. Alternatively, 'dirty' companies may need to pay a wage premium to attract such workers. This problem is especially pronounced when firms engage in innovation and R&D, as high-skilled experts often tend to be more sensitive to environmental concerns than other types of workers.

7. **Low market power.** Companies that rely on big customers (e.g., large retail chains) may find themselves being pulled up by them through 'green sourcing.' When major distributors (or monopsonists) go green, suppliers may be required to follow. Participation in voluntary certification programs such as ISO 14001 may in fact become *de rigeur* when such certification becomes a requirement when bidding for a contract.

8. **Established environmental reputation.** Last but not least, company history matters. A company's negative record often leads to extra scrutiny as society is already primed to expect bad news from such a company. It is difficult to overcome an established negative perception, and even minor issues may draw attention and may even be exaggerated in the news media. On the other hand, a positive record sets high expectations, and sometimes increasing expectations. An environmentally conscientious firm may find it difficult to top its own past successes to maintain its role as environmental leader in its industry or market.

In their book about companies' environmental strategies, Esty and Winston (2006) put forward the following dictum: *Smart companies seize competitive advantage through strategic management of environmental challenges.* Perhaps this dictum is a bit vague—after all, what is a 'smart' company? What is the metric for smartnees? On the other hand, the dictum suggests that a firm's environmental challenges should not be viewed merely as a cost factor, faced grudgingly and with disdain. Instead, a firm may be able to turn a perceived disadvantage into a potential advantage. The key idea is that other firms in the same industry probably face similar problems. By getting on top of the environmental challenge, a firm may be able to take the lead as an innovator, address the environmental problem, and at the same time realize overlooked efficiency potential. This is the idea of a double dividend. Cleverly advertised, the firm may also be able to claim environmental leadership over its competitors. This may curry favour with environmentally sensitive consumers or customers.

Sustainability has thus emerged from being a reactive strategy and has turned into a proactive strategy for businesses. Sustainability is not necessarily viewed as a burden, but instead as a strategic opportunity to capture new markets or gain economic advantages over competitors.

1.5 Corporate social responsibility

Corporate social responsibility (CSR) has become a buzzword in strategic management. Sometimes CSR is also referred to as 'corporate citizenship.' Some people have portrayed CSR as a panacea to cure the ills of the corporate world, while others have portrayed CSR as window dressing. The truth, as always, lies probably somewhere in between. CSR has its merits but it also has its limitations. CSR is certainly more than just corporate philantropy. In some way, CSR is a reflection of the information age. Stakeholders, investors, and consumers alike, are armed with much better information about what companies do, or don't do. Visibility has increased, and this means that companies may be held to higher standards of accountability and transparency than ever before. So what exactly is CSR? The following definition may be a helpful start.

> **Corporate social responsibility** is the set of activities through which companies integrate social, environmental, and economic concerns into their values and operations in a transparent and accountable manner.

With this definition in hand, the next step is to identify the 'set of activities' that is referred to in the definition, identify key principles for these activities, and delineate the scope of what is covered by CSR and what is not. Beyond the definition, CSR faces the same problem as sustainability: to make its application and success identifiable, we need a metric to identify what amounts to more CSR and what amounts to less CSR. Is it possible to quantify CSR? Are there CSR scoring techniques? Lastly, we also need to ask why companies should adopt CSR in the first place, and whether or not it is effective.

1.5.1 Characteristics of CSR

CSR is defined by activities that set it apart from other corporate activities. First and foremost, CSR involves voluntary, not government-mandated, activities. Firms decide that they want to pursue CSR activities. Therefore, firms self-select into participation. Some firms participate, and others don't. Which firms implement CSR principles (and which don't) is therefore an interesting research question that will try to link firm characteristics to CSR adoption.

In many cases CSR activities involve sacrificing profit for other (social or environmental) objectives. While in some cases firms can reap a double dividend where CSR activities generate value, in most instances firms probably have to incur expenditures without offsetting revenue in order to pursue CSR. If that is the case, firms have to be profitable to engage in CSR. Unprofitable or marginal firms do not have the resources to pursue CSR.

Ethical and social values that inform CSR practices may be heterogeneous across regions, countries, and time. Do firms in China or India have the same 'corporate values' that inform their CSR activities as do firms in the United States or Canada? In addition to the geographical heterogeneity in CSR aspirations, there is quite likely also an intertemporal heterogeneity in CSR aspirations. Will future generations of a firm's senior management share the CSR values of their predecessors? It is immediately clear that it is very difficult to find common ground across time and space with respect to a set of CSR activities that will be accepted universally. Consequently, CSR is very much a managerial practice that is in the eye of the beholder—namely, the eyes of the stakeholders that a firm cares about in some way or another. Naturally, CSR activities can be expected to evolve over time as the set of stakeholders changes.

The CSR definition referred to a set of activities. These activities fall, broadly, into four major groups: *internal conduct* (organization, governance), *external conduct* (business partners, governments), *monetary transfers* (donations, sponsorship), and *specific projects*. The latter can be any number of projects that stakeholders may value or view positively. One company may pursue a project of helping communities in poor nations install water pumps, and another project could involve scholarships for bright students. The point is that these projects are visible to stakeholders. These stakeholders may not necessarily be the public in general. For example, a car manufacturer in Brazil may run an orphanage, but not advertise it much. Instead, the company may find that involving volunteers from its workforce is a more direct way to contribute to the community and build community ties. CSR may sometimes be mostly invisible except to the stakeholders that matter.

Given the wide spectrum of possible CSR activities, putting a common structure on these activities is probably useful. In November 2010, the International Organization for Standardization launched a standard on social responsibility. ISO 26000 is a 'voluntary guidance standard' that is focused on seven principles of social responsibility applied to seven core subject areas. Table 1.3 shows these principles and subject areas. While this new standard is supposed to provide a platform for evaluating CSR activities, there is no certification attached to participation in this standard.

Table 1.3 Principles and Subject Areas of ISO 26000

Principles	Subject Areas
Accountability	Organizational governance
Transparency	Labour practices
Ethical behaviour	Environment
Respect for stakeholder interests	Fair operating practices
Respect for the rule of law	Consumers
Respect for international norms	Community involvement & development
Respect for human rights	Human rights

1.5.2 Do stakeholders recognize CSR?

Despite the fact that some companies may prefer low-key CSR activities, most CSR activities are designed to be visible to the public, and perhaps impress the public in order to create a positive image of the firm.

Investors increasingly care about the sustainability and ethical values of the firms they invest in. Over the last few years a number of groups have attempted to define portfolios of companies that meet certain sustainability criteria. The most popular of these is probably the *Dow Jones Sustainability Index* (www.sustainability-index.com), which tracks the performance of the most sustainable 20% of companies out of the largest 2,500 companies worldwide (with the exception of the alcohol, tobacco, and firearms sectors).

Since January 2000, the *Jantzi Social Index* in partnership with Dow Jones has tracked 60 Canadian companies that meet sustainability criteria. Since 2001, a mutual fund company (Meritas) has provided a related mutual fund product, and in 2007 an exchange-traded fund (XEN:TSX) was launched that tracks the index. The companies included in the index must pass a set of broadly based environmental, social, and governance (ESG) rating criteria. Inclusion in the index is governed by committee decision, which in turn compares ESG ratings for each company with a best-of-sector benchmark. Companies included in the index are then value-weighted, reflecting their relative market capitalizations.

In Britain, the *FTSE4Good Index* tracks companies worldwide that meet globally recognized corporate responsibility standards. To be included in the index, companies need to demonstrate that they are working towards (i) environmental management; (ii) climate change mitigation and adaptation; (iii) countering bribery; (iv) upholding human and labour rights; and (v) supply chain labour standards. As with all such indices, some sectors are excluded (tobacco, weapons systems).

Consumers also care about corporate reputations. While there is no easily recognizable CSR mark that identifies companies, such as an eco-label, consumers may assess a company's CSR reputation through opinion polls about 'most respected corporations' and through CSR rankings published by news organizations. For example, table 1.4 shows the top ten *Corporate Knights* CSR Ranking for Canadian companies.

Table 1.4 *Corporate Knights* S&P/TSX 60 Corporate Responsibility Ranking, 2010

Company	Sector	Envmt.	Govern.	Social	Final
1. Loblaw Companies	Consumer staples	56.2%	69.2%	92.9%	80.8%
2. George Weston	Consumer staples		36.1%	94.8%	71.6%
3. Iamgold Corp.	Materials	74.7%	68.5%	65.0%	71.2%
4. Cameco Corp.	Energy	80.7%	70.8%	43.6%	69.1%
5. Sun Life Financial	Financials		38.5%	85.6%	67.4%
6. SNC-Lavalin Group	Industrials		71.2%	55.4%	66.0%
7. Cnd. National Railway	Industrials	40.4%	69.7%	64.4%	65.2%
8. Royal Bank of Canada	Financials	34.8%	71.1%	65.4%	64.0%
9. Nexen Inc.	Energy	39.6%	68.1%	73.9%	63.8%
10. TD Bank	Financials	36.6%	72.2%	67.7%	63.8%

Source: *Corporate social responsibility rankings*, The Globe and Mail, June 18, 2010.

The environmental score in this table captures measures of energy productivity, carbon productivity, water productivity, and waste productivity. The governance score captures measures of sustainability leadership, leadership diversity, and sustainability remuneration. A social score captures the ratio of the CEO's salary to that of the lowest-paid worker in the firm, employee safety, the percentage of taxes paid, the Board of Director pensions over $200 million, and pension funding. Lastly, a 'transparency modifier' is applied to firms that make it difficult to score them along any of the dimensions. In 2010, Loblaw Companies achieved the highest CSR score; the company was also recognized as Canada's greenest employer in 2011.

1.5.3 *The economics of CSR*

A survey paper by Margolis et al. (2009) summarizes the economic analysis of CSR into four distinct questions. Are firms actually allowed to engage in CSR, as it distracts them from their main objective of maximizing profits or shareholder value? Do they have the resources to pursue CSR without jeopardizing their competitiveness? Which firms engage in CSR, and which don't? And lastly, on a normative level, should firms engage in CSR in the first place or leave philanthropic activities to shareholders, governments, and non-governmental organizations (NGOs)? We turn to these four questions, following Margolis et al. (2009) closely.

May firms sacrifice profits in the social interest?

It is generally believed that corporate directors have a fiduciary duty to maximize profits for shareholders. In 1970, Milton Friedman expressed the idea that the only responsibility of business is to maximize profits (shareholder value), while public goods (or curtailments of negative externalities) should be provided by governments with a democratic mandate. However, the legal environment leaves room for firms to sacrifice profits in the public interest.

Even if managers have a fiduciary first-order responsibility to generate shareholder value, it is also generally thought that the *business judgment rule* effectively protects managerial actions from legal challenge as long as managers can plausibly claim that their actions are in the long-term interest of the firm. By pointing to future rather than current profitability, managers can justify their CSR activities to shareholders and shield themselves from criticism.

Can firms engage in CSR on a sustainable basis?

Even if firms can engage in CSR, it does not mean that they can afford to. If CSR is expensive, CSR may become unsustainable if it hurts the bottom line sufficiently, and may even risk the very existence of the business. To understand the difference between sustainable and unsustainable CSR, it is useful to put different motivations behind CSR into a matrix as described in Kitzmueller (2008). Owners and shareholders on one side, and all other stakeholders such as consumers on the other side, may be motivated by purely monetary objectives or by a desire to improve social and environmental performance. Table 1.5 illustrates the four possible combinations of motivations.

If both sides are motivated purely by monetary objectives, there exists no rationale for CSR. The company pursues simple profit maximization. When stakeholders are motivated primarily by monetary considerations—namely, that goods are comparatively cheap—and firm owners engage in costly CSR, then there is a profound mismatch

Table 1.5 CSR Typology

		Shareholder/Owner Preferences	
		Social/Environmental	Purely Monetary
Stakeholder Preferences	Social/ Environmental	**Voluntary CSR** mixed effect on profits	**Strategic CSR** profit maximization
	Purely Monetary	**Unsustainable CSR** negative effect on profits	**No CSR** profit maximization

of objectives. Consumers will drift to cheaper goods from competitors that do not engage in costly CSR, and the firm's CSR becomes unsustainable due to these competitive pressures. CSR needs to be valued by stakeholders to exist.

Voluntary CSR is induced by shareholder or owner preferences, but the profitability of these actions depends on the extent to which stakeholders value these activities. There is a match of preferences between stakeholder and shareholders, and the key question becomes not whether there should be CSR, but how much CSR there should be. The outcome on profits depends on how well preferences match.

Perhaps the most interesting type of CSR may be coined *strategic CSR*. This type of CSR is induced by stakeholder pressures rather than owner or shareholder preference. Firms are merely reactive. As the firm maintains its purely monetary objective, strategic CSR is focused on providing activities at just the right amount valued by consumers. This could be through the provision of 'green goods' or other types of product upgrading. Ultimately, this is perhaps the world of quality differentiation where CSR is a quality signal valued by customers or other stakeholders. The key to understanding strategic CSR is the idea that firms react to external influences and forces, but entirely within the paradigm of profit maximization. There are several economic forces that could induce strategic CSR.

- **Labour economics.** Contract theory suggests the possibility that CSR could be used as a screening device to attract morally motivated agents and employees. Firms with a high CSR profile may be better able to attract and retain top-quality employees. It is also conceivable that CSR could be used as an entrenchment strategy to protect top managers' jobs. Bosses with a high CSR profile may be more immune to criticism of their other actions.
- **Product markets.** Perhaps the most appealing motive for strategic CSR is the existence of 'green consumerism' or 'socially responsible consumption.' Firms that sell experience goods or credence goods

are more likely to engage in CSR than firms selling search goods. CSR signals unobservable product attributes or general quality.

- **Financial markets.** As was discussed above, interest in 'socially responsible investing' led to the creation of related stock portfolios. In their extensive meta study, Margolis et al. (2009) report a statistically significant positive correlation between corporate financial performance (CFP) and CSR. However, this correlation disappears when allowing for CFP correlation with R&D (McWilliams and Siegel, 2000). In another study, Small and Graff Zivin (2004) consider corporate giving and private charitable giving as imperfect substitutes, and they find that CSR can maximize firm value as long as corporate philanthropy and private charity are not perfect substitutes.
- **Private politics** entails the notion of social activism, of citizens lobbying firms to engage in certain desired practices. CSR induced by social activism has two effects. In the short run, it raises the cost of the targeted firm. However, in the long run, CSR reduces the threat of being targeted by social activism. CSR thus hedges against social activism.
- **Public politics** entails regulatory intervention. CSR can be used to preempt such interventions, or influence or deflect possible future regulation that would be costly to the firm. In other words, CSR responds to 'regulatory threat,' and increased self-regulation can crowd out public regulation.

What, then, are the conditions under which CSR is sustainable for an individual firm? Essentially, there are conditions under which CSR has no or positive revenue implications. There are also conditions under which CSR reduces costs or protects against future cost increases. And lastly, there are conditions under which CSR can create competitive advantages.

There is the possibility that CSR is not costly to the firm because it involves 'surplus materials.' For example, restaurants donating left-over food to a food bank falls into that category. It is also possible that socially beneficial actions may reduce a firm's business expenses by a greater amount than their cost. An example of such a 'win-win' situation is installing energy-saving technologies that reduce electricity cost and emissions at the same time. As long as the capital cost of the new installation is offset over time by reduced energy costs, the firm realizes a positive net present-discounted value of the investment.

Socially beneficial actions may also yield an increase in revenue if CSR activities create good will or enhance a firm's reputation. Furthermore, if CSR activities amount to creating an environmentally differentiated good, consumers may be willing to pay a premium for this product.

Firms may sometimes choose to overcomply with environmental, health, or safety laws in order to deflect or influence future regulation. This type of CSR is preemptive in nature. CSR becomes a substitute for government intervention, or an excuse for government inaction. It is also conceivable that a firm may choose to overcomply with environmental, health, or safety regulations in order to spur future regulation that will disadvantage competitors that are minimally compliant. This strategic motive requires, perhaps implausibly, that regulators be more swayed by the brilliance of an overcompliant firm than by the grumblings from minimally compliant rivals. It also assumes that differences in regulatory costs are sufficiently large to create a competitive advantage. Unsurprisingly, examples of this strategic motive are hard to find.

Do firms engage in CSR? Which do, which don't?

In the last section we saw that there are circumstances in which CSR can be profitable: if it matches preferences of stakeholders and shareholders, and when it furthers strategic objectives. Indeed, many firms view CSR as a profitable business activity. They engage in it on a limited basis if the socially beneficial activity also contributes towards their financial goals. Nevertheless, there will be a fair amount of heterogeneity in the benefits of CSR. While some firms may find that CSR increases profitability, others may find them financially unrewarding even if they find them socially rewarding.

If CSR is driven by a profit motive, then it should be possible to find empirical evidence that links CSR and positive financial performance. In their large meta study, Margolis et al. (2009) looks at numerous previous studies that tried to find such evidence. Their conclusion is that CSR has in general little effect on profitability, either positive or negative.

The meta study also answers another important question: which firms engage in CSR? Not all firms engage in CSR, and thus there is a self-selection mechanism that makes somes firms adopt CSR and other firms reject CSR. Is it simply that some firms care about society and environment and others just about the bottom line? Margolis et al. (2009) find a very plausible answer to the self-selection question.

Empirical evidence suggests that companies that are profitable are more likely to engage in CSR. Companies that can afford CSR engage in CSR, and companies that cannot afford CSR will avoid it.

Profitability is closely tied to a company's market power. Firms in oligopolistic markets tend to be more engaged in CSR than firms in highly competitive markets. It is therefore no surprise to find firms with high levels of CSR in the banking and communication sectors. Private utility firms are also often engaged in CSR, in many instances because their profitability is protected through government regulation or a natural monopoly position.

Should firms engage in CSR?

The previous sections answered the questions whether firms *may*, *can*, and *do* engage in CSR. These are mostly positive questions and they can be answered by looking at legal and economic circumstances. Ultimately, there is also the normative question whether firms *should* engage in CSR.

It is useful to start with the reasons against CSR. While it may seem that all companies should be socially responsible, questions arise when one analyzes concrete manifestations of CSR activities.

The first problem is *bias*. When firms adopt particular CSR activities, they select these activities based on a number of factors that are often unrelated to social costs and benefits. As CSR activities are typically chosen by a firm's top managers, their personal preferences weigh heavily. The managers' preferences may coincide with society's preferences, but that is not guaranteed. Some well-intentioned CSR activities could put resources in an area that, given the choice, society would rather put elsewhere. Furthermore, firm characteristics may also distort the choice of CSR activities. CSR may be driven by what a firm can afford financially, or by what CSR activity is more visible rather than more effective.

A second problem is *efficiency*. Generally, firms do not make socially optimal CSR investments. Firms are driven by their own considerations and not the priorities of society at large. A socially optimal CSR activity is one that yields the greatest net social benefit, subject to budget constraints. What is optimal for society may not be optimal for the firm. It could be the case that governments are better able to deliver desired social outcomes than voluntary CSR activities that may be poorly coordinated, duplicated, or lack economies of scale.

The last problem is *legitimacy*. To the extent that CSR uses up a country's resources (capital, labour, etc.), the decision to devote part of a country's GDP to social actions rests with shareholders and not with society at large. Given a vote, society might well prefer other activities; this was the bias problem. The fact that democratic institutions do not have a vote in the allocation of these resources is a legitimacy deficit. A country could of course tax these firms and direct the tax revenue into democratically selected alternative activities.

An obvious counter argument to bias, inferior efficiency, and lack of legitimacy is that governments or other societal institutions are not necessarily better at delivering outcomes that society desires. Societal preferences are quite heterogeneous. Some people like more health care services, some want a cleaner environment, and some would really like to own a new car every other year. Some people vote for parties of the political left, centre, or right, and some people don't vote at all. Aggregating preferences is difficult and will always remain a very imperfect process. In a world with heterogeneous and evolving preferences, CSR does have some legitimacy. Governments and bureaucracies may be slow to experiment or adopt novel measures, whereas firms can move fast with CSR activities and may be less shy about experimentation.

Is it possible to make a convincing case for CSR despite the three key objections? There are some areas where CSR can indeed trump public policy. CSR decisions may benefit welfare when firms have access to *private information* that is not readily observed by regulators. This is a problem of information asymmetry. For example, a firm may be better able to understand its current and future polluting activities (especially those that are novel in scope) and can thus plan proactively, whereas regulators often intervene only reactively.

Another area where CSR can be very positive is in the context of developing countries. Here CSR can be particularly beneficial because poorer nations often have lower environmental standards than rich countries (or may enforce them less strictly). Multinational enterprises that have already adopted relatively cost-effective interventions at home may find it easy to deploy the same interventions in their offshore locations in the developing world, even if they are not required to do so by local standards.

So the bottom-line question may be: does the world need more CSR or less CSR? The answer, obviously, depends on weighing the benefits against the costs of CSR. If current government provision of socially beneficial public goods is suboptimal, then there is ample scope for CSR to increase social welfare, but not when government provision of public goods is in line with society's demands. In the case of underprovision of public goods, CSR can be a substitute for government action. If public goods are provided adequately, CSR should best be viewed as a *complement* to rather than a *substitute* for government intervention. CSR can fill the niches left unserved by governments, it can experiment with new interventions that governments may find difficult to jump start, and it can correct information asymmetries, or pursue activities that cross jurisdictional boundaries more easily than governments can.

1.5.4 CSR strategy

In practice, many businesses equate 'corporate responsibility' with 'sustainability.' RBC (formerly known as Royal Bank of Canada) defines CSR as 'behaving with integrity, sustaining our company's long-term viability, being transparent and accountable, and contributing to the future well-being of all our stakeholders.' The terms 'corporate respon-

Fig. 1.5 CSR Strategy

sibility' and 'sustainability' are simply shorthand for 'good business practices' and 'good corporate governance.'

Figure 1.5 illustrates the elements of CSR strategy as an integral part of overall business strategy, where CSR informs overall business strategy, and CSR is informed by business strategy. CSR always requires acting with integrity, which is supported by transparency and accountability. Corporate social responsibility has four main corner stones. It starts with managing the company's workplace and labour force well: by employing human resource management practices that are fair and progressive, that respect human rights, and encourage diversity in the workforce. Another corner encompasses support for community programs through donations, sponsorships, and employee volunteerism. The third corner involves working towards reducing the company's environmental footprint. The fourth and last corner involves making a positive economic impact through creating employment opportunities, opportunities for workforce training and education, paying taxes, and purchasing goods and services responsibly. These four corners are connected through the principle of integrity—consistency in CSR actions, truthfulness in reporting CSR actions, and internal consistency of CSR actions with all of the company's activities. In other words, CSR cannot be used as a 'fig leaf' approach to masquerading questionable practices elsewhere in the business.

In terms of public visibility, philanthropy stands out because it is most easily recognized. For example, a bank's good governance and business practices are often observable only to its employees and shareholders. However, sponsorship of events and worthy causes is often more recognizable to the public. For that reason, promoting a single cause with a large amount of resources rather than promoting a multitude of causes with spread-out resources can raise the profile of a company's CSR. A good example is RBC's Blue Water Project, discussed in box 1.2 on page 30.

1.6 Summary

This chapter has explored the notions of 'sustainability,' 'environmental management,' and 'corporate social responsibility.'

Sustainability is a concept that is difficult to define unambiguously, as it can be interpreted easily in a number of different ways. Sustainability is usually seen as an *objective*, whereas environmental management is usually seen as a *tool* to achieve environmental objectives. A definition proposed by the United Nations defines sustainable development as improving the quality of human life while living within the carrying capacity of supporting ecosystems. This can be viewed as maximizing social welfare subject to the biological and physical constraints of maintaining our biosphere in such a state that it can support the world's population indefinitely. A key problem with sustainability is the difficulty of operationalizing this concept, of measuring and quantifying what is and what is not 'sustainable.' Emerging empirical tools (macro measures and micro measures) are trying to address this key problem.

Environmental management is a more concrete concept than sustainability. Environmental management is a systems approach for achieving environmental objectives within a firm. It involves defining a corporate environmental strategy and implementing it through suitable tools throughout the firm. The systems approach is aimed at understanding the environmental concerns of a firm in its entirety rather than partially. For example, a firm's pollution can be mitigated through pollution abatement devices. However, a systems analysis may also reveal how changes in sourcing inputs or energy, or changing the production process, can prevent emissions.

Corporate social responsibility encompasses a wide range of beneficial activities of a firm. Through CSR activities companies integrate social, environmental, and economic concerns into their operations in a transparent and accountable manner. CSR is typically carried out by

Box 1.2: CSR and RBC's Blue Water Project

The RBC Blue Water Project is an innovative, 10-year, global commitment to help protect the world's most precious natural resource: fresh water. Through the project, RBC has committed $50 million in charitable grants to NGOs that protect watersheds and provide or ensure access to clean drinking water. Since 2007, RBC has committed more than $28 million in single and multi-year grants to over 380 organizations.

The program focuses on watershed protection and access to clean drinking water. Watershed protection can involve the protection and restoration of sensitive natural areas, community-based watershed stewardship, sustainable water use and conservation practices, or raising watershed awareness programs. Eligible to apply for a grant are organizations that are federally registered charities in Canada or have similar status in the United States.

To handle the many applications for receiving grants, RBC had to develop principles to assess them. The four principles are focus (watershed protection and access to clean drinking water), prioritization (including projects in developing nations), collaboration (leveraging of expertise and resources), and impact (measurable outcome). To run the program effectively, RBC constituted an advisory panel made up of experts from academia and prominent NGOs.

To date, the Blue Water Project has funded a large number of projects in Canada, and the United States, with additional projects in the United Kingdom, the Bahamas, and Trinidad and Tobago.

One of the largest projects funded by RBC is the *Tides Canada* project in British Columbia's Great Bear Rainforest. The Great Bear Rainforest is one of the world's largest remaining ancient coastal temperate rainforests covering 64,000 square kilometres. It is a vast ecosystem with over 100 pristine watersheds, and it is also home to the rare white Spirit bears, grizzly bears, and rare and unusual plants. It is also a vital cultural and economic resource for British Columbia's First Nations communities.

Tides Canada played a lead role in ensuring the protection of about a quarter of that land from logging through an alliance of environmental NGOs, First Nations, industry, and government. RBC contributed a half-million-dollar grant that funded conservation management and sustainable economic development in First Nations communities in the region. Tides Canada is a philanthropic services company based in Vancouver and Toronto.

firms which can afford such activities, which favours sectors that are exceptionally profitable or exhibit oligopolistic market power and thus less competition. On average, firms that engage in CSR do not tend to improve their profitability, although outcomes may vary depending on whether CSR activities are motivated by shareholder or stakeholder interests. While CSR may be criticized for a number of valid reasons, in practice it is most beneficial when it targets objectives that are complementary to those pursued by governments.

1.7 Study questions and exercises

1. Which factors decide which companies are (or should be) concerned most about the environment?
2. Why is it difficult to define 'sustainability' meaningfully?
3. How can one measure sustainability at the macro and micro level?
4. What is the role of 'intertemporal discounting' in defining environmental policies? (What role does it play in the *Stern Review*?)
5. What are the pros and cons of using ecological footprint and biocapacity measures to determine sustainability?
6. Discuss the four key questions on corporate social responsibility:
   (a) may firms sacrifice profits in the social interest?
   (b) can they do so on a sustainable basis?
   (c) do firms actually behave in that way, and if yes, which firms?
   (d) should firms engage in CSR?
7. Are firms' directors better than their shareholders at directing resources to environmental causes?

Exercises

1. For an industry of your choice, identify the ten largest companies in that industry. Go to their web sites and find out if they have a statement of corporate social responsibility. Which companies publish an annual CSR report, and which don't? Create a list of typical items (dimensions) in the CSR reports and see to what extent they overlap across companies.
2. Utilize data from the World Bank's database (data.worldbank.org). Starting with the measure of adjusted net savings (ANS) discussed in this chapter, take a recent year, and compare the ANS measure with a variety of country-level pollution metrics such as carbon dioxide emissions per capita and organic water pollutant emissions per day and worker. Put the data into a bubble plot with the size of the bubbles indicating country size (population). Interpreting the charts, how much does the ANS measure capture economic and social development relative to environmental distress?

Chapter 2
Environmental Issues

Businesses face an ever-changing world of opportunities and threats. Environmental concerns are an integral part of this ever-changing world, and almost every business will have to deal with a growing list of such environmental concerns. Businesses need to understand where and how to respond to environmental challenges and problems, government regulations and interventions, and pressures from stakeholders. They also need to see where environmental issues open up new opportunities for markets and technologies. There is a natural tension between 'green opportunities' and 'green threats' to a business. On one side, environmental issues can be costly for businesses. They have to comply with government regulations, improve products and production processes, or switch supply and distribution channels. On the other side, environmental leadership can generate revenue-generating, profitable business opportunities. Esty and Winston (2006) explore many of the issues relating to corporate environmental strategy. Following their thinking, it is useful to look at some of the environmental issues facing the planet with two questions:

- What are the negative, cost-inducing consequences for business?
- What are the positive, revenue-generating opportunities for business?

The environmental issues will be presented only in broad strokes. The main objective of this chapter is to zoom in on how these environmental issues affect businesses, positively and/or negatively. The order in which they are presented does not reflect their importance. The last section of this chapter is devoted to climate change, which is arguably the most important environmental issue facing our society today.

2.1 Energy

Modern society and all industrial production relies on a steady supply of energy. Energy use is driven by two elements: the size of the world population and world economy, and the energy intensity of our world economy. While total energy use has increased by orders of magnitude over the last two centuries, energy intensity (per unit of GDP) has actually peaked in most countries and is starting to fall. Energy intensity increases as countries industrialize rapidly. This increase is driven in particular by the energy-intensive manufacturing sector. Eventually, energy intensity levels off as other industrial sectors become more important. The service sector with light energy use becomes more and more dominant in post-industrial societies. As energy becomes more expensive, energy efficiency also increases. At the same time, energy intensities converge across countries due to energy trade, adoption of common technologies and similarities in patterns of consumption. Nevertheless, energy intensity peaks at different times in different countries. In the United States, energy intensity peaked at about 0.5 tons of oil equivalent per dollar of GDP (adjusted to 2009 purchasing power parity) at around 1910-1920, and has been falling quite steadily ever since. According to the BP Energy Outlook 2030 (2011), energy intensity has also peaked in China and India.

A key problem with energy is energy storage. Fossil fuels have the huge advantage that they can be transported and stored quite easily. Primary energy converted into electricity is much more difficult to store. This problem is pronounced when primary energy sources are intermittent, such as solar energy (day and night, seasons) and wind (varying speed and direction).

Fossil fuels are exhaustible. This implies that in the long term the remaining reserves will eventually become increasingly more difficult and costly to explore. The output of existing oil and gas wells will diminish over time as the pressure that forces these fuels up a well will dissipate gradually. This process can be slowed down with new technologies, known as enhanced oil recovery. Ultimately, wells will run dry and alternative sources will need to be found. The notion that individual oil wells reach a point of maximum output is known as Hubbert's peak. Whether or not such a peak can be observed for aggregate oil production is a matter of much discussion. Forecasts that the world has reached peak production have been proved wrong numerous times. While it must be true that a peak will be reached at some point in the future, predicting that point proves tricky.

Some fossil fuels are also much 'dirtier' than other. This can be measured in terms of emissions per unit of energy. By that measure, natural gas is cleaner than oil, and oil is cleaner than coal. Among coal types, soft coal (lignite) is often associated with higher emissions (in particular sulfur dioxide) than hard coal (anthracite). This ranking of fossil fuel sources makes fuel switching the most attractive option to reduce emissions such as carbon dioxide, especially when unit prices of these fuels are comparable. Discovery of shale gas has greatly reduced the price of natural gas, and this makes switching from coal to natural gas an increasingly attractive option environmentally as well as economically.

At this point in time, the cost of renewable energy sources remains comparatively high for several types of sources. Wind energy, and geothermal energy in favourable locations such as Iceland are among the most competitive renewable energy sources. Despite rapid decreases in production cost for photovoltaic cells, solar energy remains relatively expensive and depends heavily on subsidies from governments or utility rate payers. A key challenge for renewable energy sources is storage and transportation. Solar energy (at least on the surface of our Earth) and wind are intermittent energy sources. Storing this energy is technically challenging and costly. The best locations for wind and solar energy are also often far from where the energy is needed. Building transmission lines adds to the cost of renewables.

What are the business consequences of the changing energy landscape? As the supply of fossil fuels diminishes over time, their prices will go up. How soon is a matter of speculation. Increasing prices for fuel and energy will spur energy conservation. This poses a great opportunity for businesses developing technologies that improve energy efficiency. Higher energy prices will also stimulate innovation in renewable energy sources, in part with government assistance. Innovation has been hindered by the boom-bust cycle of energy prices because this volatility makes it difficult to predict if an investment into a new technology will eventually pay off.

Depending on the relative prices of different types of fossil fuels, fuel switching will increase. However, the direction of the fuel switching can be positive or negative environmentally. Fuel switching from oil to natural gas entails environmental advantages, but fuel switching from oil to coal entails higher emissions.

Businesses need to worry about energy prices to the extent that they are locked into particular technologies for long periods. Reliance on a secondary energy source (electricity) provides greater flexibility, albeit typically at a higher cost than relying on a primary energy source (typically a fossil fuel). Firms with high sunk costs in existing equipment will find adjustment more challenging and may wait longer to upgrade equipment when prices are volatile.

2.2 Fresh water

Businesses (industrial and agricultural) compete with households for access to freshwater resources. In most developed countries, water supplied to household and industry of drinking-water quality (i.e., it is safe for human consumption).

Water is used in one form or another virtually by every business. Probably every manufactured product uses water during some part of the production process. To give an example, an automobile coming off the assembly line will have used at least 120 cubic metres of water; two-thirds for producing its steel and one-third for its fabrication. Industries that stand out as heavy water users include metal fabrication, wood

Box 2.1: Yemen's Water Crisis

Yemen is projected to be the first Arab country that will use up all of its groundwater, but no one knows exactly when the water table will dry out or fall beyond a viable level for human use.

About 90% of Yemen's groundwater is currently used to irrigate high-value qat crops. Qat is a mildly narcotic leaf, chewed for pleasure and much-loved by Yemenis. Qat farmers rely on subsidized diesel to power their water pumps. Landowners are supposed to obtain a permit to drill new wells but the sector is poorly regulated.

Decades of random drilling have depleted Yemen's aquifers, extracting groundwater faster than rainfall can replenish supplies. Rigs are now boring well shafts to mine fossil water that was capped and sealed in the rocks during prehistoric geological times.

processing including pulp and paper production, and chemical plants. In addition, certain types of oil production and refining require vast amounts of water.

In the United States, industrial use of fresh water in manufacturing industries is usually dwarfed by two other uses: irrigation for agricultural production, and thermoelectric power generation. In Canada, agricultural water use is much less pronounced. Instead, water use is dominated by thermoelectric plants (mostly in Ontario).

The regional diversity of the United States provides a useful illustration of the different water uses. Irrigation is heavily concentrated in states such as California and Idaho. Water use for thermoelectric power production is much more diversified regionally and follows, roughly, the relative population size of individual states. Louisiana, Indiana, and Texas account for a large share of industrial water withdrawals (about 40%) due to the presnce of chemical and paper industries.

There are two major sources of fresh water: groundwater and surface water. In the United States, groundwater account for about 20% of total water withdrawals, and surface water for about 80%.

Assessing water use from an environmental perspective, there are two key dimensions: water quantity and water quality. Quantity is important because water is a scarce resource. Natural scarcity can be exaggerated by market failures due to imperfect or absent pricing mechanisms. Actual scarcity is in most cases the result of mismanagement. For example, water rights in California are heavily skewed in favour of farmers, amounting to vast subsidies for agricultural production. In Yemen, overuse of water for growing certain types of crops (see box 2.1) has depleted aquifers dangerously.

Fig. 2.1 World Water Scarcity

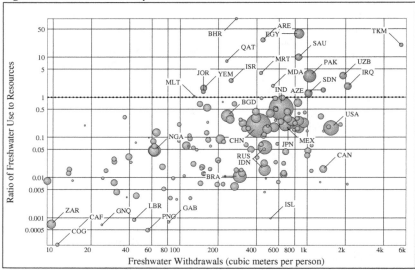

Data Source: World Bank, *World Development Indicators,*
series ER.H2O.FWTL.K3 and ER.H2O.FWTL.ZS, for 2009.

Figure 2.1 shows the availability of water around the world. The horizontal axis shows freshwater withdrawals in cubic metres per capita on a logarithmic scale. For example, freshwater withdrawals in the United States and Canada are 1,560 and 1,362 cubic metres per person per year, respectively. Canada and the United States rank among the heaviest per-capita water users in the world. European countries use significantly less water per capita. The vertical axis, also on a logarithmic scale, shows the ratio of freshwater withdrawal to internal reserves. This is an index of water stress. Countries that use more water than is renewable exhibit unsustainable water use. They either deplete underground aquifers or they import water from neighbouring countries. In some areas water is scarce due to climate, but in many places water is scarce due to economic factors.

Water quality is affected by contamination, in particular **eutrophication**, which will be explored in a later chapter. As inland waters are also used to support fisheries, there is a natural tension between that industry and other commercial uses such as pulp and paper mills.

Businesses are threatened by increasing limits on water use or contamination of water supply. Water-intensive pulp and paper plants may find themselves subject to tightening regulations or increasing water prices. Bottling plants (e.g., Coca-Cola in India) may need to subject their water supply to extensive testing and possibly treatment.

Water management also creates new business opportunities. They fall into three broad categories:

1. wastewater treatment of effluent from industrial and residential use;
2. desalination of seawater into potable water in arid regions where surface water is naturally scarce and groundwater resources are nearing depletion; and
3. development of technology for water conservation that increases the efficiency of water use, for example by minimizing leakage and evaporation.

As water becomes a more precious resource over time, in particular in light of population increases in some areas and rapidly progressing industrialization in others, business opportunities for water management and water treatment look very promising.

Desalination of seawater is very energy intensive. Using carbon-based fuels adds greenhouse gas emissions. The technological challenge will be to link desalination to renewable energy sources.

Wastewater treatment calls for technological innovation that turns blackwater (sewage) or greywater (waste water from washing machines, dishwashers, bathing) back into potable water. Greywater is less contaminated than blackwater and thus easier to treat. Untreated greywater can be recycled onsite and used for landscape irrigation. Recycling into potable or near-potable water requires advanced filtration systems and microbial digestion.

Water conservation is ultimately driven by the price of water. Scarcity of water, the cost of transporting water, and the cost of treating waste water, are all important contributing factors to the price of water. Where water has become scarce, such as in Australia's Murray-Darling basin, or around the Colorado and Rio Grande rivers in the United States, prices have risen sharply. Even where water may appear plentiful, such as in Canada's West, existing reservoir capacity may limit availability in urban areas such as Vancouver, and a downward trend in the summer flow in the Athabasca river may limit the availability of water for industrial use in Alberta's oil sands production. Increasing scarcity of water will also lead to increased interjurisdictional conflicts over water rights. Historically, this has already led to numerous water right treaties. The United States and Mexico established the International Boundary and Water Commission in 1884, which negotiated important water right treaties for the Colorado, Tijuana, and Rio Grande rivers. Canada and the United States established the International Joint Commission in 1909, which completed several treaties managing the water in the Great Lakes.

2.3 Air pollution

Air pollution is generated primarily by industrial activity, although in developing countries emissions from households burning coal for heating may contribute significantly. The major air pollutants are sulfur dioxide (in particular from burning coal), nitrogen oxides (from high-temperature combustion and often visible as brown haze over a city), carbon monoxide (a colourless, odourless, but poisonous gas from incomplete combustion of fuels), volatile organic compounds (mostly hydrocarbons, many of them suspected carcinogens), and particulate matter of fine particles suspended in the air (mostly associated with respiratory diseases). Nitrogen oxides and volatile organic compounds can interact to create ground-level ozone.

Air pollution tends to be a local or regional problem, as many air pollutants only travel relatively short distances. Emissions from plants dissipate over distance and turn into ambient emission concentrations that vary over distance and time. Because weather conditions such as wind speed and wind direction and seasonal variations in temperature and precipitation can influence emission concentrations, the health impact of emissions on the population can vary greatly. Favourable weather conditions can help mitigate air pollution, while unfavourable weather conditions can trap air pollutants and lead to 'smog' (smoke + fog). In December 1952 the British capital London experienced a period of cold weather with windless conditions, which trapped air pollutants from burning coal in what is known as a temperature inversion: cold and stagnant air trapped under a layer of warm air. The resulting fog mixed with air pollutants and created a thick layer of smog, which made 100,000 people ill and led to an estimated 4,000 premature deaths. Dangerous levels of smog remain a big problem in many large cities of developing countries, including Indonesia, China, and Brazil.

Local concentrations of pollutants are considered hot spots. From a policy perspective, curtailing maximum emission concentrations in such hot spots is of greater concern than reducing emissions overall. Therefore, many governments rely on maximum emission standards as their preferred policy tool.

With governments responding to the health hazards created by air pollution, businesses are required to deploy a variety of pollution abatement technologies. Many of these technologies are discussed in chapter 9. Businesses can either avoid emissions by deploying less-polluting production technologies (pollution prevention) or they can install abatement devices (end-of-pipe treatment). Either way, reducing air pollution will be costly for businesses. In a survey conducted by the US Environmental Protection Agency in 2005, abatement cost expenditures remain a relatively small item overall. However, pollution abatement equipment can account for 10-15% of all new capital expenditures in select industries (petroleum and coal products manufacturing, chemical manufacturing, primary metal manufacturing).

In addition to the (fixed) capital cost of deploying abatement technologies, firms also need to consider the ongoing (variable) cost of measurement and testing. Firms also need to be mindful of adverse effects on the local communities in which they operate.

While many air pollutants are local in scope, some have planet-wide effects. The most important group are greenhouse gases such as methane and carbon dioxide, which are linked to climate change. In the 1980s, another category of substances caused great concern. Chlorofluorocarbons (CFCs) were linked to the depletion of the ozone layer, in particular over the two poles. The overall decline in the ozone concentration in the Earth's stratosphere, and the widening of the 'ozone holes' over the poles, led to an increase in harmful UV radiation that is associated with skin cancer, cataracts, and other negative effects on people and the biosphere. These concerns led to a consensus among nations to restrict CFCs in the 1985 Vienna Convention. Implemented in 1987 through the *Montreal Protocol*, CFCs were to be phased out and ultimately banned. The convention was effective stopping the release of CFCs, perhaps because the sources of CFCs were readily identifiable (CFCs, in particular Freon, were used in air conditioning and cooling), and alternatives were available. While atmospheric concentrations of CFCs have decreased since the Montreal Protocol was implemented, the Antarctic ozone hole is expected to persist for decades.

The key lesson to be learned by businesses from the experience with CFCs is to think early about suitable alternatives for substances that may turn out to be harmful. In fact, there are a large number of alternative refrigerants that can be used in cooling and air-conditioning applications, many of which do not harm the ozone layer. Modern refrigerators (especially in Europe) use isobutane instead of the Freon coolant.

2.4 Waste management

The 3R mantra 'reduce, reuse, recycle' is as sensible for businesses as it is for households.[1] Waste reduction is often a 'win-win' for businesses. Waste is often costly in two ways: costly materials are discarded without being recovered, and disposing of these materials may involve costly transportation, processing, or landfilling. By reducing waste, a firm can reduce waste-management costs. Reusing and recycling materials is typically part of a more sophisticated life-cycle approach to managing products.

---

[1] A 4R version includes 'recover,' recovering energy from waste; see the section on *solid waste management* in chapter 9.

The environmental hazard from waste is particularly pronounced for toxic waste. For example, discarded electronics often contain toxic metallic contaminants such as lead, cadmium, beryllium, or traces of mercury and americium (the latter used in smoke detectors). Such e-waste poses particular dangers. The best way to process such waste is to disassemble the components, salvage working or repairable parts, and separate hazardous from non-hazardous waste. However, such methods are labour-intensive, and often bulk shredding and smelting is used to separate substances.

Firms will become increasingly responsible for thinking ahead to the end-of-life of the products they manufacture and sell. Some countries are considering voluntary and even mandatory take-back programs for manufactures. As a product is discarded, the manufacturer will be required to take it back and dispose of it appropriately. Such extended producer responsibility can perhaps even become an opportunity for a firm to design its products in a manner that makes it easy to disassemble them in the future, and recycle and reuse components more easily. While take-back programs will add costs to businesses, businesses can reduce those costs by improving design and recycling rates.

Take-back requirements can be quite costly for smaller businesses. When a take-back program for packaging was introduced in Germany in 1991, producers and retailers banded together to create a second disposal system, parallel to the public waste disposal system, that collected, sorted, and recovered recyclable materials. Products suitable for this process are marked with a (nowadays ubiquitous, widely recognized, and trademarked) green-dot label.

Chemicals, toxics, and heavy metals are a concern not only for waste management, but also for contaminating consumer products. Many substances have cumulative long-term effects rather than short-term acute effects. Thus, contamination may not lead to concerns until a product has been on the market for considerable time. Toxics can be grouped loosely in three broad groups:

(a) **known** toxics such as asbestos, lead, and mercury that are typically subject to regulation;

(b) **suspected** toxics that have been tentatively identified as problematic but with yet-insufficient evidence and have been put on a 'watch list' or 'priority reduction list' that may subject them to regulation in the future;

(c) **latent** toxics whose toxicity may be suspected but has not been researched, perhaps because of insufficient long-term data.

Dealing with toxics requires that companies carefully track their materials. Knowing where materials come from, what they contain, and where they are going, is essential. The use of latent toxics is linked to the potential of liability for harmful effects in the future, and the yet-unforeseen need to abandon materials even if they have been in use for

Box 2.2: Bisphenol-A

Bisphenol-A (BPA) is an industrial chemical used to make a hard, clear plastic known as polycarbonate, which is used in many consumer products, including reusable water bottles and baby bottles. BPA is also found in epoxy resins, which act as a protective lining on the inside of metal-based food and beverage cans.

During 2008, new research showed that BPA is a potential risk to infants under 18 months of age. BPA does not pose a risk to the general population, including adults, teenagers, and children. The Canadian government has banned import and sale of polycarbonate baby bottles that contain BPA.

In December 2007, Mountain Equipment Co-op pulled BPA products from its stores. In anticipation of Health Canada's announcement, many stores (e.g., Canadian Tire, The Bay) pulled BPA products in the spring of 2008. Nalgene Outdoor Products stopped making plastic bottles that contain BPA.

a long time. A good example is the use of bisphenol-A, explained in box 2.2.

2.5 Transportation

Perhaps like no other environmental issue, we are faced with transportation issues every day. As individuals, we make transportation mode choices every day when we decide to walk, ride a bike, drive a car, take public transit, or fly on a plane. We also make important investment decisions. Many of these decisions are driven by economic trade-offs between convenience (time) and cost (money). Long-term decisions about investments are also driven by expectations about future trends in transportation. A buyer of a new car will consider the fuel efficiency of the vehicle differently if fuel costs are expected to increase over time.

The environmental outcomes of transportation are manifold. The most noticeable is local air pollution. Motor vehicles emit a mixture of carbon monoxide, nitric oxide, nitrogen dioxide, and hydrocarbons. When exposed to sunlight, nitrogen oxides can react with volatile organic compounds (VOCs) to form ground-level ozone (smog). These emissions from motor vehicles are linked to respiratory ailments.

The combustion of fossil fuels in motor vehicles is also a major source of carbon dioxide and thus a major contributor to climate change. About one-quarter to one-third of world-ide greenhouse gas emissions are attributable to transportation. Transportation is also related to a variety of other negative effects: increasing density of transportation leads to traffic congestion (lost time and higher emissions); frequency and speed of traffic is linked with increasing noise levels as well as increasing numbers of accidents.

Because automotive transportation is linked to all these different negative effects, policy interventions can be very effective for improving environmental outcomes. Consumers react to incentives such as subsidies and taxes, even though price signals may have a much stronger effect in the long term than in the short term. Consumers and businesses make two decisions: in the short term about use (how much to drive), and in the long term about investment (what sort of vehicle to drive). Economically, these decisions involve variable costs (use) and fixed costs (investment). The owner of an automobile can vary the amount of driving in response to changing prices or incentives immediately, while the fuel efficiency of the vehicle can be changed only by replacing the vehicle every few years.

Transportation is the backbone of all industrial activity. Without transportation, virtually all commerce would cease. Therefore, businesses respond strongly to changing costs of transportation. In order to minimize transportation costs, they choose among competing transportation modes and technologies. Courier firms use virtually any form of transportation depending on local circumstances and the properties of the shipment: parcels can be shipped by bike, car, truck, train, ship, or plane.

Airlines, which often engage in intense competition with each other, are particularly sensitive to fuel cost changes. Increases in the cost of kerosene get passed on to travellers in the form of higher ticket prices or fuel surcharges. To stay competitive, airlines are opting for more fuel-efficient airplanes. Today's aircraft are 70% more fuel efficient than those operated 40 years ago. Modern aircraft achieve a fuel efficiency of 3.5 litres per 100 passenger kilometre, and the today's most advanced aircraft (the Airbus 380 and Boeing 787) achieve 3.0 litres per 100 passenger kilometre.

Rising fuel costs as well as government interventions prompt businesses to increase operational efficiency as well as fleet efficiency. Operational efficiency can be increased by utilizing the existing fleet more efficiently. For example, delivery trucks of a courier firm can be routed more efficiently through GPS-tracking and traffic congestion avoidance, and delivery routes can be planned more effectively through route optimization. Airplanes can be used more effectively by reducing taxi time on runways.

Transportation offers an enormous scope for innovation and ranks among the most lucrative opportunities for combining environmental gains with commercial profitability. Several large car manufacturers have embraced the production of hybrid-electric cars, and the production of these vehicles has now become a source of profitability. The same is not (yet) true for pure-electric cars. They remain more costly than their hybrid-electric cousins. So far, only one new car manufacturer has emerged—Tesla Motors of Palo Alto, California—that appears financially viable by targeting the high-performance end of the automotive market. Many companies focus on innovating key automotive technologies. With falling natural gas prices in North America due to the discovery of new resources, there is a significant potential for developing natural gas engines for motor vehicles. Westport Innovations of Vancouver, BC, is a leader in the development of such engines that can use compressed natural gas (CNG), liquefied natural gas (LNG), as well as biofuels and hydrogen.

European countries have invested heavily in high-speed rail. Originally pioneered in Japan in the 1960s as the 'bullet train' (shinkansen), high-speed train services in Europe and China run at speeds of 300–320 km/h. Since 2007, a French TGV has held the speed record of 574 km/h. Developing this infrastructure incurred huge up-front costs because high-speed rail tracks needed to be built to a much higher standard than conventional rail tracks. High-speed tracks are fused together and require more elaborate signalling systems; they also require less curvature and fewer inclines, which in turn requires more bridges and tunnels. High-speed rail service has shifted traffic from short-haul flights to trains. There are numerous environmental gains. The electricity used by trains in Europe is associated with far fewer emissions than equivalent air transportation. The noise footprint of trains is also much smaller than that of planes. Most importantly, downtown-to-downtown train service is often more convenient and faster than travelling by air.

The trade-off between higher up-front fixed costs and lower variable costs is pervasive in many business decisions that concern environmental outcomes. This is significant for individual choices such as buying a more expensive hybrid-electric car that saves fuel costs over time. It is also significant for investments in infrastructure such as Europe's high-speed rail network, where the magnitude of the necessary investments required some degree of government involvement in order to achieve desirable societal benefits.

2.6 Noise

Among the least-appreciated environmental hazards is noise pollution. Noise effects humans and animals. Noise of sufficient intensity and duration can induce temporary or permanent hearing loss, ranging from slight impairment to deafness. Noise can interfere with speech communication, the perception of other auditory signals, and lead to the disturbance of sleep and relaxation. Marine mammals may also get subjected to intense noise from seismic pulses originating from underwater oil exploration. This noise has been reported to affect the migration and mating of whales.

The sound pressure level that corresponds to noise is measured logarithmically in decibels (dB); an increase from 40 to 50 decibels implies a ten-fold increase in sound pressures. Noise is distributed over a wide range of frequencies of human hearing, typically from about 20 Hz to 10,000 Hz. When measuring noise levels it is therefore necessary to weight frequencies; the db(A) and db(C) weightings are most commonly used for noise measuring and acoustical standards. Transportation and construction activities are among the most important sources of noise. Acoustical standards are often found in building codes and municipal bylaws, and in assessing projects such as new airports, airport expansions, new highways, and new railway lines.

Reducing noise can create interesting business opportunities. There is a demonstrated market for noise reduction. People generally prefer quiet over noisy (except when attending sports events or rock concerts). The introduction of noise-cancelling headphones, widely used by airplane travellers, is a good example. Aircraft are increasingly using quieter engines and use different take-off and landing procedures to reduce noise impact on communities around airports. Automobiles can be made quieter by improving muffler design, reducing vibrations, and noise-insulating the engine compartment. Electric or hybrid-electric vehicles are quieter than their combustion-engine counterparts. Roads can be made quieter by paving them with hot mix asphalt concrete. In Europe, major highways and train tracks are separated from nearby houses by sound walls. Buildings can make more use of noise-insulating materials. When people are given a choice over controlling their ambient noise levels, there is clearly a market opportunity for businesses to develop noise-reduction solutions. Even whales can be protected from noise by surrounding the drilling sites with sheets of air bubble curtains.

2.7 Climate change

Climate change is the most topical environmental concern because of its far-reaching potential impact. The complexity of the issue makes it challenging to present this topic in a nutshell. Despite a growing scientific consensus that the warming trend is real and persistent, in many countries there remains political controversy over whether to take this threat seriously and what to do about it. The literature on climate change is vast, and thus the discussion below tries to provide a bird's-eye perspective on the key questions and answers.

Is the Earth's troposphere experiencing 'global warming'?

The answer to this question depends somewhat on the time horizon in which this question is framed. There is very solid scientific evidence on the geological time scale through measurements from ice core samples. The Vostok Antarctic ice core sample was drilled in 1998 to a depth of over 3 km and covers a climate record of over 420,000 years. More core samples were taken in Antarctica and in Greenland. After drilling the ice cores, the core sample is cut into fine slices and the ice samples are made to release the trapped carbon dioxide for measurement. Researchers find a close correlation between Antarctic temperature and atmospheric concentrations of carbon dioxide. Major transitions from the lowest to the highest values are associated with glacial-interglacial transitions. During these transitions, the atmospheric concentration of carbon dioxide rises from about 180 to 280–300 ppmv.[2] The present-day levels of carbon dioxide (about 400 ppmv in late 2013) are thus unprecedented.

The record on temperature changes is less conclusive. The ice core samples reveal that current global temperature averages are at the upper end of the scale, but not much outside this range. At a finer time scale, the evidence is strongly mounting that global average temperatures have been rising in the last century.

Weather and climate are often confused. Weather is the short-term variation in temperature, precipitation, and wind experienced at a local level. Climate is the long-term trend, and this requires data over many decades to be conclusive. While systematic measurement of temperatures started in earnest only about 150 years ago, coverage remained spotty until the second half of the 20th century. Coverage and standardizing measurements of ocean temperatures posed additional technical challenges. Nevertheless, the statistical evidence is increasingly reliable and shows a warming trend, visualized in figure 2.2 using data from the Global Historical Climatology Network (monthly). While there are significant short-term fluctuations in the data, the long-term trend is pointing upwards.

Is climate change anthropogenic?

While the evidence for an increase in the average global temperature is scientifically compelling, the question about the origin of this temperature rise is more difficult to answer. How much of this warming is attributable to man-made (anthropogenic) sources, and how much is attributable to natural processes?

While the increasing concentration of carbon dioxide in the atmosphere is clearly the result of human activity, there are a number of natural processes that influence the climate: volcanic activity, variations in

---

[2] ppmv = parts per million by volume.

Fig. 2.2 Global Surface Temperature Anomalies

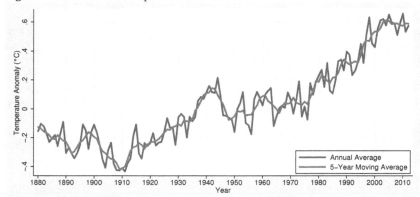

Data source: US National Oceanic and Atmospheric Administration, National Climatic Data Center (www.ncdc.noaa.gov). Temperature anomalies are relative to the 1901-2000 average. The chart shows the combined land and ocean anomaly.

Earth's orbit[3] that are linked to changes in the amount of solar radiation received by Earth and especially high northern latitudes, and changes in the sun's radiation output (solar irradiance). None of the alternative natural explanations can explain the rapid temperature changes of the last 30 years. While solar and volcanic forcings can explain certain warm and cold periods over the last two millennia, they cannot explain the recent warming trend.

Today's consensus view is expressed in the opinion of the Intergovernmental Panel on Climate Change (IPCC). The scientists who advise the IPCC conclude that most of the observed increase in globally-averaged temperatures since the mid-20th century is *very likely* (more than 90% certain) due to the observed increase in anthropogenic greenhouse gas concentrations, and that it is *extremely unlikely* (less than 5%) that the global pattern of warming during the past half-century can be explained without external forcing.

---

[3] Periodic change in three of the Earth's orbital parameters are referred to as Milankovitch cycles. Variation of the eccentricity of Earth's orbit follows a 100,000-year cycle with eccentricity varying from near circular to a peak of about 9%. parameters change cyclically over time The second cycle involves the tilt (obliquity) of Earth's axis, which varies between 22.1° and 24.5° over a 41,000-year period. The third cycle is due to the precession of the spin axis, a wobble of Earth's axis over a 25,800-year cycle. These cycles cause variations in solar radiation and can be connected to the climate record from ice core samples. Empirically, the 100,000-year eccentricity cycle appears to be most strongly linked to the ice age cycle over the last few million years.

> The case for anthropogenic forcing of climate change is compelling. 'No climate model using natural forcings alone has reproduced the observed global warming trend in the second half of the twentieth century.' (Solomon et al., 2007, p. 687)

A vocal but small minority of scientists disputes the anthropogenic cause of climate change. If they were right, there would be no reason to engage in any form of mitigation policy (reducing emissions) and all effort should be focused on adaptation policy (dealing with the negative consequences of climate change). Following the majority of scientists and the IPCC's conclusion suggests a strong focus on mitigation policy. However, exactly how much effort is needed remains difficult to pinpoint. The mitigation policy dilemma can be summarized in the double question: *how much, how soon*? Prudence suggests that a mixture of mitigation and adaptation is probably most likely to succeed, combined with a focus on implementing effective measures sooner rather than later.

What are the likely effects of climate change?

If the IPCC's conclusion is correct and anthropogenic emissions of greenhouse gases are forcing climate change, then the continuing build-up of greenhouse gases in the atmosphere due to the continued use of carbon-based fuels will lead to a continuing increase in global average temperatures and a variety of adverse weather phenomena. But how much does it matter? Will the effects be benign or catastrophic? Will they remain managable or have a deleterious effect on living standards regionally or worldwide?

The key to understanding the effects of climate change is to appreciate the regional diversity of these effects. Some countries will be significantly more challenged than others. Numerous countries may suffer greatly, while others may be able to adjust graciously.

The consequences of climate change on society are numerous. Rising global temperatures have been linked to a rise in the frequency of extreme weather events, although this link is still empirically somewhat fragile. There is strong empirical evidence that sea levels have been rising by about 0.2 cm per year over the last century. Some projections put the possible sea level rise for the 21st century somewhere between half a metre and two metres. Such a rise could threaten the habitability of parts of low-lying countries such as Bangladesh and the Netherlands. Perhaps the greatest risk of climate change is to the food supply. Higher temperatures would lead to productivity decreases for some crops in low latitudes and increases in agricultural productivity in high latitudes. This would create gainers and losers among countries.

While higher temperatures may affect precipitation adversely, higher concentrations of carbon dioxide also lead to a positive carbon fertilization effect that increases productivity. However, the magnitude of this offsetting effect remains a matter of scientific study.

What is the appropriate emission reduction *target* and how can this target be obtained *efficiently*?

If one accepts the conclusion that carbon dioxide and other anthropogenic greenhouse gases (GHGs) are responsible for climate change, then the logical question that follows is what to do about that. The scientists who advise the IPCC aim to stabilize the concentration of GHGs at 450 ppmv, which corresponds to keeping the rise in global average temperature to about 2°C above the preindustrial global average. The link between GHG concentrations and global average temperature is not instantaneous. Rather, if GHG concentrations were stabilized at today's level, there would still be an increase in temperatures in the following decades.

Scientific climate models do not provide a precise way of identifying the maximum level of GHG concentrations that would avoid catastrophic climate change. In part this is due to the feedback loop that keeps temperatures rising even if emissions were to be cut— entirely unrealistically—to zero tomorrow. In part this is also due to non-linearities in the climate system. Several such non-linearities that need to be taken into account.

First, the oceanic thermohaline current transports warm water from places such as the Gulf of Mexico to Europe. It has been argued that rising ocean temperatures may disrupt this global conveyor belt. This could actually lead to climate cooling in Europe. The full range of consequences is not yet well understood.

Second, huge amounts of methane are trapped in Arctic permafrost. Rising temperatures in the Arctic will start thawing the permafrost, which then may release this trapped methane. The greenhouse effect of methane is about 25 times that of carbon dioxide over a 100-year period, or about 72 times over a 20-year period. This is because methane has a half-life in the atmosphere of only about a decade, compared to about a century for carbon dioxide. Sudden release of methane could therefore have very pronounced climate effects.

Third, the frozen polar caps have a high albedo (light reflectivity). The melting Arctic will expose sea water under the north pole, which has a much lower albedo. This will lessen the amount of solar radiation reflected back into space, and thus contribute to further warming and further melting of the polar ice caps. This reinforcing process marks another non-linear transition.

Because of the numerous uncertainties about the course of climate change in response to rising GHG concentrations, it is very difficult to say with certainty where GHG concentrations need to be stabilized, and how aggressive GHG emissions need to be curtailed. It is entirely conceivable that we are already past the point of no return, and that the GHG concentrations we currently observe are sufficient to trigger significant changes in climate around the globe. The IPCC scientists reason that keeping within the 2°C target (and below 450 ppmv) will avoid catastrophic consequences. However, the continuing use of fossil fuels and the rapid economic growth in large countries such as China, India, and Indonesia will make it extremely difficult to keep GHG concentrations below the IPCC target.

This discussion leaves us with two dilemmas. The first dilemma is that there remains a significant degree of variation in scientific opinions about the appropriate GHG concentration target. This dilemma is a problem of science. The second dilemma is that even if we knew the GHG concentration target with precision, we also need to take into account the economic costs and benefits of getting there, and how fast. This dilemma is a problem of economics, and we will revisit this cost-benefit problem in more detail in chapter 3 on environmental economics.

What should we make of the many uncertainties surrounding the likely path of climate change? Should we wait until all uncertainties are resolved? William Nordhaus, an eminent environmental economist, answers these questions as follows:

> [W]e have discovered more puzzles and greater uncertainties as researchers dig deeper into the field. There are continuing major questions about the future of the great ice sheets of Greenland and West Antarctica; the thawing of vast deposits of frozen methane; changes in the circulation patterns of the North Atlantic; the potential for runaway warming; and the impacts of ocean carbonization and acidification. Moreover, our economic models have great difficulties incorporating these major geophysical changes and their impacts in a reliable manner. Policies implemented today serve as a hedge against unsuspected future dangers that suddenly emerge to threaten our economies or environment. So, if anything, the uncertainties would point to a more rather than less forceful policy—and one starting sooner rather than later—to slow climate change. (Nordhaus, 2012)

Studies by Nordhaus and other economists imply that reducing emissions sooner will come cheaper than reducing emissions later. Gradual adjustment will also be cheaper than abrupt adjustments a few decades from now. Current economic studies also suggest that the most efficient policy is to raise the cost of carbon emissions gradually, either through a cap-and-trade system or through a carbon tax, to provide appropriate incentives for businesses and households to move to low-carbon activities. Nevertheless, significant uncertainty remains about the appropriate speed and level of carbon pricing. Pindyck (2013) highlights the many empirical obstacles to pinning down an appropriate policy path. What we can say with great certainty, however, is that putting a price on carbon remains the best policy approach. As summarized in

Tietenberg (2013), empirical evidence from the existing policy experiments clearly supports this view. (Nordhaus, 2013) offers a thorough analysis of why earlier policies such as the Kyoto Protocol have failed, and which policy tools remain available going forward. This book is aptly titled *The Climate Casino*—the world is gambling on the trajectory of climate change.

What are the available technological options to mitigate or adapt to climate change?

If countries decide to respond to the challenge of climate change, it is possible to invest either in mitigation (reducing emissions, developing emission free technologies) or in adaptation (retooling our economy to cope with the consequences).

Considering the mitigation options, the key challenge is to select the technologies that achieve the targeted emission reduction with minimial cost. In other words, what are the 'low hanging fruit' of mitigation? The Swedish energy company Vattenfall commissioned a study (Mogren, 2007) to determine the mitigation scope and cost of different policies. A stylized version of that study's results, and the updated version from McKinsey (2009), appears in figure 2.3. The chart—now often referred to as the McKinsey curve—ranks the mitigation options by their scope and the marginal cost of abatement. Curiously, the first gigatons (Gt) of carbon dioxide reductions exhibit negative marginal cost. There is a free lunch! Virtually all of these options involve energy efficiency and energy conservation measures, through improved fuel efficiency, better insulation, and better lighting systems. Many of these efficiencies can be obtained by improving standards for buildings and transportation systems. The policy options that have a positive marginal abatement cost require an international long-term credible price of carbon. Renewable energy sources play a major role, as does nuclear power. More costly options involve carbon capture and storage (CCS). At the far end of the diagram are options that require significant technological innovation. The global GHG mitigation curve paints an optimistic scenario: with a carbon price of about €30 (about $40), about 35–40 Gt in carbon dioxide reductions could be achieved. The study also illustrates that there is no 'magic bullet' among the available options. For a particular government-mandated carbon price, climate mitigation will involve a combination of different policies and technologies.

Adapting to climate change—after its consequences have emerged—may be appealing to some countries because it postpones costly decisions. On the other hand, the wait-and-see approach may become ever more costly as the the consequences of climate change build up. Rising sea levels will cause increasing flood damage. The forestry industry will be impacted by changes to forest growth, increased number of forest fires, and new types of pests. Higher local temperatures in urban areas

Fig. 2.3 Global GHG Mitigation Cost Curve

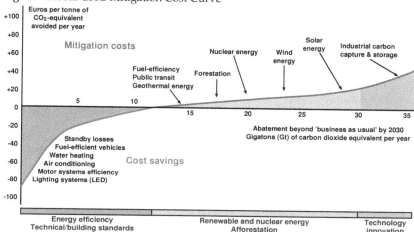

Stylized adaptation of Mogren (2007), McKinsey (2009), and UNEP/GRID-Arendal, 'Kick the Habit: A UN Guide to Climate Neutrality' (www.grida.no/publications/vg/kick). The type of chart above is often referred to as a 'McKinsey curve.'

may also affect air quality adversely, leading to higher health care costs. Adaptation technologies in the forestry sector include reducing the risk of forest fires by planting more resilient trees and actively controlling pests. Rising water levels can be countered by banning new buildings in areas at risk of flooding, and urban air quality can be improved by installing pollution control technologies that limit ozone formation. Nevertheless, the question remains whether adaptation is ultimately going to be more expensive than engaging in mitigation today.

How should firms adjust to the climate change challenge?

Firms are responding to the climate challenge through a combination of mandated and voluntary measures. Voluntary measures are primarily driven by a mixture of corporate social responsibility and the desire to discover win-win strategies that reduce costs and improve environmental performance at the same time. The task for individual firms can be broken down into several steps:

1. **Know what you emit**. Firms need to measure their releases of greenhouse gases, just as they monitor release of other (toxic) pollutants. This requires improving their environmental monitoring and information gathering. An environmental management system creates a feedback loop that can identify problems (e.g., leaks, malfunctions) and identify areas for improvement. Measuring emissions is not al-

ways easy, however. Box 2.3 discusses the approaches to measuring and estimating greenhouse gas emissions.

2. **Find win-win solutions**. Firms are (mostly) motivated by maximizing profits, and thus finding cost-reduction opportunities that also benefit the environment is making good business sense.

3. **Anticipate regulation**. Sooner or later governments will mandate environmental policies that tackle climate change. Knowing what options are available to respond cost effectively requires exploring substitution options: changing inputs such as fuels, and developing products that perform better. The objective is to reduce transition costs to new regulatory regimes.

4. **Invest in R&D**. In a changing competitive world it is imperative to stay ahead by being an innovator and technological leader. Falling behind often means losing the market. Firms need to invest in improving their productivity and develop novel solutions that reduce their environmental footprint.

2.8 Summary

Firms face a variety of environmental challenges. Some are local in nature, often related to particular production activities. Some are global in nature (such as climate change) and individual firms contribute only a small part to the overall problem. Environmental challenges create both opportunities and challenges for businesses. Improving environmental quality requires development of new technologies, from energy generation to pollution abatement. It also requires developing new products that respond to buyers' needs for better environmental performance, such as more fuel-efficient cars. In a competitive landscape, the key challenge is innovation. Stricter environmental regulation and changes in consumer demand will drive this process.

Which environmental challenges are the most important? How should firms prioritize which to respond to first? Governments play an important role in setting the environmental standards and price signals that reflect society's priorities. As environmental problems are often negative externalities from industrial activity, putting an appropriate price on the externality is often the best public policy. Firms can then figure out the most cost-effective technological option conditional on that price, and prioritize their activities accordingly.

Box 2.3: How do firms measure their carbon dioxide releases?

Firms are increasingly required to monitor their carbon dioxide releases. What technical methods are at their disposal? The ideal method involves continuous monitoring and direct measurement, such as stack sampling with gas analyzers and volumetric gas flow meters. While such devices are appropriate for large-scale industrial operations, they are often too expensive for small and mid-size businesses.

Alternative methods involve the use of mass balance, emission factors, and engineering estimates. Mass balance calculates the difference in input and output of a chemical reaction. Emission factors can often be applied quite easily to fuel use in a business; emissions are equal to the activity (fuel use) times the emission factor. For example, burning coal to generate a kWh of electricity involves a fixed amount of carbon dioxide per kWh, and thus knowing the amount of electricity generated is sufficient to estimate the amount of carbon dioxide released. Examples of carbon dioxide emission factors are:

- Natural gas (electric utilities): 1891 g/m^3.
- Light fuel oil: 2830 g/l.
- Heavy fuel oil: 3080 g/l.
- Coal: 1480–2390 g/kg (varies by type of coal)
- Gasoline vehicles: 2360 g/l fuel.
- Diesel vehicles: 2730 g/l fuel.

Fugitive emission factors are used when leaks, venting of natural gas, or gas flaring is involved (especially in the oil and gas industry). Emission factors can also be used in agricultural production, where methane emissions are converted into carbon dioxide equivalent emissions. Methane is released from enteric/intestinal fermentation (dairy cattle produce about 130 kg of methane per head per year) and manure management (another 30 kg of methane per head per year for dairy cattle).

2.9 Study questions and exercises

1. For each of the discussed environmental issues, what are examples of how individual companies are facing challenges to respond or adapt, and what are examples where these environmental issues create opportunities for entrepreneurship?
2. Businesses often face multiple environmental challenges simultaneously. How should businesses set priorities about which environmental problems they should tackle in which order?
3. In the debate about climate change, what do we know about the long-term pattern of carbon dioxide emissions and the long-term pattern of average global temperature change?
4. Explain the problem of 'how much? how soon?' with regard to climate change policies.

5. What are regional differences in climate change? Which regions may gain, which regions may lose, and which regions may experience catastrophic changes?
6. How does climate change affect Canada's Arctic both environmentally and economically?

Exercises

1. Look around the community you live in (your city or region) and itemize the most pressing *local* environmental issues facing your community. What are the available options to deal with them? Try to rank the solutions in terms of their environmental outcomes and likely cost.
2. Recently, claims have been made that climate change has 'disappeared' because the global average temperature has not increased substantially over the last fifteen years. See, for example, the articles 'A sensitive matter' in *The Economist* on March 30, 2013, or 'What to make of a warming plateau' in *The New York Times*, June 10, 2013. This exercise will require the use of a statistical software package such as Stata or SAS. Go to the web site of the National Climatic Data Center of the US National Oceanic and Atmospheric Administration (www.ncdc.noaa.gov) and download the global surface temperature anomalies data (monthly global land and ocean combined). This text file contains three columns for the year, month, and temperature anomaly ($°C$) relative to the 20th-century average.

   a. Using the data from 1880 through 2012, run a simple linear regression of the monthly temperature anomaly on a time trend variable (year+month/12)/100 that captures the temperature increase per century. Repeat this regression for the 1998–2012 period. Is the time trend statistically insignificant over the latter period at a conventional 95% confidence level?
   b. Now repeat the linear regressions for all 15-year periods from 1880–1929 through 1998–2012. How many times is the time trend statistically significant or insignificant? What do you conclude from the 15-year regression for 1941–1955?
   c. Repeat the analysis once more for all 50-year periods from 1880–1929 through 1963–2012. What do you conclude from these results for the path of climate change? Which time horizon is needed to identify climate trends conclusively?
   d. Can you find any empirical evidence that the increase in the global average temperature has been accelerating? Try using an exponential time trend exp((year-1950+month/12)/100). Does this provide a better fit to the data than a linear time trend?

Chapter 3
Environmental Economics

Protecting the environment is embraced widely, but businesses and society often differ about the scope of protection. How much environmental protection is too little, and how much protection is too much? There is often no scientific answer to that question. Ultimately, it comes down to a trade-off where the costs of environmental protection (or pollution abatement) are weighed against the benefits of a cleaner (less polluted) environment. Often an important consideration is whether environmental harm is reversible or irreversible. With reversible harm, economic policy does not necessarily have to 'get it right' on the first try; but when harm is irreversible, policies that are insufficiently stringent will lock in the damage permanently. Environmental economics is a useful tool for designing environmental policies. In essence, environmental economics rests on the assumption that there are market failures for environmental goods (such as air and water), and that policy interventions (ideally using market and price mechanisms) can be used to correct these market failures. This chapter explores the fundamental concepts of environmental economics with a view towards how economic policies affect businesses and their choices.

While covering some of the basic elements of environmental economics, it is important to note that this chapter does not cover a sibling area: resource economics. A discussion of the economics of renewable and non-renewable resources is beyond the scope of this book.

The material in this chapter leans to some extent on the coverage of environmental economics in a number of popular introductory texts in this area. There are four texts that are highly recommended as further reading. First, Field and Olewiler (2011) is a widely used introductory text on environmental economics with a focus on Canadian applications. Goodstein (2010) is the U.S. counterpart, written with a focus on recent topical issues. Some of the examples in this chapter were adapted from this source. A book with a wider scope (it includes an excellent coverage of resource economics) is Perman et al. (2003), which aims at both undergraduate and graduate readers by including advanced material in chapter appendices. Last but not least, McKitrick (2011) is an advanced text that focuses on the economic analysis of environmental policy, and is aimed at graduate students who are comfortable with mathematical modelling and econometric tools. All four books are excellent sources to gain a deeper understanding of environmental economics. Considering the wide interest in emissions trading markets, another useful source is Tietenberg (2006). This is one of the few rigorous treatments of the topic that includes a thorough discussion of transaction costs, spatial and temporal dimensions, market power and enforcement.

3.1 Basic economic concepts

3.1.1 Pollutants and externalities

The starting point for economic analysis of the environment is the notion of a negative externality, a spillover from an economic activity that is costly to a third party. Pollution is the classic example of a negative externality. It is a cost that is not borne by the buyer and seller but by the public at large. Because negative externalities are not captured by the price of the good that is being sold and bought, they constitute a type of market failure that is caused by a lack of property rights. The extreme case of a lack of property rights was described as the tragedy of the commons by Garrett Hardin in 1968. It describes a situation where multiple parties, acting only in their own self-interest, destroy an open access shared resource even though this is not in their long-term interest. Overfishing that leads to fish stock collapse (see discussion in section 11.3) is an example of such a tragedy of the commons. Environmental economics has an effective recipe for dealing with such negative externalities and property right deficiencies. The general solution to the externality problem is to find a way to internalize the externality, which involves compensating the affected parties for the pollution they are exposed to, or to create property rights over the affected environment or resource. A large part of the analysis in environmental economics is concerned with finding the most efficient way to internalize negative externalities. Often this involves allocating and managing property rights effectively.

Before exploring specific tools in the toolbox of environmental economists, it is useful to step back and first look at the nature of the negative externalities that we are dealing with. Figure 3.1 provides a simple schematic of the economic-environmental system. Industrial activity generates a flow of pollution. Such pollution flow generates some immediate (short-term) environmental damage due to the exposure of humans and the ecosystem at large. Nature is able to absorb many pollutants over time and render them harmless; this ability is described as nature's assimilative capacity. This process can be relatively quick (especially when dispersion and dilution are involved), but often it is rather slow. When nature is not able to cope with long-lived pollutants, there is a build-up of a pollution stock, with damage to humans and the

Fig. 3.1 Pollution Sources and Sinks

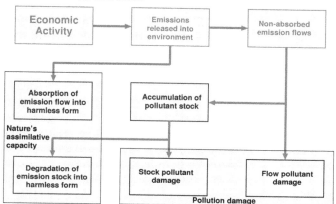

ecosystem. This means that the harm from these pollutants may continue well after the emission flow has been discontinued.

The environmental consequences of pollution flows and pollution stocks are transformed through the ecosystem itself. A pollutant's health hazard evolves over time as the pollutant may undergo chemical or biological transformations. For example, nitrous oxide emitted from soil fertilizers breaks down when it reaches the stratosphere and forms ozone-destroying nitrogen oxides. Biological processes can also increase the health risk from pollutants. Two important processes are bioaccumulation and biomagnification.

Bioaccumulation describes the build-up of toxic pollutants in the tissue of living organisms due to ambient exposure to the pollutant. The effect is more pronounced in organisms that are unable to metabolize or excrete the pollutant. Contaminated food supply may increase the pollutant dosage that an organism is exposed to by orders of magnitude from the ambient level. While the ambient pollution concentration may be harmless, the accumulated long-term dosage may be harmful or even lethal to the organism.

Bioaccumulation is often accompanied by biomagnification, where pollutants are passed on from lower organisms in the foodweb (a lower trophic level) to higher organisms in the foodweb (a higher trophic level). For example, prior to 1972 the insecticide DDT was used in the United States to combat mosquitoes, which transmit diseases such as malaria. Rain washed DDT into rivers and lakes and into the fish stock. A number of predatory bird species ate contaminated fish, and the DDT's thinning effect on the birds' egg shells led to their premature breaking, thus decimating these bird species.[1] DDT has also been linked with direct health effects on humans, including miscarriage, premature birth, difficulty breast-feeding, and developmental neurotoxicity.

Bioaccumulation (within a trophic level) and biomagnification (across trophic levels) require that the toxin is (i) long-lived (it does not decay rapidly), (ii) mobile (typically airborne or waterborne), (iii) soluble in fats, and (iv) biologically active (has a measurable effect on cell metabolism).

The effect of pollutants has both a time and a space dimension. The time dimension is reflected in the process of bioaccumulation and biomagnification. Temporal clustering is also important with respect to the dose-response relationship of a pollutant—i.e., the change in effect of an organism caused by differing levels of exposure. The ambient concentration (the dose) of a pollutant often has a non-linear effect on health (the response). Therefore, short-term exposure to a high dose may have more detrimental effects than long-term exposure to a low dose. This non-linear relationship has important consequences for the design of environmental policy. Emission standards need to take into account the temporal clustering of exposure and set separate limits for short-term exposure and long-term exposure. For example, Canada's recommended ambient air quality standard for carbon monoxide limits the maximum acceptable level to 30 ppm over a one-hour averaging period and to 13 ppm over an eight-hour averaging period.

The spatial dimension of pollutants matters as well. One needs to distinguish between local pollutants (with adverse effects limited to a few kilometres from a point source), regional pollutants such as sulphur dioxide that travel over tens or even a few hundreds of kilometres, and global pollutants such as the greenhouse gas carbon dioxide. Technically, local and regional pollutants are referred to as non-uniformly mixed pollutants, while global pollutants are referred to as uniformly mixed pollutants. The spatial clustering of pollutants creates what is known as hot spots, areas with very high ambient pollution concentrations. In the 1960s it was quite common to solve the hot-spot problem by building higher smoke stacks and following the mantra 'the solution to pollution is dilution.' While spreading out the pollutant more equally over a larger area reduces ambient concentrations, it is not a particular effective method because adverse weather conditions can still lead to extreme local concentration levels.

The spatial dimension matters in yet another way. Pollution can cross jurisdictional borders. Such transboundary pollution is very common and limits the ability of a single jurisdiction to tackle environmental problems effectively. The need for policy coordination is often

---

[1] The 1962 book *Silent Spring* by biologist Rachel Carson, which describes the ill effects of DDT, is often considered one of the defining events in launching the environmental movement in the United States, and perhaps even worldwide.

paramount but limited by the constitutional allocation of responsibilities or the inability to conclude effective cross-jurisdictional or international treaties. These problems are examined later in the chapter on environmental law.

3.1.2 Public goods and property rights

Private goods differ in two key dimensions from public goods, which are goods enjoyed in common. Public goods are described by two features: non-excludability and non-rivalry. Excludability requires that it is possible to prevent people who have not paid for the good from using it. A rival good cannot be consumed by two consumers simultaneously. Conversely, a non-rival good is one which can be supplied at zero marginal cost to a second and further consumers, and thus can be consumed by an unlimited number of consumers. The two dimensions form a classification matrix with four different types of goods:

	Excludable	Non-excludable
Rivalrous	Private goods food, clothing, cars, toys	Common goods fish, forests
Non-rivalrous (simultaneous consumption)	Club goods cable television, cinemas	Public goods lighthouses, air, national defence

While public goods are characterized by non-excludability and non-rivalry, common goods and club goods are cousins with only one of these characteristics. Common goods such as fish and forests are non-excludable (or at least not easily excludable) but rivalrous: a fish I eat you can't eat; a tree I log you can't log. Club goods such as cable television are easily excludable, but to the extent that households already have a cable connection, adding another subscriber comes at practically zero marginal cost to the cable company. Put another way, if I watch a television show, any number of people can watch the same show at the same time.

The environment is a public good and as such encounters the problem of free riding. Consumers can take advantage of public goods without contributing sufficiently to their creation, and with respect to the environment, the environment can be used freely without contributing to keeping the environment clean. Free riding is a consequence of poorly defined property rights. A solution is therefore to create property rights. Property rights can create excludability, or rivalry, or both, depending on the particular nature of the property rights.

Restoring property rights is the crucial step in fixing a problem with a negative externality. The concept was pioneered by Nobel Prize laureate Ronald Coase in the 1960s and is known as the Coase theorem.

> **Coase theorem**: When trade in an externality is possible and when there are no transaction costs and free riding, bargaining will lead to an efficient outcome regardless of the *initial* allocation of property rights.

As far as the environment is concerned, the Coase theorem suggests that governments should create property rights over its use. Regardless of who owns the property rights, the externality will be internalized. Who owns the property rights is important only in regard to the distribution of income from these property rights.

If the government endowed the polluter with a right to pollute, then the pollution victim would bargain to pay the polluter to reduce pollution. If, on the other hand, the government endowed a city or province with a right to clean air, then the polluter would bargain to pay the city or province for permission to pollute. Of course, in the first case revenue would flow to the polluter, and in the latter case to the city or province. The outcome will be economically efficient either way, but the two solutions will be perceived as differently fair.

The Coase theorem acknowledges one major caveat: the presence of transaction costs. The efficient outcome may not be feasible when the parties find it difficult to negotiate and transact. For example, the victims of pollution may find it difficult to coordinate among themselves, and firms would find it difficult to contract with thousands of individuals rather than a single other party. Where such transaction barriers exist, governments may need to play the role of the contracting party and exercise the property right on behalf of a large number of people.

There is a second caveat: incomplete information. When property rights are allocated to one party, that party has an incentive to withhold crucial information to strengthen its bargaining position. In the absence of complete information, the efficient outcome may not be possible to achieve. Furthermore, when the negotiation between parties occurs over multiple rounds, reputation effects can arise that distort the outcome.

In practice, the Coase theorem points us in the right direction (create property rights) without telling us the precise destination (whom to allocate the property rights) or the shortest route there (with the least transaction costs, and with the most complete information). Nevertheless, property rights can be used quite effectively in many instances. For example, individual transferable quotas (ITQs) are used to manage rights over fish stock, and tradeable emission permits (TEPs) are used to manage emissions into air. In both cases, though, initial allocation matters in practice. While property rights can be very efficient, big questions remain about fair allocation of such rights.

3.1.3 Efficiency and fairness

In the discussion about the allocation of property rights and the Coase theorem, it was seen that outcomes involve both efficiency and fairness. An outcome that is economically efficient may be viewed as unfair, while an economically inefficient outcome may be regarded as fair. How does economics reconcile these notions?

Economic efficiency is a straight-forward optimality concept involving a state without scope for further improvement. In environmental economics, the notion of Pareto efficiency is crucial:

> Pareto efficiency describes an outcome in which it is impossible to make one person (or contracting party) better off without making anyone else (or the other contracting party) worse off.

Finding economic efficiencies often involves allocating property rights and letting the different parties bargain over the outcome, which may make both parties better off. Box 3.1 illustrates the situation of water rights in California and the potential for a Pareto-improvement.

Efficiency does not imply fairness. Both polluter or victims can pay to reduce pollution and achieve an efficient outcome. Yet most of us would probably instinctively object to giving polluters the right to pollute rather than citizens the right to clean air. In economics, fairness is a notion that applies to the distribution of income and wealth, and thus fairness is closely linked to distributive equality. Good social outcomes are 'fair.' Suppose two equally productive people R and P started out with an income of $50,000, so that the total is $100,000. Now double the total income and give all of the extra income to person R and none to P. This is Pareto-efficient (nobody is made off worse), but probably not very fair. The notion of fairness goes beyond economics and is ultimately political in nature: what is fair—or not—is defined by societal norms, which may change over time, and may differ across cultures. Much of the following analysis is therefore focused more on efficiency and less on notions of fairness. The problem with many environmental policies, though, is that many policies that are economically efficient also create winners and losers—and this becomes quickly a matter for political battles.

Fairness is also concerned when it comes to the location choice of polluting firms. There have been concerns about environmental jus-

Box 3.1: Water Rights in California

California is legendary for its water wars (which came to Hollywood fame in the 1974 movie *Chinatown*). The unending thirst of a growing Los Angeles led to the building of aqueducts and the draining of lakes, resulting in battles between the city and rural communities. California is also a state of water extremes, with years of strong rainfall and other years of drought. The perceived shortages of water in California are at least in part an example of mismatched supply and demand.

When California was settled, the settling farmers were endowed with most of the water rights. Today, they use more than three-quarters of the available water at a price that is set by the state and the federal government as low as 1 cent per cubic metre. By comparison, residents of Los Angeles pay 9.25 cents per cubic metre, almost ten times as much as farmers pay. This is clearly inefficient and explains why irrigation is overused to produce agricultural output. This can also be viewed as a huge subsidy to farming.

Is there a Pareto-improvement? Imagine there was a single market price for water that equalized supply and demand for water in California. If farmers were allowed to sell their water entitlements to urban dwellers, quite a few would probably find it profitable to sell water to city dwellers or commercial users rather than use it to produce crops. Reallocating water through a market mechanism could boost California's economy through increased efficiency.

There are, of course, other inefficiencies in California's management of water. As in many other jurisdictions, water use is often not metered and is essentially provided at a flat rate, thus offering little monetary incentive to conserve water.

tice when polluting firms are concentrated in poor neighbourhoods or neighbourhoods with larger shares of demographic minorities. While there may be some self-selection involved (people choosing to live close to the plants they work for, rather than plants choosing to move into neighbourhoods with particular demographics), studies have found unfavourable correlations between poverty and the presence of hazardous waste sites.

In the real world there are large transaction costs between the many individuals in society and the few polluting firms. Efficiency can be achieved under a polluter pays principle. Requiring a polluter to pay for the right to pollute is likely to be more efficient than the other way around because it reduces transaction costs and free riding. What is more important is that endowing firms with a right to pollute would lower their overall cost, lead to more firm entry into the industry, and create yet more pollution.

What is an efficient solution to pollution abatement? Firms all have different capabilities to reduce emissions. For some it will be very expensive to reduce emissions on a per-unit basis, and for others it will be much less expensive. Who should reduce emissions more: the 'dirty' or the 'clean' firm? To rank the ability of individual firms to reduce their emissions, we need to know each firm's per-unit marginal abatement cost (MAC). Marginal abatement cost is usually expressed in dollars per physical unit (e.g., metric tonne of emissions). Firms usually have different MACs at different levels of output or emissions. As a firm's share of abated pollution rises, the cost of the extra abatement continues to rise. Reducing 80% of emissions may be relatively cheap, but moving from 80% to 90% abatement efficiency may become more costly, and going from 90% to 99% abatement efficiency may involve yet more costly abatement technology. As a result, firms usually have an upward-sloping MAC curve with respect to the abatement level (or abatement efficiency).

Efficient pollution abatement: the least-cost pollution abatement regime requires that the marginal cost of abatement is equalized across all firms undertaking pollution abatement.

A least-cost solution will in general not involve equal abatement effort by all polluters: some polluters will have higher per-unit abatement costs than others. When MACs differ across firms, cost efficiency implies that relatively low-cost abaters will undertake most of the total abatement effort, but not all of it. On the other hand, the relatively high-cost abaters will carry out less abatement effort. This may lead, counterintuitively, to the 'dirty' firms abating less than the 'clean' firms. But as we are only interested in an overall reduction of emissions, it does not matter who reduces the emissions as long as we achieve the desired emission reduction at the lowest overall cost. But how do we get the low-cost abaters to do most of the pollution abatement? What are the best policy instruments to achieve the efficient outcome?

3.2 Policy instruments

The economic answer to the problem of negative externalities is quite simple: put a price on the negative externality. The fundamental problem with negative environmental externalities is that there is a gap between the private cost and the social cost of the polluting activity. The social cost is borne by society, but not the producer. Therefore, the efficient solution is to close the gap. Arthur Pigou discovered the solution to this problem in 1920:

Pigouvian principle: pollution should be priced at its marginal external cost.

The marginal external cost is the cost resulting from the production of one additional unit accruing to a different party than either the producer or consumer of the product. A Pigouvian tax is intended to cover the social cost (negative externality) of an economic activity and restore the efficient outcome. It is important to understand that a Pigouvian tax is efficient only when it is applied to the pollutant (or the externality) directly on a per-unit basis. For example, a tax on automobiles to combat carbon emissions is not as effective as a tax on carbon emissions (or gasoline) because cars differ in fuel efficiency and the mileage they are driven.

When we look at individual firms, a Pigouvian tax will increase the firm's pollution abatement effort. The firm's marginal abatement cost will rise as it steps up this effort. This means that the MAC curve will be upward sloping in abatement effort, or downward sloping in actual emissions. Reducing emissions by 10% will be less costly per unit of output than reducing emissions by 80% per unit of output. In other words, there are low-hanging fruit of pollution abatement (e.g., switching fuel sources) that are relatively cheap, and there are costly capital investments in pollution abatement equipment (e.g., installing a scrubber, perhaps connected to an electrostatic precipitator).

Armed with data on the abatement cost of firms and thus the 'supply' of pollution, what do we know about the 'demand' for pollution? It may seem counterintuitive to think that anyone would 'demand' pollution, but in fact we all do. Any time we get behind the steering wheel in a conventional automobile and drive, we emit pollutants such as carbon monoxide and carbon dioxide. By deciding to drive this particular car we 'demand' the pollution that goes along with this activity. Of course, if this pollution costs us extra money (in the form of carbon taxes or higher gasoline taxes), we may decide to drive less or drive a more fuel-efficient vehicle. Our demand for pollution is leading to environmental damage, and this damage tends to increase on a per-unit level as emissions increase. This is another way of saying that there is a nonlinear dose-response function. Technically speaking, marginal damage is upward sloping in emissions. Neoclassical economic analysis tells us that the efficient outcome is where pollution supply meets pollution demand, and this happens when marginal abatement cost equals marginal damage. This clean theoretical result encounters an empirical dilemma, unfortunately.

While marginal abatement cost is observable (at least by the individual firm, if not the regulator), marginal damage is often very difficult to pinpoint. In practice, the regulator steps in to reflect society's belief about the marginal environmental damage—and this may be on target or off target. In the discussion about the different policy instruments we need to keep an eye on the effect of uncertainty about marginal damage. What happens when the regulator gets it wrong? Furthermore, the regulator may not always be able to observe correctly each firm's marginal abatement cost. This is a situation of information asymmetry: one side (the firm) knows more than the other side (the regulator).

Policy instruments fall into three broad categories:

- **Information-based** policy instruments are voluntary in nature. They induce firms to make public information about their emissions in the hope that pressure from stakeholders, along with knowledge sharing among firms within an industry, will lead to emission reductions without direct government intervention. The *Toxics Release Inventory* in the United States and the *National Pollutant Release Inventory* in Canada are tools that inform the public. Governments promote cooperation among firms through voluntary challenge programs. In the United States, the 33/50 program targeted 17 priority chemicals and set as its goal 33% and 50% emission reduction by 1992 and 1995, respectively. In Canada, the ARET program targeted a wider set of pollutants for virtual elimination between 1995 and 2000. Consumers armed with more information alone are not necessarily putting a lot of pressure on firms: the empirical evidence for green consumerism is relatively weak. Another popular information-based approach involves product labelling or certification whereby firms signal environmental performance to consumers. Consumers who value such environmental credentials may be willing to pay a green price premium for such products.
- **Mandated** (or direct) policy instruments are command-and-control measures: they give firms a precise set of rules that they are required to follow. Such rules come in two flavours: an emission standard regulates the environmental performance of production facilities (such as a maximum level of emission concentrations), while a technology standard regulates the production process by mandating specific production methods or pollution abatement equipment.
- **Incentive-based** policy instruments work indirectly through price signals and the market mechanism. The simplest form is a Pigouvian tax in the form of an emission tax that sets a price for the pollutant. The carbon tax in British Columbia ($30/tonne since 2012) is an example of such a tax. An alternative is the use of tradeable emission permits whereby the regulator auctions or allocates emission rights to firms. Once in possession of these permits, firms can trade freely in them but at the end of a reference period must possess sufficient permits to cover all their emissions. Governments can also use a variety of other taxes to influence environmental outcomes, albeit less directly. As particular intermediate goods and ser-

vices are linked to emissions, input taxes can target them. A fuel tax can target simultaneously a variety of pollutants associated with the burning of such fuels. Instead of using taxes, governments can also pay firms directly to reduce emissions. Governments often prefer subsidies over taxes for political reasons: everybody loves getting money from the government, but nobody likes paying money to the government.

3.2.1 Instrument choice criteria

There is a large number of possible environmental policy instruments. How should a regulator choose among them? Which instruments are preferred by firms? Regulators and regulated need to consider a number of criteria. Below there are grouped together into four main categories:

1. **Environmental effectiveness**
    - **Directedness** is the degree to which the policy is aimed at the environmental problem. First-best approaches target the environmental problem directly, while second-best approaches take aim through a secondary mechanism. For example, reducing automotive emissions through a fuel tax is a direct approach, while taxing vehicles (rather than the amount of driving) is an indirect approach.
    - **Short-term effectiveness** is achieved by going after the biggest pollution sources first. These are often the 'low-hanging fruits' of policy intervention, such as shutting down old and highly-polluting facilities before designing policies that encourage further emission reductions across all facilities.
    - **Long-run effectiveness** requires that the policy's potency does not diminish over time, for example through substitution effects. If firms or households can avoid the policy by switching to other (unregulated) products or processes with other adverse environmental effects, the policy will become increasingly ineffective.

2. **Economic efficiency**
    - **Static efficiency** is achieved when the emission reduction target is obtained at the lowest possible abatement cost. Incentive-based policies are more efficient than mandated policies.
    - **Dynamic efficiency** is achieved when the policy creates persistent and predictable incentives to innovate into pollution abatement, emission-reducing products or emission-reducing manufacturing processes.

- **Flexibility** is necessary to ensure that a policy instrument can be adapted quickly and effectively to new situations and circumstances. Firms have a high degree of autonomy in choosing appropriate technologies to achieve the desired environmental outcomes.
- **Robustness** ensures that the policy remains economically efficient even in the presence of high uncertainty (or incomplete information) about abatement costs or environmental damage.
- **Simplicity** is related to informational costs. A policy that is complex and has numerous transaction costs is less desirable than a policy that is simple and does not require much information gathering, monitoring, or enforcement action by regulators.

3. **Fairness and participation**

- **Fairness** is the notion that the environmental policy does not favour one societal group over another, or put undue burden on a small group in society.
- **Involvement** that is wide and deep across society ensures that stakeholders take ownership of the policy, especially if the policy targets modification of behaviour. Involvement helps entrench a policy against opportunistic abandonment of the policy.

4. **Political considerations**

- **Political feasibility** requires that an environmental policy is supported by the electorate and elected representatives. Widely unpopular policies may be difficult to adopt even if they are environmentally sound.
- **Budget implications** are the effects of the policy on the government budget. Taxes raise revenue, while subsidies incur costs. Revenue-neutral policies are often preferred.
- **Ancillary benefits** arise when a policy has beneficial secondary effects. Such a policy is said to have a double dividend. For example, tax revenue from the environmental policy can be recycled to offset inefficiencies in other parts of the economy, the tax system, or to pursue other environmental objectives.

This is a long catalogue of criteria, and while the economic efficiency theme stands out among them, it is quite apparent that no single instrument is clearly superior along all the dimensions relevant to policy choice. Significant trade-offs arise in the choice of instruments. In addition to considering economic efficiency and fairness (distributional equity), regulators often find that political feasibility imposes the most important constraints on deploying particular policy instruments.

> No single environmental policy instrument is superior along all dimensions; hybrid instruments, or a combination of instruments, are often able to strike a better balance among economic efficiency, distributional fairness, and political feasibility.

In the presence of conflicting choice criteria, hybrid regimes may sometimes become preferable over pure instruments (Goulder and Parry, 2008). For example, one can make strong case for a regime of tradeable emission permits with upper and lower price ceilings—i.e., a hybrid system of emission quotas and emission taxes. For a given environmental problem, multiple market failures may be involved. In this case, multiple instruments may need to be deployed simultaneously on efficiency grounds. There is also the possibility of potential interactions among environmental policy instruments. If hybrid regimes are not designed carefully or emerge through overlapping jurisdiction, interactions among these policy instruments may reduce their overall efficacy.

Yet another problem is that environmental policy instruments may need to be adjusted to allow for existing market distortions. Specifically, when an industry is imperfectly competitive, an emission tax may lead to an overly strong output reduction. This implies that emission taxes ought to be somewhat lower in oligopolistic than in competitive markets.

When regulators deploy environmental policy instruments, they affect a firm's choice of (i) input mix (especially different types of energy); (ii) use of abatement technology; (iii) output level; and (iv) innovation activity (with respect to redesigning products or processes). When we look at the individual firm, an environmental policy may affect one or more of these at the same time, and this may not always lead to effects working in the same direction.

3.2.2 Technology and emission standards

Governments often feel at greatest ease setting a technology standard, as this can be accomplished through the process of granting a development permit for the construction of a new plant. This is a very simple once-and-for-all minimum standard that the firm has to adhere to, and that can be monitored and enforced easily through an inspection.

In general, technology standards are specific requirements regarding the production process and production technology. They can involve a mandate for an end-of-pipe treatment (such as installing a scrubber or other pollution abatement device) or the use of particular inputs (e.g., natural gas instead of coal).

Although technology standards are appealing because of their relative ease of implementation and monitoring, heterogeneity among firms makes it very difficult for the regulator to possess all necessary information to maximize the cost-effectiveness. Technical standards suffer from the information asymmetry problem, where the firm knows more about its own abilities than the regulator. Technical standards can easily evolve into a hodgepodge of plant-specific rules that vary over time and across jurisdictions. But even when technical standards are set as a single mandate that is equal across firms, they will not always result in a cost-effective outcome because different firms will face different marginal abatement costs due to differences in their production process, plant age, inputs, or other factors.

An emission standard is aimed at a firm's output rather than inputs or production technology. Such standards are typically expressed as emission intensity (pollutant per unit of output). Just like technology standards, emission standards are subject to the information asymmetry problem. In practice, emission standards are often sufficiently modest that they can be met by reducing emissions through input substitution and relatively benign end-of-pipe treatment. Emission standards such as fuel efficiency limits for automobiles—in particular, the Corporate Average Fuel Economy (CAFE) standard in the United States—often do not sufficiently encourage output reduction (e.g., number of automobiles on our roads) or output use (e.g., kilometres driven). On the other hand, emission standards are also relatively easy to enforce and monitor, and thus remain popular with regulators.

Despite their relative economic inefficiency, technology and emission standards also remain popular with regulated firms. The reason is their predictability and certainty. Technology standards are often once-and-for-all requirements that can be fulfilled during the construction stage of a new plant. Emission standards often evolve gradually, and are sometimes easily subverted. For example, the CAFE standard for automobiles was eroded by classifying the popular sport-utility vehicles as light trucks rather than cars, which were subject to different standards.

3.2.3 Environmental taxes

Among incentive-based policies, environmental taxes (also referred to as 'green taxes') stand out as providing the most immediate and stable price signal to firms and consumers. Unlike mandated policies, incentive-based policies are usually able to achieve economic efficiency because they let firms figure out how to respond optimally to the price signal. It is entirely up to the firms to find the cheapest way to reduce emissions. An individual firm will increase pollution abatement until the marginal abatement cost equals the price of the pollutant as defined by the environmental tax or through the price in a tradeable permit market. The regulator does not need to know each firm's marginal abatement cost curve, and thus information asymmetry is not a problem. As long as the regulator knows that firms will equate the emission price to marginal abatement cost, the cost-efficient outcome will emerge. The regulator simply needs to figure out the correct price for the negative externality.

How should environmental taxes be introduced? The answer is: gradually. Like any regime shift, businesses require time to adapt. It is therefore highly advisable that government phase in an environmental tax over a number of years and raise the tax once a year until it has the desired effect. Such a gradual introduction avoids the risk of overshooting when regulators have imprecise knowledge about the market equilibrium that corresponds to the desired emission reduction.

Fig. 3.2 Cap-and-Trade versus Green Tax

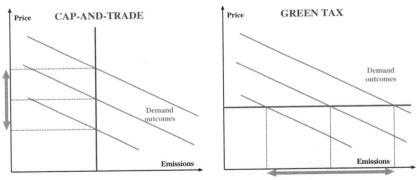

Environmental taxes and tradeable emission permits are equally efficient in a static sense (comparing their effect in a single period). They can achieve the same outcome at the same abatement cost. For any environmental tax there is an equivalent cap-and-trade emission target. Figure 3.2 illustrates how the two policy regimes differ. The two diagrams show consumer demand as a downward sloping curve, which mirrors a normal demand curve with output and price. The only difference is that the horizontal axis shows emissions rather than output. Emissions are simply a by-product of output. Fluctuating demand will move the demand curve lower or higher.

With an emission tax (right panel in figure 3.2), the regulator sets a tax rate (horizontal line) and may thus hit or miss the emission target as demand shifts up or down. This is a case of quantity uncertainty. With a cap-and-trade regime (left panel in figure 3.2), the regulator sets the emission target (vertical line) and the market discovers the price through the trading of emission permits. As demand shifts up or down, the market price fluctuates. This is a case of price uncertainty.

Fig. 3.3 Effect of Green Tax on Firm

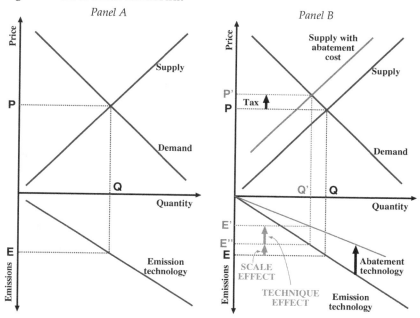

The effect of an environmental tax on an individual firm is illustrated in figure 3.3. The economic logic for a cap-and-trade system is identical; it is different for a subsidy, however. Panel A in figure 3.3 shows a double diagram where the upper part depicts a conventional supply-and-demand diagram. Demand is downward-sloping: higher prices reduce demand. Supply is upward-sloping: higher prices will increase supply. Given supply and demand, the market equilibrium will emerge where the supply curve and demand curve intersect, with an optimal price P and quantity Q. In the lower half of the diagram, output Q translates into a corresponding amount of emissions E as governed by the currently used technology without abatement.

Panel B in figure 3.3 demonstrates the effects of an environmental tax, which shifts up the supply curve by making output more expensive for any given amount of output. The distance between the two supply curves is the tax rate. The tax-induced upward shift of the supply curve leads to a new market equilibrium, with a higher price $P' > P$ and a lower output level $Q' < Q$. There are now two effects to consider. First, the reduction in output will reduce emissions from E to E'' before abatement technology is deployed. This is the scale effect. Second, the environmental tax induces the firm to deploy abatement technology until its marginal abatement cost equals the environmental tax. This amounts to a rotation of the emission technology line in the lower half of the diagram. The blue line rotates into the red line. At the new and lower output level Q', the new emission technology line translates output Q' into the new final emission level E'. This further reduction in emissions from E'' to E' is the technique effect. With an environmental tax and cap-and-trade regime, scale effect and technique effect work in tandem and complement each other. Which of the two effects is larger or smaller depends on the steepness of the firm's supply curve and the rotation of the emission technology curve. A flat supply curve magnifies the scale effect, which is usually not welcome. Lost output also means lost revenue for a firm. What is welcome, however, is a large rotation of the emission technology curve, which reflects low abatement costs and magnifies the technique effect.

Emission taxes generate government revenue, and this may make emission taxes politically unpalatable. In principle, governments can take the revenue from an emission tax and redistribute it in the form of lower taxes elsewhere. This has been described as a (revenue-neutral) green tax reform. British Columbia's carbon tax, introduced in 2008, returned the revenue to its citizens in the form of lower personal and corporate income taxes, as well as a one-time $100 per head 'dividend payment.' Governments can also funnel the revenue into other environmental projects, from public transit to 'green subsidies.' This dual environmental benefit of green taxes is often described as the double dividend. Despite the possibility of revenue neutrality or a double dividend, many politicians consider proposing (let alone introducing) an environmental tax 'toxic' for their electoral prospects. Of course, this raises the question whether there is a method to construct an environmental tax that generates very little revenue while preserving the emission price. There are hybrid emission standards plus emission taxes that can accomplish this. Consider an environmental tax on firms only, where firms' MAC is ranked on an abatement ladder: the best firm with the lowest MAC firm is at the lowest rung, and the worst firm with the highest MAC is on the highest rung. The best firm probably uses state-of-the-art technology while the others are catching up technologically. The regulator can set an efficient emission tax based on a firm's excess emissions over an emission standard. If the emission standard is based on the best firm's emission intensity, the best firm will pay no tax, and firms that are performing worse pay increasingly more. If, instead, the regulator sets the emission standard at an industry average, the over-performers would in fact collect a subsidy that is paid for by revenue from the under-performers. Such a hybrid regime might be as appealing to firms as an emission permit system with grandfathering.

3.2.4 Tradeable emission permits

Emission permits are known as cap-and-trade systems. The government allocates a fixed number of emission permits (the cap on pollution) and firms trade their allowances among each other in order to balance their emissions optimally in response to the emerging market price for the emission permits. When an emission permit is traded, the buyer is paying for the right to emit more pollution, while the seller is giving up that right because the seller does not need it. The buyer profits from the purchase because buying the permit is cheaper than reducing pollution through costly pollution abatement. The seller profits from the sale because the permit price is higher than the seller's marginal abatement cost. Thus the buyer can increase pollution until that firm's MAC equals the permit price, whereas the seller is reducing pollution until its MAC matches the permit price. Both firms gain from the trade.

Trading benefits

To illustrate the key idea of emissions trading, consider two firms A and B with different abatement costs. Let C_i denote firm i's total abatement cost, and let Z_i denote firm i's emission abatement. In panel A of figure 3.4 the marginal abatement cost (MAC) curves are upward sloping. Specfically, let $C_A = 100 + 1.5Z_A^2$ and $C_B = 100 + 2.5Z_B^2$, so that $\text{MAC}_A = 3Z_A$ and $\text{MAC}_B = 5Z_B$. The MAC curve for firm A is flatter than for firm B, suggesting that firm A is the 'clean' firm that finds it easy to abate, while firm B is the 'dirty' firm that finds it difficult to abate. The industry-wide $\text{MAC} = (Z_A + Z_B)/(1/3 + 1/5) = 1.875Z$, where $Z = Z_A + Z_B$. In the diagram, the industry-wide MAC can be thought of as stacking together horizontally the MAC_A and MAC_B curves. If the regulator requires abatement of $Z = 40$ units, this implies a permit price of $P = \text{MAC}(40) = \$75$. Both firms face the same emission price, and at \$75 firm A will carry out more abatement (25 units) than firm B (15 units).

Let us now consider a scenario where we start with original unabated emissions equal to 100 units, 50 from each firm. The regulator wants to reduce emissions by 40 units to a final emission level (the 'cap') of 60 units. The regulator allocates the 60 permits corresponding to this cap equally to both firms, so both firms receive 30 permits. This scenario is illustrated in panel B of figure 3.4. With 30 permits in hand, each firm still has to abate 20 emission units. When abating 20 units, firm A faces an MAC of \$60, while firm B faces an MAC of \$100. They both can do better.

Fig. 3.4 Firm Heterogeneity and Marginal Abatement Cost

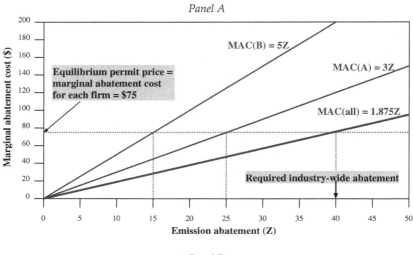

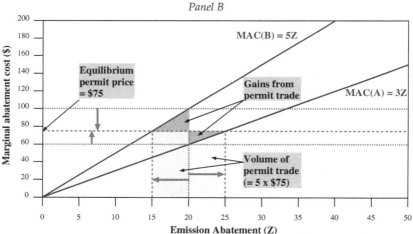

If firm A increases abatement by five units, it could sell five of its emission permits that it then no longer needs. Increasing abatement from 20 to 25 will cost firm A $337.50, or $67.50 per unit. If it could sell those five permits for $75, it would get paid $375 and thus make a profit of $37.50. If firm B were to purchase these five permits at $75, it would pay $375 for them. Being able to increase emissions by 5 units and reduce abatement by 5 units would allow firm B to reduce abatement cost by \$437.50, which generates profits of \$62.50 for firm B. Note that the profits from the trade do not have to be equal for firms A and B. As long as their profits are positive, they will trade. Initial allocation determines which firms gain more from trade, and which will gain less from trade. How the firms allocate abatement effort among themselves is summarized in the table below:

	Firm A	Firm B
Initial unabated emission	50	50
Initial permit allocation	**30**	**30**
Initial necessary abatement Z°	20	20
Initial $MAC(Z^\circ)$	60	100
Optimal $MAC(Z^*)$	75	75
Optimal abatement Z^*	25	15
Permit demand $Z^\circ - Z^*$	–5	+5
Final permit allocation	**25**	**35**

Initial allocation

Before emission trading can commence, permits must be allocated in some form to firms. The way in which this initial allocation takes place generally does not affect the efficiency of the trading outcome; this is an application of the Coase theorem. Nevertheless, the initial allocation has distributional implications and creates winners and losers.

One way to allocate emission permits is through lotteries, a type of random access. This is a cheap method with the advantage of placing all permits into the hands of firms without creating government revenue or favouring one firm over another. It is a method immune to lobbying. Nevertheless, this method is favoured neither by governments nor by businesses.

The methods most widely used involve grandfathering and auctions. Grandfathering involves the allocation based on eligibility criteria or past performance such as output and employment, or in some cases previous-year emissions. Eligibility criteria can become problematic if they can be manipulated easily or when they create perverse incentives. For example, if the emission levels of the year before the start of the permit system are used as the basis for the allocation, firms would have an incentive to increase emissions purposefully in the benchmark year in order to obtain more emission permits the next year. This is a problem of moral hazard. Firms generally like grandfathering because it places all permits in their hands without paying the government. Payments for traded permits end up in the hands of other firms, not the government.

Governments generally prefer auctions of emission permits because auctions generate revenue for them, just like emission taxes. In fact, if firms get their initial allocation just right during the auction, there would be no need to engage in further emission trading.

What are the pros and cons of both methods of initial permit allocation? Grandfathering creates immediate winners and losers as the government decides the initial allocation. Governments will try to use allocation criteria that are perceived to be fair, but the allocation formula is very likely subject to intense lobbying from interested parties. At the very least the allocation formula will need to reflect the relative size of the firms, which can be captured by measures of employment, output, sales, or value added. Grandfathering will result in substantial trading volume because the government's initial allocation will be suboptimal. On the plus side, grandfathering will be politically easier to sell because it does not generate revenue for the government and thus is not perceived the same way as a tax. An initial auction of permits has the opposite advantages and disadvantages. It is more likely to provide an initial allocation that is closer to the optimal allocation, and thus there will be less trading volume during the year. As trading is costly for firms (especially smaller firms), auctions tend to have lower transaction costs than grandfathered allocations.

Smart governments may choose a hybrid allocation method that involves both auctions and grandfathering. The grandfathering component buys political acceptance as it keeps a lid on the regime's overall cost for firms. The auctioning component reduces overall transaction costs and allows governments to take the revenue and correct other distortions in the tax system that ultimately benefit firms.

Intertemporal issues

Emission permits provide companies with the right to emit a given quantity of emissions over a fixed period, typically one year. At the end of each year, each company must surrender enough allowances to cover all its emissions. Companies that exceed their allowance (including those they bought in the permit market) are fined. It can happen that a cautious firm keeps too many allowances because of variability in output and emissions. Because of the fine, a company does not want to end up with too few permits, and thus it may want to hold an inventory of permits that is slightly too large. So what should the company do with the leftover permits at year's end? And what should a company do if it ends up, unexpectedly, with too few permits at year's end and wants to avoid a penalty? Such intertemporal issues can make a permit system less attractive than an environmental tax unless there is a way to smooth out the variability in permit demand over more than the reference period for the permit. Emission volumes can be quite volatile over time due to changes in output or because of technical problems (spills and leaks). Flexibility in permit trading can be obtained through permit banking and permit borrowing.

Permit banking helps firms with an unused inventory of allowances at year's end. The firm can use up the unused allowances in the next reference period. Thus, a firm can keep a contingency reserve of allowances in case there is an unexpected need for them without having to worry that the permits expire at year's end. Permit banking allows firms to hold a permit beyond its designated date for later use.

Permit borrowing works in the other direction. If a company runs unexpectedly short of permits at year's end, it can borrow permits from next year's allotment and apply them against the excess emissions of the current year. Permit borrowing thus allows firms to use permits before their designated use period.

The use of permit banking and permit borrowing enhances the dynamic efficiency of emission permit trading. This flexibility lowers the cost of participation in the emission trading system significantly. There is a downside to this flexibility, however. If firms can borrow and bank permits, they may be able to have very large emissions in one year and much lower emissions in other years. This temporal clustering of emissions can lead to high peak concentrations of emissions at certain points in time. With greenhouse gas emissions such as carbon dioxide this hardly matters because temporal clustering is not an issue: the time horizon for climate change is measured in decades rather than years. However, for many local pollutants with a strong non-linear dose-response function, high peak concentrations matter. Then, banking and borrowing may exacerbate temporal clustering.

From a firm's perspective, the ability to engage in permit banking has another advantage. If the firm expects that the regulator will increasingly tighten the emission cap over years to come, the permit price will necessarily increase over time. A firm may thus find it useful to buy permits when they are still cheap and use up (or sell) them when they are more expensive. If the expected price increases are substantial, banking permits could even become a speculative investment. To keep a lid on such speculative activities, regulators typically will limit the scope of banking (and borrowing) to a few years at most.

3.2.5 Hybrid regimes

Hybrid regimes that involve both emission permits and emission taxes can provide beneficial effects that limit the fluctuations of prices and/or emissions. Lesser variability may have economic end ecological advantages.

Figure 3.5 illustrates two important hybrid systems. In an influential contribution, Roberts and Spence (1976) made the case for a hybrid emission permit trading system that includes a price floor and price ceiling, which confines the permit price to the range between floor and

Fig. 3.5 Hybrid Regimes

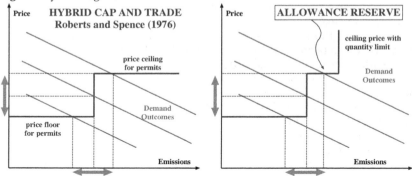

ceiling and thus dampens price volatility. The left panel in figure 3.5 shows how the price range of the permits is limited. As demand for permits shifts, the permit price fluctuates within the price range. The hybrid regime thus involves a limited amount of price uncertainty *and* a limited amount of quantity uncertainty.

A price floor can guarantee a minimum abatement effort if the permit price falls below the price floor. A permit price may drop unexpectedly due to an economic slowdown, recession, economic shock, or significant technological change. The price floor will guarantee that firms will retain a sufficient incentive to innovate (see section 3.2.8 below). In practice, a price floor can be maintained by governments' buying back permits in the open permit market, by setting a reserve price at the initial permit auction, or by charging an extra environmental tax on each used permit.

A price ceiling is implemented as a safety valve to protect firms from runaway costs if there is an unexpected shortage of permits, perhaps due to an economic boom or another (positive) economic shock. A price ceiling can be managed in different ways. One way is for the government to sell extra permits at the ceiling price. Another way is to release an extra allotment of allowances. This is shown in the right panel of figure 3.5. When the permit price reaches the price ceiling, the regulator will release an allowance reserve that will keep prices at the price ceiling. If permit demand exhausts even the allowance reserve, permit prices will continue to increase.

Regardless of which hybrid method is used, the rationale for using such a system is compelling because it limits uncertainty and makes the cap-and-trade system more predictable and less worrisome for participating firms.

3.2.6 Subsidies

For obvious political reasons, governments prefer popular over unpopular measures. Because subsidies inject money into the economy, they rarely receive much criticism despite the fact that governments often exhibit favouritism in their selection of subsidy recipients. Taxpayers still end up footing the bill, but the source of funding is more opaque than with a new tax or fee. But are subsidies as efficient as taxes?

Subsidies can provide the same incentive for emission reduction as emission taxes or cap-and-trade systems. However, there is one major difference in the way subsidies work. Let us assume that a government pays firms a carbon reduction fee of $20 per tonne rather than taxing firms at the same rate. So, for every tonne of carbon emissions that a firm reduces relative to a baseline, it would receive $20 from the government. This subsidy will have one unintended effect: it will lower the firm's overall production cost and, in a competitive environment, the firm will pass on these cost savings to its customers. The lower prices will induce consumers to buy more output, and this in turn will increase emissions along with the increased output. As output increases, the original emission reductions will be partially offset. The scale effect and the technique effect work in opposite directions.

Fig. 3.6 Feebate

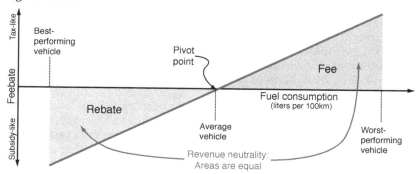

It is also possible to combine subsidies and taxes into a hybrid regime known as a feebate—a combination of fee and rebate. Such a system has been used to promote fuel efficiency in vehicle purchases. Figure 3.6 illustrates the concept. Consider the fuel consumption x_i for vehicle i, and assume that the average fuel consumption for the entire vehicle fleet is $\bar{x}$. Then a feebate would be calculated as $\tau(x_i - \bar{x})$, where τ is the feebate rate. If a vehicle's fuel consumption is above the average, the feebate turns into a tax (it is positive), and when the fuel consumption is below the average, it turns into a subsidy (it is negative). Thus a feebate penalizes gas-guzzlers and rewards fuel-thrifty hybrid cars. Different types of feebate systems have been used by the federal government of Canada and the province of Ontario. What makes feebates particularly attractive to policy makers is that they can be revenue neutral; the revenues from the fee part of the program exactly offset the cost of the rebate part of the program if the pivot point $\bar{x}$ is chosen appropriately. In figure 3.6, the area of the triangle to the right matches the area of the triangle to the left of the pivot point. The revenue neutrality of new environmental policies can be important to win citizens' approval. As mentioned earlier, when the British Columbia carbon tax was introduced in 2008, it was designed to be revenue neutral by providing offsetting tax cuts and a one-time 'climate dividend' cheque to each household.

3.2.7 Second-best approaches

Interventions such as tradeable permits and emission taxes are considered first-best approaches because they price the negative environmental externality directly. To the extent that regulators can assess marginal damage correctly, they will set the price on the tax or quota of permits correctly; this leads to an efficient economic outcome. However, in many instances a first-best approach is not feasible for political or other institutional reasons. In such cases, regulators often need to rely on second-best approaches, which involve targeting activities that are highly correlated with the negative environmental externality.

A good example of a second-best approach is the fuel tax on gasoline and diesel fuel. A fuel tax can be used to target carbon emissions. On one hand, the carbon content of fuel is fixed at 2.328 kg of carbon dioxide (CO_2) per liter of gasoline and 2.614 kg/l for diesel. Thus, a fuel tax is equivalent to a carbon tax for these two fuel types. However, a fuel tax only covers the transportation sector and not CO_2 emissions from industry and households. A fuel tax is therefore an imperfect substitute for a carbon tax. Nevertheless, a fuel tax also addresses other negative externalities. By discouraging driving, it can relieve traffic congestion and motor vehicle accidents in cities. As vehicles emit a variety of air contaminants such as carbon monoxide, nitrous oxides, and hydrocarbons, a fuel tax also helps to reduce air pollution. Because emissions of such air contaminants are predominantly local, the high traffic density in urban areas leads to higher ambient pollution concentrations in those areas. It is therefore sensible to have higher fuel taxes in urban areas than in rural areas. Some jurisdictions actively pursue such a strategy. For example, as of May 2012, the provincial tax on gasoline in British Columbia varies across regions. It is highest (25.5 cents) in the densely populated south coast district that includes Metro Vancouver; it is lower (18.0 cents) in the capital district that includes Victoria, the provincial capital; and it is lowest in the rest of the province (14.5 cents). The resulting price differences are remarkably immune to arbitrage; few drivers drive dozens of kilometres to refuel, or cross the border to the United States to refuel even more cheaply.

The fuel tax is also an example of a multi-purpose environmental intervention. It has multiple targets: global carbon emissions, local air pollutants, and traffic congestion. Fuel taxes are also quite efficient to collect, and they require relatively little administrative overhead. Such administrative efficiency may be an important consideration when the first-best policy instrument is difficult or costly to implement.

Another example of a second-best approach is the fuel efficiency fee-bate discussed in the previous section, or the CAFE standard used in the United States. Fuel efficiency standards target the negative externality (CO_2 emissions) only indirectly because the actual emissions depend on how much each vehicle is used. A 15 l/100 km gas-guzzler that is driven only 5,000 km per year emits fewer emissions than a 5 l/100 km hybrid car that is driven 20,000 km per year. Feebates are more efficient than the CAFE standard because the fee or rebate for individual cars is directly linked to each vehicle's fuel efficiency, rather than to the fuel efficiency of a manufacturer's entire vehicle fleet.

Economists dislike second-best policies because the rationale for not pursuing first-best policies is often weak. Embracing second-best policies may lead to the slippery slope phenomenon: if a second-best policy is good enough, a third-best policy may be good enough too. If there are obstacles to pursuing a first-best policy, it may be better (or cheaper) to remove these obstacles than to pursue a less-efficient second-best policy.

3.2.8 Static and dynamic efficiency

Time plays a significant role when comparing different environmental policies. Different policies can have different dynamic effects. In general, market-based instruments have better **dynamic efficiency** than command-and-control policies because they generate persistent incentives for innovation in pollution abatement technologies. With an emission standard, once it is achieved, there is no further incentive for reducing emissions. However, with an incentive-based policy, every further emission reduction will also reduce costs further. Companies will invest in R&D for abatement technology as long as the gains from the resulting innovations are offset by the savings from lower emission charges. In other words, with an emission tax or emission permit, every unit of

emission reduction is rewarded with a tax saving or fewer permits that
need to be purchased.

The four panels of figure 3.7 illustrate the dynamic effect of an emission tax and an emission permit system. Each panel shows the emission
price on the vertical axis and the abatement activity on the horizontal
axis. In panel A, the dashed line on the right shows the level of pre-
abatement emissions. At a given emission price τ, the firm will conduct
pollution abatement until its MAC equals τ. The firm's total abatement
cost is therefore the (blue) triangle plus the (green) rectangle; the former
captures the total cost of the actual abatement activity, and the latter
captures the cost of the emission permits or emission tax.

Now consider a technological innovation in abatement technology,
shown in panel B. This rotates the firm's MAC curve clockwise from
MAC_1 to MAC_2, and this generates cost savings. This will increase the
amount of abatement carried out by the firm, leaving fewer emission to
be covered through permits or to be paid for through an environmental
tax. In panel B, the triangular area for the total abatement cost has now
increased because the firm is abating more, but the rectangular area for
the emission tax or permit purchase has decreased by a larger amount.
The net savings are visualized in panel C as the two highlighted triangular areas combined. The left triangle captures the savings from
cheaper abatement, and the right triangle captures the net savings from
reduced tax payments or reduced permit purchases. The two triangles
combined capture the firm's innovation incentive. A firm invests into
R&D for new abatement technology if the total cost of developing and
installing the new technology is less than the present discounted value
of the savings in abatement costs *and* taxes or permit purchases.

How do emission permits and an emission tax differ with respect
to the size of the innovation incentive? With a permit system, the market price for emissions fluctuates, while it is fixed (by the regulator)
with an emission tax. For an individual firm, the emission tax leads to
a predictable innovation incentive. By comparison, the size of the innovation incentive varies with the emission market price in the cap-and-
trade system. This effect is illustrated in panel D. As τ shifts up and
down, the size of the triangular innovation incentive becomes larger
or smaller (dark or light shading). The price uncertainty introduced by
the cap-and-trade system reduces the innovation incentive if firms are
modestly risk averse. With an emission tax, the emission price is more
predictable, and thus the innovation incentive is also more predictable.

Why does it matter if the innovation incentive fluctuates over time?
The firm invests in R&D up-front, while the future cost savings from
the new abatement technology arrive in the future. If the firm miscal-
culates, the R&D cost will exceed the discounted future cost savings. A
risk-averse firm that wants to avoid losses will work with a low (lower
than average) market price as the planning scenario. The innovation

Fig. 3.7 Abatement Costs and Innovation

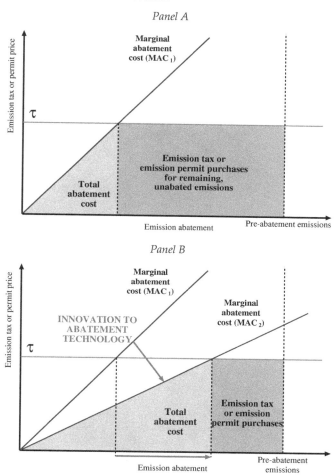

incentive penalty of emission permit systems will grow along with the price volatility of the permit market. The more volatile the market price, the less the innovation incentive.

Fig. 3.7 Abatement Cost and Innovation (continued)

Panel C

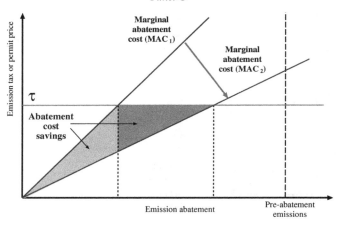

Panel D

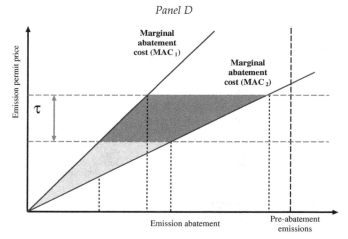

Emission taxes and emission permits are generally equally efficient at achieving a targeted emission reduction in the short term. However, emission taxes are dynamically more efficient than emission permits because emission taxes provide steadier innovation incentives for pollution abatement technology.

3.2.9 Dealing with uncertainty

For the regulator there are two types of uncertainty for incentive-based instruments: uncertainty about firms' (or plants') abatement costs, and uncertainty about marginal damage.

In the presence of uncertainty about plants' abatement cost. the regulator sets an emission tax or permit allocation where the assumed marginal abatement cost (MAC) equals marginal damage (MD). This means that the resulting emission tax or permit allocation may be suboptimal as a result of the information asymmetry between firms and the regulator. If the regulator assumes that firms' abatement costs are higher than they actually are, a tax will be too high or a permit allocation will be too generous. A tax that is too high generates excess abatement costs, whereas the overallocation of permits generates excess damage. On the other hand, if the regulator assumes that abatement costs are lower than they actually are, the emission tax will be too low, while a permit allocation will be too restrictive. Now the tax that is too low generates excess damage, whereas the underallocation of permits generates excess abatement costs.

With uncertainty about the MAC curve, do taxes or permits perform better? This depends on the shape of the MAC and MD curves and thus on the relative size of excess abatement costs and excess damage. When the MD curve is steep relative to the MAC curve, permits are preferred over taxes, and when the MD curve is flat relative to the MAC curve, taxes are preferred over permits. A flat MD curve implies that large changes in emissions have relatively small changes in terms of damage, whereas a steep MAC curve suggests that abatement opportunities are limited and costly. This scenario is somewhat more likely than the scenario where pollution abatement is easy and environmental damage sits at a trigger point. Consequently, when there is uncertainty about firms' abatement ability, taxes are better able to get the equilibrium right at once rather than iterating towards the equilibrium in multiple rounds of policy adjustment.

When there is uncertainty about the marginal damage rather than the marginal abatement cost, taxes and permits perform equally. Both instruments generate the same equilibrium outcome.

3.3 Environmental markets in action

The International Energy Agency (IEA), an energy forum for 28 advanced economies established in 1974, maintains a very useful database of energy efficiency policies and measures for each of its member countries, including Canada and the United States. The list of activities is remarkably long and consists primarily of subsidies, accelerated depreciation allowances (known as a capital cost allowance in Canada's tax system), R&D incentives, education and outreach activities, and various voluntary technical standards. In the United States, some of the most recognized programs are the Energy Star program for products and home improvement (launched in 1992) and the CAFE standard for improving fuel efficiency of vehicles (launched in 1974).

In recent years, a number of jurisdictions have introduced a **feed-in tariff** for electricity to subsidize renewable energy such as solar and wind power. One of the most lucrative such programs exists in Germany. Operators of various types of renewable energy installations (hydro, biomass, geothermal, wind, and photovoltaics) receive a guaranteed feed-in tariff when they supply electricity to the grid. In 2009 a photovoltaic installation was paid €0.3194/kWh if installed on open land and €0.3300–€0.4301/kwH if installed on buildings (depending on installation size). The feed-in tariff was guaranteed contractually for twenty years. These feed-in tariffs are very generous when compared to the typical production cost of electricity from conventional sources. As a result, solar power and wind power blossomed in Germany, from rooftop solar panels on individual homes to large wind farms. Farmers have redefined 'farming' by turning their potato fields into solar farms.

Other jurisdictions have also pursued feed-in tariffs. Spain has guaranteed €0.2694/kWh for 25 years for solar thermoelectric installations. Between 2009 and 2011, Spain completed the installation of two 150 MW, four 100 MW, and eight 50 MW solar-thermal power plants. The largest solar-thermal installation is currently being built in the Mojave desert of the United States with a capacity of 354 MW. In Canada, the Ontario Power Authority offers a feed-in-tariff of $0.42/kWh for photovoltaics and $0.11/kWh for wind and biogas. These incentives serve a dual purpose. On one hand they are meant to build renewable energy capacity, while on the other hand they are meant to stimulate investment and innovation in the green-tech sector of the economy. In 2010, a 97 MW photovoltaic solar farm was built by Enbridge and First Solar near Sarnia, Ontario.

Permit markets

There are several emission permit markets in operation in the United States and Europe, albeit none in Canada at this point. One of the first emission permit markets was established through the Acid Rain Program in the United States. This cap-and-trade system was established under the 1990 *Clean Air Act* and sought to reduce sulfur dioxide emissions by 50% between 1980 and 2010. Trading commenced in 1995 and initially affected 263 units at 110 mostly coal-burning electric utility plants located in 21 eastern and midwestern states. The second phase of the program commenced in 2000 and eventually encompassed over 2,000 units, virtually all power plants with more than 25 MW capacity.

Allowances are grandfathered on an emission baseline (the average fossil fuel consumed from 1985 through 1987 multiplied by 1.2 pounds of sulfur dioxide per million British thermal units).

The state of Illinois has adopted a cap-and-trade system for volatile organic compounds (VOCs) for eight counties, named the *Emissions Reduction Market System*. It was launched in 2000 with over 100 participants. Ten northeastern states agreed on a cap-and-trade system called the *Regional Greenhouse Gas Initiative* (RGGI) for carbon dioxide emissions from power plants. This system was launched in 2009 with quarterly auctions of permits and is aimed at reducing emissions by 10% below 1990 levels by 2020. Allowance prices typically range between $2 and $3 per ton of carbon dioxide.

By far the largest permit market in the world is the *EU Emission Trading System* (ETS) launched in 2005. The ETS now operates in 30 countries (27 EU member states plus Iceland, Liechtenstein, and Norway) and covers carbon emissions from power stations, combustion plants, oil refineries and iron and steel works, as well as factories making cement, glass, lime, bricks, ceramics, pulp, paper, and board. The total amount of emissions from these industrial sectors were originally capped by each government separately. This led to an overallocation of permits during the first (2005–2007) phase of the trading system as governments were not careful coordinating targets. As a result of the overallocation, the permit price for the 2007 allocation crashed. During the third phase of the ETS, which started in 2013, allocations are determined directly at the EU level rather than the national level. Permit trades are carried out on private futures exchanges; the largest and most liquid market is the ICE Futures Europe exchange, previously known as the European Climate Exchange (ECX). Permit prices remain quite volatile. In 2012, prices for the second ETS phase target (2008–2012) dropped to €6–8 per tonne. In 2013, prices for the third ETS phase (2013–2020) dropped to under €3 at times but have since stabilized at about €5 per tonne.

Offset Markets

Markets for carbon offsets have sprung up either as voluntary schemes or as compliance markets following a government mandate. Offsets are meant to take carbon dioxide or other greenhouse gases out of the atmosphere in exchange for other entities putting them into the atmosphere. This only works if the carbon dioxide is truly sequestered, such as accumulation in trees or through underground injection. To make carbon offsets effective, several criteria need to be met effectively:

- additionality: the emission reductions would not occur without the offset (e.g., because they are financially worthwhile anyhow);
- permanence: the emissions are sequestered permanently as well as irreversibly;

- verifiability: the reductions can be verified and audited by an independent third party (which may be difficult outside one's own jurisdiction); and
- no leakage: implementing the emission reduction project does not lead to higher emissions elsewhere such as through substitution effects or international trade.

Many offsets today are based on 'emissions avoided' concepts; few are based on true sequestration. Nevertheless, some progress has been made certifying offsets through the ISO 14064 standard. Box 3.2 discusses the use of carbon offsets in British Columbia.

Several airlines offer their customers to buy carbon offsets for their flights. For a Toronto-Vancouver round-trip with an estimated 703 kg of carbon dioxide emissions, Air Canada passengers can purchase carbon offsets for between \$14-\$20/tonne from a forest restoration project, a landfill gas recover project, and a tire recycling program. These three projects are among the better ones in the offsetting industry as they involve, at least in part, true sequestration. As of December 2011, Air Canada's partner Zerofootprint had sold \$285,160 in (voluntary) offsets, equivalent to 17,749 tonnes of carbon dioxide. In 2010, Air Canada consumed a total of 3.378 billion litres of turbo fuel at 2.5 kg carbon dioxide per litre. This amounts to about 8.4 million tonnes of carbon dioxide. So less than 0.02% of its emissions were offset voluntarily.

A voluntary market for carbon offsets was launched as the Chicago Climate Exchange (CCX). However, this market crashed in 2009 as firms retreated from voluntary offsets in the wake of a major economic recession.

3.4 Valuing the environment

When businesses develop new mines or build new plants, pipelines, power transmission lines, or other infrastructure, they often impact the local environment. Regulators and businesses alike need to know the cost of such activities: regulators because they may want to assess the overall cost and benefits of such a project, and businesses because they may need to compensate anyone affected by the planned new activity. Environmental economists have developed approaches to valuing the environment, but this task is not easy because the environment does not come with a simple price tag.

There are two major approaches to valuing the environment and the services provided by the environment. One approach is based on measuring or estimating the market benefits of the environment. Because this approach is based on observable market data, it is called the revealed-preference approach. When such market data are not observable because there are no markets for the services of the environment,

Box 3.2: Carbon Offsets in British Columbia

In British Columbia, the provincial government mandated the public sector to become 'carbon neutral.' Because the public sector cannot suddenly stop heating schools and universities, these public sector entities have to buy offsets.

The Pacific Carbon Trust (PCT) that was established as British Columbia's clearing house for carbon offsets does not necessarily achieve actual sequestration. Instead, most offsets (or 'carbon credits') are based on hypothetical reductions against a business-as-usual scenario.

For example, consider supplementing the natural gas heating of a warehouse with solar power. The owner of the warehouse offers to instal solar panels in exchange for a payment equivalent to the reduced carbon dioxide emissions times a negotiable carbon price. As public sector entities have to pay $25 per tonne for their carbon offsets, the PCT can afford to pay up to $25 for carbon credits. So what is the catch? Perhaps the warehouse owner would have installed solar panels anyhow. This is a problem of free riding. If someone offers you money to buy a hybrid-electric Toyota Prius in order to reduce emissions, you might take the money even if you would have bought the Prius anyhow because it reduces your fuel consumption and fuel costs. If the proportion of free riding is large, offsets will become ineffective.

As the $25/tonne carbon offset price is fixed for public sector entities, a supply-demand mismatch may occur. The PCT may run out of viable projects at a price below $25/tonne to offset all public sector GHG emissions. Then the public sector will no longer be 'carbon neutral.' Alternatively, if the PCT can supply all necessary offsets at a price below $25/tonne, the public sector entities are overpaying. Many current offsets are in fact available well below $25/tonne.

The PCT refuses to make public the prices it pays for individual carbon offset projects. This secrecy and lack of accountability is disturbing and calls into question the veracity of claims made by the PCT. Nurturing an 'infant industry' is no excuse for secrecy. The PCT may be more interested in developing politically opportune showcase projects than in finding least-cost carbon offsets (which are likely to be found in afforestation and reforestation projects).

In November 2013, the British Columbia government announced that it will eliminate the PCT. However, the carbon offset program will continue within the Environment Ministry's Climate Action Secretariat. A revised program may expand an exemption to health agencies and post-secondary institutions that was adopted originally for elementary and high schools.

economists rely on estimating the non-market benefits of the environment. This is called the stated-preference approach.

The results from any of the valuation methods are often input into a cost-benefit analysis (CBA); see Boardman et al. (2010a) for a thorough treatment of this subject. CBA is a policy assessment method that quantifies in monetary terms the value of all consequences of a policy to all members of society. Fundamentally, CBA is based on the principle that a society can make economic trade-offs among its members; it allows for some people to win (gain benefits) and some to lose (incur costs) from a new project. CBA also allows for intertemporal trade-offs to be made, allowing for benefits and costs to materialize at different points in time (costs now and benefits later, or benefits now and costs later). Section 3.5 explores this topic further.

3.4.1 Revealed-preference approaches

Consumers reveal preferences through market transactions. This implies that a researcher can observe market prices (and quantities) and infer how consumers value a particular resource. Sometimes the market valuation is indirect because the use of an environmental resource may involve another activity that can be measured. One such indirect method is the travel-cost approach. For example, it is is possible to measure the value that consumers place on the use of parks and other recreational sources by observing the time they are willing to travel to get there. As time is costly, the travel time and distance implies a travel cost.

A more direct method is the use of hedonic regressions, an econometric tool where an observed market price is explained statistically through a number of observable characteristics. This method tries to capture the change in prices of (complementary) goods to infer consumers' willingness to pay for a cleaner environment or some other environmental amenity. Hedonic regressions are widely used in real estate appraisals. For example, a hedonic regression was used to estimate how PCB contamination of sediments in the harbour of New Bedford, Massachusetts affected real estate prices. A study by Mendelsohn et al. (1992) showed that in 1982 real estate prices were depressed by $9,000 in the most affected zone, controlling for numerous property characteristics, including size and quality of homes.

Real estate valuations are affected by a large number of environmental issues. For example, the construction of pipelines, electrical transmission lines, roadways, bridges, railway lines, or subway tunnels affects property values. For urban environments, using real estate valuations is often the most promising avenue for estimating environmental impacts.

Yet another revealed-preference approach uses the value of a statistical life (VSL). The value of a statistical life captures the trade-off between mortality risk and other goods and services. It is defined as the ratio of the marginal utility of a small reduction in mortality risk to the marginal utility of a small change in income, and it is measured in dollars per unit of risk reduced. At first glance it may appear unethical to put a price on a life, but this is a profound misunderstanding of the VSL concept (Cameron, 2010). A common misconception about VSL is that it puts a price on human life, and even provides different figures for different groups in society (such as old and young people). VSL is not about putting a price on any specific life or person. Instead, it merely captures individuals' willingness to pay for reducing mortality risk. Keeping this important distinction in mind, VSL calculations can yield very insightful policy recommendations. Workers who pursue careers that involve a higher-than-average risk of death (such as police officers, firefighters, or coal miners) typically accept a wage premium that compensates them for this increased risk. Combined with actuarial statistics on death rates, the wage premium computes into a monetary measure, the VSL. Studies of wage premia from risky jobs put the value of a statistical life at about $5 million (in current dollars of the reference period). Based on a review of numerous studies, the US Environmental Protection Agency currently uses a VSL of $7.4 million in 2006 dollars.

A useful example of how the VSL can be used in practice is to look at various environmental regulations and calculate the implied VSL. This can be compared with what we know from other studies about VSL. Viscusi (1996) examined numerous US environmental regulations to determine the cost of a statistical life saved, yielding widely different estimates shown in table 3.1. Putting seat belts in cars saves about 1,850 lives per year in the United States, and at a cost of $300,000 per life saved it is relatively cheap. By comparison, banning formaldehyde in the workplace costs about $72 billion per life saved, which is hugely expensive compared to the $5 million VSL used in that study. The line in the middle of the table marks that threshold, indicating that the the policies above the line are sensible, while the policies below are too expensive and should be reviewed.

3.4.2 Stated-preference approaches

Often there is neither a direct nor indirect market through which consumer preferences can be gauged. Many environmental resources only exhibit non-market benefits. Such resources can exhibit use value, option value, and existence value. The total value of an environmental resource or feature is the sum of use, option, and existence value.

Table 3.1 The Value of a Statistical Life (VSL)

US regulation (selected examples)	Agency	Initial Risk (per year)	Expected Lives Saved	Cost/Life ($ millions)
Unvented space heaters	CPSC	2.7 in 10^5	63	0.10
Airplane cabin fire protection	FAA	6.5 in 10^8	15	0.20
Auto passive restraints/belts	NHTSA	9.1 in 10^5	1850	0.30
Hazard communication	OSHA	4.0 in 10^5	200	1.80
Grain dust	OHSA	2.1 in 10^5	4	5.30
Arsenic/glass manufacturing	EPA	8.0 in 10^4	0.11	19.20
Arsenic/copper smelter	EPA	9.0 in 10^4	0.06	26.50
Asbestos	EPA	2.9 in 10^5	10	104.20
Formaldehyde in workplace	OHSA	6.8 in 10^7	0.01	72,000.00

Source: Viscusi (1996). Initial annual risk indicates annual deaths per exposed population. Agency denotes the US agency responsible for issuing the regulation; FAA: Federal Aviation Authority; NHTSA: National Highway Traffic Safety Administration; PHSA: *Public Health Services Act*; EPA: Environmental Protection Agency; CPSC: Consumer Product Safety Commission. Valuations are expressed in 1984 current-price US dollars.

Use value is based on consumers' use of an environmental resource. For example, a clean river is more suitable for swimming, boating, fishing, and for obtaining drinking water. Option value is intertemporal in nature. For example, preserving the Amazon forest may allow for the discovery of new medicines derived from yet-undiscovered plants or animals. Option value is rooted in preserving future use and limiting current use. Existence value looks at benefits that are intrinsic to the existence of the resource, whether it is scenery, a plant or animal species, or a historic artifact. For example, an endangered species such as polar bears may have an aesthetic value (they are cute to look at) or an ecosystem value (they contribute ecosystem functions to habitat or other species).

Stated preferences are captured through a method known as contingent valuation; see Alberini and Kahn (2009) for a thorough discussion of this topic. Contingent valuation is a survey-based technique for the valuation of non-market resources that provide utility to people. Whenever there is a lack of a market due to the inability to transact in an environmental resource, survey-based methods may be able to help. Surveys ask people about their willingness to pay (WTP) to maintain or preserve an environmental feature or their willingness to accept (WTA) compensation for degrading or losing that environmental feature. In theory, both questions should elicit the same response. In practice, that is not the case, and the stated willingness to pay is smaller than the willingness to accept for the same environmental feature. The WTA > WTP paradox is a central feature of contingent valuation. Economic theory is trying to explain this paradox.

The willingness to pay or accept is closely linked to the economic concept of consumer surplus, which is defined as the difference between what one is willing to pay for a good or service and what one is actually paying for the good or service. With common access, the price for most environmental resources is zero. The price that people are willing to pay for a public good such as an environmental amenity is close to the increase in consumer surplus they enjoy. WTA should be a little higher than consumer surplus because people are better off with the compensation payment, whereas WTP should be a little higher than consumer surplus because people are made poorer by paying to preserve the environmental amenity.

The WTA > WTP paradox goes beyond the small deviations from consumer surplus that can be explained by a wealth effect. For example, the estimated willingness to pay for remedying a contaminated landfill is typically much less than the willingness to accept compensation for enduring the environmental hazards from the contaminated landfill.

Economists offer two leading explanations for the WTA > WTP paradox. One is based on prospect theory, and the other is based on poor substitutability. Prospect theory was developed by behavioural researchers, most prominently Nobel laureate Daniel Kahneman and his co-researcher Amos Tversky. They demonstrated that people suffer from loss aversion when making economic decisions. People tend to weight losses larger than an equal amount in gains; losing $1,000 is psychologically more intense than gaining $1,000. Prospect theory suggests that utility is not an absolute measure (as used in neoclassical economics) but a relative measure. Consumers adopt the status quo as their reference point when evaluating (expected) gains and losses. Because of loss aversion, the marginal benefits of environmental cleanup tend to be smaller than the marginal benefits of accepting environmental degradation.

Another explanation may be rooted in the poor substitutability of monetary compensation and non-tangible costs such as the risk of death or environmental degradation. If an individual faces income constraints, he or she might not be able pay for a large reduction in the risk of death from, say, an environmental contamination, the WTP will be low, whereas the individual may demand a very large amount in compensation for being exposed to that risk, which implies a high WTA.

Whether WTA or WTP questions are used on a contingent valuation survey also depends on how the property rights are assigned. When people own the right to an environmental amenity, it makes sense to ask them about their WTA. If, however, they do not own the environmental amenity, it makes sense to ask them about their WTP to preserve it.

Carrying out a contingent valuation survey carries with it numerous pitfalls inherent in all surveys. Among them is the risk that people articulate protest answers that exaggerate their true WTP or WTA. Similarly, respondents may engage in strategic behaviour by exaggerating their true WTP and WTA if they believe that their answer on the survey will influence the decision in their favour; this leads to strategic bias. Another common problem is response bias in surveys, where respondents tell the pollster what they think they are expected to respond rather than their true belief. If the respondent believes that the survey is conducted on behalf of a particular interest group, they may be more inclined to articulate a position favourable to that interest group. People are often conflict averse and vary their opinion depending on whom they talk to. There is also the possibility of free riding when asked about WTP: why offer to pay anything when others are willing to pay?

Contingent valuation surveys also suffer from something called embedding bias. Answers to survey questions may depend on the context in which they are provided. The WTP may depend on the order in which two or more projects are embedded in the survey. This is a question of sequencing and nesting that can sometimes be overcome by asking questions in random order, or by varying the ranking of competing options in random order from one survey participant to the next. Surveys can be compromised by asking a number of leading questions that may influence the critical WTP or WTA question. A related problem arises from asking multiple WTP or WTA questions for partial but additive policies. The sum of the partial WTPs or WTAs may exceed the WTP or WTA for the joint policy.

If contingent valuation surveys are fraught with problems, why bother? The answer is simple: in the absence of market prices, surveys provide the only way to elicit useful valuation information. The key is therefore understanding, preventing, or correcting the various survey biases discussed above. Randomization of survey questions and avoidance of leading questions can help address several of the problems. The usefulness of contingent valuation is self-evident; box 3.3 illustrates a typical application.

3.5 Cost-benefit analysis

There are two major types of cost-benefit analysis (CBA). Ex-ante CBA is more common and involves assisting in a decision about implementing a proposed project. Ex-post CBA is performed during or after a project's life and informs the decision about continuing or repeating a project.

Box 3.3: The Glen Canyon Dam and Recreation

Image by Christian Mehlführer, reproduced under Creative Commons License.

The Colorado River has been dammed extensively. Lake Powell was created through building the Glen Canyon Dam in 1956–66, and Lake Meade was created through building the Hoover Dam in 1931–36. A large share of water is diverted to irrigation and to nearby cities. The Colorado River used to flow into the Gulf of California in Mexico, but the river delta has shrunk to 5% of its original size.

The Glen Canyon dam provides peak-load power for residents of Nevada and California, which adversely affects downstream ecosystems in the Grand Canyon and reduces the quality of recreational rafting along the canyon. The US Bureau of Land Reclamation and the National Park Service were interested in assessing the value of recreational rafting compared to the market value of peak-load power supply. The study was meant to inform a decision about modifying the water flow from the dam that would permit greater recreational use of the Colorado River. The two agencies conducted a contingent valuation survey and found substantial economic values for rafting with increased water flows worth $2 million per year. This survey helped inform the *Grand Canyon Protection Act* of 1992.

Further contingent valuation surveys explored the willingness to pay for different flow regimes. The lack of the natural high spring water flows threatened endangered fish species, native vegetation, and birds. The survey revealed strong support for a more natural flow regime. This resulted in changes to the flow management, including large spills during the spring of 1996 to emulate the natural high spring flows. These large spills were repeated several times, most recently in 2004 and 2008.

CBA decision rule: Among a set of candidate projects or options, a decision maker should choose the project or option that maximizes the net social benefit (benefits minus costs) expressed in present-discounted terms.

The use of net social benefit in cost-benefit analysis is crucial. Net social benefit is the difference between social benefits and social costs, expressed in dollar amounts. Policy efficiency is a different concept: the ratio of benefits to costs. One policy may be more efficient than another but may still be outranked if the other policy's net social benefit is larger.

The four panels in figure 3.8 illustrate the key concepts of CBA. In panel A, a particular policy is evaluated with a benefit of $50 million and a cost of $40 million. The net social benefit is therefore $10 million. However, the benefit-cost ratio of 1.2 is very low. Many parameters that were estimated to obtain the two point estimates for benefit and cost are 'noisy' and therefore may vary over a certain range. To reflect this uncertainty, it is customary to draw an error ellipse around each cost-benefit point estimate, based on the standard error of each of the two point estimates. In panel A, both the 50% and 95% error ellipses cut across the efficient frontier and suggest that it is possible that the policy may be inefficient—i.e., costs may exceed benefits. This policy would be considered marginal, and regulators should probably consider alternative policies that are unambiguously efficient.

In panel B, policies A and B are both efficient and the benefit-cost ratio greatly exceeds 1. Policy A has a net benefit of $150 − $20 = $130 million, while policy B has a net benefit of $100 − $40 = $60 million. Clearly, policy A outranks policy B both in terms of net social benefit and efficiency. The situation in panel C demonstrates that two policies can be equally efficient but still dominate each other in terms of net social benefit. Policy A has a net benefit of $90−$30 = $60 million, while policy B has a net benefit of $150 − $50 = $100 million. Both policies have an equal benefit-cost ratio of 3:1 and are thus equally efficient. However, policy B generates $40 million more in net social benefit than policy A.

Panel D in figure 3.8 illustrates the most difficult case. The policy ranking is ambiguous. Policy A has a net benefit of $120 − $52 = $68 million, while policy B has a net benefit of $100 − $40 = $60 million. Policy B is more efficient than policy A because its benefit-cost ratio of 2.5 is larger than the benefit-cost ratio of 2.3 for policy A. However, policy A generates $8 million more in net social benefit. Should the regulator therefore adopt policy A? The error ellipses of the two policies overlap a fair bit, and it may not be possible to say with confidence that policy A is better than policy B. There is a significant region where both policies may deliver the same outcome. In this case, the regulator may

Fig. 3.8 Cost-Benefit Analysis and Uncertainty

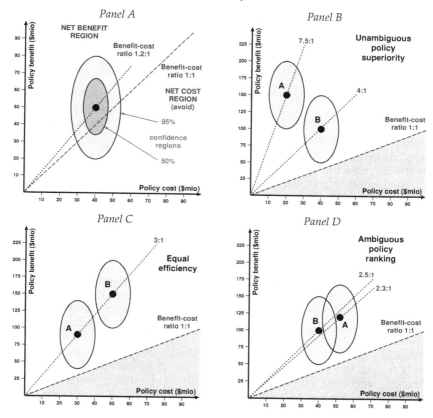

in fact prefer policy B, which is 23% cheaper than policy A. This example demonstrates how important it is to carry out a rigorous analysis of the parameter uncertainty in the cost-benefit model. Simply basing a policy decision on the 'best' point estimates could lead to expensive policies that do not deliver a superior outcome.

Often the most important challenge in cost-benefit analysis is the time horizon. Costs may need to be incurred immediately while benefits accrue over many years. Table 3.2 provides the discount factors that correspond to particular discount rates and time horizons.[2]

---

[2] For a given discount rate r, the discount factors are $[1 - (1 + r)^{-T}]/r$ for the finite time horizon T and $(1 + r)/r$ for the infinite time horizon.

Table 3.2 Cost-Benefit Analysis and Discount Factors

Time horizon	Discount rate										
[Years]	2.0%	2.5%	3.0%	3.5%	4.0%	4.5%	5.0%	6.0%	7.0%	8.0%	10%
10	8.98	8.75	8.53	8.32	8.11	7.91	7.72	7.36	7.02	6.71	6.14
20	16.35	15.59	14.88	14.21	13.59	13.01	12.46	11.47	10.59	9.82	8.51
50	31.42	28.36	25.73	23.46	21.48	19.76	18.26	15.76	13.80	12.23	9.91
∞	51.00	41.00	34.33	29.57	26.00	23.22	21.00	17.67	15.29	13.50	11.00

For example, a project or policy with a 20-year time horizon and a discount rate of 3.5% has a discount factor of about 14. A project or policy that costs $100 million today (and nothing henceforth) would need to generate annual benefits of $100/14.21 = $7.04 million in each of the 20 years to be considered worthwhile

The importance of the choice of discount rate is best seen in the case of an infinite time horizon as shown in the last row of table 3.2. Suppose a particular environmental policy generates annual benefits of $100 million in perpetuity. At a discount rate of 10%, this amount is equivalent to 11 times $100 million today, or $1.1 billion. At a discount rate of 4.0%, the same policy is valued at $2.6 billion dollars today. The regulator with the 4% discount rate would be willing to spend $2.6 billion to implement the policy, while the regulator with a 10% discount rate would only be willing to spend less than half of that amount. While economic analysis can guide us to a reasonable choice of discount rate (Boardman et al., 2010b; Moore et al., 2013), there remains great uncertainty about the choice of the appropriate time horizon. How long will a policy remain in place unchanged to generate the continual benefits? Or how long will an infrastructure project last before it will need to be replaced? These uncertainties make it necessary to engage in a rigorous analysis of possible scenarios and develop appropriate error ellipses around the cost-benefit point estimates.

If one does not want to commit to using a particular discount rate, there is another way of analyzing a cost-benefit scenario. One can ask which discount rate would drive the net social benefit to zero. This critical rate at which present-discounted benefits equal present-discounted costs is known as the internal rate of return. Calculating this quantity requires numerical approximation techniques. The decision to proceed with a particular project is made when the internal rate of return exceeds the cost of capital—i.e., the interest rate at which funds can be borrowed. This tool is less useful for evaluating an environmental policy because such policies may not involve investments. The internal rate of return is also not useful for ranking competing projects; it is only a tool for analyzing a single project.

3.6 International trade repercussions

Environmental policies can be affected by repercussions from a country's international trade regime. An open economy is vulnerable to opportunistic behaviour by firms. Strict environmental policies could motivate companies to shift production outside the regulated jurisdiction. This phenomenon is called the pollution haven effect.

It has been argued that poorer countries tend to maintain lower environmental standards than richer countries. Therefore, poorer countries may become pollution havens in response to ever stricter environmental regulations in rich countries. Theoretical and empirical economic work has demonstrated that the effect is likely small because of an offsetting effect. Richer countries also tend to be more capital intensive, and because capital-intensive industries are also pollution intensive, richer countries therefore tend to be more pollution intensive. This factor endowment effect works in the opposite direction of the pollution haven effect. The two sources of comparative advantage work against each other. Which one dominates depends on their relative strength and thus varies from country to country. Trade liberalization shifts the composition of industrial activity in a country, and thus the composition effect of trade liberalization depends on whether a country's comparative advantage tilts towards pollution-intensive industries. In addition to the composition effect of trade liberalization, the overall gains from trade also boost a country's income and thus generate a technique effect whereby richer countries adopt stricter environmental rules. The idea behind this effect is that the environment is a normal good, and that when societies grow richer they will demand more of the 'clean environment' good. Empirically, this technique effect tends to dominate the picture for a pollutant such as sulfur dioxide. However, the above statements do not apply in the same way for global pollutants such as carbon dioxide.

When a country adopts a carbon policy, there is a considerable risk of carbon leakage. When one country reduces carbon emissions as a result of adopting a related carbon policy, another country may increase emissions due to goods production moving from the country with the carbon policy to the country without the carbon policy. There are two transmission channels for such carbon leakage:

- **Supply-side leakage** occurs through the physical relocation of production facilities to escape pollution control regimes. This is the pollution haven effect discussed above, and is influenced strongly by a country's comparative advantage. Supply-side leakage is bounded by the cost of relocating production, plants, or entire industries to a foreign country. Furthermore, international trade adds transportation costs that may dampen the relatively small cost advantages from the absence of a carbon policy. When pollution is local rather than global, relocation may not necessarily be a bad thing. If the firms migrate to areas with lesser population density, negative externalities may actually be reduced.

• **Demand-side leakage** occurs when local environmental regulation depresses demand for a polluting good in one region (by increasing its price), and this demand shifts to lower-priced imports from an unregulated region.

Leakage is a phenomenon that applies not only to carbon policies but potentially to any other environmental policy. Nevertheless, the potential of leakage is always associated with global pollutants because for global pollutants only the world total emissions matter, but not where the emissions occur.

Yet another international trade phenomenon is known as reshuffling. This phenomenon can also occur among different states and provinces within a country. Consider regulations that are imposed at the point of purchase so that consumers in one country or region are subject to the policy and others are not. For example, assume that California accounts for 10% of the world's sea bass market, and that California adopts regulation that only sea bass caught using sustainable fishing techniques can be sold there. If more than 10% of sea bass in the world market is *already* caught using sustainable methods, these fish can be diverted for sale in California. The California regulation may not have any effect at all on how fish are caught. Reshuffling becomes more likely when the share of products that already comply with an environmental policy is larger than the share of consumers who are subject to it.

Another example is a firm's decision to contract with a wind farm operator to supply 100% of its electricity from clean renewable energy, albeit delivered through the conventional electric grid. While it may appear that the firm is boosting demand for renewable energy, the wind farm operator would have sold the electricity to the grid anyhow. Electricity merely got reshuffled from the average consumer to the particular firm. In fact, electrons do not carry identification tags, and thus once electricity enters a distribution grid it is anonymous. There is no way of earmarking electricity. The firm's commitment to renewable energy is thus meaningless.

3.7 Summary

Environmental economics provides an analytic framework for designing environmental policy interventions and making decisions about the relative merit of different environmental policy options. Generally, incentive-based policy interventions such as environmental taxes and cap-and-trade systems are more efficient economically than mandated policy interventions such as technical standards. No environmental policy is superior along all relevant dimensions, and thus a strong case can be built for hybrid environmental policies that mix elements from different policies. Long-term considerations are particularly important when considering the effect of environmental policies on innovation in pollution abatement and pollution prevention technologies. Regimes that provide predictable and stable innovation incentives (in particular, environmental taxes) have a significant advantage.

Valuing environmental amenities and natural resources can be accomplished through revealed-preference approaches based on market values, and when this is not feasible, through stated-preference approaches that are based on contingent valuation surveys. Results from such an analysis can be incorporated into a cost-benefit analysis. The CBA framework suggests that among competing projects the one with the highest total net benefit should be chosen. When two or more projects are statistically indistinguishable as top contenders, the lowest-cost project should prevail.

3.8 Study questions

1. In the presence of a negative environmental externality, how does the market equilibrium without a policy differ from a market equilibrium in which the externality has been priced correctly?
2. What is bioaccumulation, and what is biomagnification?
3. What does the 'Coase theorem' teach us about achieving efficient environmental outcomes and about the initial allocation of property rights?
4. Why do market-based interventions (green taxes, cap-and-trade) tend to deliver more efficient outcomes than mandated interventions (standards, technology mandates)?
5. What are key criteria for choosing among different environmental policy instruments?
6. Why is no single environmental policy instrument superior along all dimensions relevant to policy choice? Compare emissions standards with a green tax.
7. Explain how a green tax or a cap-and-trade system leads to distinct *scale effects* and *technique effects* for individual firms.
8. When you compare a subsidy for pollution reduction and a tax on pollution emissions, are *scale effect* and *technique effect* working in the same direction?
9. In the presence of firm heterogeneity in abatement technology (and thus marginal abatement cost), what is the optimal way of allocating abatement effort across firms, and which policy instruments can achieve this efficient outcome?

10. Does the method of issuing emission permits in a cap-and-trade system (auctioning or grandfathering) affect the efficient outcome?

11. What are the (political) trade-offs for allocating emission permits by way of auctioning or grandfathering in a cap-and-trade system?

12. What is the benefit of using *permit banking* and *permit borrowing* in a cap-and-trade system?

13. What are the practical problems associated with the European Emission Trading System? What works, what doesn't?

14. Discuss the advantages of a hybrid cap-and-trade system that includes a price floor and price ceiling, or an allowance reserve.

15. What is 'carbon leakage' and why should policy makers be concerned about it?

16. What is 'reshuffling' and why should policy makers be concerned about it?

17. Why are green taxes superior to a cap-and-trade system when a policy maker is concerned about providing incentives for innovation into pollution abatement technology?

18. Consider Germany's generous feed-in-tariff (FiT) for electricity from photovoltaic systems on house roofs and on farmers' fields. What is economically sensible about a FiT subsidy, and what is not?

19. Describe key approaches for valuing environmental assets based on market benefits (revealed preference) and non-market benefits (stated preference).

20. When using *contingent valuation* surveys, why do questionnaire respondents often indicate a greater willingness to accept compensation for environmental degradation than a willingness to pay to prevent the environmental degradation?

21. What are *hedonic regressions* and how are the used?

22. How does one calculate the 'value of a life,' and how can one use such calculations to identify the 'low hanging fruit' of environmental policies?

23. In cost-benefit analysis, what objective is being maximized: the benefit-cost ratio or the net benefit?

24. How can one compare different options in cost-benefit analysis when point estimates of costs and benefits are subject to substantial measurement error?

25. What is captured by the measure 'value of a statistical life'? How can it be used to inform policy decisions?

Chapter 4
Life Cycle Assessment

From the perspective of environmental management, one of the most useful practical tools for businesses is the life cycle analysis (LCA) of their products and production processes. (The terms life cycle assessment and life cycle analysis are used interchangeably.)

LCA is an evaluation of the environmental effects associated with any given industrial activity, from the initial gathering of raw materials from the earth until the return of all residuals to the earth. This is often described as a cradle-to-grave analysis, and cradle-to-cradle analysis. The difference between cradle-to-grave and cradle-to-cradle analysis is that the latter incorporates the recycling of materials when a product is discarded. Waste management considerations play an important part of cradle-to-cradle analysis.

LCA intends to capture the environmental impact generated both *directly* through the manufacturing process and *indirectly* through energy use, raw material extraction, product distribution, consumer use, and disposal.

An integral part of manufacturers' product stewardship is the determination of their products' environmental externalities (e.g., pollution) as well as resource and energy use. Through life cycle analysis, manufacturers can determine the environmental footprint of their products and manufacturing methods. Life cycle analysis helps inform decisions about competing production methods or competing product designs by taking into account explicitly the environmental costs during the entire life of the product, from cradle to grave or (ideally) from cradle to cradle.

LCA is an area of rapidly evolving standards. A widely used standard is the *Code of Practice* for LCA published by the Society of Environmental Toxicology and Chemistry (SETAC). SETAC has partnered with the United Nations Environment Program to widen the use of LCA worldwide. The International Organization for Standardization (ISO) is developing standards known as the ISO 14040 series for supporting life cycle assessment. These standards are voluntary and—unlike the ISO 14001 standard for adopting an environmental management system—do not lead to certification or third-party review.

Fig. 4.1 Life Cycle Assessment

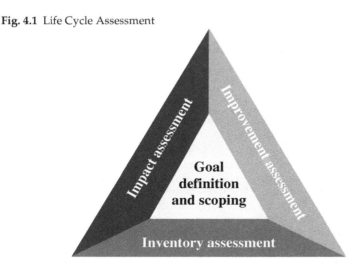

4.1 Concepts

Box 4.1 provides an introductory example of a life cycle analysis: are fluorescent light bulbs more environmentally friendly than incandescent light bulbs when mercury emissions are taken into consideration? As it turns out, the answer depends on taking both direct and indirect emissions into account.

Figure 4.1 visualizes the LCA 'tripod,' which consists of a central goal definition and scoping that in turn is surrounded by the three stages of LCA. The first stage, inventory analysis, compiles a list of all the environmental effects associated with a product. This is essentially a data-gathering stage. The second stage, impact analysis, is concerned with classifying, characterizing, and valuing the identified environmental impacts. The third and last stage, improvement analysis, attempts to identify measures through which the current production process and value-chain activities can be improved in order to reduce the environmental impact of the product.

The LCA practitioner will find a number of databases and software tools quite helpful. The Swiss *ecoinvent Centre* has put together a very useful set of databases for LCA. The European Commission also maintains an extensive *Life Cycle Inventory* (LCI) database. A consortium of universities has put together an input-output life cycle model known as *Open IO*. There are also several software platforms for LCA modeling. The *openLCA Project* is in the process of assembling public domain soft-

Box 4.1: Fluorescent or Incandescent?

Compact fluorescent (CFL) light bulbs are significantly more efficient than incandescent light bulbs in terms of electricity use. For example, a typical 60 Watt incandescent light bulb can be replaced by a 13 Watt CFL light bulb. The cost difference between these light bulbs has shrunk significantly over the years and nowadays they cost about the same. (The same is not true for the even more efficient LED bulbs.)

If only energy use was considered when CFL bulbs are compared with conventional bulbs, CFLs would win easily. CFLs consume only about 25% of the power that incandescent bulbs consume. In a life cycle analysis, other types of externalities are considered as well. One particular concern is the mercury that is used in CFLs. If only mercury content was considered, incandescent bulbs would outperform fluorescent bulbs because the latter contain about 4 milligrams of toxic mercury. However, there are also indirect sources of mercury to be considered. Coal-burning power plants emit considerable amounts of mercury into the air, and in the United States

coal plants are used more widely than in Canada. In the United States, each kilowatt-hour (kWh) of electricity generates about 0.012 mg of mercury.

The table below shows a simple life cycle analysis of fluorescent versus incandescent light bulbs, assuming that both are used for 8,000 hours. (Because incandescent bulbs do not contain mercury, we do not need to worry about the fact that conventional bulbs do not last as long as CFLs and need to be replaced more often.)

Once *direct* (landfilling) and *indirect* (electricity generation) effects are taken into consideration, CFLs actually outperform incandescent light bulbs with respect to mercury emissions. The indirect effect trumps the direct effect. CFLs outperform conventional light bulbs even more because they last longer than conventional light bulbs. Mercury is also more dangerous when airborne. A milligram of mercury from burning coal for electricity generation is worse than a milligram of mercury in a landfill from discarding CFLs.

	Fluorescent	Incandescent
Watts	13	60
Hours of use	8,000	8,000
kWh Use, lifetime	104	480
Mercury from power generation (mg/kWh)	0.012	0.012
Mercury from electricity (mg)	1.2	5.8
Mercury from landfilling (mg)	0.4	0.0
Total mercury (mg)	**1.6**	**5.8**

ware modules for LCA, and the *EIO-LCA* project at Carnegie Mellon University maintains an economic input-output LCA database.

4.2 Goal definition and scoping

In order to use LCA, it is crucial to define what the analysis is meant to accomplish and what is taken into consideration. For example, the mini-LCA about compact fluorescent and incandescent light bulbs in box 4.1 only took mercury emissions into account and nothing else. The *goal* was to compare only the two types of light bulbs (and exclude LED light bulbs), and the *scope* was restricted to mercury emissions.

The *goal* of an LCA can be quite varied, but typically involves some kind of comparison of two or more competing alternatives. The most straight forward LCA goal is to compare competing products (e.g., different light bulbs) or competing production methods (e.g., bleaching pulp with chlorine, chlorine dioxide, or ozone). LCA can also be deployed to: achieve a particular environmental standard; improve the delivery of a product by considering packaging, distribution methods or transportation distances; or improve the use of the product by a client or consumer (e.g., water use by different types of shower heads or toilets).

After the goal of the LCA has been defined, the scope of the LCA needs to be limited. In most cases it is not feasible to characterize all environmental externalities associated with a product. In many cases data limitations impose constraints on the scope of the analysis. Therefore, most LCAs focus on a limited number of environmental effects, typically those that are of primary concern. This means that the LCA needs to draw a line between what is considered in the LCA and what is excluded from the LCA. This is the *scope* of the analysis. Logically, the scope of the LCA follows the value chain of the firm and the cradle-to-grave steps of the product and its parts:

- Raw materials and energy acquisition;
- Manufacturing (including intermediate inputs);
- Transportation;
- Packaging/distribution;
- Use/reuse/maintenance by consumer;
- Recycle/waste management after use.

4.3 Inventory analysis

After completing the goal definition and scoping, the first practical step in the LCA involves building an inventory of the environmental effects of the product or process. This requires quantifying energy and raw materials use, emissions into air and water, and generation of solid and hazardous wastes. All these environmental effects need to be tracked over the entire product life cycle. The challenge for the individual firm is often the lack of solid data about environmental effects caused by intermediate parts suppliers and environmental effects caused by consumers who use the firm's product. The data-gathering aspect of the inventory analysis is often the most time-consuming and most challenging part of a LCA. Even where data are available, they may be proprietary and costly to acquire, or they may be confidential.

Inventory analysis often involves building a computer model in which one can vary assumptions about different key parameters. This allows the LCA analysis to explore different scenarios. Often such scenarios are couched in terms of low-level, mid-level, and high-level assumptions about these parameters. For example, when taking into consideration behavioural assumptions about end users of a product, there is often a wide range of usage patterns. If the empirical distribution of the behaviour patterns can be established, the mean and standard deviation can be used to establish a baseline scenario and two alternative scenarios at the plus/minus one standard deviation points. Another typical use of an empirical distribution is to use the median as the baseline and the first and third quartile (at the 25% and 75% marks of the distribution) for the alternative scenarios.

Another source of variation in an LCA is the location context of the analysis. For example, when using electricity, there is great variation in power generation methods across countries. An LCA study that took into account electricity use in Canada and the United States might come to quite different conclusions. Electricity in Canada tends to be much cleaner than in the United States because Canada employs lots of hydroelectricity while the United States relies much more on coal-fired power plants. On average, an electric car in Canada emits fewer indirect pollutants than in the United States. As a general rule, great care needs to be applied when LCA results are applied outside the geographic boundary of the original analysis.

Inventory analysis concludes with interpreting the results and drawing conclusions about potential sources for reducing resource use, energy use, or emissions. The evaluation of these potential improvement areas is reserved for the improvement analysis, however.

4.4 Impact analysis

The purpose of the impact analysis is to translate the raw data obtained from the inventory analysis into measures of actual harm. This follows an approach that is also used in a somewhat different context for environmental impact assessment, which we will encounter in chapter 6.

Impact analysis commences with classification, which assigns items from the inventory assessment to a number of different impact categories, such as human health, ecological quality, or natural resource depletion. Each of these impact classes is then itemized by the relevant stressors, such as specific contaminants (individual substances), human health effects (e.g., carcinogen, irritant, odours), or wildlife effects (e.g., habitat destruction, diseases).

The second step involves characterization, which converts the measured or estimated emissions or effects (assessment data) into their actual consequences (impact data). For example, carcinogenic air or water emissions translate into a projected number of new cancer cases caused by that pollutant. The key challenge for characterization is to express the different types of consequences into something that is comparable: adding apples and apples and not apples and oranges. To tackle the 'unit of measurement' problem, characterization employs three different techniques.

The loading technique adds up data in each impact category and compares totals. However, this technique only works when the units of measurement are comparable. Even when the physical units are the same (say, kilograms), it does not mean the impact is comparable. A kilogram of mercury does not have the same effect as a kilogram of arsenic.

More common is the use of an equivalency model, which converts data into comparable units based on equivalency factors (e.g., acute toxicity risk). For example, the United States Environmental Protection Agency has developed a system of *Risk-Screening Environmental Indicators* for toxic chemicals, allowing for different forms of human contact (inhalation, ingestion).

Yet another method employs the critical dilution volume of a pollutant. This converts the emissions into units of dilution required. For example, how much water flow is needed to dilute the leakage of a certain amount of arsenic into a river to a level meeting a particular environmental standard (provided that suitable standards exist and are meaningful)?

The third and final step in the impact analysis involves impact valuation, which assigns relative values or weights to different impacts or impact categories. Whereas characterization often involves scientific models, assigning weights is often somewhat problematic because it may be prone to value judgments. This problem is particularly pronounced when the impact categories are in very different domains (say, human health and animal health). How should human health be weighted relative to animal health? Or what are appropriate weights when such diverse categories as energy consumption, climate protection, toxicity reduction, and biodiversity are involved? LCA studies can become quite subjective if the weights are arbitrary. As a general rule, the wider the scope of the LCA, the more analytic robustness is required. This means the weights should be varied and it should be demonstrated if the qualitative results are susceptible to subtle changes in the weights.

Because weights can be subjective, it is important to demonstrate that the weighting is not influenced by the desire to generate a particular outcome. In the absence of scientifically rigorous methods, a useful practical approach is to survey a number of experts at arm's length and use the average weight for each impact category. A variation of this method employs a broader survey or poll of citizens. Such methods are also explored in greater detail in chapter 6, which discusses environmental impact assessment.

The valuation exercise in the LCA is also often referred to as ecoscoring, and the resulting empirical score is sometimes referred to as ecopoints or environmental load units.

4.5 Improvement analysis

The purpose of the inventory analysis is to identify opportunities to reduce emissions, waste, energy consumption, or material use. The purpose of the impact analysis is to identify those areas that are contributing the greatest environmental impacts and should be prioritized for improvements. The final step in the LCA is therefore the improvement analysis, which aims to develop strategies for guiding the improvement of the product or production process. Improvement analysis needs to make a compelling business case for changing the status quo. Improvement analysis is not just an engineering exercise where one demonstrates that things could be done better. Improvement analysis is meant to support decision making, and this means looking at improvement options and quantifying their implementation costs and environmental benefits.

Improvement analysis faces numerous hurdles. Suggested improvements or novel innovations may have little data to quantify their impacts. Without solid data to back up decision making, firms take a risk, and this risk needs to be contained. Small 'evolutionary' improvements are therefore often more acceptable than large 'revolutionary' improvements. Generating new ideas in the improvement analysis often means going back to the earlier LCA stages to model new outcomes or collect relevant data. LCAs may therefore involve several iterations through the three stages of inventory, impact, and improvement analysis.

During the improvement analysis, it is often helpful to look at products, production processes, and projects from a whole-life cost perspective. This leads to the method of life cycle costing (LCC), which is appealing to managers because it involves quantifying alternative options in dollar terms. LCC is particularly useful for appraising projects or new products as it looks at all phases of ownership of a product or asset: purchase and installation; operation; maintenance and repair; performance monitoring; and removal and disposal. Because of the intertemporal perspective of the analysis, it is necessary to use discount rates to translate future costs into net present value (NPV). This involves two

Box 4.2: An LCA Battle: Disposable or Reusable Diapers?

A study by the U.K. Environment Agency from October 2008 estimates the environmental impact of a child using cloth or disposable diapers for the first 2-1/2 years of its life (using 2006 reference data). The study includes the environmental effects of disposable nappy manufacturing, disposable nappy disposal choices, and laundry choices for cloth nappy use.

The table below shows the key results for different types of handling reusable diapers. The environmental impacts of reusable diapers can be higher or lower than using disposables, depending on how they are laundered. It is consumers' behaviour after purchase that determines most of the impacts from reusable nappies.

CO_2	Reusable	Disposable
Baseline	570 kg	550 kg
Line-drying	475 kg	—
Washing at 90°C instead of 60°C	620 kg	—
Tumble-drying	785 kg	—

important parameters: the discount rate and the project lifetime. LCC is sensitive to these two numbers, and variations of these need to be explored carefully.

LCC can be illustrated by looking at the total cost of ownership of an automobile. A cheap car may be poorly built and cost more in maintenance and repair than an expensive car that incurs little maintenance costs. And the greater initial expense for a vehicle with a diesel engine or hybrid engine may be offset by greater fuel efficiency of these types of engines. Which vehicle has the lowest total cost of ownership depends crucially on parameters such as the driver's annual mileage, the expected lifetime of the vehicle, and fuel cost expectations.

Box 4.2 provides a concluding example of LCA: the battle between disposable and reusable diapers. The example illustrates nicely that variation in how consumers use a particular product can influence the outcome of the LCA significantly.

4.6 Environmental input-output analysis

A key component of a life cycle analysis for a product is environmental input-output analysis (EIO). The problem is that final products contain intermediate products, and therefore an LCA needs to take into account energy use, waste, and pollutant emissions that are generated not only by the production of the final good, but also those generated by the

production of all of its parts. Producing one more unit of one good generates both *direct* emissions in its own industry and *indirect* emissions
in all other industries that supply intermediate goods.

EIO is a numerical tool that makes use of industry-wide data on immediate goods use. Statistical agencies collect such data and assemble
them into an **input-output matrix**, which tells us, for every dollar of
output in industry i, how many dollars worth of inputs we need from
industry j. With EIO we can tell how a change in demand for a particular product will impact emissions or the environment. EIO is a compromise, however. Ideally, we would like to know about each individual
good's specific components rather than an industry average. But often
such information is not available or is confidential. Looking at industry averages instead of specific intermediate goods suppliers is a useful
approximation.

EIO is not without problems. First, approximating true input-output
relationships by using aggregate industry data may lead to significant
errors when there is much heterogeneity across firms within the industry. Second, using a domestic input-output matrix may be misleading
when intermediate goods are imported from foreign countries, which
may have rather different input-output relationships or pollution intensities across industries. Therefore, more sophisticated EIO models use
multi-country and highly disaggregated data.

Mathematically, let y_i denote final demand for good i, and let x_j denote output of industry j. Further, let $a_{ij} \geq 0$ denote input coefficients.
Coefficient a_{ij} is measured in units of good i needed for the production of one unit of good j. Therefore, $a_{ij}x_j$ is the total amount of good i
needed by industry j. Then the accounting identity $x_i = y_i + \sum_j a_{ij}x_j$
holds: industry output x_i is either consumed directly as final demand
(y_i) or is used as inputs elsewhere in the economy ($\sum_j a_{ij}x_j$). In matrix
form, this can be written more compactly as

$$\mathbf{x} = \mathbf{y} + \mathbf{Ax} \quad,$$

where $\mathbf{A}$ is an $n \times n$ input-output matrix and $\mathbf{x}$ and $\mathbf{y}$ are $n \times 1$ vectors
of total output and final demand. There are n industries in total. Manip-
ulating this matrix equation by solving for $\mathbf{x}$ yields the expression

$$\mathbf{x} = (\mathbf{I} - \mathbf{A})^{-1}\mathbf{y} \quad,$$

where $\mathbf{I}$ is the identity matrix and $(\mathbf{I} - \mathbf{A})^{-1}$ is known as the **Leontief
inverse matrix**. In practice, the mathematical operations are solved in a
computer model.

So far we have only addressed the input-output relationship among
industries. What about emissions? We need to know each industry's
per-unit emissions for each pollutant, which we can collect in a matrix

$\mathbf{P}$ of size $p \times n$, where p is the number of pollutants (e.g., CO_2, CO, SO_2, NO_x). Total emissions are the sum of direct and indirect emissions:

$$\mathbf{m} = \mathbf{P}\mathbf{x} = \mathbf{P}(\mathbf{I} - \mathbf{A})^{-1}\mathbf{y} \quad ,$$

The coefficients in the $\mathbf{P}$ matrix are expressed in units of pollutant per dollar of output. Now that we have a vector of total emissions $\mathbf{m}$, the remaining task is to aggregate these into an impact measure. When the pollutants are from the same domain (e.g., air pollutants), it is often possible to aggregate them into **environmental load units** (ELUs) using equivalency factors or weights, which are collected in the $1 \times p$ vector $\mathbf{w}$. To conclude the analysis, we can now look at a change in final demand $\Delta \mathbf{y}$ and calculate the corresponding change in environmental load:

$$\Delta\text{ELU} = \mathbf{w}(\Delta\mathbf{m}) = \mathbf{w}\mathbf{P}(\mathbf{I} - \mathbf{A})^{-1}\Delta\mathbf{y} \quad .$$

Let us consider a numerical example for environmental load units. We wish to calculate the ELUs due to air emissions from one kilogram of ethylene production. Emissions are 0.53 kg of carbon dioxide, 0.006 kg of nitrogen oxides, 0.0009 kg of carbon monoxide, and 0.009 kg of sulfur oxides, respectively (Boustead, 1993). Impact studies have provided equivalency weights for the different pollutants, shown in the table below. All that is left to do is to convert the emission intensities into ELUs (per 1 kg of ethylene), and sum up.

Emission	Weight	ELU	
0.53 kg CO_2	0.09 ELU/kg CO_2	0.0477	95.2%
0.006 kg NO_x	0.22 ELU/kg NO_x	0.0013	2.6%
0.0009 kg CO	0.27 ELU/kg CO	0.0002	0.4%
0.009 kg SO_x	0.10 ELU/kg SO_x	0.0009	0.2%
		0.0501	100%

What is useful in this exercise is to look at the relative contributions from the different pollutants. Carbon dioxide contributes by far the most to the total environmental load from ethylene production.

Now let us us consider a numerical example for EIO with just two industries: electricity production (EL) and manufacturing (MF). EL provides $500 of output to MF; EL purchases $200 of inputs from MF. EL uses $150 worth of its own output, and MF uses $100 of its own output. In the table below, rows disaggregate output into its constituent part: EL's total output of $1,000 is consumed as $350 final demand and $150 + $500 = $650 intermediate demand. The columns in the table disaggregate inputs: to produce $2000 of MF output, $500 + $100 = $600 worth of inputs are needed, and $1,400 is value added in the MF industry. Production of EL and MF is associated with pollution. Let us assume that EL generates 100 grams of toxic waste (e.g., mercury) per dollar of output, while MF generates only 5 grams of toxic waste per dollar of output.

	EL	MF	Final demand	Total output	Waste intensity	Toxic waste
Electricity (EL)	$ 150	$ 500	$ 350	$ 1,000	100 g/$	100 kg
Manufacturing (MF)	$ 200	$ 100	$ 1,700	$ 2,000	5 g/$	10 kg
Value added	$ 650	$ 1,400	$ 2,050			
Total inputs	$ 1,000	$ 2,000				110 kg

Now let us consider a 20% increase in the final demand for electricity (i.e., $70 worth of extra EL output) perhaps due to an increased use of power-hungry 'server farms' for 'cloud computing' in this economy. How much more toxic waste is generated by this increase? Converting the input values into shares (e.g., $500/$2000 = 0.25$) provides the coefficients a_{ij} for the input-output matrix. With total output of $1,000 electricity and $2,000 manufacturing goods, this economy generates 110 kg of toxic waste. The full calculation is then

$$\Delta m = \begin{bmatrix} 100 \\ 5 \end{bmatrix}^T \left(I - \begin{bmatrix} 0.15 & 0.25 \\ 0.20 & 0.05 \end{bmatrix} \right)^{-1} \begin{bmatrix} 70 \\ 0 \end{bmatrix}$$

$$= \begin{bmatrix} 100 \\ 5 \end{bmatrix}^T \begin{bmatrix} 1.2541 & 0.3300 \\ 0.2640 & 1.1221 \end{bmatrix}^{-1} \begin{bmatrix} 70 \\ 0 \end{bmatrix}$$

$$= \begin{bmatrix} 100 \\ 5 \end{bmatrix}^T \begin{bmatrix} 87.79 \\ 18.48 \end{bmatrix} = 8871.3 \quad .$$

As a result of the increase in final demand for electricity by 20% (i.e., $70), output of electricity increases by $87.79 and output of the manufacturing good increases by $18.48. Toxic waste increases by 8,871 g (i.e., 8.1%). Another way to portray this change is as an elasticity. Based on the numbers just calculated, a 1% increase in final demand for electricity generates an 0.4% increase in toxic waste: the elasticity is 0.4.

4.7 Summary

For individual firms, life cycle analysis (LCA, often combined with environmental input-output analysis) provides a useful decision tool to consider the cradle-to-grave or cradle-to-cradle environmental impact of the products they sell. LCA can help firms improve product design and 'green' their sourcing and distribution systems. Once the goals and boundaries of the LCA have been defined, an LCA conducts an inventory, impact, and improvement assessment.

Environmental input-output (EIO) analysis is often used as a supplementary tool when detailed firm-level data are not readily available. EIO uses industry-level data and therefore employs industry averages. This is an approximation for true firm-level relationships. EIO can be used to predict how a change in demand for a good translates into more direct and indirect output in all industries in that economy, which in turn can be used to calculate the change in emissions and, when aggregated across pollutants, the change in environmental load units.

4.8 Study questions and exercises

1. What is the objective of LCA?
2. What are typical applications of LCA? Find examples of competing types of products.
3. What is the difference between cradle-to-grave and cradle-to-cradle analysis?
4. How does *life cycle costing* compare to *life cycle analysis*?
5. What is the 'measurement problem' during impact analysis? What are viable solutions to this measurement problem?
6. How can environmental input-output analysis help determine the total environmental impact of certain production activities?
7. What are the merits and constraints of the EIO approach?

Exercises

1. Sales of bottled water have skyrocketed in the last decade. Should consumers continue to buy drinking water packaged in plastic bottles or use tap water in reusable containers?

    a. Explore the controversy surrounding bottled water. What are the arguments in favour of bottled water, and those against it? What explains consumers' demonstrated willingness to pay an enormous premium for bottled water?
    b. Have someone administer a blindfolded taste test. Can you tell the difference between bottled water and tap water?
    c. Carry out a life cycle assessment of bottled water versus tap water. Start with scoping: what are the pertinent environmental issues, and which health issues need to be taken into account for users of bottled and tap water? Continue with the impact assessment. Conclude with recommendations to inform consumer behaviour.
    d. Differentiate your LCA based on the assumption that plastic water bottles are: (i) reused twenty times before being recycled;

(ii) used once and then fully recycled; (iii) used once, then recycled or landfilled with 50% probability; or (iv) used once and then landfilled.

2. Ethanol has become a common supplement in gasoline. Many gas stations sell blended fuel that contains either 5% or 10% ethanol, and some vehicles are capable of E-85 fuel (85% ethanol) even though few stations sell E-85.

    a. Carry out a limited life cycle assessment for ethanol and gasoline production in terms of the energy footprint, assuming that ethanol is generated from corn. For ethanol production, the scoping should include key agricultural inputs (fertilizer, natural gas, electricity, diesel fuel), while for petroleum production the scoping should include the production stages extraction, transportation by pipeline or railway, and refining.
    b. If you have been able to keep track of the different fuel sources in the LCA process, expand your analysis to greenhouse gas emissions. Use country-wide average emission intensities for the different fuel sources coal, natural gas, or petroleum.

3. Conduct goal definition and scoping for the choice among four different methods of hand-drying: (1) using a paper towel dispenser; (2) using a cotton roll towel dispenser; (3) using a conventional low-speed electric hand dryer; (4) using a high-speed Dyson electric hand dryer. Which issues should be considered when comparing these options?

4. Conduct a life cycle analysis and life cycle costing for the choice among three different methods of heating water in a home: (1) a conventional natural gas heater with tank; (2) a high-efficiency condensing tankless natural gas heater; (3) an electric tankless heater. Compare fixed (purchase) costs and variable (operation) costs over a 20-year period. What are the carbon dioxide emissions associated with each method?

5. Explore the freely available Open-LCA software (www.openlca.org). The web site has a few case studies that provide suitable tutorials and instruction in the software's use. The 'aluminum can vs PET bottle' case study available on the Open-LCA web site is a particularly suitable starting point.

Chapter 5
Environmental Law

Environmental law is a relatively young area of jurisprudence. Many of the core environmental laws, rules, and regulations have only been developed over the last few decades. Because of a relative paucity of case law, many important questions have not yet been fully settled.

Environmental law has a distinctly local component, and there are major differences in the way different countries have enacted environmental laws and regulations. This chapter discusses the foundations of environmental law in Canada and the United States, highlighting major differences as well as the similarities. Historically, US environmental law is somewhat older than Canadian environmental law, and the approach in the United States tends to be more centralized than in Canada. This chapter is rounded out with a discussion of international law and international environmental treaties, with a special focus on how environmental issues interact with international trade law and the special obligations under the *North American Free Trade Agreement*.

There are also not very many textbooks on Canadian or US environmental law. Benidickson (2008) is the most thorough treatment on the Canadian side, although it is primarily directed at law students. On the US side, Salzman and Thompson (2010) provide a thorough and up-to-date discussion of environmental law an policy. This chapter draws on the discussions in both books, along with numerous other sources, and attempts to distill some of the key concepts into a managerial perspective.

5.1 Pollution as a legal concept

The legal definition of pollution poses unique challenges. Whereas science can measure or estimate pollutant emissions on a continuous scale, the law prefers a more tangible, discrete scale. Designing a suitable test to ascertain whether pollution is present in the environment is not trivial, however. Different jurisdictions have developed different approaches to defining pollution.

In the United States and in Quebec, pollution is defined through a standard: a pollutant is a contaminant or mixture of several contaminants present in the environment in a *concentration or quantity greater than the permissible level* determined by laws or regulations.

By comparison, the definition of pollution in British Columbia focuses on the harm: pollution is the presence in the environment of substances or contaminants that substantially alter or impair the usefulness of the environment. Such a definition effectively requires evidence of harm before a substance can be said to be a pollutant.

The definition used in Saskatchewan is perhaps the broadest among the different approaches as it captures a range of adverse effects: 'pollution [...] is the addition or removal of any substance that (i) will render the environment harmful to the public health; (ii) is unsafe or harmful for domestic, municipal, industrial, agricultural, recreational or other lawful uses of the environment; or (iii) is harmful to wild animals, birds, or aquatic life.'

A related legal concept is conservation, which can be defined as maintaining resource stocks and ecological capacity. Conservation is usually a balancing act. There are trade-offs between short-term economic benefits and long-term environmental benefits. For example, the Canadian *Fisheries Act* stipulates that the 'the conservation of Canada's fisheries and their management on a sustainable basis are central to the economic viability of persons engaged in fishing and fish processors and the well-being of communities that are dependent on fisheries resources.' The regulator is therefore required to weigh the long-term benefits from conserving the fish stock against the short-term benefits of maintaining employment and income for the local fisheries communities. In the past, the Canadian Department of Fisheries and Oceans (DFO) has often sided with the short-term economic benefits, and this has contributed to the collapse of several fisheries such as the cod stock off the coast of Newfoundland. While the law provides the tools for conserving resources such as fish, ultimately it is the political determination of the regulator which decides if these tools are fully used.

Several Canadian laws make reference to notions of sustainability and sustainable development. An earlier chapter has already explored the difficulty of giving precise meaning to this term. It is easy to see that using this terminology in a legal framework gives rise to questions about the definition and meaning, let alone implications. How can these concepts be made operational? Ultimately, what it comes down to is to specify specific actions that comply or do not comply with the law, and to specify corresponding standards, penalties, or taxes. Making references to sustainability in a legal context also necessitates the development of quantitative tools that can capture what is and what is not sustainable. In the absence of such metrics, laws requiring sustainable development remain weak if not unenforceable.

Among the most important principles in environmental law is the notion that a polluter is responsible for damages, known as the polluter pays principle. What that means in practice is that harmful conduct implies monetary responsibility for polluters. Implicitly, the cost of pollution should remain private and polluters should not be subsidized by direct public expenditures for the environmental harm they cause.

The polluter pays principle maintains that anyone who creates an adverse effect on the environment must take remedial action and pay for the costs of that action.

Whereas the polluter pays principle is rather uncontroversial, the precautionary principle poses conceptual challenges. Its application has often been marred by controversy. An example is the dispute about genetically-modified organisms, discussed in box 5.1. The precautionary principle demands early preventative action even in the absence of conclusive scientific evidence when delaying action would risk greater environmental harm. The lack of full scientific certainty that underlies the precautionary principle has been used by some to demand action even in the complete absence of scientific evidence. This is a misinterpretation of the notion of precaution. On one side, the lack of full scientific certainty should not be used as a reason for inaction when there is a threat of serious and *irreversible* damage. On the other hand, invoking the precautionary principle when scientific evidence is completely absent is equally problematic. Scientific uncertainty should not be mistaken as an invitation for (un-)scientific speculation.

In the absence of full scientific certainty, the precautionary principle shifts the burden of proof to those who propose innovations whose environmental consequences are not yet fully understood. The principle demands rigorous study before deploying new technologies. Precaution also calls for wide margins of tolerance when implementing new technologies. New products and technologies should be fault-tolerant (with respect to safety), and they should allow nature to adjust to any environmental consequences gradually. In other words, worst-case scenarios for a new technology should not overwhelm an ecosystem.

Companies can apply the precautionary principle directly when they shift effort from end-of-pipe treatment of pollutants to pollution prevention (also known as 'P2'). Pollution prevention involves any action by a company that avoids or minimizes the creation of pollutants or waste and thus reduces the overall risk to the environment or human health.

5.2 Environmental law in Canada

When the United States adopted its constitution in 1787 and when Canada confederated through the *Constitution Act* in 1867, the notion of environmental protection was unknown and found no place in either

Box 5.1: The Genetically Modified Organism (GMO) Dispute

The dispute over genetically modified organisms (GMOs) illustrates the application of the precautionary principle. GMOs include transgenic microbes, plants, and even animals. Proponents of GMOs maintain that their use increases agricultural yield and productivity, makes certain crops more resistant to pests, and helps ensure food safety. Opponents of GMOs suspect that their use may pose long-term risks for human consumption (such as increasing allergenicity) and to the diversity of species. At this point, there is no conclusive scientific evidence that points to long-term harm from GMOs.

In the United States, a large number of GMO-based products are produced and marketed commercially. In Canada, the approach to GMOs has been mixed. One province, Prince Ed-ward Island, has banned GM potatoes. Nevertheless, Canada is also one of the world's largest producers of GM canola. In the European Union, scepticism about GMOs prevails, and in 1998 the EU placed a de facto moratorium on new GMO products. This moratorium affected US exports of maize gluten and soybeans to the EU, and the United States has filed a related complaint with the World Trade Organization (WTO).

In 2006 the WTO ruled that the EU restrictions did indeed violate international trade rules, but by 2004 the EU had already lifted the moratorium and replaced it with new labelling and traceability requirements. Products that contain GMOs of more than 0.9% are now required to be labelled. Labelling shifts the choice over GMOs from governments to consumers.

document. This means that legal authority over the environment has evolved gradually through interpretation and extension of other rules. In particular, there is no clear assignment of responsibilities to the federal level or to the provinces and states. In practice, both levels of jurisdiction exercise some control over environmental issues, sometimes in cooperation and sometimes in competition with each other.

Interpreting the constitutional framework in Canada follows three guiding principles. First is a focus on legal instruments such as regulations, application of criminal law, issuing of licences, and setting of standards. Which level of jurisdiction can deploy the instrument most effectively? This depends to some extent on which has constitutional authority over related realms of law (e.g., criminal law, building permits) and on which can monitor and enforce such law effectively. Second is a focus on the environmental media—in particular, air, water, and land. Which level of jurisdiction can protect the medium most effectively? This depends in part on the local or regional nature of pollutants and whether their adverse effects are confined to one jurisdiction or spill over into neighbouring jurisdictions. It also depends in part on the importance of local expertise and the need for local flexibility in setting and enforcing environmental regulations. Third is the focus on geographic demarkation. Which jurisdiction has legal responsibility for particular territories—for example, parks, aboriginal lands and native reserves, or coastal waters?

5.2.1 Federal jurisdiction

In Canada, federal authority over the environment is rooted in several constitutional powers: trade and commerce (s.91[2] of the *Constitution Act*); navigation and shipping (s.91[10]); seacoast and inland fisheries (s.91[12]); federal works and undertakings (s.91[29], s.92[10]); and aboriginal lands (s.91[24]). Federal authority is thus quite strong with respect to environmental protection of rivers, lakes, and coastal waters. The federal *Fisheries Act* takes a prominent role in establishing jurisdiction over all water resources.

The federal government also has sole jurisdiction over international treaties and international trade. International environmental agreements are concluded by the federal government, and international trade rules also have repercussions on environmental regulation. Nevertheless, authority over international treaties is not a backdoor through which federal authority can be established over particular environmental domains because entering into an international agreement on the environment does not automatically supersede provincial jurisdiction. In most cases, the federal government relies on the cooperation of lower levels of jurisdiction.

In the presence of transboundary pollution, federal power can be established if individual provinces are unable to protect the environment effectively. Different provinces may have competing interests, and one province's action (or inaction) may cause significant harm to residents of another province.

The federal government has unambiguous jurisdiction over criminal law (s.91[27]).[1] This power can be used to prohibit blameworthy or wrongful conduct but cannot be used to regulate conduct. It is therefore challenging to protect the environment through criminal law alone. It is possible to criminalize the act of dumping toxic waste into a river; however, it is not possible to regulate emission intensities through the criminal law channel. Criminal law requires an absolute standard of conduct, not a relative or gradual standard of conduct. This means that the use of criminal law powers is probably restricted to penalizing the most dangerous consequences for human health.

---

[1] This is quite different from the United States, where criminal law is primarily the purview of the states.

The *Constitution Act* contains a general clause that grants the federal government a residual power to maintain *peace, order, and good government* (POGG). While this clause may seem to open the door to a wide interpretation of federal power, the courts have interpreted it quite narrowly. The courts apply the national concern doctrine: subject matter must have a *singleness, distinctiveness, and indivisibility* that clearly distinguishes it from matters of provincial concern to justify federal authority under the POGG clause. Therefore, the invocation of POGG is probably limited to environmental issues that are predominantly extra-provincial or international in scope.

The Canadian government has expanded its jurisdiction over the environment through two major legal bodies: the *Canadian Environmental Protection Act* (CEPA, 1999) and the *Canadian Environmental Assessment Act* (CEAA, 1992). Environment Canada is the department of the government of Canada charged with the responsibility of coordinating environmental policies and programs at the federal level. There are a number of related agencies, such as the Canadian Environmental Assessment Agency or the National Energy Board, that have been assigned particular duties with respect to environmental issues. There are also 'neighbouring' government departments, such as Fisheries and Oceans Canada (DFO) and Natural Resources Canada (NRCan). The DFO has the lead role in managing Canada's fisheries and safeguarding its waters. NRCan is the responsible authority for a number of projects related to resource extraction and energy, and for this purpose is involved in environmental assessments.

The current *Canadian Environmental Protection Act* came into effect in 1999; it was updated from the first CEPA, which was introduced in 1988. Its main objective is to regulate environmental conduct. When the original CEPA was introduced, it provided a comprehensive framework for managing toxic substances across their entire life-cycle that included development, manufacturing, transportation, distribution, use, storage, and ultimate disposal. CEPA also opened the door to federal authority over the wider introduction of regulations and environmental quality objectives. A main feature of the updated 1999 CEPA is a greater recognition of voluntary efforts by industry, improved consultation with the provinces and territories, and strengthened provisions on information gathering and publication. The 1999 version of CEPA also makes pollution prevention the cornerstone of national efforts to reduce toxic substances in the environment.

What exactly constitutes a toxic substance that is subject to regulation is of great practical significance. Section 64 of CEPA defines a substance as toxic 'if it is entering or may enter the environment in a quantity or concentration or under conditions that: (i) have or may have an immediate or long-term harmful effect on the environment or its biological diversity; (ii) constitute or may constitute a danger to the environment on which life depends; or (iii) constitute or may constitute a danger in

Canada to human life or health.' To identify which toxic substances are potentially problematic and require more detailed investigation, CEPA introduced a priority substance list. Following further study, some of these listed substances may be deemed toxic by the minister of the environment and are added to Schedule 1. Substances placed on the CEPA Schedule 1 are not automatically controlled. Rather, listing them as toxic allows the government to proceed with regulations, pollution prevention (P2) plans, environmental emergency (E2) plans, or target them for virtual elimination.

CEPA is enforced by federal enforcement officers who are authorized to: enter premises, examine any substance, product, fuel, cleaning product, or water conditioner; take samples; seize evidence; conduct tests or take measurements; and open and examine any books, records, electronic data, or documents.

The maximum penalties include fines of up to $1 million a day for each day an offence continues, as well as imprisonment for up to three years or both. CEPA includes mandatory penalties such as the cost to remedy the damage done to the environment. Violators may also have to pay for clean-up costs or forfeit any profits earned as a result of an offence. Very importantly, corporate officials can be prosecuted if they authorize, accept, or participate in any violation of CEPA or its regulations.

CEPA can be enforced in a number of ways. Most typical is the warning when there is minimal or no threat to the environment or human health. A warning is meant to assert a violation so that the alleged violator can correct the problem and return to full CEPA compliance. For the purpose of preventing the release of toxics, CEPA officers can also issue specific directions or instructions. CEPA officers can also issue tickets for such thing as failing to provide a report. Beyond these relatively informal measures, there are compliance orders and court injunctions to prevent or stop a violation; ministerial orders requiring remedial measures; and lastly prosecution. Despite the large potential penalties set forth in sections 272 and 273 of CEPA, penalties are rare. In a three-year period from March 2008 to March 2011 there were only 23 convictions under CEPA totalling $242,500 in fines. CEPA officers carry out about 5,000 inspections per year and issue between 1,000 and 2,000 written warnings per year. There are about 40-60 formal investigations and perhaps about 10 prosecutions per year.[2]

Under CEPA, the minister of the environment may issue ministerial orders that can: (a) prohibit activities that involve novel substances; (b) compel the recall of a regulated substance or a product containing that substance; and (c) put a production and importation moratorium on a new product or substance during the evaluation of that substance for its toxicity. The minister can also seek an injunction against a firm in

---

[2] Source: W. Amos et al., 'Getting tough on environmental crime?' ecojustice.ca, 2011.

order to stop or prevent a violation of CEPA, and where a violation has already occurred, the minister can pursue prosecution or civil action in order to recover the cost of remedial actions. Prosecution will always be pursued when the environmental damage involves death or bodily harm to a person, or serious harm to human life or health. Prosecution also takes place when a violation happens due to a firm's failure to comply with a ministerial order or directions by an enforcement officer. Prosecution may lead to a less serious summary conviction (without the right to a jury trial, and with a half-year time limit on laying charges) or a more serious conviction by indictment (no time limit for charge or trial).

Informed policy-making requires information about where pollutants enter the environment, and how much. The nation-wide tool for such information gathering is the *National Pollutant Release Inventory* (NPRI), established in 1992 and recording data since 1993 through mandatory annual reports from all facilities that meet reporting requirements. CEPA sections 46–50 now provide the legal mandate for gathering and publishing the information collected through the NPRI. By 2011, over 8,400 facilities were reporting to the NPRI on more than 300 listed substances. Unlike its US counterpart, the *Toxics Release Inventory* (TRI), the Canadian NPRI covers all industries. CEPA has systematically expanded its coverage and over the years has added micropollutants such as dioxins and furans and air contaminants from stationary combustion facilities. The reporting requirement is triggered if any of the listed substances is emitted, *and* if the total number of hours worked at the facility exceeding a 20,000 hour-employee threshold (approximately 10 full-time employees).

The *Canadian Environmental Assessment Act* (CEAA) of 1995 aims to ensure that projects under federal jurisdiction do not cause significant adverse environmental effects. The CEAA applies to any proposed construction, operation, modification, decommissioning, or abandonment of a physical work. It covers projects described on an inclusion list that covers national parks, protected areas, oil and gas projects, nuclear facilities, waste management, fisheries, wildlife, and projects on aboriginal land. Additional criteria about the size and form of the project will trigger a CEAA review. The review process consists of several stages. During an initial phase, the proposal is screened and studied comprehensively. At the decision stage, the review panel makes a recommendation on proceeding with the project, proceeding with mandatory mitigation, or rejecting the proposal. In the last stage, the minister of the environment exercises relatively wide discretion in adopting the panel's recommendations, or appoints a mediator or review panel to reexamine the proposal.

Because many projects with an environmental impact are related to energy generation and transmission, the National Energy Board (NEB) plays a crucial role alongside the Canadian Environmental Assessment Agency. The NEB was established in 1959 with the mandate to regulate international and interprovincial aspects of the oil, gas, and electric utility industries. This includes in particular the construction and operation of pipelines and power lines. The NEB has authority to consider aspects of environmental protection in its review of new projects, covering the entire life cycle of a project from planning, through construction and operation, to abandonment.

5.2.2 Provincial jurisdiction

Provincial jurisdiction over environmental matters is derived from a number of constitutional provisions that seem to grant provinces somewhat larger scope over environmental issues than the federal government. These constitutional powers include: property and civil rights in the province (s.92[13] of the *Constitution Act*); generally all matters of a merely local or private nature in the province (s.92[16]); management and sale of public lands and timber (s.92[5]); municipal institutions (s.92[8]); licensing for local, municipal, and provincial revenue (s.92[9]); enforcement powers (s.92[15]); and, significantly, natural resources (s.92a). In addition, section 92[10] gives the provinces jurisdiction over local works and undertakings, which includes hydro dams, power stations, and power distribution systems within the provinces. Also relevant is the provincial taxation power (s.92[2]), as it enables provinces to introduce environmental taxes (e.g., a carbon tax). The rights of ownership and proprietary rights over natural resources weigh heavily in the provinces' favour. Many environmental issues arise over the extraction of natural resources (e.g., oil and gas) or the harvesting of renewable resources (e.g., forests). The bottom line is that the related constitutional powers probably form a stronger basis for environmental authority than the federal powers discussed above.

The constitutional jurisdiction over property and civil rights provides the most important provincial power for regulating environmental issues relating to businesses operating within provinces. Combined with the power over municipal institutions, provinces can assert authority over water treatment, land-use planning, waste management, air pollution, and noise control.

While the authority over environmental issues in Canada is a shared federal-provincial responsibility, provinces and the federal government are not required to coordinate and harmonize their policies. As a result, most provinces have their own environmental assessment acts that work in parallel with, and overlap with, the corresponding federal act. Thus it is entirely possible for a province to grant a permit under its own assessment act while the federal government denies a permit. For example, the proposed Prosperity Mine project by Taseko Mines Ltd. in the Chilcotin region of British Columbia was approved by the provincial government in January 2010 but was rejected by the federal government over concerns that the project would cause significant adverse effects on fish habitat, grizzly bears, navigation, local tourism, and would infringe on certain aboriginal rights.

Beyond understanding actual constitutional allocations of responsibilities lurks the question how such responsibilities should be allocated most efficiently. One of the organizing principles of federalism is the subsidiarity principle, which can be applied to allocate environmental responsibilities among jurisdictions.

> The subsidiarity principle suggests that environmental issues should be handled primarily at a local level of jurisdiction and that only those tasks which cannot be performed effectively at a local level should be delegated to a central authority.

A central government is more efficient at managing environmental issues: (i) if there are transboundary issues where the central government can coordinate policies and facilitate interjurisdictional trade-offs, or (ii) if the central government has operational economies of scale. On the other hand, provincial governments may sometimes better understand local environmental concerns, or balance them against economic interests. Provincial governments, and state governments in the United States, can also become incubators for new environmental policies or pioneer technological solutions. New areas of environmental policy are often first addressed at the level of provinces and states, and later adopted by the federal authority.

5.2.3 Municipal jurisdiction

Under Canadian law, municipalities are 'creations of the provinces.' Municipal governments lack constitutional autonomy and thus their powers are obtained through delegation by means of provincial law. However, once such powers are conferred, municipalities have the capacity to enact and enforce municipal bylaws. There is one important caveat, however. Municipal bylaws cannot exceed or contradict the intent of corresponding provincial legislation. Cities cannot set stricter environmental standards than the province has set already. It is generally recognized that municipalities have authority over planning and zoning; licensing businesses; maintaining public health; regulating the storage and transportation of dangerous substances; and regulating environmental matters (e.g., pesticide use bylaws, noise bylaws).

There is ample scope for municipalities to develop environmental initiatives. The courts have tended to give municipalities leeway in claiming ground for regulating environmental issues as long as such regulations are not inconsistent with federal or provincial law. In practice, the ability of municipalities to develop and pursue environmental standards is probably hampered more by their fiscal constraints to implement and enforce regulations than by their legal constraints over jurisdiction.

5.2.4 Interjurisdictional cooperation

Pollution is often transboundary in nature.. This necessitates cooperation among jurisdictions. Such coordination may be difficult to achieve if jurisdictions have strongly competing interests.

From an economic point of view, there is an important trade-off in choosing the level of jurisdiction that is best suited to deal with an environmental issue. Greater centralization (federal authority) is desirable when dealing with an environmental issue that requires uniformity, consistency, and comprehensiveness of standards and regulations, and when a higher level of jurisdiction exhibits economies of scale in implementing and monitoring such standards and regulations. On the other hand, greater decentralization (provincial authority) fosters more innovation and experimentation with environmental policies, and may lead to greater sensitivity to local conditions and thus more flexible regulations tailored to these local conditions. This trade-off is often couched in terms of the subsidiarity principle: a higher level of jurisdiction should perform only those tasks which cannot be performed effectively at a lower (more local) level of jurisdiction.

Because of the shared responsibility over the environment, cooperation among provinces and between the provinces and the federal government often takes the form of a consultation process. The National Round Table on the Environment and Economy (NRTEE) was established in 1988 by the Canadian government to foster cooperation and innovation at all levels of governments—and provide non-partisan policy advice. The federal government decided to terminate NRTEE at the end of March 2013.

Decisions on cooperative regulations are made by the Canadian Council of Ministers of the Environment (CCME). The CCME has set a variety of country-wide standards for substances such as particulate matter, mercury, benzene, dioxins, and furans. The CCME has also adopted a prohibition on bulk water exports.

Interjurisdictional cooperation is increasingly focusing on developing bilateral federal-provincial agreements ('accords') that try to avoid duplication. For example, the parallel environmental assessments at the federal and provincial levels may be streamlined into a joint environmental assessment process that satisfies both federal and provincial concerns. Two types of federal-provincial agreements are used to further interjurisdictional coordination. Saskatchewan (1994) and Quebec (1994-2005) have entered into administrative agreements with the federal government to streamline administering regulations and to cover inspections, enforcement, monitoring, and reporting. Alberta (1994) entered into an equivalency agreement with the federal government to avoid duplication and to enable the best-suited jurisdiction to handle environmental issues. Specifically, when an instrument already exists at the provincial level that achieves the same environmental outcome as a federal CEPA regulation, the provincial or territorial instruments take precedence.

Carrying out an environmental impact assessment (EIA) may fall under federal or provincial jurisdiction, and in numerous instances under both. Particular criteria may trigger assessments at two levels of jurisdiction. In this case there is the potential for duplication as well as divergent outcomes. It is entirely possible for one jurisdiction to approve a project and the other jurisdiction to reject it. Some effort has gone into EIA harmonization. A 1998 CCME accord on EIA harmonization attempted to avoid duplication by creating joint review panels (while retaining separate decision authority). A 2012 revision of the *Canadian Environmental Assessment Act* abolished a large number of federal EIAs and imposes strict time limits on the decision-making process.

Individual provinces may also enter into equivalency agreements with the NEB, which reviews new energy projects, including pipelines and transmission lines. For example, British Columbia has an agreement with the NEB that accepts an NEB assessment as equivalent to a provincial environmental impact assessment. It is important to note, though, that such equivalency agreements do not fetter or limit the applicability of provincial permits or authorizations. This leaves the door open for a province to pull the plug on a project that is approved federally but is economically or socially undesirable from a provincial perspective.

Despite the potential for federal-provincial conflict, the CCME has made slow and steady progress in finding a common denominator on environmental policy. In October 2012, the CCME adopted a comprehensive *Air Quality Management System* (AQMS) that sets country-wide Canadian Ambient Air Quality Standards (CAAQS), establishes air zone management within provinces and territories, and defines six regional airsheds to facilitate coordination for air pollution that crosses jurisdictional boundaries.

Table 5.1 shows the CAAQS for fine particulate matter and ozone. The standard takes effect in 2015, with slightly lower standards taking effect in 2020. The CAAQS also defines air management thresholds for

Table 5.1 Canadian Ambient Air Quality Standards

Pollutant	Averaging Time	Standards 2015 (2020)	Management Thresholds	Metric for standard
$PM_{2.5}$	24 hours	28 (27) $\mu g/m^3$	10 / 19	3-year average of the annual 98th percentile of the daily 24-hour average concentrations
$PM_{2.5}$	1 year	10.0 (8.8) $\mu g/m^3$	4.0 / 6.4	3-year average of the annual average concentrations
Ozone	8 hours	63 (62) ppb	50 / 56	3-year average of the annual 4th-highest daily maximum 8-hour average concentrations

Source: CCME *Canadian Ambient Air Quality Standards (CAAQS) for Fine Particulate Matter (PM$_{2.5}$) and Ozone*, October 2012. Management thresholds explained in text.

four management levels: green (actions for keeping clean areas clean); yellow (actions for preventing air quality deterioration); orange (actions for preventing the exceeding of CAAQS); and red (actions for achieving air zone CAAQS). In table 5.1, management thresholds are indicated for the yellow and orange management levels. The red management level is triggered by exceeding the standard. Implementation of air zone management actions is left to the provinces.

The 2012 CCME agreement also establishes Base-Level Industrial Emissions Requirements (BLIERs): quantitative or qualitative emissions requirements for new and existing plants and equipment types. BLIERS focus on nitrogen oxides, sulfur dioxide, particulate matter, and volatile organic compounds. The idea behind adopting BLIERS is to identify best practices based on standards or codes of practice adopted in leading domestic and foreign jurisdictions.

The CCME has also adopted standards for mercury emissions as well as dioxins and furans. Because these types of emissions are tied to particular sectors, the standards have been tailored to these sectors. For example, mercury standards exist for base metal smelters, waste incinerators, and coal-fired power plants. Exhaust gas from incinerators must not exceed a maximum concentration of $20\mu g/m^3$ for municipal waste, $50\mu g/m^3$ for hazardous waste, and $70\mu g/m^3$ for sewage sludge. Base metal smelters are regulated according to their production of finished metal in tonnes. Existing base metal smelters must not emit more than 2g/tonne of mercury, and new or expanding base metal smelters must stay below 0scepticism.2g/tonne for zinc, nickel, and lead smelters, and below 1g/tonne for copper smelters.

5.2.5 *Aboriginal rights*

Many environmental issues are related to resource extraction industries and their related activities. Aboriginal communities, referred to in Canada as First Nations, hold claims to large swaths of land, and the legal status of these claims has not yet been resolved in many instances. Unsettled land claims have created uncertainty over resource development. Such land claims overlap in jurisdiction and are both federal and provincial responsibility.

Aboriginal rights are protected by the *Constitution Act* (s.35). Judicial interpretation of the Constitution obliges the Crown[3] to consult with and accommodate First Nations. The Supreme Court ruled in 1990 that '[this] provision gives a measure of control over government conduct and a strong check on legislative power. The government is required to bear the burden of justifying legislation which has some negative effect on any aboriginal right protected under section 35(1).' The duty to consult and accommodate, which invokes the Honour of the Crown, must be met and cannot be delegated to third parties.

Modern treaties between aboriginal communities on one side and the federal and provincial governments on the other side create certainty for communities and resource developers, and also liberate these communities from restrictive regulations of the *Indian Act*, which is generally regarded by these communities with scepticism. Many aboriginal communities view the *Indian Act* and as an impediment to their self-determination and an obstruction to their road to prosperity.

In the absence of treaties, aboriginal communities and their people can hold an effective veto power over developments that intrude into their lands or could cause serious negative repercussions, such as those that occur through pollution of land and rivers. For example, the proposed development of the Northern Gateway pipeline would cross through aboriginal lands in British Columbia. The provincial government has made it clear that they require First Nations to be accommodated, as the Constitution requires. However, neither the developer (Enbridge) nor the federal government have yet moved to accommodate these communities, or accept their refusal for such development to cross their land. Many First Nations do not object to the transport of natural gas or refined petroleum, but many object to the transport of diluted bitumen (dilbit) and other crude oils. Without the required accommodation, federal approval of such resource projects undoubtedly will end up in litigation.

At the federal level, the government of Canada consults with aboriginal people during an environmental impact assessment conducted

---

[3] Canada is a constitutional monarchy, and the state is therefore referred to as 'Her Majesty the Queen in Right of Canada,' the 'Crown in Right of Canada,' or simply the 'Crown.' It encompasses the federal, provincial, and territorial governments.

by a review panel of the Canadian Environmental Assessment Agency. Aboriginal communities are provided an opportunity to comment on potential environmental effects of a new project and how such a project may impact established aboriginal or treaty rights. They can also comment on (or propose) mitigation measures and follow-up programs. The *Canadian Environmental Assessment Act* also obliges the federal government to specifically consider environmental effects, including any change in the environment that affects the current use of lands and resources for traditional purposes by aboriginal people. The Act also provides the opportunity to include aboriginal traditional knowledge in the assessment process.

Consultation would be meaningless without the potential for accommodation, which aims to avoid, eliminate, or minimize adverse impacts on aboriginal communities. Where it is not possible to accommodate, the government may also choose to compensate aboriginal communities for adverse impacts. In some situations, however, appropriate accommodation may involve cancelling a proposed project. While the duty to consult does not oblige the Crown to accept accommodations suggested by the aboriginal communities themselves, it does oblige the Crown to act in good faith during the process.

5.3 Environmental law in the United States

The previous section highlighted the mixture of competition and cooperation between provincial and federal governments in Canada. Because the Canadian constitution did not settle environmental policy responsibilities clearly, a complex web of overlapping jurisdiction has emerged. The situation in the United States is somewhat simpler because the US Constitution tips the balance of power over environmental matters to the federal government. The 1789 Constitution does not contain any explicit references to the environment. References to 'general welfare,' 'domestic tranquility,' and 'the blessings of liberty to ourselves and posterity' in the preamble may be interpreted as encompasing a vague mandate for protecting the country's environment. As the federal government has seized responsibility over large domains of environmental policy, the US Supreme Court has effectively confirmed federal jurisdiction in a number of its rulings. In particular, three major acts of Congress have shaped environmental policy in the United States since the 1970s: the *Clean Air Act of 1970* and the amendments passed in 1980; the *Clean Water Act of 1977* followed by the *Water Quality Act of 1987*; and the *Comprehensive Environmental Response, Compensation, and Liability Act of 1980*, more commonly known as the *Superfund Act*.

The constitutional basis for federal jurisdiction in the United States is the commerce clause, which gives Congress the power to regulate interstate commerce. Most environmental regulations will have some impact on commercial transactions among the states, and the Supreme Court has affirmed the broad federal authority over the environment. Some environmental issues are clearly local in scope (such as protection of wetlands), but courts have upheld federal jurisdiction even where the link to interstate commerce is tenuous. Congress can also invoke the property clause for dealing with environmental issues on federal lands and parks. Congress can also use its spending power to pay for environmental policies, tax environmental externalities, or withhold funds from states or other entities that fail to comply with federal laws.

The establishment of the Environmental Protection Agency (EPA) in 1970 followed in the wake of the *Clean Air Act*. With more than 17,000 employees, ten regional offices, and several laboratories, the administrative functions of the EPA have expanded substantially over its history. The EPA is charged with administering, monitoring, and enforcing federal environmental laws. Because many of the mandates established in environmental law are relatively unspecific, the EPA has a significant role in establishing precise standards. The nature of federal environmental law promotes the use of command-and-control approaches to environmental regulation. The use of market-based instruments has largely evolved around initiatives of single or small groups of states.

The role of individual states is characterized by federal preemption. The federal government has filled the regulatory space for environmental law and environmental regulations so that there is little incentive for individual states to exceed the federal mandates. For the most part, states simply exercise regulatory authority to the extent that federal law delegates it to them. The primary role of states is the implementation and enforcement of federal environmental laws. For this purpose. Congress provides funding to individual states, and can cut off (or threaten to cut off) funding if states are not complying with federal regulations.

An important question is whether states can exceed federal regulations or pass environmental laws in areas that are not already covered by federal law. Even when Congress has not taken the lead on a particular environmental issue, the courts have taken a dim view on local environmental laws that may discriminate against out-of-state businesses unless there is a compelling case for a local interest that cannot be met through non-discriminatory policies. Federal law can effectively preempt states from pursuing their own measures, and courts do not permit states to fill any voids left by the federal government. Thus US environmental law is heavily biased towards uniform standards across the country.

In some cases federal laws carve out a niche for states to exceed federal standards. For example, states may adopt 'California standards' for vehicle emissions that are stricter than national standards. This allows for a two-speed process where California leads the nation in pioneering tighter environmental regulations. Under the *Clean Water Act*, states are permitted to adopt water quality standards for particular rivers and lakes that exceed federal norms. Federal law requires polluters to meet the stricter of the two standards. In all cases, states can act only to the extent that their own environmental policies are at least as strict as the federal rules and standards.

Where states have some degree of autonomy is with respect to implementing national policies and standards. Whereas federal regulations set environmental quality standards (for example, emission concentration limits), individual states must design the path to attainment. Federal regulators review and approve state implementation plans and determine if a state has the capacity (personnel, expertise, funding, etc.) to fulfil its enforcement obligations. After a state implementation plan is approved, the federal regulator (the EPA) tends to remain in the background unless the state fails to achieve the federal environmental targets. This delegation is crucial. States retain significant flexibility in designing compliance schedules and compliance priorities. States also retain leeway in determining appropriate sanctions for violations. As a result, despite relatively uniform national targets for environmental performance, state environmental programs vary significantly in quality. It has been argued that in some instances states possess too much discretion rather than too little. The ability of federal regulators to punish states for failing to attain environmental targets is limited. The EPA could take over enforcement action from a state entirely, but this intervention-of-last-resort is impractical and politically inopportune.

Beyond the regulatory context lies the domain of litigation. Unlike Canada, where environmental lawsuits are rare, in the United States non-governmental environmental organisations (ENGOs) have played a major role in bringing lawsuits against companies as well government agencies. Most federal environmental laws contain a provision for a citizen suit that allows individuals and organizations to sue (a) anyone who violates an environmental law; and (b) any relevant government official who fails to carry out a non-discretionary statutory obligation. The introduction of citizen suits has opened the door for citizens to help enforce environmental law. There are limits to the scope of such lawsuits. For example, allegations of wrong-doing cannot target past violations but must demonstrate that violations are ongoing or intermittent. A citizen who brings forward an environmental lawsuit must also have standing by demonstrating that the challenged action or infraction (a) causes 'injury in fact' to the plaintiff, (b) can be traced to the defendant, (c) can be redressed by a court action, and (d) must be within the 'zone of interests' of the underlying federal statute. Most challenges to standing hinge on the notion of injury, although courts have interpreted injury broadly, encompassing more than merely economic or pesonal losses.

5.3.1 The Clean Air Act

The introduction of the *Clean Air Act* is a milestone in environmental legislation in the United States. It was the first environmental law that could be said to be truly national in scope and ambition. Introduced in 1970, it was prompted primarily by widespread dissatisfaction with poor air quality in many urban areas around the country. The *Clean Air Act* is fairly comprehensive and rather complex. The regulatory framework needs to take into account that air pollution originates both from point sources (industrial facilities) and non-point or mobile sources (transportation). The main element of the law is a command-and-control approach for setting emission standards. Amendments to the law opened the door for more market-based approaches, including emission permit trading. However, market-based instruments have been used only sparsely.

The starting point of the *Clean Air Act* is the identification of **criteria pollutants** that are deleterious to public health and welfare. Once a substance has been declared a pollutant, it creates an obligation for the EPA to regulate it. The main instrument of regulation is a set of uniform national attainment targets known as *National Ambient Air Quality Standards* (NAAQS). Table 5.2 provides descriptions of the pollutants, the limits, and the form in which these limits are calculated. The NAAQS have been updated several times. Primary standards (type P in the table) aim to provide public health protection, especially for higher-risk populations such as asthmatics, children, and the elderly. Secondary standards (type S in the table) are aimed at protecting animals, crops, vegetation, and buildings. The NAAQS amount to a classic one-size-fits-all approach to regulating emissions. Uniformity makes it easier to enforce the standards and avoids the pollution haven effect where one state could gain a competitive advantage over another state by maintaining lower standards.

Which substance is declared a pollutant is not always determined through wide consensus. In April 2009, the EPA declared carbon dioxide and five other greenhouse gases to be pollutants that endanger public health and welfare. This administrative declaration opens the door to regulation under the *Clean Air Act*, and it is expected that the Obama administration will introduce targets and specific rules by 2015. Congressional inaction on climate change left the government with the sole option of using regulatory powers under existing legislation. While market-based approaches would be more efficient economically, the command-and-control approach of the *Clean Air Act* appears to be the only available road to mitigating greenhouse gas emissions in the short term.

Once standards have been set for particular pollutants, each state is required to develop a **state implementation plan** (SIP) for achieving the targets. NAAQS levels are monitored in 247 different air quality control

Table 5.2 US National Ambient Air Quality Standards (2013)

Pollutant	Averaging Time	Level	Type	Calculation Method for Exceeding Threshold Level
Carbon monoxide	8 hours	9 ppm	P	no more than once per year
(CO)	1 hour	35 ppm	S	no more than once per year
Nitrogen dioxide	1 hour	100 ppb	P	not to be exceeded
(NO_2)	annual	53 ppb	S	not to be exceeded
Sulfur dioxide (SO_2)	1 hour	75 ppb	P	99th percentile of 1-hour daily max. concentrations, 3-year avg.
	3 hours	0.5 ppm	S	no more than once per year
Ozone (O_3)	8 hours	0.075 ppm	P+S	annual fourth-highest daily max. concentration, 3-year average
Particulate matter	annual	12 $\mu g/m^3$	P	annual mean, 3-year average
($PM_{2.5}$)	annual	15 $\mu g/m^3$	S	annual mean, 3-year average
	24 hours	35 $\mu g/m^3$	P+S	98th percentile, 3-year average
PM_{10}	24 hours	150 $\mu g/m^3$	P/S	no more than once per year on average over 3 years
Lead	3 months	0.15 $\mu g/m^3$	P+S	not to be exceeded

Units of measurement are: parts per million (ppm) by volume; parts per billion (ppb) by volume; a micrograms per cubic metre of air ($\mu g/m^3$). Source: EPA.

regions, allowing states to implement different measures in different regions. States have indeed used a wide array of specific measures to achieve the NAAQS targets. The EPA's role is to approve the SIPs and then monitor whether states achieve the targets. If a state fails to meet the targets, the EPA may take over administration of the law through a federal implementation plan (FIP). However, FIPs have not been much used in practice and remain largely an empty threat. Many states have failed to achieve the targets for particular criteria pollutants in one or more of their air quality control regions, which is described as non-attainment. Such non-attainment can be the result of unforeseen local conditions, but it can also be the result of non-compliance with state regulations. As a last resort, the EPA has the ability to impose specific standards on new industrial facilities to employ best-of-class pollution abatement solutions (with the lowest achievable emission rates). The EPA can also demand that existing facilities in non-attainment areas employ reasonable (although not best-of-class) pollution abatement solutions. In such cases, the EPA still requires the cooperation of the states to enforce these rules. In order to make interventions more manageable, the 1990 amendments to the *Clean Air Act* introduced five levels of non-attainment: marginal, moderate, serious, severe, and extreme. The required steps to achieve compliance with the NAAQS vary with the degree of non-attainment.

While NAAQS standards are based on ambient emission concentrations, regulations target emissions at source. The *Clean Air Act* gives the EPA the ability to set new source performance standards (NSPS), which effectively set minimum standards for new point sources as part of the permitting process for building new industrial facilities. The standards depend on whether a proposed new facility is in an attainment area or a non-attainment area. Existing industrial facilities that undergo major modifications are subject to the same review process. However, most existing industrial facilities are grandfathered and do not need to meet the NSPS requirements. As a consequence, emission intensities of old plants can exceed emission intensities from new plants substantially. While targeting new plants is politically less costly than targeting existing plants, it is economically inefficient.

Mobile sources of pollution, such as trucks and automobiles, contribute a large share of air pollution, in particular nitrogen oxides, volatile organic compounds, and carbon monoxide. The *Clean Air Act* gives the EPA the authority to set standards for tailpipe emissions of motor vehicles as well as for the quality of fuels (e.g., the amount of sulfur in diesel fuel). The emission targets forced automobile makers to adopt new technologies, in particular the catalytic converter. Regulating vehicle emissions has a checkered history in the United States. California was the first state to regulate emissions from automobiles when the state enacted the 1960 *Motor Vehicle Pollution Control Act* (Vogel et al., 2010). The automobile industry first opposed emission standards and in the mid-1960s shifted towards advocating federal standards. Congress passed its own federal regulation, preempting all state regulations bar an exception for California. When the federal government introduced the *Clean Air Act*, California was permitted to retain or enact more stringent standards than those specified federally. In the 1990 amendment of the *Clean Air Act*, the scope of the exception was enlarged to allow any state to adopt the tougher California standards. Effectively, federal law permits states to choose between two sets of standards: the pioneering California standard or the default federal standard.

California continues to pioneer new environmental policies. For example, in 1990 it adopted a policy to help promote and develop the market for low-emission vehicles (LEVs) and zero-emission vehicles (ZEVs). Car makers are required to meet Corporate Average Fuel Economy (CAFE) standards under the 1975 *Energy Policy and Conservation Act*, a law that was passed more in response to the 1973 oil crisis than in response to environmental concerns. It is important to note that CAFE captures a fleet-wide average.[4] The original California program extended these requirements and mandated that the market share of ZEV vehicles had to increase to 10% by 2003. The minimum ZEV requirement for each manufacturer is rising to 12% for model years 2012–14, and to 14% for model years 2015–17. Considerable flexibility is built into

---

[4] Technically, CAFE is computed as the harmonic mean, not the arithmetic mean, of the fuel efficiency of vehicles sold.

this program. Manufacturers are allowed several methods to meet the ZEV requirements with credit substitution ratios for different classes of LEVs (typically, for hybrid cars).

Meanwhile, CAFE standards are evolving continuously and are administered by the National Highway Traffic Safety Administration (NHTSA). The EPA's role is limited to providing measures of vehicle fuel efficiency. Originally specified in terms of two specific miles-per-gallon fuel efficiency targets, separately for passenger cars and light trucks, a 2012 revision to the CAFE standards adopted a new system of setting targets with respect to the vehicle footprint—a measure of vehicle size based on the product of wheelbase length and track width. Vehicles with a smaller footprint must achieve higher fuel efficiency targets than vehicles with a larger footprint. Fuel efficiency targets are specified for each new model year. The different targets for passenger cars and light trucks allowed car manufacturers to escape the stringency of the regulation as the market share of SUVs (classified as light trucks) rose from one-tenth to about one-half over the course of three decades. Companies that fail to meet the CAFE standard can be assessed a hefty penalty.[5] In addition, sales of vehicles under 6,000 pounds that do not meet a fuel efficiency target of 22.5 miles per gallon are subject to a gas guzzler tax (paid by the manufacturer or importer) under the *Energy Tax Act*; heavier vehicles are exempt from this tax. CAFE standards hovered at 27.5 mpg for passenger cars and 20.7 mpg for light trucks until 2004, with standards for light trucks improving to 23.5 mpg by 2010. CAFE standards are set to rise to about 50 mpg by model year 2025 under the new footprint-based rules announced in 2012.

A significant caveat of the *Clean Air Act* is its reliance on command-and-control interventions. As the discussion in the chapter on environmental economics made clear, market-based interventions such as pollution taxes and cap-and-trade systems are much more economically efficient at achieving particular targets. The EPA has slowly expanded the use of cap-and-trade schemes. As lead in gasoline was being phased out starting in 1982, EPA allocated lead permits to refiners and allowed trading among them. The most comprehensive trading system in place to date targets sulfur dioxide emissions, the major source of acid rain. The 1990 amendments to the *Clean Air Act* replaced the requirement for technology standards (specifically, installing scrubbers for removing sulfur dioxide) with a nation-wide emission permit system. The first phase of the program (1995–99) covered only large power plants, with permits allocated on the basis of a historic baseline. The second phase of the program started in 2000 and covers all power plants with

---

[5] The 2007 *Energy Independence and Security Act* established a CAFE credit transfer and trading system. Credits from overcompliance in one year can be applied to a shortfall from undercompliance in a subsequent year, or credits can be purchased from an over-compliant competitor.

more than 25 MW capacity. Since 2010, sulfur dioxide emissions have been capped at 8.95 million tons per year. Participants buy and sell allowances through brokers and can also participate in an annual EPA auction of a small contingent of allowances. Prices in the SO_2 market have varied and typically hover around the $150-200/ton mark, except for a period between 2004 and 2008 when prices spiked to $1,600/ton in anticipation of stricter regulations that eventually did not come to pass. The future of the SO_2 market is in serious doubt as prices collapsed in 2012 following the announcement of the *Cross-State Air Pollution Rule* (CSAPR), which reduces the scope for cost-effective interstate trades hugely. States with caps under CSAPR must reduce their emissions to comply and cannot buy permits to offset non-compliance.

5.3.2 The Clean Water Act

The *Clean Water Act* was introduced in 1972, two years after the *Clean Air Act*. The *Clean Water Act* has contributed significantly to reducing pollution from point sources of water pollution—industrial facilities and municipal water treatment plants. However, the Act has been inadequate in dealing with non-point pollution sources—contaminated run-off from agricultural land, construction sites, and mines. The Act set ambitious targets for pollution reduction; it called for the elimination of all discharges of pollutants into rivers and lakes by 1985. This zero-emission target was unattainable since implementing such a policy would be prohibitively expensive. In practice the *Clean Water Act* has led to many pragmatic policies that have focused on point sources of water pollution. Provisions in the Act for regulating non-point sources of water pollution were left mostly to the discretion of the states, and this explains why there has been insufficient progress in this area.

The *National Pollutant Discharge Elimination System* (NPDES) requires anyone who discharges effluent or wastewater into rivers, lakes, or oceans from a point source to obtain a permit. NPDES permits are issued for a period of time (usually five years) and are renewable. Once issued, they can still be amended or cancelled. Permits are issued by individual states that have achieved the qualification to issue them, while the EPA issues permits for the remainder of states. A permit requires the permit holder to report any discharges (usually monthly) to the EPA and the issuing state. Information on permits and discharges is publicly available through the EPA's integrated compliance information system, which can be accessed through the EPA's web site.

The particular limitations imposed by an NPDES permit depend on whether the point source is a publicly owned wastewater treatment plant. Because wastewater treatment plants receive contaminants rather than generate them, NPDES permits for wastewater treatment plants specify particular technologies that they are required to use, whereas NPDES permits for regular point sources of wastewater stipulate specific numeric limits on effluent discharges. Because of the high cost of upgrading treatment plants, municipalities have often failed to meet the NPDES requirements for adopting wastewater treatment practices despite generous federal grants.

For point sources that are covered by regular NPDES permits, the EPA calculates a numeric effluent limit based on a suitable 'end-of-pipe' treatment technology. The EPA has considerable leeway in choosing the appropriate technology, and this choice is not necessarily based on a cost-benefit analysis. The technology choice is also the object of intense lobbying and political interference. Most permit holders choose to adopt the technology that was used in the evaluation process, even though in principle they are free to choose another technology as long as the alternative technology meets the effluent limit. The *Clean Water Act* allows the EPA to set effluent limits for categories and classes of point sources, and courts have interpreted this provision so that the EPA can set industry-wide standards rather than facility-level standards. The EPA has indeed established technological standards for about fifty different industries. However, individual facilities can ask for variances from the industry-level standard if the assumptions underlying the standard (i.e., the choice of treatment technology) are somehow inapplicable to them. The technological standards that are used for calculating effluent limits differ by type of point source.

Existing point sources are usually required to adopt the 'best available control technology economically achievable,' known as a BAT standard. This requirement is applied to toxic pollutants (itemized in the *Clean Water Act*) and non-conventional pollutants. The technological standards for five conventional pollutants—five-day biochemical oxygen demand, total suspended solids, acidity or alkalinity (pH), fecal coliform bacteria, and oil and grease—are somewhat more relaxed, and can also involve pollution prevention approaches instead of end-of-pipe treatment.

New point sources have to meet higher standards than existing facilities. The rationale is the same as for the *Clean Air Act*: demanding higher standards from new facilities is politically easier. Existing facilities often favour this approach as well because it raises the barrier to entry for potential competitors. It also encourages existing facilities to keep their outdated technologies in place for longer than necessary. New point sources must meet best-of-class approaches currently available, without consideration of costs.

Whereas point sources of effluents are tightly regulated under the *Clean Water Act*, non-point sources such as run-off from agricultural land are virtually unregulated. Several efforts have been made to expand the scope of the *Clean Water Act* in this direction, but these efforts have met strong political opposition.

5.3.3 Hazardous pollutants and the superfund

Many industrial activities involve hazardous substances—substances that are toxic and involve elevated levels of morbidity or mortality. Defining what exactly constitutes a hazardous substance is inevitably contentious as many of the risks are relatively low for an individual. However, elevated risk levels turn up for entire populations, and in particular in regional clusters. As empirical evidence is growing through more and better scientific research, the list of hazardous substances is growing as well. There are several options for dealing with a toxic substance. A toxic substance can be banned. Its use can be limited. It can also be phased out gradually. It is also possible to simply limit exposure to the toxic substance through protective measures. The regulatory approach to hazardous substances is evolving and often involves balancing health risks against the benefits from using the substances. When the EPA banned asbestos due to its cancer risk, it did so after amassing a large body of evidence that showed that the cost of the ban would be reasonable compared to an estimate of the number of lives saved. Essentially, the EPA adopted a test based on the value of a statistical life, discussed earlier in this book.

In addition to the acute risk from emissions of hazardous substances, there is also the long-term risk from hazardous waste. Industrial activity over the last century and a half has left many contaminated industrial sites. Cleaning up hazardous waste sites poses significant challenges. Which sites need to be cleaned up? In which order? And who should pay for the clean-up?

Federal action was prompted through the discovery of major hazardous waste sites such as the Love Canal neighbourhood in Niagara Falls, New York. In this case, the city had acquired land from Hooker Chemical (now Occidental Petroleum) in 1953. The land had been used as a dump site for 21,000 tons of toxic waste. Eventually, houses were built on the land, and unknowing residents started to experience severe medical conditions in the late 1970s. The federal government declared an emergency, relocated 700 families, and ordered a clean-up of the site. This incident and a similar environmental disaster in Times Beach, Missouri, prompted Congress to pass the *Comprehensive Environmental Response, Compensation, and Liability Act* (CERCLA) in 1980. CERCLA established a superfund, providing federal funds to aid in the clean-up of hazardous waste sites. The intention was to recover these funds from parties responsible for the environmental hazard.

CERCLA is designed to expedite dealing with contaminated sites. To determine the priority of contaminated sites, the EPA has developed a hazard ranking system that is based on the toxicity of the contaminants, the proximity to populations, and the likelihood of a release into drinking water, the food chain, or sensitive environments. Separate scores are calculated for different pathways, such as groundwater, surface water, soil exposure, and air migration. The result of the analysis determines which sites are included in the *National Priorities List*.

Sites that are identified in such a manner are subjected to a remediation study that investigates clean-up alternatives. A particular approach is selected and implemented. Different remediation options are explored in chapter 6 on environmental impact assessment, but in short, remediation can involve complete disposal and destruction, concentration (extracting contaminants from surrounding soil), or dilution (often through pumping water through a mildly contaminated site).

While initial funding for site clean-up is available through CERCLA's $8.5 billion superfund, the fund is meant to sustain itself indefinitely through operating on a cost recovery basis. Funds drawn from the superfund are reimbursed through application of the polluter pays principle. The cost of the clean-up is charged to the potentially responsible parties (PRPs): current owners and operators of the contaminated site; prior owners or operators of the contaminated site at the time of the waste disposal; arrangers of disposal or treatment; and transporters of the hazardous waste if they helped select the disposal site. Which of these parties ultimately pays is determined through an application of the standard of strict, joint, and several liability. Simply put, strict liability avoids the need to prove causation through negligence or intent; it is sufficient to demonstrate that the accused party is one that is potentially responsible. Joint and several liability implies that the responsible parties will have to pay collectively for the damage, and even a single party can be on the hook for the entire cost if other parties are unable to pay their share (perhaps because they have gone out of business). This standard of joint and several liability raises important questions about fairness because it could shift an inappropriate burden onto a marginal contributor to the damage that happens to be large and wealthy. Joint and several liability can only be avoided if particular contributions to the hazardous waste can be traced back to its origin *and* if the waste has remained separate since its disposal on the site. This will not be the case if the hazardous waste has leaked and cross-contaminated other waste since its disposal on the site.

5.4 Civil liability for environmental harm

When businesses cause environmental harm, they face sanctions not only from regulators or governments; they are also subject to civil liability. In common law countries such as Canada and the United States, a civil wrong is known as a tort. Tort law deals with situations where someone's behaviour has unfairly caused someone else to suffer loss or harm. A tort does not necessarily involve an illegal or criminal act. All that is necessary is that someone's (a company's) action has caused harm, and therefore the harmed parties may recover their losses. Unlike criminal law, where a case is brought forward by the state, tort law allows anyone who has suffered a loss to bring forward a case before a court. When it comes to environmental harm, there are several causes on which a tort case can be built. The party who initiates a lawsuit before a court is known as the plaintiff (complainant), and the accused party is known as the defendant.

The first tort cause is nuisance, which could be caused by toxic fumes, chemical spills, smoke, unpleasant odours, or excessive light or noise. To become a nuisance, such environmental effects need to *substantially and unreasonably* interfere with the plaintiff's own reasonable use of the land, resulting in actual physical damage to property, personal injury or risk to health and safety, or discomfort and inconvenience. In other words, the harm must be direct—and ideally measurable. There is also an important legal distinction between private nuisance and public nuisance. Public nuisance is a matter for the attorney general, whereas only individuals can pursue private nuisance claims. Some (public) nuisances may be statutorily authorized, such as noise from a nearby airport.

One of the most common causes of torts is negligence. In this case, a plaintiff must first establish a defendant's failure to meet a reasonable *standard of care* to which the plaintiff was entitled. Furthermore, the plaintiff must also demonstrate that the plaintiff owed the defendant a *duty of care*. Compensation can be sought for personal injury or property damage, but not economic losses. In practice, negligence is not easy to prove. The plaintiff has to prove damages such as physical injury or property damage; pure economic losses typically do not qualify. Negligence can become quite important in cases where the claims are not made against the originator of the environmental harm but against others whose acts or omissions have exposed the plaintiff to harm. For example, if someone buys contaminated land from an owner who did not disclose the contamination caused by a previous owner, the seller of that land is negligently misrepresenting the condition of the property and may thus be liable for damages.

The concept of strict liability applies even when a party exercises reasonable care in preventing environmental harm. If someone stores dangerous substances on his property and these dangerous substances (e.g., sewage, pesticides, fuel, chemicals) escape and cause damage on someone else's property, such a leak or spill causes liability. Strict liability applies strongly when scientific knowledge makes the risks of environmental harm foreseeable.

The intentional and direct entry onto someone else's land is known as trespass. More importantly for environmental harm, placing or allowing some substance or material onto someone else's land may also constitute trespass. Discharging refuse or sewage into a stream passing through a plaintiff's property falls into that category. Trespass requires directness, not just merely coincidental intrusion such as drifting smoke. It is often quite difficult to demonstrate trespass if there was no clear intent to place the substance on a specific property.

Lastly, there are also riparian rights that concern rivers and other water streams. A riparian owner has the right to a river's water and its natural flow, without significant alteration of its character or quality. For example, pollution from a pulp mill that causes damages to owners downstream would constitute a cause for initiating a tort.

Despite the existence of multiple causes for initiating torts that deal with environmental harm, there are numerous pitfalls. Environmental harm to individuals may be small or not immediate even if the aggregate environmental harm is substantial. Pursuing tort cases with an uncertain outcome can be risky. Because environmental harm often involves damage to multiple injured parties and potential plaintiffs, many jurisdictions offer the possibility of launching a class action lawsuit. For a court to certify a class action, however, the injured parties must be identifiable and the case must resolve an issue common among them. If injured parties have been affected in different ways, the case for a common issue is weak. Similarly, if individuals may have been exposed to potential environmental harm but have not been injured *demonstrably*, it is not possible to delineate the set of injured parties clearly.

5.5 Corporate and personal duties

There is a tension between a company's collective liability and the personal liability of the company's officers. Is a company liable even when an environmental offence was committed by one of its employees without its knowledge or approval? Is an employee liable for environmental offences that the employee was asked to carry out by senior company officers? Are employees obliged to refuse to carry out orders when they suspect that the requested action would result in environmental harm? The possibility of personal liability of officers of a corporation may also lead companies to offer indemnity to these officers by offering to pay any personal penalties for environmental infractions.

Corporate and personal liability coexist. One does not exclude the other. It is therefore important that a company whose activities involve the potential of environmental harm develop suitable defence strategies to prevent its officers from facing personal liability in the case of an environmental accident. Willful violations of CEPA or other acts always remain individual responsibility, but companies should demonstrate that their officers carried out their duties responsibly with respect to environmental laws. Two strategies are useful in this context.

First, firms should carry out due diligence in managing their environmental portfolio. This means that firms should take all reasonable measures to comply with applicable laws and regulations. Firms have a 'duty to take all reasonable care.' This duty of care implies (a) a high standard of awareness, and (b) decisive, prompt, and continuing action when an environmental problem occurs. A high standard of awareness can be achieved through implementing an environmental management system that helps implement environmental codes of conduct and monitor compliance with such a code.

Second, companies should carry out an environmental audit, which should be repeated at regular intervals. Such an audit is a systematic, documented, and objective evaluation of a facility's management, operations, and equipment. It is often part of implementing an environmental management system, or the certification of such a system through a third party. An important function of the audit is to verify the company's compliance with legal requirements and adherence to its own internal policies and standards, such as its environmental code of conduct and its pollution prevention plan.

In addition to responsibilities under pertinent federal or state/provincial environmental legislation, publicly traded companies also have a duty of accountability with respect to their shareholders. Under generally accepted accounting principles (GAAP), firms are required to itemize any potential environmental liabilities, for example when they decommission an existing facility. Similarly, securities legislation (which is a provincial matter in Canada) requires full disclosure of obligations concerning environmental liabilities. This includes a general obligation to disclose risk factors in a prospectus for offering securities. There is also a special obligation for companies whose equity or revenue exceeds $10 million. Large firms are subject to an annual filing requirement for information about the financial or operational effect of environmental protection requirements on capital expenditures, earnings, and competitive position. Companies are increasingly turning this necessity into a virtue: they prepare an annual environmental statement for shareholders that describes their actions towards environmental protection as well as any risks and potential liabilities emerging from their activities.

Box 5.2: Directors' Responsibility

A factory near the city of Cambridge in southwestern Ontario leaked toxins—primarily the metal degreaser trichloroethylene—into the groundwater underneath nearby homes. The company responsible, Northstar Aerospace Inc., has since gone bankrupt. In an attempt to apply the polluter pays principle, in November 2012 the Ontario Ministry of the Environment ordered twelve former members of the board of directors to pay for the clean-up of the site, which is estimated to cost $15 million. The directors are fighting the provincial order.

More than 200 homeowners installed indoor air mitigation systems to capture potentially dangerous vapours. The company paid about $20 million for this remediation effort before it went bankrupt, but bankruptcy left the continuing clean-up unfunded.

Did the directors really do everything they could to deal with the potential liability from environmental risks? The Ontario government asserts that the directors failed to ensure that sufficient funds were put aside to finish the remediation, and permitted the discharge of pollutants to occur.

As of mid-2013, the case is before the judge dealing with the company's insolvency case, but it may also be brought before the Ontario Environmental Review Tribunal. The tribunal is an arbitration panel that holds public hearings on appeals arising from government orders issued under an extensive list of provincial environmental laws. The tribunal decides whether to grant permission to appeal the order, and may also grant a stay of the order. Whatever the outcome, it will set an important precedent for future similar cases.

5.5.1 The Canadian legal context

In Canada, federal law defines a number of environmental offences that are subject to sanctions under CEPA sections 273 and 274. Obvious violations concern breaching a statutory prohibition against discharging a contaminant into the environment. Penalties also apply when a firm fails to comply with a regulatory requirement or administrative order, or when it fails to obtain a required licence, permit, or regulatory approval. Firms are also liable for disregarding or interfering with the regulatory process. This includes providing false or misleading information or obstructing enforcement officials in carrying out inspections.

Liability for environmental offences is both a responsibility of the firm as well as the individuals within the firm who carry responsibility for the particular actions. CEPA s.274(1) stipulates a number of offences where a person may be guilty and liable 'on conviction on indictment to a fine or to imprisonment for a term of not more than five years, or to both, who, in committing an offence under subsection 272(1) or

273(1), (a) intentionally or recklessly causes a disaster that results in a loss of the use of the environment; or (b) shows wanton or reckless disregard for the lives or safety of other persons and thereby causes a risk of death or harm to another person.' Beyond CEPA there is also the possibility of individual criminal responsibility when criminal negligence is involved. CEPA s.274(2) specifically invokes sections 220 and 221 of the Criminal Code when contraventions cause death or bodily injury.

CEPA s.280 unequivocally holds officers and directors of a corporation responsible for environmental offences: '(1) Where a corporation commits an offence under this Act, any officer, director or agent of the corporation who directed, authorized, assented to, acquiesced in or participated in the commission of the offence is a party to and guilty of the offence, and is liable to the punishment provided for the offence, whether or not the corporation has been prosecuted or convicted.' Responsibility for environmental offences does not stop at senior officers and the board of directors; it permeates the entire corporate structure and concerns all managers and workers. However, directors and officers of a corporation carry an additional responsibility for due diligence: they need to take reasonable care to ensure that the company complies with all regulations, orders, and directions that are imposed by the regulator or by enforcement officers. Additional director responsibility may also come under provincial jurisdiction, as the recent legal case described in box 5.2 illustrates.

5.5.2 The US legal context

In the United States, the most important statutes that stipulate corporate liability are the CERCLA (discussed earlier) and the *Oil Pollution Act of 1990*. Importantly, CERCLA applies equally to historic and current releases of pollutants. As noted above, CERCLA imposes strict, joint, and several liability, which means that each party involved in an operation has full liability and may thus have to cover any shortfalls from other participants. Furthermore, liability under CERCLA is also retroactive. An individual or company may be held liable for actions that were entirely legal at the time they were initiated.

The *Oil Pollution Act* attempts to reduce civil liability from oil spills by requiring oil companies to engage actively in pollution prevention, and prepare for the possibility of leaks and spills through the development of containment and clean-up plans. In many instances the required tasks in case of a spill or accident exceed that of a single corporation. As a result, the oil industry created the Marine Spill Response Corporation to deal with emergency responses.

Unlike in Canada, the responsibility of corporate directors is more limited. CERCLA s.107(a) imposes liability on 'operators' of facilities where there has been a release of hazardous substances. The courts have interpreted the term 'operator' relatively narrowly. In most instances, the officers and directors of corporations cannot be held directly liable for environmental infractions. Directors and officers are liable only if and when they are directly, actively, and personally involved in the environmental infraction. The courts have rarely strayed from this rule, although in some instances directors have been found liable if they exercised control over the facility even where they had no explicit involvement.

Despite CERCLA's statutory protection of corporate directors, corporate shareholders may initiate a derivative suit to hold officers and directors liable based on their fiduciary duty of care. Under the duty of care, a director's fiduciary responsibility is to perform his or her duties with the diligence of a reasonable person in similar circumstances. A breach of fiduciary duty occurs when the board of directors acts negligently or fails to avoid a preventable loss. Such a breach may be the result of insufficient managerial monitoring and control.

Another key question concerns the responsibility of parent companies under CERCLA. The bedrock principle holds that a parent corporation is not liable for the acts of its subsidiaries. In line with this long-established legal prinicple, CERCLA does not easily pierce the "corporate veil" of ownership. Exceptions arise only when the parent company is actively controlling and directing the facility of its subsidiary that is involved in an environmental infraction. From a policy perspective, ownership structure can be misused to limit environmental liability despite CERCLA's provisions to implement the polluter pays principle.

5.6 Damage, compensation, and remediation

When an environmental incident causes significant environmental harm, firms need to assess the extent and cost of that damage. The first step in preparing an incident analysis is to assess the scope of the damage and to identify the specific dimensions of the damage by impact group, source, and mitigation potential.

There are four broad impact groups for environmental harm: human health (or life); physical damage to own property or property of others; economic losses of persons (income losses of workers) or the company itself (lost revenue if a facility is shut down temporarily); and damage to the ecosystem (wildlife, nature). Damage can be assessed separately for each impact group.

Understanding the source of the incident is also crucial. A planned or authorized action typically involves the continuing release of a pollutant into the environment. Here the concern is often about compensating other parties who will be subject to continuing environmental harm. Unplanned or unauthorized incidents involve accidents or spills, which are by their very nature unpredictable. Here the problem is often assessing the damage as it progresses, developing damage scenarios, and readying financial and logistical resources to contain and minimize the damage.

Lastly, there is the question of mitigation potential. Environmental harm may be reversible or irreversible. Where harm is reversible, firms may have to pay for remedial actions (e.g., clean-up), whereas when harm is irreversible, firms may have only the option of compensating the harmed parties.

Once the scope of the damage has been identified, a company experiencing an environmental incident needs to quantify the monetary size of the damages. The methodology for this was explored in section 3.4. Wherever possible, market values should be used in accordance with the revealed-preferences approach. Where such information is available, compensation is measured as the difference between pre-damage value and post-damage value. Often the environmental damage touches on intrinsic values, such as recreational, aesthetic, or historical value. Here, the environmental loss is best measured in terms of the replacement cost or remediation cost. Lastly, when market values are not available, firms may have to relay on stated-preference approaches such as contingent valuation.

When environmental damage has occurred, how are the damages assessed and distributed? Claimants could be individuals, other firms, and the state. The scope of compensations can involve personal injury, damage to property, and in some cases even economic loss (e.g., due to damaged fish habitat). It is likely that disputes about the scale of the damage will ensue that will be decided by a court. This can be a drawn-out process that takes several years. However, certain types of damage require immediate remedial action—for example, cleaning up an oil spill, or providing medical treatment to injured people. In some cases, immediate responses can be triggered by an environmental protection compliance order, with the company becoming responsible for shouldering the cost of the ordered action. Beyond that, statutory duties may arise even prior to a court settlement where adverse effects (e.g., injuries) can be ameliorated through quick response.

Remediation of an environmental harm involves both a short-term and a long-term strategy. The short-term objective is clean-up: elimination or neutralization of the contaminants. The long-term objective is restoration: returning the affected area to its original environmental state.

Applying the polluter pays principle is hampered by two problems. First, who pays when the company that caused environmental damage ceases to exist? There are a number of reasons companies may cease to exist. There is the possibility of bankruptcy, or a foreign company folding its domestic subsidiary. In this case, a private environmental liability may quickly turn into a social environmental liability. To prevent such opportunistic behaviour by firms, some governments require firms to contribute to a type of insurance fund that covers environmental disasters. In some cases, governments have moved to partially indemnify companies from environmental liabilities. For example, the Price-Anderson *Nuclear Industry Indemnity Act* that was passed in the United States in 1957 provides a no-fault insurance whereby the first $13 billion (approx.) of damage from a civilian nuclear incident is industry-funded and any excess damage is covered by the government. Some foreign governments require firms to make a refundable deposit before investing in a sector where environmental incidents may occur.

Yet another problem is remediation of a brownfield site, an existing industrial site that has been sold to a new owner. (The alternative is a greenfield site for building a new plant.) What happens when the new owner discovers that the existing site is contaminated, and the previous owner did not disclose this fact (knowingly or unknowingly)? Who pays for the remediation? Can the new owner sue the old owner? Application of the polluter pays principle suggests that the owner who caused the contamination should pay. To help with such situations, the government of Canada maintains an *Environmental Damages Fund* (EDF) that follows the polluter pays principle. The EDF, administered by Environment Canada, is helping to ensure that those who cause environmental damage take responsibility for their actions. It is funded by receiving fines, court orders, and voluntary payments. These funds are then directed towards priority projects that will benefit remediation of environmental damage. However, the size of the EDF is minuscule because fines and other such contributions are rare and very small. A sensible reform would be to institute mandatory payments to such a fund and turn it into a capable insurance fund of last resort. The Canadian EDF mimics the US superfund discussed in section 5.3.3.

5.7 International environmental treaties

International environmental treaties are either bilateral or multilateral in nature. Bilateral environmental treaties usually involve neighbouring countries and issues such as transboundary air and water pollution, or sharing water resources from rivers and lakes. When the scope of the environmental problem is global, related international treaties are necessarily multilateral in scope and are typically negotiated under the auspices of the United Nations. Today there are dozens of such international environmental treaties that cover atmospheric pollution, freshwater resources, hazardous substances, maritime law, conservation of natural resources, biodiversity, and nuclear safety.

Some of the more prominent multilateral agreements include the 1973 *Convention on the International Trade in Endangered Species of Wild Flora and Fauna*; the 1979 *Convention on Lon-Range Transboundary Air Pollution*; the 1985 *Vienna Convention for the Protection of the Ozone Layer* along with its 1989 *Montreal Protocol* implementation; the 1992 *Framework Convention on Climate Change* along with the 1997 *Kyoto Protocol* under which countries committed themselves to reductions of greenhouse gases; and the 1989 *Basel Convention on the control of Transboundary Movements of Hazardous Wastes and Their Disposal*.

Beyond treaties that focus on particular environmental issues, there are also broad agreements that are based on geographic scope and that touch on environmental issues. The 1959 Antarctic Treaty establishes Antarctica as a scientific preserve. The *Convention on the Law of the Sea* (UNCLOS) was first concluded in 1958 and 1960 and revised in 1982 (referred to as UNCLOS III). UNCLOS has its own international court, the International Tribunal for the Law of the Sea (ITLOS) based in Hamburg, Germany. The United States is one of the few countries that has signed but not ratified the Convention, although in practice it honours almost all of its provisions. UNCLOS III establishes the International Seabed Authority with is own dispute resolution tribunal, which remains a point of contention. One of the important aspects of UNCLOS III is its establishment of a maritime exclusive economic zone (EEZ) for coastal states through which those states have exclusive rights over the exploration of marine resources. A country's EEZ covers 200 nautical miles (370 km) from its coastal baseline. The inner 12 nautical miles are considered territorial waters in which the country exercises full sovereignty; the outer 188 miles are considered international waters. Beyond the EEZ, states also have rights to the seabed of what is called the continental shelf up to 350 nautical miles (648 km) from the coastal baseline. Upon ratification of UNCLOS, a country has a ten-year period to make claims to an extended continental shelf. Canada, Russia, Norway, and Denmark are all actively pursuing related territorial claims in the Arctic.

There are also important bilateral agreements between Canada and the United States. In the 1991 *Canada-United States Air Quality Agreement*, the two countries agreed to reduce emissions of sulfur dioxide and nitrogen oxides, the primary precursors to acid rain. In 2000 an annex was added that covers ground-level ozone, a major contributing factor to smog.

Lastly, international trade law has significant repercussions on environmental issues. A separate section below is dedicated to discussing the implications of the *General Agreement on Tariffs and Trade* and the World Trade Organization, as well as the *North American Free Trade Agreement* (NAFTA).

5.7.1 International law

International environmental treaties often involve the terms 'agreement,' 'convention,' 'covenant,' 'protocol', and 'treaty.' The differences between them are more a matter of nuance than of substance. Generally, an international treaty is any express agreement under international law entered into by sovereign states (and in some cases supranational organizations). The terms 'convention' and 'treaty' are often used for the more fundamental agreements on particular topics. The term 'protocol' is often used for an annex to an existing treaty.

International treaties come into effect in three steps: signature, ratification, and implementation. Multilateral treaties are first signed by participating states in order to indicate their approval of the negotiation process. However, a simple signature is not binding until a country ratifies the treaty. A signature therefore merely obliges a party to act in good faith towards ratification, and to refrain from actions to defeat its ratification. The process of ratification establishes a country's consent through its internal constitutional process. This is usually a two-step process that involves (1) approval by a national parliament and (2) notifying the other contracting parties. Often (but not always) a third step involves passing national laws that implement the purpose of the treaty. For example, the *Kyoto Protocol* to reduce greenhouse gases left it to individual countries to decide how they want to implement their reduction targets.

In the United States, the president may negotiate a treaty, but the treaty must be approved by a two-thirds vote in the US Senate. Only after the Senate approves the treaty can the president ratify it. Ratification also makes the treaty binding on all US states under the Constitution's Supremacy Clause. In the United States, an international treaty automatically becomes national law upon ratification and thus, in principle, enforceable law. In practice, however, additional implementation legislation is required in most instances.

In Canada, treaties are negotiated by the minister of foreign affairs and international trade. The minister can proceed to sign an international treaty after requesting approval from the governor in council (i.e., the governor general acting on advice of the federal cabinet). Then the federal cabinet prepares an Order in Council authorizing the minister of foreign affairs to ratify the treaty. The treaty does not need to be tabled in the House of Commons prior to ratification. However, in 2008 the federal government announced that future treaties would be tabled in the House of Commons prior to ratification. Nevertheless, in Canada it is necessary to introduce an implementation law in order to transport the international treaty into domestic law. Accordingly, Canada could not ratify an international treaty without putting implementation law into place, which requires parliamentary approval (in both the House of Commons and the Senate).[6]

Ratification does not necessarily imply that an international treaty is in force right away. The treaty itself may establish a date when it takes effect, or it may include a trigger clause that requires a minimum number of participants. For example, The *Convention on the Law of the Sea* had to be ratified by 60 signatory states in order to take effect. It had been signed by 119 countries in 1982, but it did not come into force until 1994, one year after the 60th country had ratified it.

International law and national law are quite different. National law is characterized by the power of the state to legislate and enforce its own laws. A nation's justice system is a collection of institutions to uphold these laws, equipped with the power of the state to maintain public law and settle disputes among conflicting parties in civil law cases.

International law is different in two major ways. First, it only concerns nations, not individuals. Parties to an international treaty are sovereign states. Individuals are not party to such treaties, and thus disputes about the interpretation or application of an international treaty are the exclusive domain of national governments. There are important implications of this principle insofar as sub-national levels of government in a federal state (Canadian provinces, US states) have no standing in international treaties. This can lead to internal conflicts between levels of government within a country.

Second, international law lacks enforceability. Whereas national law can be enforced by a country's justice system, international law lacks the ability to sanction non-compliance effectively. A state that does not comply with a treaty may simply decide to withdraw from it. The ability of the world community to sanction opportunistic behaviour of sovereign countries is very limited. The ability to impose sanctions is marred in political friend-and-foe considerations, and weighing the sanctions' benefits against their cost.

How can governments be held accountable for implementing an international environmental treaty? A treaty that has been ratified but not implemented through national law may linger in legal limbo. Canada ratified the *Kyoto Protocol* but never implemented it through appropriate legislation to curb greenhouse gas emissions. Citizens cannot sue their government for failing to implement a treaty that it acceded to; the only effective recourse is the ballot box.

As well, in Canada, international treaties may encroach on provincial jurisdiction and cause federal-provincial frictions. As discussed earlier, the environment is a shared responsibility under the Cana-

---

[6] It is extremely rare for an implementing act not to be passed by Parliament. In 1988 the Senate refused to pass the proposed Canada-United States Free Trade Agreement Implementation Act, thereby triggering an election. A similar bill was passed shortly afterwards by a new Parliament.

dian Constitution. The federal government cannot enforce compliance with international treaties in areas beyond its jurisdiction. Specifically, the federal government cannot use the need to comply with international treaties as justification for encroaching on areas of provincial jurisdiction. Therefore, the federal government must cooperate with the provinces when relevant measures need to be implemented under provincial jurisdiction. Because of these potential conflicts between jurisdictions, some international treaties contain an explicit federal state clause that informs the other treaty parties that the federal government may encounter difficulties implementing the treaty if it fails to secure the cooperation of some or all sub-national jurisdictions.

International law can be used to establish international institutions that monitor compliance and provide a mechanism for dispute resolution. Among the more prominent such institutions are the WTO (which adjudicates international trade disputes) and ITLOS (which adjudicates maritime disputes). There are also important bilateral institutions. Among the oldest bilateral institutions in North America is the International Joint Commission (IJC) for the Great Lakes, established in 1909. The IJC expresses a commitment of both countries to 'equal and similar rights,' which is formalized through a hierarchy of water uses in order to prioritize rights and responsibilities. The IJC has several important practical functions. It is a quasi-judicial body that is charged with the approval or rejection of works such as water diversion. It has investigative powers, and in principle it has the ability to arbitrate disputes. However, this arbitral power has never been used because of a lack of necessary approval from the US Senate.

One of the peculiarities of international law is that international treaties do not need to be internally consistent with each other. There is no supreme court which could sort out conflicting requirements. Multilateral treaties do not take precedence over bilateral treaties. Nevertheless, in interpreting treaty obligations, it is often assumed that newer treaties take precedence over similar older treaties (*lex posterior* rule) and that more specific treaties take precedence over more general treaties (*lex specialis* rule). Yet, it is entirely conceivable for a country to enter into binding international environmental treaties that involve contradicting, opposing, or offsetting requirements. In such cases, it is up to the participating countries to sort out the problems among them. They can decide to revise one treaty and uphold the other and make the rules compatible with each other. They can also decide to do nothing and let the conflicting rules stand.

5.7.2 The GATT, the WTO, and NAFTA

The *General Agreement on Tariffs and Trade* (GATT) was concluded in 1947 with the purpose of promoting freer trade among nations based on transparent and fair rules rather than the often arbitrary trade policies of the first half of the 20th century. While the GATT treaty made progress through several rounds of negotiations, this process culminated in 1995 in the formation of the World Trade Organization as the GATT's permanent successor. In addition to reducing trade barriers, the GATT aimed to put trade on principles of fairness and non-discrimination. Specifically, the GATT was founded on two non-discrimination principles:

> The most favoured nation (MFN) principle requires that a concession granted to one member country must be granted to all other member countries. This ensures that foreign countries are treated equally and fairly.
>
> The national treatment (NT) principle requires that imports and domestic products must be treated alike. This ensures that foreign and domestic companies are treated equally and fairly.

There are important exceptions to these noble principles. The key exemption to the MFN principle is the establishment of a free trade area (FTA) or a customs union. An FTA exempts the vast majority of trade among the FTA partners from tariffs. A customs union establishes a region with common customs rules and common external tariffs. This allows the member countries to dismantle their internal borders.

Environmental concerns were certainly not at the top of the agenda when the GATT was introduced in 1947. However, important exemptions in the GATT have been used in recent years to allow countries to develop environmental policies that are compatible with international trade obligations. For example, a country might wish to exclude imports of products that have been produced with high level of emissions, or give subsidies to domestic firms that produce green-tech products. Such actions can easily come into conflict with GATT/WTO obligations.

GATT Article XX provides several exceptions that allow countries to establish domestic laws and regulations that may be in conflict with GATT obligations. The word 'environment' is not mentioned anywhere, but Article XX(b) provides an exception for measures that are necessary to protect human, animal, or plant life or health, and Article XX(g) provides an exception for measures relating to the conservation of exhaustible natural resources. Certain restrictions apply. Domestic regulations that invoke Article XX exemptions must not constitute disguised trade restrictions or arbitrary or unjustifiable discrimination be-

Box 5.3: The Mexico-US Tuna-Dolphin Case

In eastern tropical areas of the Pacific Ocean, schools of yellowfin tuna often swim beneath schools of dolphins. When tuna are harvested with purse seine nets, dolphins are trapped in the nets and often die unless they are released. The US *Marine Mammal Protection Act* established dolphin protection standards. Countries exporting tuna to the United States had to meet the US standards or their exports to the United States were embargoed. This included Mexico.

In 1991, Mexico asked a GATT panel to rule on the dispute. The panel produced a report in which it concluded that the United States could not embargo imports of tuna products from Mexico simply because Mexican regulations did not satisfy US regulations, and that GATT rules did not allow one country to take trade action for the purpose of enforcing its environmental laws outside its own jurisdiction.

The panel's concern was that allowing the United States to maintain its policy would open the door to a flood of possible protectionist abuses. If countries were allowed to ban imports of a product from another country because that country maintains different (lower) environmental or health standards, this would become a way for countries (especially larger ones) to force their own laws and standards on other countries.

The GATT panel report was circulated but never adopted. The United States and Mexico settled their dispute through bilateral negotiations and Mexico dropped the case. In 1992 ten countries (including the United States and Mexico) adopted the *La Jolla Agreement*, which established an international limit on dolphin mortality rates among tuna fishers. The agreement has been credited with a significant reduction in dolphin mortality.

tween countries. More importantly, they must be the 'least restrictive' with respect to trade among alternative measures that are equally effective. Lastly, trade restrictions cannot be applied to further extra-jurisdictional environmental objectives, which was a core issue in the US-Mexico tuna-dolphin dispute discussed in box 5.3.

During the first decade of the 21st century, the WTO increasingly opened the door to considering environmental concerns in decisions. The WTO Appellate Body, a standing body of seven persons that hears appeals from reports issued by panels in disputes brought by WTO members, has indicated its willingness to receive so-called *amicus curiae* ('friend of the court') briefs from environmental non-government organizations (ENGOs) in some circumstances. In considering such briefs, the ENGOs must demonstrate that there is a 'sufficient nexus' to permit trade measures to protect the environment (e.g., migrating birds, transboundary air pollution). The landmark decision is the 1997 shrimp-turtle case discussed in box 5.4.

WTO case law is pointing in the directions through which environmental standards can be made compatible with international trade law. The first and foremost requirement is that environmental standards should be applied fairly to all countries; they cannot single out individual countries. Countries may restrict imports from countries that do not meet environmental protection standards, but in doing so the importing country must allow for the exporting country's application of environmental protection measures that are *comparable in effectiveness* to the domestic protection scheme. This means that a country cannot impose particular solutions or methods on other countries as long as the other country can meet the environmental standard. There is a catch, however, when applying country-wide certification for allowing or restricting imports. Some producers in the foreign country may meet the environmental standard, while other producers in the same country may not. For example, in the shrimp-turtle dispute, some shrimp fishers may indeed catch shrimp in a turtle-friendly manner and banning their imports would be unfair. Using shipment-by-shipment certification avoids this problem. The best solution is therefore to certify countries as compliant if they have implemented a suitable environmental standard, to certify individual producers in a non-compliant country so that they are exempt from trade restrictions, and otherwise to apply trade restrictions only to non-compliant producers in a non-compliant country.

Canada, Mexico, and the United States are also bound by the *North American Free Trade Agreement* (NAFTA), which took effect in 1994. A NAFTA side agreement is the *North American Agreement on Environmental Cooperation* that established the Commission for Environmental Cooperation (CEC), based in Montreal. This side agreement recognizes the treaty parties' rights to establish their own levels of of domestic protection as well as environmental development policies and priorities. The treaty obliges all parties to provide for high levels of environmental protection, although this is not given much more specific meaning other than to share information. The environmental side agreement makes the treaty parties subject to a dispute settlement mechanism if a party persistently fails to enforce its own environmental laws. So far, the main value of the CEC has been to conduct an analysis of NAFTA's impact on the environment.

Most contentious has been Chapter 11 of NAFTA, which includes investment measures and thus goes beyond the domain of international trade covered by the GATT/WTO. Specifically, NAFTA article 1110 prohibits the member countries from taking measures that are 'tantamount to expropriation.' In such cases it allows aggrieved companies to sue member states for compensation. But how does environmental regulation amount to expropriation? The idea is that an environmental reg-

Box 5.4: The Shrimp-Turtle Case

A few years after the tuna-dolphin case (see box 5.3), the issue of extra-territorial application of domestic environmental law by way of trade policy resurfaced. In 1997, several Asian countries challenged a trade embargo by the United States under its 1973 *Endangered Species Act* that aimed to prevent shrimp fishing techniques that produce high mortality rates of sea turtles (an endangered species). The United States required that US shrimp trawlers use 'turtle excluder devices' (TEDs) in their nets when fishing in areas where there is a significant likelihood of encountering sea turtles. The trade embargo only permitted imports of shrimp from countries that used similar fishing techniques. Complainants claimed a violation of GATT Article XI, which bans non-tariff import restrictions.

The WTO panel sided with the complainants and did not consider the Article XX(g) exception for natural resource conservation. Instead, it invoked the *chapeau* (introductory clause) of Article XX and considered the import restriction causing damage to the integrity of the world trading system because of the the proliferation of discriminatory domestic and trade-related policies.

In a landmark decision, the WTO Appellate Body reversed the panel's decision in part and accepted an Arti-

cle XX(g) defence but upheld the violation of the Article XX *chapeau*. However, the Appellate Body imposed a duty to negotiate seriously with trade partners before applying unilateral measures that require protection schemes abroad *comparable in effectiveness* to the domestic protection scheme. This ruling also opened the door to *amicus curiae* briefs from interested parties such as ENGOs.

The United States lost its WTO case essentially on technical grounds. It lost not because it sought to protect the environment but because it discriminated between WTO members by providing some countries (mainly in the Caribbean) with technical and financial assistance and longer transition periods for their fishermen to start using TEDs, but not to those in the four complainant countries (India, Malaysia, Pakistan, and Thailand).

Photo: U.S. National Oceanic and Atmospheric Administration.

ulation can exclude a foreign company from a particular market, thus expropriating its market and profits:

- When Canada banned imports of MMT (a fuel additive), US-based Ethyl Corporation claimed that its Canadian subsidiary's assets had been 'indirectly expropriated.' The dispute was settled for $19 million for cost and lost profit and the repeal of the MMT ban.
- Canadian Methanex supplied methanol for the MTBE gasoline additive, which California banned in 1998 for health reasons. Methanex sued the United States under NAFTA articles 1102, 1105, and 1110. However, a NAFTA tribunal dismissed all claims in 2005. In its dismissal, the tribunal reaffirmed that non-discriminatory regulations in the public interest (such as environmental laws) will almost never be considered expropriation. The ruling also set a precedent for allowing an *amicus curiae* brief from the Canadian-based ENGO International Institute for Sustainable Development.

The implications of NAFTA's chapter 11 remain controversial and can also lead to conflicts between levels of jurisdiction in Canada. In November 2012, U.S.-based Lone Pine Resources Inc. filed a notice of intent to sue the Canadian government under NAFTA's Chapter 11, demanding $250 million in compensation for Quebec's stand against fracking. Quebec had passed legislation in June 2012 that amounted to a moratorium on fracking. The legislation also cancelled permits for oil and gas exploration, including the permit held by Lone Pine. Quebec's moratorium on fracking is meant to stay in place until the province completes a review of the environmental consequences of this technology. Under NAFTA, the federal government is also responsible for actions by provincial governments even though the provinces are not signatories to the trade agreements.

Environmental regulations also pose the risk of being used as an instrument of protectionism. Countries may use environmental regulations purposefully to disadvantage foreign producers. Box 5.5 discusses the example of Ontario's excise tax on aluminum cans that put US beer brewers at a competitive disadvantage.

5.7.3 Environmental border adjustments

Environmental border adjustments are tariffs or non-tariff barriers that subject imported goods to domestic environmental policies. They are intended to equalize the playing field between domestic and foreign producers. This is an area where international trade law and environmental law may clash.

Conflicts between trade and environmental law may arise when countries start implementing some form of carbon pricing (by carbon

Box 5.5: Green Protectionism?

Environmental policies can be used to promote domestic environmental objectives. Sometimes these objectives can clash, intentionally or unintentionally, with the non-discrimination principles of free trade. When environmental policies are used intentionally to protect domestic producers from foreign competition, this amounts to 'green protectionism.' Even when there is no intent to disadvantage foreign producers, environmental policies can sometimes have unintended trade consequences.

In 1992 Ontario introduced a 10-cent environmental recycling fee on aluminum beer cans in order to encourage greater use of returnable glass bottles for beer. Provincial officials contended that glass bottles are more environmentally efficient, since they can be used an average of fifteen to eighteen times and they are less likely to end up in landfills. Ontario further maintained that the excise tax was needed to protect the province's extensive recycling efforts, because without the tax consumers would switch to less expensive imported beer sold in aluminum cans, thus forcing Canadian producers to switch to aluminum cans as well.

The Ontario measure offered a marketing advantage to Molson and other Canadian breweries that used glass bottles, whereas most US breweries used aluminum cans. Around 80% of Canadian beer was sold in bottles, of which 97% were recycled. Beer imported in cans is less costly to transport than beer in bottles. The environmental tax applied only to aluminum beer cans, not to aluminum cans for soft drinks, which suggested that the measures may have been discriminatory and directed against US breweries. The United States retaliated with a $3/case (50%) tax on beer imported from Ontario, and Canada countered with an equal tax on the major US exporter of beer to Ontario.

In 1993 the beer dispute was settled within a larger set of negotiations involving the beer industry. The Ontario levy on aluminum cans was allowed to stand, but the settlement provided for improved access for US breweries to the Ontario distribution system. The settlement also rescinded the retaliatory duties.

Over time, US brewers started bottling in Canada, or entered licensing agreements. Eventually, the beer industry started to consolidate across the border. Molson and Coors merged in 2005, and in 2007 merged further with UK-based SABMiller. The world's largest brewer, Anheuser-Busch InBev acquired Canadian-based Labatt Breweries in 1995.

taxes or a tradeable carbon permit system). If a country adopts carbon pricing, its imports will be advantaged over domestic producers because the domestic producers would be subject to the carbon price but not the foreign producers. The playing field for domestic and foreign firms could be levelled through a carbon border adjustment—in particular, a carbon tariff that imposes a carbon price on the carbon emission embodied in the imported goods. The idea of a carbon border adjustment is theoretically compelling, as it would prevent leakage. However, it is also fraught with practical as well as legal problems.

The practical problem relates to the measurement of the carbon content of imported goods. As different countries use different production technologies, the carbon content of otherwise identical goods may differ greatly. Consider aluminum for example. This is a homogeneous good but it requires lots of electricity to produce. Therefore, it matters whether the electricity for aluminum smelters is produced by geothermal energy (as in Iceland) or with a large share of coal (as in the United States).

Longer supply chains complicate matters even further. Exporters may find it extremely difficult to measure the carbon content of their products even with the best of intentions. Many producers may not be able to account for the carbon content of their intermediate goods, some of them perhaps imported from third countries. For example, how should a computer manufacturer in China know about the carbon content of the screens it imports from suppliers in South Korea and the microchips it imports from suppliers in Japan if there is no requirement for them to carbon-label their exports? Without a comprehensive global system of carbon accounting, it would be very difficult to provide accurate measures of the carbon content embodied in specific goods. It may be possible to approximate the carbon content by using averages based on national or sectoral data, but this may penalize the firms that use state-of-the-art low-emission technologies. While the carbon border adjustment is intended to rectify a distortion between domestic and foreign producers, it may create a new distortion among competing foreign producers.

Even if it was possible to compute the actual carbon content of imported goods precisely, carbon border adjustments may not be fully compatible with international trade law. It is very likely that the first country to introduce a border adjustment will get challenged by other countries under WTO rules. Because otherwise-identical imported goods may have different levels of carbon content, border adjustments would need to be set at different levels for different countries, and set at zero for countries that maintain identical carbon pricing. This may run afoul of the WTO's MFN principle, which requires that tariffs on imported products be the same across countries (with the exception of free trade partners and certain poor countries). Carbon border adjustments may also run afoul of the NT principle if the level of the carbon tariff differs from the domestic carbon price, and in particular if a domestic carbon policy is standard-based (without an explicit carbon price) rather than incentive-based.

The practical and legal difficulties of implementing a carbon border adjustment make it unlikely to succeed politically (risk of a major trade dispute) or economically (too costly to implement).

5.8 Summary

In Canada, the constitutional allocation of responsibilities makes the environment a shared responsibility of the federal and provincial governments. Natural resources are generally the domain of the provinces. The federal government has authority over international environmental treaties and surface water, and it can apply statutory powers over criminal law to harmful environmental conduct (albeit not to setting explicit emission standards). Federal law imposes requirements on firms that prompt many to develop pollution prevention (P2) plans, environmental emergency (E2) plans, and introduce environmental management systems. Provincial governments often act as incubators for exploring novel types of environmental regulation. For example, British Columbia has pioneered a carbon tax, and Quebec has pioneered a number of agri-environmental policies for protecting watersheds. Federal and provincial governments both maintain rules (in parallel) for environmental impact assessment prior to approving new industrial projects. They also cooperate through the Canadian Council of Ministers of the Environment, which has become the source of many country-wide emission standards. Provincial governments have also concluded equivalency agreements with the federal government to streamline the process of environmental impact assessment.

Environmental law in the United States is characterized by a hybrid system of national standards and statement implementation and enforcement. States maintain a degree of flexibility to impose standards that go beyond federal norms, and they can set their own priorities for enforcing federal standards. The main bodies of legislation in the United States, the *Clean Air Act*, the *Clean Water Act*, and the *Superfund Act*, provide significant powers and relative uniformity of environmental law. These acts also enable citizen suits, which opens the door for citizens and environmental organizations to commence litigation in the case of regulatory inaction or alleged infractions by polluters. The administrative clout of the Environmental Protection Agency has helped ameliorate many environmental problems in the United States.

As many environmental problems are transboundary in nature, international environmental treaties have become increasingly important.

However, they suffer from poor enforceability, free riding, and coordination problems. On the positive side, early conflicts between adopting stricter environmental standards and international trade policy are making way for a more environmentally conscious international trade regime based on flexible certification processes.

5.9 Study questions and exercises

1. How can one define *pollution* legally? How do approaches to defining pollution differ?
2. Which constitutional provisions provide jurisdiction over the environment to the federal government, and which provide jurisdiction to the provinces?
3. Which mechanisms do the Canadian federal government and the provinces use to coordinate environmental policies among them?
4. Canada has competing jurisdictions over the environment where federal and provincial authority overlap. What are the advantages of overlapping jurisdiction, and what are disadvantages of overlapping jurisdiction?
5. What role do First Nations play with respect to environmental policy in Canada?
6. What are the instruments available under the US *Clean Air Act* to regulate emissions? What is the scope for variation across states with respect to emission standards and implementation methods?
7. Explain the differences between point sources and non-point sources with respect to the US *Clean Water Act*
8. What are the core principles of the US *Superfund Act*? Explain the liability of polluters.
9. What is the *precautionary principle* and what are key problems applying it in a legal context?
10. Why is it difficult to (a) negotiate and conclude, and (b) enforce international environmental treaties?
11. Domestic environmental laws may conflict with obligations under international treaties such as the *General Agreement on Tariffs and Trade* (GATT). Under which conditions can countries invoke GATT Articles XX(b) and XX(g)? What are the requirements to make domestic environmental law 'compatible' with GATT requirement?
12. Consider the shrimp-turtle case. How can certification help solve trade disputes about environmental policies? Should environmental certification be done on a country-by-country or shipment-by-shipment basis, and why?
13. Describe the range of compliance mechanisms available in environmental law. What can a regulator do to enforce regulations?
14. Which environmental offences are covered by criminal law?

15. What are the legal obligations of officers of a corporation with respect to environmental mandates? Is their responsibility personal or collective (corporate)?

Exercises

1. Consult the archive of a major national newspaper and identify the most recent legal cases that involve corporate liability and environmental issues. Which laws are invoked? Summarize the key arguments by plaintiffs and defendants. How have these cases set precedents for future similar cases?
2. Draw up a list of all recent international environmental treaties. Which countries have joined, and which have not? Which countries that have joined have fully implemented that treaty? Which of the treaties appear to be effective, and which seem to have failed?
3. For the state or province that you live in, identify the regulatory bodies that are of relevance to environmental issues. (For example, Ohio has three major agencies: the Ohio Department of Natural Resources, the Ohio Environmental Protection Agency, and the Ohio Air Quality Development Authority.) Determine the particular responsibilities of these agencies and the legal mandate under which they operate. Where does authority overlap or compete with federal jurisdiction?

Chapter 6
Environmental Impact Assessment

Regulators need a set of procedures to review and approve proposed projects with respect to their environmental consequences. This process is formalized as environmental impact assessment (EIA) under US and Canadian law. Generally, EIA can be used to review the introduction of any new technology, project or program with respect to the full range of environmental consequences. Environmental consequences are typically explored in multiple dimensions: time (immediate versus long-term effects); space (local effects versus regional or global effects); and intent (direct anticipated versus indirect unanticipated effects).

EIA is a comprehensive and systematic process designed to identify, analyze, and evaluate the environmental effects of proposed projects. It is meant to integrate public concerns over environmental considerations into the decision-making process. It is thus a hugely important tool to help decision-makers achieve the goal of sustainable development. The term 'environment' in EIA is usually considered quite broadly and is meant to encompass both human effects (culture, health, community, financial) and biophysical or ecosystem effects (air, water, land, plants, animals).

In the United States, the enactment of the *National Environmental Policy Act* in 1970 provided the basis for an environmental assessment of any federal action. An environmental assessment leads either to a more detailed environmental impact statement or to a finding of no significant impact. Several US states have mirrored the federal procedures. For example, California requires an environmental impact report under its own *California Environmental Quality Act*.

EIA became entrenched in Canadian federal law in 1995 through the *Canadian Environmental Assessment Act* (CEAA). Thousands of EIAs are completed each year, ranging from local initiatives to large-scale resource development projects such as pipelines or hydroelectric dams. Almost all Canadian provinces have their own EIA systems. The federal body conducting EIAs is the Canadian Environmental Assessment Agency.

Environmental Impact Assessment (EIA) takes a prominent role when it comes to developing new projects. Noble (2006) provides a compact introduction into this topic with applications to Canada. Hanna (2009) is a more extensive edited volume with numerous contributions from leading experts on EIA in Canada. The book also includes detailed discussions of different provincial EIA procedures.

6.1 Objectives and process overview

EIA has both short-term and long-term objectives. Short-term objectives are procedural in nature and focus on the process of addressing environmental concerns in the the the design of a proposed development or project. A key objective of EIA is to identify or anticipate any adverse effects that could harm the environment, and propose solutions to avoid, minimize or offset these adverse effects. From a short-term perspective, EIA is an information tool for deciding on a proposed project.

EIA also involves long-term objectives, which can be viewed as outcome objectives rather than as process objectives. EIA is meant to promote development that is sustainable and facilitate participatory approaches to such development. Ultimately, EIA is about protecting human health and safety as well as the productivity and capacity of human and natural systems and their ecological functions.

These short-term and long-term objectives are all somewhat vague, and thus it is more useful to look at EIA as the set of procedures defined in law, which businesses need to comply with. From that perspective EIA can be broken up into individual steps of the review process:

1. **Project description**: description of proposed action sufficient for assessment, including project alternatives.
2. **Screening**: determination of whether the action is subject to EIA and determination of what level of assessment is required.
3. **Scoping**: delineation of key issues and assessment boundaries, including baseline conditions and scoping of alternatives.
4. **Impact prediction**: prediction of environmental impacts and determination of impact significance.
5. **Impact management**: identification of mitigation strategies and development of environmental management and protection plans.
6. **Review and decision**: technical and public review; recommendation on proceeding, and under which conditions.
7. **Implementation** of project and environmental management measures; compliance monitoring; monitoring of effectiveness of impact management measures and accuracy of impact predictions.

6.1.1 The EIA process in the United States

The legal framework for environmental impact assessment depends on the jurisdiction. Canada and the United States follow rather different procedures. The basis for EIA in the United States is the *National Environmental Policy Act* (NEPA), enacted in 1970. Canada's legislation followed fifteen years later and is more evolved as a result, having absorbed many of the critical lessons from the US experience.

The US NEPA mandates an environmental assessment for projects falling under federal jurisdiction, unless the projects are categorically excluded from review. An environmental assessment is an initial stage in which a federal agency prepares a preliminary analysis of potential impacts if the significance of the environmental impact is not yet known. This process can result in two outcomes. First, the process can end with a 'finding of no significant impact,' in which case the project can get implemented. Second, the process can end with the conclusion that an environmental impact statement (EIS) is needed.

In terms of the seven steps outlined above, environmental assessment covers the first two steps, 'project description' and 'screening.' The EIS covers the remaining steps. The environmental impact of a proposed project is rated as one of four distinct categories:

- Lack of objections (LO): no potential environmental impacts.
- Environmental concerns (EC): the review has found environmental impacts that require suitable mitigation measures.
- Environmental objections (EO): the review has found significant environmental impacts that need to be avoided and thus require substantial changes or consideration of a project alternative.
- Environmentally unsatisfactory (EU): the project must not proceed as proposed because (a) it would violate a national environmental standard; (b) it would have particularly severe, lasting, and widespread environmental consequences; or (c) it would threaten national environmental resources.

Environmental assessments can involve different federal agencies. The lead agency (in some cases multiple agencies) is the one that is directly involved in the project. The Environmental Protection Agency (EPA) has multiple roles in the process. As a cooperating agency it assists other federal agencies in preparing an EIS, and it has a mandate under the *Clean Air Act* to comment on the environmental impact of all major federal actions. If the EPA considers a proposed project to be environmentally unsatisfactory, the case is referred to the White House Council on Environmental Quality for arbitration.

Whenever an EIS is required, the process goes through several stages. A draft EIS is prepared by the lead agency. This version covers the entire range of environmental impacts and outlines possible alternatives. A comment period follows the circulation of the draft EIS. Feedback from the public is taken into consideration when the lead agency prepares the final EIS and suggests the proposed action. In some cases, a supplemental EIS can be required when deficiencies in the final EIS are discovered or the scope of the proposed project changes significantly. The process concludes with a record of decision by the lead agency. The only recourse against it is through suing the lead agency in federal court.

6.1.2 The EIA process in Canada

The Canadian legal framework for environmental impact assessment distinguishes different types. This recognizes the different levels of environmental impact from projects of different types: some have the potential for major impacts, while other projects may have minor impacts and can be subjected to a template-type screening.

The **Screening EIA** systematically documents the potential environmental effects of a proposed project, identifies mitigation measures, and determines the need to modify a project. If a project is found to have significant environmental impacts, it may be referred to a mediator or a review panel.

For routine projects, a **Class Screening EIA** may suffice. There are two variants of this type of EIA. Model class screenings are generic assessments in which certain design standards and mitigation measures are implemented. This also establishes a template for future projects of the same type. Replacement class screenings do not require location-specific or project-specific information, and are used for generic types of projects, such as special holiday events or activities in a national park.

A **Comprehensive Study EIA** is mandated for large-scale projects described under the *Comprehensive Study List Regulations* of Canada's EIAA. Such EIAs require additional screening steps that include: a detailed project description; specification of technical project alternatives; where applicable a discussion of the effect on renewable resources; and the need for follow-up to assess environmental impacts. EIAs of this type are triggered by meeting certain criteria during the screening phase, discussed below. Alternatively, a similarly comprehensive EIA can be formed as a **Review Panel EIA** appointed by the federal minister of the environment. The minister can exercise this discretionary privilege if the potential environmental effects of the proposed project are uncertain or are potentially very significant.

Panel reviews are common for major projects. Panels can be convened as joint panels with other regulatory bodies. It is common to convene a joint review panel for energy-related projects such as the construction of pipelines or power lines. Regulatory bodies that may participate include: the National Energy Board (NEB), Fisheries and Oceans Canada, as well as local regulatory entities. The NEB has federal jurisdiction for approving interprovincial and international oil and gas pipelines (exceeding 40 km in length), and international power lines. Pipelines or power lines that fall entirely within the territory of a province are subject only to provincial approval.

The 2012 revision of the *Canadian Environmental Assessment Act* mandates strict time limits on the review process. The Canadian Environmental Assessment Agency has 45 days to determine whether an assessment is needed, and it has 12 months (24 months for a review panel)

Box 6.1: Mackenzie Valley Gas Project EIA

In 2003 Imperial Oil, Shell Canada, ConocoPhillips, ExxonMobil Canada, and the Mackenzie Valley Aboriginal Pipeline Ltd Partnership submitted a preliminary information package describing the proposed Mackenzie Valley Gas Project and its related environmental and socio-economic issues.

The project involves the $7 billion development of natural gas reserves in the Mackenzie River Delta in the Northwest Territories, as well as natural gas processing and the construction of a 1,220 km pipeline with a capacity of 34 million cubic metres per day for shipping the natural gas through the Mackenzie Valley to northern Alberta. Employment is expected to peak at 8,000 during construction and drop to 150 during operation of the pipeline. Up to 32 communities will be affected by the project.

The project is subject to an EIA under the CEAA, the *Mackenzie Valley Resource Management Act*, the *Western Arctic Claims Settlement Act*, as well as the National Energy Board. These bodies formed a joint review panel. Among other issues, the panel considered alternative locations for infrastructure sites, alternative routes for the pipeline, and alternative methods of construction and reclamation.

The joint review panel made 176 recommendations to the minister of the environment in May 2010, 115 of them within federal jurisdiction. The minister accepted only 11 outright and asked 77 recommendations to be changed. The minister accepted only the intent of these 77 recommendations, but not the proposed implementation. The minister also rejected 27 recommendations, 20 of them because he deemed them to be outside the mandate (subject matter or geographic scope) of the review panel, and 7 because he disagreed with the panel's recommendations.

Federal cabinet approval of the project was granted in March 2011. The project's lead firm, Imperial Oil, had until the end of 2013 to make a decision on whether to proceed with the pipeline. In December 2013 the company announced that the project's original cost estimate of $7 billion more than doubled to over $16 billion. Because of the recent glut of natural gas from hydraulic fracturing (tracking), the Mackenzie Valley Gas Project remains uneconomic at this time.

to complete an assessment. The 2012 revision also allows the federal government to delegate the review process to a province if the federal government is satisfied that the province's review process is a sufficient substitute.

Box 6.1 illustrates the process and outcome of a joint review panel EIA for the Mackenzie Valley Gas Project. It illustrates the complexity of the decison-making process, as well as the political dimensions of that process.

6.2 Screening

In the United States, the screening process is essentially established through a federal agency's mandate and where a project is subject to federal permitting, licensing, or funding. In Canada, the process is more elaborate because specific screening criteria trigger the review process. These criteria differ federally and provincially, which may result in situations where a project requires only federal, only provincial, or both types of assessment. Where both federal and provincial EIAs are required, it is not certain that the outcome will be identical. For example, the Prosperity Gold-Copper Mine project by Taseko Mines Ltd. in the Chilcotin region of British Columbia was approved by the BC government in January 2010, but rejected by the federal government in November 2010.

The Canadian federal EIA only applies to projects, which includes activities in relation to physical works as well as other activities that are described in the *Inclusion List Regulations*. A project must then fulfill three additional criteria: (i) the project must not be specifically excluded from environmental assessment in the *Exclusion List Regulations*; (ii) the project must involve a federal authority; and (iii) there must be a trigger to initiate the assessment.

The inclusion list is relatively long. It contains any project carried out in a national park, a variety of oil and gas projects including pipelines, nuclear facilities, defence projects, transportation, waste management, fisheries, and projects on aboriginal and northern lands. The exclusion list is much shorter and exempts a variety of minor projects.

Comprehensive Study List Regulations identify projects likely to cause significant adverse effects or significant public concern (e.g., activities in a national park, nuclear facilities, mining and mineral processing operations) for which an EIA is required, and are subject to categorization according to project thresholds. A few examples of screening thresholds illustrate the concept. A Comprehensive Study EIA is required for the proposed construction, decommissioning, or abandonment of: (i) a fossil fuel fired electrical generation station with a capacity of 200 MW or more; (ii) a heavy oil or oil sands processing facility with an oil production capacity of 10,000 m^3/day; (iii) a metal mine, other than a gold mine, with an ore production of 3,000 tonnes/day or more. A Comprehensive Study EIA is also required for the construction of: (iv) an electrical transmission line with a voltage of 345 kV or more that is 74 km or more in length on a new right of way; and (v) the proposed construction of a railway line more than 32 km in length on a new right of way. These examples illustrate the regulator's need to delineate major and minor projects. These thresholds are often rules of thumb and may in some cases trigger opportunistic behaviour to avoid a particular type of EIA in favour of a less comprehensive examination.

6.3 Scoping

Scoping determines the important issues and parameters that should be addressed in an environmental assessment. Scoping also establishes the boundaries of the assessment, and focuses the assessment on these relevant issues and concerns. It defines those components of the bio-physical and human environment that may be affected by the project and for which there is public concern. Scoping may be either open or closed. In the case of closed scoping, the scope of the EIA is predeter-mined by law. In the case of open scoping, issues and boundaries are identified through stakeholder consultation.

Scoping involves a number of separate steps. The starting point is the detailed project description, and based on this the development of project alternatives. Alternatives serve an important function in the as-sessment process. They provide the assessment panel with an opportu-nity to consider variations that may better satisfy environmental con-cerns. Even though the applying company may favour the main pro-posal on cost grounds, sometimes trade-offs need to be made. If the applying firm proposes only a single alternative, the assessment panel is forced to make an up-or-down decision. However, with reasonable alternatives it is possible to salvage an application. For example, when proposing a route for a new pipeline, it may be necessary to consider alternative routing as unforeseen environmental concerns may come to light that make the proposed route less attractive. There are three di-mensions of project alternatives:

- alternative projects that achieve the intended project purpose in dif-ferent functional ways (for example, an above-ground skytrain sys-tem versus a below-ground subway system)
- alternative locations (for plants or mines) or routing (for transmis-sion and transportation systems);
- alternative designs (technological implementation).

These three dimensions of project alternatives rank from more challeng-ing to less challenging. Alternative projects often involve hugely dif-ferent costs and thus the set of alternatives is often very constrained. Alternative locations may also not be readily available because of: (i) fixed location (e.g., mines); (ii) topographical constraints (e.g., pipeline routes); and (iii) land-use constraints (e.g., proximity to settlements, or ownership). Alternative designs are often the most readily available as the variations can be minor. For example, when building a power plant, different pollution abatement devices may accomplish different emis-sion reduction targets.

The next steps in the scoping process involve identifying the assess-ment boundaries for the impact areas that will be considered, and the environmental baseline against which alternatives can be compared. Boundaries are established in three dimensions:

- **media**: the parts of the ecosystem (e.g., air, water, wildlife) that need to be included in the assessment;
- **space**: the jurisdictions that need to be considered in the assessment, which in turn depends on the spatial extent of the possible environmental impacts; and
- **time**: the time horizon for the environmental assessment, for physical projects typically from construction to decommissioning plus five years.

The last step in the assessment process involves identifying potential impacts and environmental issues along these dimensions. This process results in a list of impact indicators. These indicators are arranged in an impact matrix where each project action can be quantified or ranked.

6.4 Impact prediction

Scoping puts boundaries around which environmental impacts will be assessed, and which alternatives will be considered. Quantifying all the possible environmental impacts is perhaps the most difficult step—this is the task for impact prediction. Often the main challenge is finding solid and reliable data.

For predicting impacts, direct measurement is always preferable but in many instances not feasible. Such direct measurements typically come from similar projects that already exist elsewhere, and the challenge is adapting these data to local circumstances and conditions. When measurement is not possible, impact prediction through a scientific model is the next-best choice. Such a model can be calibrated to existing observables, and then simulation exercises can be performed to predict changes to the model. The drawbacks of simulation models are that the numerical calibration may be coarse or that the model is driven by particular assumptions that are difficult to verify empirically. Nevertheless, scientific models of one kind or another remain the main tool for impact prediction.

Where direct measurement or simulation is not possible, qualitative scoring is used. A commonly used technique for qualitative impact assessment is the Delphi method, in which experts are questioned in two or more rounds, often involving questionnaires. After each round of questioning, the experts are presented with a summary of the other experts' assessments and their reasoning for arriving at their conclusions. This process is meant to facilitate an (anonymized) dialogue among the experts that will help them converge to a consensus in multiple rounds of questioning.

What exactly is meant by the term *impact*? There are two elements to assessing impact: quantifying a measurable effect on the environment ecosystem, or health; and assessing the relative importance of the measured effect. Assessing relative importance involves putting weights on different impact categories, a process which almost always involves expert panels. Two important methods for obtaining weights will be discussed below: fixed-point scoring and analytic hierarchy process.

Impacts can be direct or indirect. A proposed project always has a direct impact. For example, the proposed construction of a hydroelectric dam may cause a decrease in the growth rate of fish. Many projects also have indirect (second-order) effects. In the example of the proposed hydro dam, the decline in fish growth may diminish opportunities for downstream recreational fishing, or threaten other species that depend on a supply of fish. A dam may cut off salmon from their spawning habitat (a direct effect), and the lack of salmon may adversely effect upstream bear populations (an indirect effect).

Table 6.1 Classification System for Environmental Impacts

Type of Impact	Temporal Dimension	Impact Magnitude
adverse	duration	size
incremental	continuity	degree
additive	immediacy	concentration
synergistic	frequency	
antagonistic	regularity	

Spatial Extent	Reversibility	Impact Probability
on-site	reversible	likelihood
off-site	irreversible	risk
		uncertainty

Table 6.1 describes the multitude of impact categories and impact dimensions that can be considered. The type of impact describes its positive or negative, additive or multiplicative effect. In most instances, a proposed project will result in **adverse** effects that can be described as level changes in environmental conditions directly attributable to the proposed project. Such adverse effects can be magnified by becoming **incremental**, where the changes are not in one-off level changes (a jump from one level to another) but in changes to growth rates (where the level continues changing indefinitely). When a single effect is present, it may occur in multiple instances. Such effects can be **additive**. Even when the consequences of separate or related actions are minor individually, their overall effect may be major. For example, the exhaust from one car has relatively minor environmental effects, but thousands of cars on a city's road may have a major effect.

It is also possible to find situations where different effects interact in a positive or negative way. One speaks of **synergistic** effects when interactions between different effects result in a total effect that is larger than the sum of the individual effects. For example, a paper mill effluent may (i) change water temperatures, and/or (ii) lower dissolved oxygen content in water. Effects (i) and (ii) may be tolerable to fish separately, but not when they are combined. It is also possible that interactions result in one adverse effect offsetting another adverse effect; these are considered **antagonistic** effects. For example, a water body may receive effluents containing (i) chlorine and/or (ii) phosphates. Each effect alone leads to eutrophication, but when (i) and (ii) are combined the eutrophication effect cancels out partially.

All environmental impacts have a time dimension. The temporal dimension can be characterized in five categories. First is the **duration** of the impact. Duration can be short term and temporary (such as during a construction project) or long term and permanent (such as riverbank erosion or downstream loss of arable land from a hydro dam). Second is the **continuity** of the impact. Some effects may be continuous (such as the energy field associated with a transmission line), while others are discontinuous (such as blasting noise at a mine). Third is the **immediacy** of the impact, which is closely related to the distinction between flow pollutants and stock pollutants. For example, odour from livestock has an immediate impact, while toxics slowly accumulating in groundwater have a delayed impact. Fourth is the **frequency** of the impact. The impact of a proposed new airport runway or new railway line may differ dramatically depending on the number of planes taking off and landing, or trains passing through. Fifth and last is the **regularity** of the impact, which describes the temporal predictability of the disturbance. For the effect on a nearby population, it may matter significantly if occurrences of adverse effects are regular (predictable) or irregular (unpredictable). A new railway line may have predictable effects as the trains run on a schedule, while the blasting noise from a highway construction project may occur at unpredictable times during the day.

The spatial extent of impacts depends crucially on the environmental medium that is impacted. Noise does not travel far under normal circumstances. The impact of a high-voltage power line is in the order of tens of metres. The impact of a proposed new airport runway can be localized in terms of a few kilometres. The impact of sulfur dioxide emissions from a new coal power plant is measured in tens or even hundreds of kilometres. The impact of carbon dioxide emissions is global. Defining the scope in spatial terms not only touches on environmental concerns but also touches on concerns about jurisdiction. For example, should an environmental impact assessment in Ontario consider adverse effects in the neighbouring province of Quebec? Should Ontario consider adverse effects in New York State? Will jurisdictions weight impact on their own territory the same as impacts on neighbouring jurisdictions?

A useful tool for capturing the spatial extent of environmental impacts is a dispersion model, a mathematical model that predicts pollution concentrations as a function of distance from the source, along with a variety of attenuating factors. For air pollution, such attenuating factors can be the height and diameter of a plant's stack, the stack gas exit velocity, temperature of the exiting gas and surrounding atmosphere, as well as wind speed and direction. For water pollution, a river's width, depth, speed, and curvature may all affect how fast pollution concentrations will diminish with distance.

The severity of environmental impacts often depends on their reversibility or irreversibility. A reversible impact allows the environment to return to its pre-disturbed condition. For example, a surface mining operation may restore a disturbed forest to its original condition once the mining activity has ceased. Other effects may be irreversible. Razing the forest for the mining operation may also lead to the extinction of, say, a bird species. Many impacts are partially reversible. In that case it is not feasible to restore the environment to its prior *pristine* state but to a posterior *acceptable* state. For example, in Germany's Rhineland, many townships were moved and forests removed to facilitate large open-pit soft-coal mining, but after the mines were decommissioned the affected areas were restored to lakes and parkland, and in part resettled. Nevertheless, the success of remediation depends on whether it is possible to reactivate the original ecological functions. For example, it is possible to revegetate disturbed soil rather than restore it to its original function (such as a boreal wetland). Remediation practices may therefore lead to the reclamation of an industrial site rather than restoration of the original ecosystem. Reclamation is easier than restoration.

Environmental impacts are not always certain. Some impacts arise only with a certain likelihood or probability. Impact assessment may thus turn into risk assessment. If it is possible to quantify the uncertainty by attaching probabilities to different outcomes, the potential damage can be assessed by multiplying corresponding effects and their probabilities, and summing across the different impact groups or potential outcomes. For example, elderly people and young children may be more vulnerable to exposure to air toxics than are other age groups. Uncertainty about impacts on these different groups can be averaged using statistical techniques. Another example is the likelihood of oil spills of different magnitude. Historical data suggest a certain probability distribution, with small spills more frequent than large spills. Statistical averaging provides a useful tool for tackling uncertainty.

The notion of uncertainty can mean two different things. Some impacts may be uncertain but their likelihood of occurrence, or the likelihood of different levels of severity, can be quantified. In this case, risk analysis can be carried out by capturing the environmental impact as the expected average (perhaps along with a statistical range or standard deviation). It is perhaps useful to describe this concept as *statistical uncertainty* or *risk*. The other type of uncertainty is not measurable and cannot be conquered using statistical techniques; it is sometimes referred to as *true uncertainty*. In environmental impact assessments, unmeasurable types of uncertainty surface in the form of speculative impacts. Lack of scientific research on a particular impact, or scientific research that is inconclusive or lacking in robustness, may lead to a particular type of impact being excluded from an assessment. For example, there exists a degree of uncertainty about the potential effects of genetically modified organisms (GMOs) because such GMOs are relatively novel. Their environmental impact remains a subject of intense study, but with results not yet fully conclusive (despite claims to the contrary from both proponents and opponents alike).

6.4.1 Fixed-point scoring

There are several methods available to assign weights to different impact categories. The method of fixed-point scoring involves defining weights w_i for each impact category i such that $\sum_i w_i = 1$. This always involves trade-offs. Increasing the weight of one impact category implies reducing the weight of all other impact categories.

Weights are obtained through polling panels of experts and decision-makers, for example through the Delphi method described above. Assigning weights is always a subjective process, and therefore using a technique that leads to some form of consensus through multi-round dialogue is perhaps more useful than simply conducting a survey and averaging results.

Table 6.2 provides an example of the fixed-point scoring technique. The rows identify different impact categories such as air quality and water quality. The columns identify a variety of activities related to the construction of a new highway, such as blasting and dredging. Impacts are rated on a −5 to +5 scale.

The total impact for each impact category is obtained by multiplying the impact scores by the pre-defined weights. For example, in the first row (air quality), the sum of scores (−3) is multiplied by the weight (0.26) to yield −0.78. Scores are then added up to a grand total. This grand total can then be compared across project alternatives.

Table 6.2 Example of a Weighted Magnitude Matrix

	weight	blasting	side cleaning	dredging	road construction	waste disposal	equipment transport	Total impact
air quality	0.26	−1			−1	−1		−0.78
water quantity	0.10	−2	−3	−3				−0.80
water quality	0.22	−2	−4	−2				−1.76
noise	0.04	−2			−1	−2	−2	−0.28
habitat	0.08		−5			−3		−0.64
wildlife	0.08	−2	−4			−2		−0.64
human health	0.22	−2				+3	−3	−0.44

Impact scale: + = positive ; − = negative; (blank) = none; 1 = negligible; 2 = minor; 3 = moderate; 4 = major (long-term); 5 = severe (permanent)

6.4.2 The analytic hierarchy process

Multi-criteria decision analysis is a very subjective process. One way to reduce the complexity of the problem is to take the catalog of environmental assessment criteria and sort them into a hierarchy of assessment areas, groups, and subgroups as necessary. For each group at each level one can conduct pairwise comparisons of the relative importance of the assessment criteria in this area. This procedure of organizing the assessment criteria in a tree-like structure is known as the analytic hierarchy process (AHP), developed by Saaty (1980).

Pairwise comparisons are rated on a scale from 1 to 9, where 1 indicates equal importance of the two factors and 9 indicates extremely more important. The intermediate values 2-8 indicate increasing importance; see the left panel in table 6.3. These pairwise comparisons are collected in a decision matrix $\mathbf{A}$ where element a_{ij} indicates the intensity of importance of option i over option j. For example, if option i is absolutely more important than option j, then $a_{ij} = 9$ and $a_{ji} = 1/9$. With n options, the elements of the $n \times n$ decision matrix $\mathbf{A}$ are reciprocal so that $a_{ji} = 1/a_{ij}$. By construction, $a_{ii} = 1$. The top right panel in table 6.3 provides a numerical illustration for three environmental criteria: air quality, water quality, and noise. In this environmental assessment, the experts judged that air quality is weakly more important than water quality (score 3) and strongly more important than noise (score 7). Water quality was considered slightly more important than noise (score 2).

To calculate the weights w_i, we obtain the principal eigenvector of the decision matrix A. With linear algebra software it is easy to calculate the eigenvalues λ and corresponding eigenvectors $\mathbf{v}$ that satisfy $\mathbf{Av} = \lambda \mathbf{v}$. The eigenvector that corresponds to the largest eigenvalue $\lambda^{\max}$ is the principal eigenvector. Because the $\mathbf{A}$ matrix is positive, the elements of the principal eigenvector are also positive. We then normalize the elements v_i of the principal eigenvector so that the weigths $w_i \equiv v_i / \sum_j v_j$ sum to 1. Column w in table 6.3 reports the results of this procedure. Air quality is most important (weight 0.68), followed by water quality (0.22) and noise (0.10).

Table 6.3 The Analytic Hierarchy Process

Intensity Score of Pairwise Comparisons

	Relative Importance
1	equal
2	equal to moderate
3	moderate
4	moderate to strong
5	strong
6	strong to very strong
7	very strong
8	verty strong to extreme
9	extreme

Numerical Example

	i	1	2	3	w
Air quality	1	1	3	7	0.682
Water quality	2	1/3	1	2	0.216
Noise	3	1/7	1/2	1	0.103

Random Consistency Index (RCI)

n	3	4	5	6	7	8
RCI(n)	0.4913	0.8264	1.0363	1.1699	1.2576	1.3197
n	9	10	11	12	13	14
RCI(n)	1.3639	1.3978	1.4250	1.4468	1.4650	1.4802
n	15	16	17	18	19	20
RCI(n)	1.4931	1.5039	1.5141	1.5224	1.5298	1.5368

Pairwise comparisons do not have to be consistent with each other. Consistency would require that for any $i \neq j \neq k$, it should hold that $a_{ij} a_{jk} = a_{ik}$. The experts may not always rank choices consistently, and fortunately the principal eigenvector method is relatively robust to such judgment errors. One can judge the consistency error by the ratio of the consistency index CI $\equiv (\lambda^{\max} - n)/(n - 1)$ and a random consistency index (RCI), shown in the bottom right panel of table 6.3 for matrices of size 3–20.[1] If the ratio of CI to RCI exceeds 0.1, the consistency problem is considered unacceptable and the resulting weights may not be reliable. In our example, the CI is 0.0013 and the corresponding RCI is 0.4913, so the CI/RCI ratio is well below 0.1.

The last step in applying the AHP framework is to consider the tree-like hierarchical structure of the assessment criteria. Every branch has a set of criteria whose weights add up to 1. It is now straight forward to successively aggregate criteria from the branches down to the root

---

[1] Own calculations based on one million random matrices.

using these weights. To keep everything in comparable units of measurement, it is necessary to score each assessment criterion on the same scale (e.g., a 0–100 scale or a –10 to +10 scale).

6.5 Impact management

When particular environmental impacts have been identified, EIA can help develop strategies to tackle these impacts in order to reduce their severity. Impact management tries to identify ex-ante (before implementation) and ex-post (after implementation) strategies that:

1. **avoid** environmental impacts, perhaps by considering project alternatives;
2. **mitigate** environmental impacts, either by considering alternative ways to implement a project, or by deploying technologies that contain or reduce the impact;
3. **remedy** environmental impacts after they have occurred; and
4. **compensate** victims of environmental impacts.

Strategies are considered in this priority order. The last of these options, compensation, is therefore considered only when all else fails. Compensation can involve monetary benefits when individuals are involved. When plant and wildlife habitat is concerned, compensation may also involve the creation of an offsetting habitat in a different location so that there is no net loss of habitat.

6.5.1 Avoidance and mitigation

Avoiding environmental impact is obviously the first and best option wherever feasible. This can involve using substituting substances with less toxic or non-toxic substances. For construction activities, traffic congestion can be avoided by scheduling trucks to arrive outside rush hour.

Mitigation is designed to minimize environmental impact where some impact is unavoidable. For example, building a new road will have some adverse effects during the construction phase as well as the operation phase. During the construction phase, dust build-up can be minimized by watering gravel surfaces frequently. Noise disruptions can be minimized by limiting construction work to certain hours of the day. During the operation phase, wildlife habitat fragmentation can be reduced by building wildlife overpasses or underpasses.

To provide another example, logging operations can erode the forest soil and lead to excessive water run-off. While soil erosion is not avoidable completely, its magnitude can be controlled through the use of **buffer zones** of undisturbed vegetation.

6.5.2 Remediation techniques

There exists a plethora of remediation techniques that can be deployed to clean up a spill or leak, or restore a contaminated site. The first set of options aims to contain the contamination. This can involve the use of: walls, liners, or other means to contain a contaminant in a particular ares; the installation of treatment walls in the ground to capture contaminants in groundwater flowing through these filters; or using other methods of stabilization or encapsulation that capture or transform contaminants into stable solids that will render them immobile or inert.

The next set of options involves *in situ* treatment. A variety of physical, chemical, or biological treatments can help reduce the level of contamination, depending on the type of contamination. With air sparging, air is injected into contaminated soil, and the air bubbles that rise to the surface will carry trapped and dissolved contaminants with them. Air sparging can also be used to inject air into contaminated groundwater to enhance biodegradation or volatize contaminants. Contaminant vapours can also be collected through vacuum extraction wells, a procedure known as soil vapour extraction. Air sparging has been found to be effective in reducing concentrations of volatile organic compounds found in petroleum products at underground storage tank sites. It works best for lighter gasoline constituents and less well for diesel fuel or kerosene. At about $20–$50 per tonne of saturated soil, air sparging is often less costly than above-ground treatment options.

With soil washing, a contaminated area is flooded with water or a solution that moves contaminants to a location where the they can be collected and treated. Contaminated soil can also be treated with thermal desorption, whereby the soil is heated to vaporize contaminants. Chemical dehalogenation can convert halogen contaminants into less toxic substances through furthering chemical reactions that bind or break down the halogens. Halogens are a class of chemical elements that includes chlorine, bromine, iodine, and fluorine. The process involves removing the soil, treating it in a dehalogenation reactor, and post-treating it in a separator/washer. The cleaned soil can be returned to the original site. Chemical dehalogenation is frequently used to separate and remove chlorine from PCBs and dioxins contained in polluted soil, sludge, or sediment.

With bioremediation, organic contaminants can be rendered harmless through the injection of a mixture of bacteria and nutrients into the soil. Bioremediation can be performed *in situ* or *ex situ*. Bioremediation can sometimes be used in areas that are inaccessible without (expensive) excavation. Bioremediation can also be used effectively for hydrocarbon (e.g., petrol) spills. A related method, phytoremediation, involves planting vegetation that takes up contaminants from the soil. This process concentrates the contaminants, and the polluted vegetation can eventually get collected and disposed of suitably. Phytoremediation is often used when heavy metals such as arsenic, cadmium, or lead are key contaminants. Plans that work well as accumulators are sunflower (for arsenic), willow (for cadmium), and ragweed (for lead).

Another set of options involves *ex situ* treatment. In turn, this involves transporting the contaminated material, water, or soil to a site that is better suited to store or process these substances. This can involve pumping contaminated groundwater to the surface for treatment and injecting it back into the water table after treatment, or excavation of contaminated soil and removal to an off-site landfill for disposal (also known as 'dig-and-dump'). Last on the list is natural attenuation, which relies on natural biological or physical processes to decrease the level of contamination over time.

Which remediation options work best at a given site are a combination of the contamination substance, the accessibility of the site, and the severity of the contamination. Cost considerations give *in situ* treatment an advantage over *ex situ* treatment.

6.6 Summary

Environmental impact assessment (EIA) is a comprehensive and systematic process to identify, analyze, predict, and evaluate the environmental effects of proposed projects. The EIA process allows for the participation of the public and for the consideration of public concerns. EIA is a decision-making tool that may result in approval or rejection of a proposed project, as well as recommendation of modifications and improvements to a proposal. In the United States, EIAs are mandated under the 1970 NEPA statute and are organized into a two-step framework: an environmental assessment and an environmental impact statement. In Canada, EIAs are mandated by federal and provincial law, and may overlap in many instances. EIA is triggered by a screening process, and the size and scope of a project determine how the EIA process is conducted. Larger projects typically require a panel review, while routine projects may be handled by a template-type class screening review. EIAs are conducted through public consultations and expert reviews. Key steps involve 'scoping' (determining the spatial, temporal, and media-specific boundaries of the analysis), 'impact prediction' (scoring the environmental impact of project activities along different impact categories, and weighting these impact categories), and 'impact management' (avoiding, mitigating, or remedying adverse effects). The process results in the recommendation of improvements to the project proposal, the consideration of project alternatives, or the suggestion of particular impact management strategies. Recommendations by EIA panels are subject to discretionary and selective ministerial approval.

6.7 Study questions and exercises

1. Describe the environmental impact assessment (EIA) procedure and explain the distinct steps that lead towards project approval.
2. What are major types of EIA?
3. What is 'scoping,' and under which conditions can it become controversial?
4. What are the steps for 'impact prediction'?
5. Consider the classification system for environmental impacts. What are the major *categories* of environmental impacts, and in particular, what are specific *types* of environmental impacts?
6. How can *fixed-point scoring* and the *analytic hierarchy process* be used to develop weights for different impact categories?
7. Are the recommendations from an EIA panel binding, or can the Canadian minister of the environment pick and choose among recommendations?
8. If both provincial and federal EIAs are conducted in parallel, is it sufficient to get approval from one regulator or is it necessary to get approval from both?
9. Compare the US and Canadian approaches to EIA. Discuss the similarities and differences. Which approach involves more political discretion?

Exercises

1. Develop a template for an EIA for a gasoline station, with a particular focus on scoping and impact prediction. Separate the environmental issues during the operation of the gas station from the environmental issues after its closure. What are the legacy risks? What remediation techniques can be used for cleaning up an abandoned gas station site?
2. Obtain the report of a major EIA that was completed about a decade ago; such reports are publicly available in Canada and the United States. Summarize the crucial elements of the EIA and determine which recommendations were in fact implemented. Analyze the efficacy of these measures ex-post.

Chapter 7
Environmental Management Systems

What environmental impact assessment is for planning a new project, an environmental management system (EMS) is for operating a project or plant. An EMS is a voluntary and proactive tool for implementing an internal information system about the environmental performance of a business, exercising control over its environmental performance, and preparing plans for environmental contingencies. Importantly, the ISO 14001 standard provides a process for certifying the adoption of an EMS. ISO 14001 has become popular with businesses because a well-tuned EMS can help an organization balance business needs with environmental responsibility. This section will explore the design of an EMS as well as the ISO certification process. It is also useful to look at which businesses adopt ISO 14001, the reasons why they adopt it, and how adoption works out in terms of environmental performance.

An environmental management system is that part of the overall management system of a business which includes organizational structure, planning, activities, practices, procedures, processes, and resources for developing, implementing, achieving, reviewing, and maintaining its environmental policy.

In practice, an EMS provides a framework to balance and integrate economic and environmental interests through a firm-internal information and control system: a feedback loop. The building blocks of this feedback loop are explored in the next sections.

7.1 EMS components

An EMS is a set of internal procedures to deal with a company's environmental affairs. However, it is not simply a set of environmental targets. Put another way, an EMS is process-oriented but not outcome-oriented. The procedures defined by the EMS are supposed to be followed tightly. If the EMS is ISO 14001 certified, the procedures are subject to independent third-party review to compare plans and results. An EMS encourages companies to consider implementation of the best available technology, but does not mandate any particular practice or technology.

Fig. 7.1 The Enviromental Management System Pyramid

Figure 7.1 identifies the building blocks of an EMS, which can be thought of as a pyramid. The foundation of the EMS pyramid is the commitment by the senior executive of the company to environmental objectives. This includes a commitment to pollution prevention and compliance with applicable environmental laws. This commitment must be put into a set of objectives that are communicated to the firm's employees and the public. This often takes the form of an environmental code of conduct.

Once a company has committed itself to pursuing a set of environmental objectives, the next step is to codify these objectives in an environmental management plan that defines these goals explicitly, and in some cases defines targets for environmental performance metrics. Setting specific targets is not always necessary, as the EMS requires only a commitment to procedures, not to targets.

With a plan drawn, the next level involves the implementation of specifies procedures to ensure that the goals and objectives are met. Concretely, this requires assigning certain responsibilities to employees. For mid-size and larger firms, this involves appointing dedicated environmental managers or even a chief sustainability officer. The people charged with carrying out the objectives of the EMS must be equipped with the necessary resources to monitor environmental performance, intervene if necessary, and involve other employees for training and emergency preparedness.

On top of the EMS pyramid sits the need for continual review and improvement of the company's environmental procedures and performance. To facilitate this, an EMS requires a layer of monitoring, measurement, and constant evaluation of environmentally relevant activities and environmental performance. An EMS feedback loop is incomplete without continual performance measurement.

7.2 Code of conduct

A company's commitment to environmental objectives can be furthered by adopting a specific code of conduct. The purpose of the code of conduct is to communicate clearly what is expected of all employees in an organization. It defines which behaviour is acceptable and which is unacceptable. Environmental conduct is often subsumed into a larger catalog of objectives that may also include business ethics and health and safety practices. Rather than discussing such codes of conduct in an abstract manner, it may be more useful to examine a specific code of conduct. Teck, one of Canada's largest resource and mining companies (and until 2009 known as Teck-Cominco), has had a charter of corporate responsibility and code of sustainable conduct for many years, as activities of resource companies often pose particular environmental concerns. Below is Teck's 15-point *Code of Sustainable Conduct*, slightly edited for the purpose of highlighting important features:

1. **Obey the law** and conduct business in accordance with Teck's Code of Business Ethics.
2. Ensure that **no discriminatory conduct** is permitted in the workplace. Decisions on job selection, advancements, and promotions will be unbiased, based on merit and ability, and in keeping with commitments to local communities.
3. Foster open and **respectful dialogue** with all communities of interest.
4. Respect the rights and recognize the aspirations of people affected by our activities.
5. **Support local communities** and their sustainability through measures such as development programs, locally sourcing goods and services, and employing local people.
6. Continually improve safety, health and environmental policies, management systems and controls, and ensure they are fully integrated into each company activity.
7. Promote a culture of safety and recognize safety as a core value.
8. Continually reinforce company-wide efforts to achieve zero safety or health incidents.
9. Ensure programs that address workplace hazards are applied to monitor and **protect worker safety** and health;
10. Conduct operations in a sound environmental manner, seeking to continually improve performance.

11. Integrate biodiversity conservation considerations through all
    stages of business and production activities.
12. Design and operate for closure.
13. Promote the **efficient use of energy and material resources** in all
    aspects of our business.
14. Practice **product stewardship** and promote research to enhance the
    benefits of our products to society.
15. Conduct **regular audits** to ensure compliance with this code.

There are several key ingredients in a code of environmental (or sustainable) conduct. Compliance with the law is the first and central ingredient; it sends a clear signal to employees that taking shortcuts that flout regulatory requirements is not acceptable. Several provisions deal with the work environment, which includes a mandate to prohibit discrimination of any sort, foster respectful communication within the company and with local communities, and protect workers' health and safety. The latter part of the Code turns towards environmental performance and resource efficiency, mandating environmental performance improvements, material and energy efficiency, biodiversity conservation, and product stewardship. A central element is also the last item: expressing the readiness to undergo regular (independent, third-party) audits to ensure compliance with the Code. Important for mining companies is also point 12, which considers the fact that mines eventually shut down and may bequeath an environmental legacy to local communities.

7.3 Environmental management plan

The bridge from objectives to implementation is the environmental management plan. There are two key ingredients in this: the pollution prevention (P2) plan, and the environmental emergency (E2) plan. While other components can be added to an overarching environmental management plan, the P2 and E2 plans are indispensable. The P2 and E2 plans recognize the fact that the best possible outcome is pollution avoided rather than abated, and that even if everything has been done to avoid accidents, they may happen (perhaps due to natural disasters), and a business has to be prepared for environmental contingencies. In some cases P2 and E2 plans are mandated by law. For example, any firm (or individual) that handles or stores critical substances (flammable or otherwise hazardous) in quantities above a prescribed minimum is required to maintain an E2 plan and notify relevant emergency response authorities.

While P2 and E2 plans are concerned with environmental issues during the operation of a business, special consideration needs to be given to what happens at the end of life of an operation. Box 7.1 tells the story

Box 7.1: A Tale of Two Mines

Many industrial sites eventually reach the point where they are at the end of their useful life and need to be dismantled. Mining operations reach that point when ore and mineral deposits have been fully mined. What happens afterwards is of significant environmental concern because the mining operation can leave environmental legacies that require treatment for decades after the mining operation has been shut down.

The Brittania copper mine, located near the scenic Sea-to-Sky Highway from Vancouver to the ski resort at Whistler in British Columbia, operated between 1900 and 1974 and was owned by Anaconda Mining after 1963. After its closure, it was turned into a mining museum in 1975. Unencumbered by any environmental requirements at the time, the owner abandoned the mine without any serious environmental cleanup or reclamation. Rainwater started seeping through the mine's tunnels and rock surfaces and generated acid rock drainage into the nearby Britannia Creek, which drains into Howe Sound. Acid rock drainage occurs naturally when metal sulfides come into contact with water and oxygen. Bacteria also play an important role in this process. The process generates sulfuric acid and dissolved metals in the run-off. The highly acidic effluent polluted the local waters in Howe Sound with a daily load of about 300 kilograms of copper, as well as an array of other heavy metals including cadmium, iron, and zinc. This pollution had significant adverse effects on local salmon populations.

British Columbia took over the mine for $30 million, in exchange for indemnifying the owner against any future environmental liabilities. The province built a water treatment plant, which became operational in 2006. The water treatment plant neutralizes the acids with lime slurry. This raises the pH level from acidic to alkaline. The metals dissolved in the water precipitate out and become metal particles. A customized polymer is added in the next step that binds the metal particles and makes them sink to the bottom of a tank, where the metal sludge can be removed. The dewatered metal sludge is transported to a mining pit for storage.

The Island Copper Mine near Port Hardy on Vancouver Island is owned by BHP Billiton, a large resource company. Unlike the Britannia Copper Mine, the Island copper mine has become a model for reclamation. The Island copper open pit mine closed in 1995 and produced about 50,000 tonnes of ore per day. At one point it was Canada's third-largest mine. After it was closed, the pit was flooded to produce a layered lake that provides passive treatment of acid rock drainage. Over half a million trees have been planted on 759 hectares of land (out of a total of 769 hectares). The Island copper mine reclamation is generally regarded as a success story. Unlike the Britannia mine, the retirement of the Island mine involved stakeholder engagement and extensive consultation with experts and regulators.

of two mines in British Columbia that reached the end of their operational life. One closure was managed haphazardly, while the other was managed proactively by the owner. An environmental management plan needs to include planning for a facility's retirement and environmental restoration.

7.3.1 Pollution prevention (P2) plan

As one of the fundamental components of an overarching environmental management plan, the pollution prevention plan is a corporate policy statement that focuses on eliminating or reducing pollution, preventing spills and leaks, and enhancing recovery and recycling of materials. A P2 plan can be looked at as an itemization of corporate pollution prevention activities and procedures. The core ingredients of a P2 plan are:

- an itinerary of pollution sources that includes:
    - a description of processes that use or release hazardous substances or toxic materials; and
    - a list of treatment, disposal, and recycling facilities currently used;
- a description of firm-internal objectives and processes that includes:
    - a reference to a corporate policy statement (e.g., a code of conduct) or overarching environmental objectives;
    - a description of the P2 team, its members, its authority with respect to making decisions within the firm or giving specific directives to employees, and a specification of specific responsibilities (or 'chain of command') of P2 team members;
    - a description of how all company groups (production, R&D, maintenance, shipping, marketing, etc.) will work together and report to the P2 team; and
    - a communication plan for publicizing the P2 program within the company, and for informing employees about the success or failure of P2 measures or P2 training;
- a review of specific pollution prevention measures that includes:
    - a description of current and past P2 activities (see below);
    - a review of the cost of pollution control and waste disposal measures;
    - an evaluation of the effectiveness of past and ongoing P2 activities; and
    - a list of criteria for prioritizing candidate facilities, processes, and streams for P2 activities.

The description of current and past P2 activities obviously depends on the nature of the production processes and activities of each firm and is thus specific to each industry. P2 activities broadly fall into preventative measures and control measures. Examples of these include:

- **preventative measures:**

  - material or feedstock substitution;
  - product design or reformulation;
  - equipment or process modifications;
  - spill and leak prevention;
  - on-site reuse recycling or recovery;
  - inventory management or purchasing techniques;
  - good operating practices or training;

- **control measures:**

  - pollution control or pollution abatement;
  - energy recovery;
  - on-site waste treatment;
  - incineration with energy recovery;
  - off-site recycling;
  - off-site disposal.

Prioritizing P2 activities becomes a strategic challenge for businesses. Prioritizing involves allocating different levels of resources to these activities; it is not merely a matter of putting check marks behind each category. It is therefore crucial to quantify the costs and benefits of competing alternatives and make informed decisions based on a cost-benefit analysis. For example, is an extra P2 dollar better spent on prevention than on control? And if it is better to spend it on control measures, which among competing options delivers the highest reduction of emissions per dollar? The difficulty often lies in making trade-offs. The most harmful emissions may not necessarily be the most visible, and thus a firm's P2 plan may be influenced more by public perception than by quantitative analyses of costs and benefits. Another key problem is the challenge to prevent accidents, which often constitute a major source of pollution. Accident prevention involves two closely linked approaches. The first approach is technical and involves deploying engineering solutions that prevent or contain an accident. Technical prevention often involves monitoring devices that measure system performance and provide an early-warning system. The second approach is human-resource based. It involves training employees in procedures to respond to technical problems proactively. Many major environmental disasters can be attributed to the actions or inactions of untrained or poorly trained staff. A P2 plan depends crucially on the quality of training and the human resources devoted to it. This human element is even more important for environmental emergencies, considered next.

7.3.2 *Environmental emergency (E2) plan*

An environmental emergency is an uncontrolled, unplanned or accidental release of a substance into the environment or the reasonable
likelihood of such a release that may affect the environment or human
health. In Canada there are an estimated 20,000 environmental emergencies annually. Most of them are minor. Only about half of the emergencies get reported to Environment Canada, and only about 1,000 of
these require some further action. Such incidents are primarily the result of accidents, improper maintenance, or human error.

There are different types of events that cause emergencies that involve different response scenarios. Natural emergencies include forest
fires, earthquakes, tsunamis, floods, hurricanes, ice storms, and similar
such naturally occurring events. In some way, these emergencies have a
certain level of frequency and thus predictability, and one can take certain preventative actions if there is sufficient alert time before the event.
Weather-related events usually provide sufficient time to prepare, and
even earthquakes can be responded to with automated shut-offs. (Fa-
mously, the Japanese bullet trains are stopped at the first sign of earthquake waves of a certain magnitude.) The other class of emergencies
involves accidents and the unplanned release of hazardous substances,
often due to ruptured containment vessels of some type. Accidents are
difficult to predict, and accident scenarios may sometimes be difficult
to envision unless that type of accident has happened before, perhaps
somewhere else. Preparing for accidents requires a fair bit of creative
thinking to generate plausible scenarios and effective responses.

An E2 plan contains four central ingredients that can be summarized as **prevention, preparedness, response,** and **recovery.** Prevention
entails complying with all regulations that ensure operational safety.
Many accidents happen due to insufficient vigilance in maintaining
proper maintenance standards. Next, an E2 plan describes a variety
of measures to prepare for an environmental emergency. This includes
identifying and prioritizing potential risks through sensitivity mapping. Once these risks have been identified, employees and emergency
responders can be trained to deal with these contingencies through
workshops, courses, simulations, and exercises. Crucial is the way in
which this emergency response knowledge is retained and remem-
bered. A one-off course is not sufficient. Instead, emergency response
procedures have to be tested through regular exercises and emergency
drills. This is similar to military training where recruits are drilled again
and again in the same procedures until they can carry them out in their
sleep. Crucial emergency response activities have to be honed and refined through repeated drills, especially where time is of the essence to
prevent catastrophic consequences.

When an emergency has occurred, a quick and effective response is essential. This requires a system of escalation of responsibility and involvement that depends on the scale of the emergency: an escalation ladder. If an emergency is too large to be handled internally, provincial and federal emergency responders need to get involved. To streamline this process, Environment Canada has set up Regional Environmental Emergencies Teams that can activate larger-scale emergency responses and provide suitable assistance. Once the emergency has been contained and brought under control, the focus turns towards recovery. The first step involves damage assessment. Subsequent steps focus on planning remedial measures and restoration.

What type of information should be contained in an E2 plan filed with emergency response authorities? According to Environment Canada, a detailed E2 plan should include:

- the properties and characteristics of the substance and the maximum expected quantity of the substance at the place at any time during a calendar year;
- an identification of what types of emergencies might possibly occur, including both on-site and off-site consequences, and the associated prevention efforts under way as well as the preparedness, response, and recovery capabilities;
- the characteristics of the place where the substance is located and of the surrounding area that may increase the risk of harm to the environment or of danger to human life or health;
- the potential consequences of an environmental emergency on the environment and on human life or health;
- the identification of any environmental emergency that can reasonably be expected to occur at the place and that would likely cause harm to the environment or constitute a danger to human life or health, and identification of the harm or danger;
- a description of the measures to be used to prevent, prepare for, respond to, and recover from any environmental emergency;
- a list of individuals who are to carry the plan into effect in the event of an environmental emergency and a description of their roles and responsibilities;
- a description of the training required for each of these individuals;
- a list of the emergency response equipment included as part of the plan, and its location; and
- the measures to be taken to notify members of the public who may be adversely affected by an environmental emergency.

For the regulator, it is important to be aware of the firm's capabilities for emergency response and recovery. In a crisis, the different levels of authority up the escalation ladder need to know how to interface with each other. When an emergency emerges, often the first question asked is: who is in charge?

7.4 Environmental audit

Whereas P2 plans and E2 plans provide the foundation for an environmental management system, they do not provide comprehensive feedback for informing corporate decision-makers about what works and what does not. At regular intervals (every few years), it is therefore desirable to conduct a more rigorous environmental audit that assesses the state of environmental conduct within a firm. Such audits can be conducted both internally or externally. Major consulting firms and specialized environmental consulting firms provide such services, often with the objective of obtaining ISO 14001 certification for a firm's environmental management system. External audits are mandated for ISO certification, but may also precede a proposed acquisition or merger in order to determine potential environmental liabilities. An environmental audit can involve a variety of more specific audits, such as financial, compliance and performance audits.

The financial audit establishes whether the firm has appropriately recognized, valued, and reported environmental costs, liabilities (including contingent liabilities), and assets using generally accepted accounting practices. Financial audits can be mandated for publicly traded companies as part of their regular filings with financial regulators, but they also precede mergers and acquisitions.

The compliance audit establishes whether the firm has conducted its environmental activities in compliance with all applicable obligations from national laws, international treaties, binding standards, voluntary covenants, or codes of professional practice. Part of the compliance audit can be a policy audit that establishes whether the firm's activities meet its own environmental code of conduct.

Finally, the performance audit establishes the validity of performance indicators when reporting publicly, and determines whether environmental activities have been conducted in an effective, efficient, and economical manner.

Environmental audits are conducted with a number of different auditing tools. The first step is usually a full records and procedures audit of EMS components, such as the P2 plan or the E2 plan. This is followed by a checklist that establishes compliance with the various regulations and internal and external codes of conduct. Wherever possible, performance audits rely on observation and measurement, ideally through independent third parties. Compliance and performance audits often employ questionnaires and involve conducting interviews with employees. Audits are typically followed by a clarification process that involves discussion of preliminary findings, and ultimately a written report.

7.5 ISO 14000

The practical importance of environmental management systems is reflected in the need to standardize them so as to make the underlying processes and procedures internally rigorous, comparable across firms, and transparent to stakeholders. The ISO 14000 family of standards by the International Organization for Standardization (ISO) addresses various aspects of environmental management. The most important standard is ISO 14001 (now in the 2004 revision and thus referred to as ISO 14001:2004) that defines environmental management systems. ISO 14001:2004 provides the requirements for an EMS, and the corresponding ISO 14004:2004 gives general EMS guidelines. ISO 14001 is implemented by some 200,000 organizations in 155 countries. The other standards and guidelines in the family address specific environmental aspects that include eco-labelling, life cycle analysis, and environmental audits. It is important to understand that ISO 14000 is conceptually similar to ISO 9000 quality management: both focus on *processes* rather than on *outcomes*. Table 7.1 lists the most important standards in the ISO 14000 family.

Table 7.1 The ISO 14000 Family

14001	Environmental management system
14004	Guidelines on principles, systems, and supporting techniques
14010	Environmental audits
14015	Environmental assessment of sites and organizations
14020–14025	Environmental labelling
14031	Assessment of environmental performance
14040–14049	Life-cycle assessment
14060	Environmental aspects of products
14064	Greenhouse gas assertions (carbon offset certification)
19011	Quality/environmental management system auditing

Figure 7.2 shows the organizational logic of the ISO 14000 family. There are two branches to the family. One branch is about evaluating organizations (companies) and includes environmental management systems, environmental auditing, and other types of performance evaluation. The other branch is about product evaluation and includes environmental labelling, life cycle assessments and other environmental aspects in product standards.

The ISO 14001 standard takes a preeminent role in the ISO 14000 family because this standard is associated with a well-defined certification process. Other standards in the ISO 14000 identify 'best practices' but do not lead to certification. Certification would be desirable for several standards in the ISO 14000 family. For example, carbon offsets are often of dubious quality because the ways they are created do not need

Fig. 7.2 Environmental Management Standards

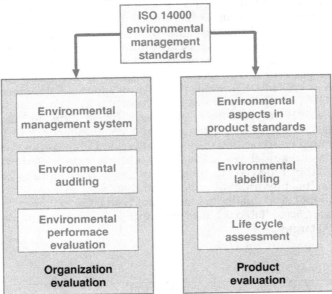

to meet internationally accepted and verifiable standards, but are often merely subject to local standards designed to subsidize local businesses rather than to promote efficient and permanent greenhouse gas reductions.

Because of the preeminence of the ISO 14001 standard, it will be explored in greater detail below. The process of ISO 14001 certification proceeds in several steps. First and foremost is the adoption decision. A company must decide whether or not ISO 14001 is worth the time, money, and effort. Of course, a company can adopt an EMS without achieving certification, but certification serves two purposes. First, it is a verification process through a third party that ensures that the EMS adopted by the firm is comprehensive, consistent, and effective. Second, certification sends a signal to stakeholders that the firm follows a rigorous process and subjects itself to independent third-party audits. Such a signal can be desirable from a marketing perspective as well as a community-relations perspective. More importantly, ISO 14001 certification may become a precondition for being selected in a procurement process of another company. In this case, ISO 14001 can make the difference between being included or excluded from a bidding process for a contract.

The next and most important step is the assessment by an external auditor. This process will be explained in detail below. Upon passing the assessment, the company achieves ISO 14001 certification, which is known as registration and is valid for three years. When the registration expires, a company can apply to renew the certificate, which involves undergoing another assessment (which is normally less involved—and less costly—than the original assessment).

7.5.1 *The certification process*

ISO certification is obtained through retaining the services of a registrar. In Canada, the Standards Council of Canada accredits the registrars as certification bodies. These registrars are often consulting firms. Examples of such registrars include BSI Management Systems, Canadian General Standards Board, KPMG Quality Registrar, Intertek Systems Certification, and QMI/SAI Global.

The first step in the ISO 14001 certification process is a review of documents. The ISO registrar prepares a checklist for the company that lists the various requirements of the standard, and the company works towards preparing all required documents, which includes assembling all required information for these documents.

During the following pre-assessment stage, the ISO auditor conducts a type of dress rehearsal for the real audit. This phase is meant to identify any problem areas that need to be addressed. This pre-assessment can be at different levels of rigour. The more rigorous version involves talking to company personnel, gathering information, and walking through the steps of the formal audit. At the end of this process, the company should have reviewed all relevant documents for completeness, conducted an internal audit, and identified and corrected any weaknesses. When this is complete, an audit schedule is adopted. Usually, the registrar that carries out the audit will not proceed to the audit stage until everything is in place to ensure a high likelihood of a positive completion of the audit.

The formal ISO 14001 audit often takes place in two stages. During the first stage, the lead auditor will finalize the document review and carry out a thorough facility inspection. The auditor will review all necessary permits (compliance audit). The first stage will be limited to senior personnel in the company. During the second stage, the audit team explores the implementation and effectiveness of the environmental management system. During this stage, interviews and more detailed inspections are conducted, often involving multiple members of the audit team and employees at all levels of the company. After a satisfactory conclusion of the audit, the registrar issues a certificate that is valid for up to three years.

7.5.2 *The adoption decision*

Which companies should seek ISO 14001 certification? Which should not? The ISO 14001 certification process can be costly, and a rational firm will invest in achieving certification only if the process leads to value added for the firm.

When is ISO 14001 certification desirable? Companies can adopt an effective EMS without certifying it. For a firm that currently has no EMS at all, adopting a certified EMS may be an expedient way of ensuring the quality of the EMS. However, for a firm that already has a functioning EMS, what additional value can be obtained from certification? In other words, adopting an EMS and seeking certification of the EMS are two separate decisions. Some firms will implement an EMS, but not seek certification.

What makes firms more likely to seek ISO 14001 certification? The reasons can be quite diverse depending on the type of firm. ISO certification can be a response to a regulatory mandate. If a firm is working towards compliance with a regulatory mandate, putting an EMS in place can help attain compliance in a verifiable manner. Key elements of an EMS such as the P2 plan and the E2 plan may already be mandated by the regulator, and thus ISO certification provides reassurance that these plans meet the standards required by the regulator. Thus the EMS can help meet the regulatory requirements more efficiently.

ISO certfication also signals a firm's good intentions to the regulator. It signals that a firm is proactive about meeting environmental challenges and thus may be in overcompliance; adopting a certified EMS exceeds what is required by the regulator. The benefits of overcompliance can be twofold. First, the regulator may inspect a certified facility less frequently than an uncertified facility. If inspections are costly in terms of time and effort, both the regulators and the regulated benefit. Second, overcompliance may create opportunities to meet regulatory challenges more flexibly. Whereas meeting minimum requirements often results in using a default method, exceeding the regulatory requirements allows for using alternative and novel methods that ultimately may create long-term benefits to a firm. For example, companies can pioneer new environmental engineering solutions that can be sold to other firms, or raise the bar for other firms to meet. Along that line, a company that discloses environmental infractions proactively will find the regulator more inclined to consider novel or more flexible ways to correct these infractions.

ISO certification may also be in response to the threat of litigation. A company that has a well-run EMS in place demonstrates that due diligence has been applied, which may protect it against accusations of negligence (and corresponding litigation) in case of an environmental accident. This suggests that a higher propensity for litigation may motivate firms to put an EMS in place, and also to seek ISO certification. But a higher propensity for litigation cuts the opposite way too. Firms that face a higher propensity for litigation may feel less inclined to be proactive about disclosing environmental infractions, and instead 'hush up' such incidents for fear of costly litigation. The risk of litigation can push firms in either direction. Which direction prevails depends on the nature of the litigation and the characteristics of the firm. Where litigation outcomes are more punitive than corrective, firms may be wary of disclosing 'too much' information that may be used against them.

Stakeholders also play a role in motivating firms to adopt and certify their EMS. In affluent and well-educated societies, consumers may be more environmentally conscious. They may prefer firms, brands, and products through acts of green consumerism that punish environmental laggards and rewards environmental pioneers. Companies that wish to signal their green credentials to consumers can use ISO 14001 certification as a means to that end. Certification can improve firm branding, although not necessarily product branding; ISO certification is a firm characteristic, not a product characteristic. When firm branding is more important than product branding, ISO certification may be more recognizable and thus more valuable for signalling green credentials.

Market characteristics may also influence the ISO certification decision. Where markets have low barriers to entry, greater competition ensues. Faced with the pressure from more intense competition, firms tend to differentiate their brands and products to occupy separate market niches. To the extent that consumers value green products, product differentiation allows firms to pursue these green consumers.

Last but not least, green sourcing can also motivate firms to pursue ISO certification of their environmental management system. An increasing number of producers demand ISO certification of their suppliers. Producers that want to achieve a high level of environmental responsibility need to push their suppliers to meet the same high standards. Rather than a 'race to the bottom,' where firms gain a comparative advantage from exploiting low environmental standards, green sourcing can lead to the opposite effect: 'a race to the top' as suppliers improve environmental performance to remain competitive bidders. ISO 14001 certification can be used as a selection criterion for accepting bids from suppliers. This can have positive cross-country effects as countries with high environmental standards require their foreign suppliers (where environmental standards may be lower) to achieve ISO certification.

Governments also see benefits in promoting ISO certification. They do this for three reasons. First, governments purchase goods and services, and requiring ISO certification is simply evidence of green government procurement. Second, governments promote ISO certification as a low-cost environmental policy, hoping that such voluntary pro-

Box 7.2: ISO 14001 and Parks Canada

Gros Morne National Park was designated a UNESCO World Heritage Site in 1987 for its exceptional universal value. The park protects thousands of square kilometres of extraordinary landscape on Newfoundland's west coast. The Long Range Mountains, the northernmost extent of the Appalachians, contain numerous glacially carved fjords. One of the most spectacular, Western Brook Pond, is also the Park's largest lake. Drawing about 25,000 visitors annually, provincial campaigns promote its image widely as a tourism icon.

Along with tourism however, the popularity of Western Brook Pond has brought with it the risk of environmental degradation. Concerned about the pressure on the ecosystem, Parks Canada revised its Request for Proposal (RFP) process, making ISO 14001 registration a mandatory requirement for companies seeking to operate concessions within the Park. In response, Norock Associates Ltd., which operates the Western Brook Pond Boat Tour, became the first boat tour company in North America to be registered to ISO 14001. Owner Reg Williams embraced the notion of certification, convinced that it would mean a lot not only for Parks Canada, but for his company as well.

One of the most important environmental objectives for any boat tour operation is the prevention of diesel fuel spills. Although Norock had leak detection procedures in place prior to adopting ISO 14001, the implementation of the standard established very vigilant daily documentation recording procedures aboard the ships, at the underground storage tank, and during fuel deliveries over the trail to dockside. The company believes the standard is delivering the performance goals Norock has set, including no fuel spills and recycling 50% of the solid waste generated at the site.

Certification did not come cheaply for Williams. When Williams had to replace an existing tour boat on Western Brook Pond, the new one was specially designed so that it could be built in sections. To avoid scarring the landscape by carrying the pieces over an ice road in the winter, the pieces were instead flown in by helicopter over the three kilometres of coastal lowland situated between the entrance to the trail at the highway and the dock. This proactive action avoided damaging a sensitive environment.

For his efforts Williams won the 2003 Sustainable Tourism Award, which is offered jointly by Hospitality Newfoundland and Labrador and Parks Canada. The award recognizes the operator who most demonstrates a commitment to protecting the natural heritage resources.

(Based on a report from the Standards Council of Canada, Consensus Magazine 30, 2003.)

grams reduce emissions. This crucially depends on how effective ISO 14001 is in improving outcomes, not just environmental procedures. As discussed below, there is some evidence that ISO 14001 is modestly effective in this direction. Third, governments care about the international competitiveness of their firms. As green sourcing is becoming more widespread, ISO certification is simply the cost of doing business. Falling behind cuts out firms from international markets. For these reasons, some governments provide incentives for firms to pursue ISO 14001 certification. The nature of these incentives can be quite diverse. For example, in the federal state of Saxony, Germany, government procurement policies favour ISO-14001-certified companies. Since 2008, industrial sites in France that are ISO 14001 certified will be subject to less frequent inspections (every 10 instead of every 5 years). In Thailand, ISO-14001-certified companies are exempted from paying annual manufacturing licence fees to the Ministry of Industry for five years. How governments can influence the ISO 14001 adoption decision is illustrated in box 7.2, which describes how Parks Canada has made ISO certification a mandatory requirement for tourism companies operating in one of its parks.

There is a slew of reasons for adopting ISO certification. What does empirical research tell us about which of these reasons matter most? Berthelot et al. (2003) conducted a survey of Canadian businesses to determine the ranking of reasons, shown in table 7.2. The researchers looked at firms that already had an EMS and those that started without an EMS. The table shows results for both groups. Responses were on a 1–7 scale ranging from not very important to very important. Among the responding firms, the strongest reason was an improved corporate image, followed by improving environmental performance and gaining a competitive edge. For the firms which already had an EMS, improving the existing EMS was another important reason to pursue certification.

7.5.3 Effectiveness

The main objective of ISO 14001 is not to reduce emissions. Its main objective is to improve the management of environmental processes in a firm through implementing an information and control system. In other words, the focus is on process, not outcome. Nevertheless, once firms are ISO certified, they often discover areas where they can improve their environmental performance, and proceed to make the necessary changes. The certification process can provide a strong motivation to review the environmental status quo and identify strengths and weaknesses of the current approach to managing a firm's environmental portfolio. It is very likely that ISO certification will, on average,

Table 7.2 Reasons for obtaining ISO 14001 certification

	Has EMS		No EMS	
	Mean	S.D.	Mean	S.D.
Improved current EMS	5.84	1.32	—	—
Improved environmental performance	5.78	1.43	5.63	1.35
Improved manufacturing process	3.78	2.09	3.72	1.91
Improved employee working conditions	3.98	2.07	4.07	1.70
Cost savings	4.09	1.98	4.15	1.90
Openings to international markets	4.14	2.31	4.55	2.10
Increased client base in Canada	3.61	2.18	4.10	2.03
Improved corporate image	6.09	1.19	6.17	1.15
Respond to current client demands	4.25	2.25	4.71	1.96
Respond to public pressure	3.52	2.12	3.83	2.05
Respond to environmentalist criticisms	3.43	2.03	3.50	2.20
Gain a competitive edge	5.14	1.87	5.48	1.51
Keep up with the competition	3.81	2.16	4.11	2.00
Company protection against lawsuits	3.95	1.91	4.45	1.86
Management protection against lawsuits	3.71	1.86	4.40	1.71
Shareholder protection against lawsuits	3.68	1.86	3.61	1.99
Improved bank loan facility	2.97	2.11	2.81	1.74

Source: Berthelot et al. (2003).

generate some positive improvements to environmental outcomes. But how large are these improvements?

ISO 14001 is a voluntary program. This makes it difficult to evaluate effectiveness with respect to environmental outcomes because the firms participating in the program are self-selecting. Which firms participate depends on the firms' characteristics and their prior environmental performance. It is entirely conceivable that the only firms that participate are those that are already well on their way to improving environmental performance. Ideally, we are interested in identifying the treatment effect of participation. If we can randomly choose firms and make them achieve ISO 14001 certification, and then look at the change in their environmental performance, we could get a good sense of the environmental 'value added' of ISO certification. However, we cannot pick firms randomly; we can only observe which firms choose to participate. It is therefore necessary to control for the self-selection of firms through appropriate econometric techniques.

In an extensive study of voluntary environmental programs, Prakash and Potoski (2006) have looked at the benefits of ISO 14001 certification. They find evidence that certification reduces emissions and increases regulatory compliance, but these beneficial effects are small. Some of the benefits from implementing an EMS come from reducing the risk of environmental accidents. As the frequency of such accidents is low, it is difficult to compare outcomes before and after ISO 14001 certification as one would need to look at a sufficiently long time horizon. Some metrics are also more encouraging than others. For example, while EMS certification may contribute less to reducing air pollution (which often depends on capital-intensive pollution abatement devices), it may help uncover opportunities for energy conservation, and it often helps improve solid waste management through improved reuse and recycling.

7.6 Summary

An environmental management system is a tool through which firms exercise control over their environmental policy throughout the organization. The EMS also acts as an information system that provides systematic feedback about a firm's environmental performance. Starting with a corporate policy statement, an EMS implements the policy through developing detailed pollution prevention (P2) and environmental emergency (E2) plans. While P2 and E2 plans are oriented towards action and control, the other key component of an EMS, the environmental audit, is oriented towards information gathering, regulatory compliance, and identifying areas for improvement.

An EMS can get certified under the international ISO 14001 standard by accredited registrars. Companies often choose certification to improve an existing EMS, enhance their corporate image, or gain a competitive advantage. While an EMS is process-oriented and not outcome-oriented, firms still hope to achieve improvements in environmental performance. After controlling for self-selection in pursuing ISO certification, there is empirical evidence that certification generates significant, albeit small, improvements in environmental performance.

7.7 Study questions

1. Identify the key elements of an environmental management system.
2. What are the key components of P2 and E2 plans?
3. How should firms plan and prepare for the eventual closure of and decommissioning of an industrial site?
4. What are the different types of an environmental audit?
5. What is the purpose of the ISO 14001 standard? Concretely, what is it meant to accomplish, and what not?
6. How does a firm pursue ISO 14001 certification, and what are the steps along that route?
7. Which reasons motivate firms to seek ISO 14001 certification?
8. Does ISO 14001 certification help improve environmental performance? What does the empirical evidence tell us?

Chapter 8
Corporate Environmental Strategy

A search on Amazon.com for books with the word combination 'green business strategy' results in over 550 matches (in November 2012). There is no shortage of advice for businesses on how to reinvent themselves with the 'green' mantra. Few books stand out among the crowd, however, and many suffer from overemphasizing case studies that other firms may find difficult to imitate. What works for one firm may not work for other firms if their situations differ in some way or another. There is no single strategy that leads to a 'greener' business, but there is usually a combination of strategic approaches that help businesses become more environmentally responsible—and not stray into 'greenwashing.' This chapter is geared towards identifying green opportunities and challenges, while at the same time pointing out the stumbling blocks and the danger of putting green ambition over green reality.

A useful resource on corporate environmental strategy is Esty and Winston (2006). It is one of the few books that approaches the subject matter systematically with a clear focus on the the strategy space. Green strategy is inextricably part of every firm's overarching business strategy. Each and every firm ought to take responsibility for its effects on the environment. Some firms do so proactively, others hesitantly, and some not at all. 'Smart' firms get ahead of the curve and create a competitive advantage through innovation in green technology, whether it is designing greener products or finding efficiencies in the production process. A book along similar lines is Makower (2009), which looks at how businesses relate to consumers and how companies can build up their 'green credentials' effectively. This book also stresses the potential for win-win strategies that are beneficial both environmentally and economically. Lastly, Harvard Business Review (2007) is a collection of eight short articles from the *Harvard Business Review*. This volume covers a diverse range of topics, from green buildings to risk management, and many other environmental business scenarios.

8.1 Strategy space

The business literature often attempts to identify the dimensions that categorize different business models: the strategy space. Many approaches use a simple two-by-two matrix to highlight competing and interacting influences. For example, the SWOT approach distinguishes long-term and short-term influences, and upsides and downsides, to arrive at a matrix of strengths (S) versus weaknesses (W) and opportunities (O) versus threats (T). Matrix approaches have also been developed for corporate environmental strategy.

To identify the strategy space for corporate environmentalism, Esty and Winston (2006) focus on two dimensions: revenue versus costs, and long-term versus short-term. This technique is useful to identify some of the core strategies but ultimately faces important limitations. For many strategic decisions, the time horizon is not discrete but continuous. Strategic decisions are not merely revenue-enhancing or cost-saving, but often involve complicated interactions.

A different matrix framework was introduced in Hart (2007) as the sustainability portfolio. Again, one dimension is the time horizon of long-term versus short-term. The second dimension is firm-internal versus firm-external. In this framework, firm-internal strategies such as pollution prevention and clean technology development are contrasted with firm-external strategies such as product stewardship and development of a sustainability vision. Both frameworks ultimately provide insufficient systematic guidance to understanding the corporate environmental strategy space because even the strategies that do not really fit the matrix need to be squeezed into it.

Figure 8.1 develops a new framework for the corporate environmental strategy space based on functional areas of competence. From left to right, it starts with the key driver of green strategy—technology—and ends with the place where success and failure is determined—the market. In the middle are two strategic target areas: the production process (which includes the value chain) and the products. Fundamentally, these two areas are linked to technology through process innovation and product innovation. The production process is surrounded by its inputs and outputs. All strategy areas are influenced from the outside by a number of actors, from suppliers to distributors, from governments to utilities, and from competitors to complementors.

The strategy space depicted in figure 8.1 also highlights the importance of market-focused strategies. A green product needs to find its market, and this can be facilitated through product marketing and firm branding, and in particular through consumer information, third-party certification, and effective pricing. The market also provides feedback that informs the product development. In particular, product differentiation helps firms establish recognition and credibility, and understanding consumer needs may help turn products into services.

Markets connect firms in myriad ways to outside influences. Competitors force a firm to define its environmental core competence, often through product differentiation. At the same time, firms need to cooperate with distributors to reach consumers, especially for retail (e.g., household) products. Many companies also depend on complementors:

Fig. 8.1 The Corporate Environmental Strategy Space

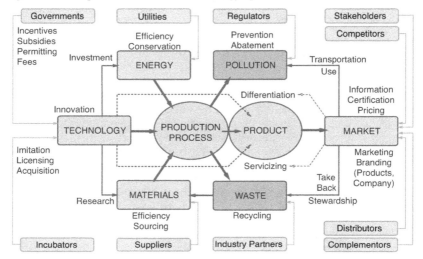

firms that produce complementary products or services (e.g., batteries for electric vehicles, hydrogen for fuel cells). Last not least, a variety of stakeholders (consumers, investors, communities) also influence a firm's green market position.

Companies need to be aware of two crucial feedback loops from the product market: transportation of goods to the market; and the use of a product over its lifetime. Both can contribute to pollution or waste. Companies can initiate take-back programs for their discarded products and engage in product stewardship.

8.2 Green innovation and technology

Technology plays a pre-eminent role in defining the corporate environmental strategy space. Technology affects a business model in two key areas: the production process and product development. The production process has input and output dimensions. On the input side, environmental issues arise through the use of energy and materials. On the output side, environmental issues arise through the products themselves (in particular, their use and final disposition) as well as through the by-products of the production process, pollution and waste.

Technological innovation can come from internal or external sources. Companies can develop new technologies through research and development, in many instances accelerated by government incentives, subsidies, permitting requirements, or (green) taxes and other levies. Companies can also obtain ideas from external sources through imitation, licensing from other companies, or acquisition of intellectual property or start-up companies. Many green ideas come from incubators, small start-ups that experiment with new technologies but lack the capacity to develop them fully or integrate them into other consumer products.

8.2.1 Process innovation

Process innovation can target inputs—energy and materials—or the by-products of production—pollution and waste. Each of these four strategic areas are connected to particular business strategies. Energy conservation and energy efficiency are explored in section 10.7, and box 10.2 illustrates this strategy with examples from the pulp and paper industry. Pollution strategies focus either on prevention or abatement (see Chapter 9). A key objective of pursuing energy efficiency is cost reduction, while a key objective of pursuing pollution reduction is avoidance of regulatory costs or interventions. Similarly, improving materials efficiency and reducing waste can save costs, but in some cases changes in materials can also generate additional revenue through improved product performance. These strategies can permeate the value chain. The related concept of green sourcing is explored below in section 8.3.

The most valuable corporate environmental strategy that focuses on the production process involves the simultaneous improvement of productivity and the reduction of environmental impact: a win-win strategy. For example, improving energy efficiency can reduce electricity or fuel costs while lowering greenhouse gas emissions. When it comes to productivity enhancements, vintage effects often play an important role. Older production facilities tend to be less efficient and less environmentally friendly, so upgrading facilities often leads to a win-win. What is holding back such upgrading is often the initial capital cost, which in times of greater market volatility poses a significant financial risk. The capital cost of an older plant may have already been fully amortized, and keeping it running for another few years seems less of a risk.

Win-win strategies are also feasible in the consumer market. Changes in the use of materials, or reductions in wasteful packaging materials, can generate significant environmental performance improvements. The example of Apple's green strategy for its laptop computers, discussed in box 8.1, highlights that improvements in environmental performance may sometimes go hand-in-hand with improvements in product performance.

Materials efficiency can also be achieved through improved system integration: developing 'closed loop' systems that involve product

Box 8.1: Apple's Green Notebooks

Apple is a world-leading innovator in computing technology. The company's visionary smartphones, tablets, computers, and online services have made it the world's most valuable brand, according to a 2013 study by Interbrand Corp., followed by Google, Coca-Cola, IBM, Microsoft, and GE.

As premium products, Apple devices strive to be cutting-edge not only in computing performance but also in environmental performance. The company even advertised the green credentials of its 13-inch MacBook on television. Apple's strategy is a classic win-win: improved environmental performance goes hand-in-hand with quality improvements in other areas. For example, a new type of battery that Apple introduced in the 17-inch MacBook Pro is expected to last five years instead of one-to-two years. The company is so confident in the performance of its batteries that in newer models it has eliminated the compartment door for accessing and replacing the battery. It expects that the typical update cycle for laptops is shorter than battery lifetime.

Apple is particularly successful at eliminating many harmful toxins in its products. The company's engineers managed to remove mercury from the CFL backlights by switching to LED backlights, and they removed arsenic contained in the glass of conventional LCD displays. The circuit boards, internal cables, and connectors no longer use PVC.

There are also more modest environmental improvements. Reducing the size of packaging boxes by 40% reduces waste—and costs. The enclosure is made of aluminum and the screen is made out of glass rather than plastic; both are recyclable. These appear to be relatively minor changes, but they amount to a more significant environmental improvement because of the large number of devices that Apple sells.

Apple also participates in the EPEAT (Electronic Product Environmental Assessment Tool) global rating system for greener electronics, and obtained the gold certification in that program. Managed by the non-profit Green Electronics Council based in Portland, Oregon, products certified by the EPEAT system must meet strict environmental criteria that address the full product life cycle.

Apple can afford to be a green leader because its devices command a high price premium. It is therefore tempting to belittle the environmental improvements. However, Apple's technological choices have a strong influence on competitors who try to imitate its products and strategies. Eventually, many of the environmental performance improvements pioneered by Apple will doubtlessly be adopted by competitors. This positive externality is reinforced through the connection between environmental improvement and product performance.

stewardship and recycling processes in which waste is condensed while recovering a reusable resource. For example, slightly contaminated water from a scrubber can be treated to extract the sludge and reuse the water. Waste-to-energy plants are another example.

Another example of a business strategy that targets materials efficiency is Ikea, the popular Swedish manufacturer of flat-pack assemble-yourself household furniture. Ikea spent much research on optimizing the packaging of the furniture components into cardboard boxes, reducing the use of styrofoam and other fill material. By adjusting the dimensions of the flat packs judiciously to match the size of trucks and cargo containers, Ikea has been able to improve the utilization of truck loads. This in turn reduces transportation costs. Ikea is also in an advantageous position to introduce other environmentally friendly products to consumers, and it is promoting the switch to energy-efficient LED lighting. The company also ensures that the wood it sources for its furniture products comes from forests that are certified as responsibly managed by the Forest Stewardship Council.

Process innovation is sometimes driven by external events. For example, Coca-Cola and Pepsi faced a significant public outcry over the discovery of trace pesticide residues in their products in India (*Business Week*, 10 August 2006). The dispute escalated when India's Kerala state banned their Indian subsidiaries from making or selling their beverages. Crisis management required a quick and determined identification of the source of the problem and the implementation of a satisfactory solution. Coca-Cola discovered that the pesticide residue came from the locally sourced sugar. Two responses were possible: import the sugar from trusted sources elsewhere in the world, with adverse effects on the local agricultural sector, or continue sourcing the sugar locally and purify it at significant cost. Ultimately, this became more of a political than an economic decision. Either way, the damage to the company's reputation required a determined public relations effort to set the record straight and restore confidence in its products.

As firms are becoming increasingly aware of the environmental impacts of their products and production methods, they are embracing the concept of product stewardship. For producers, this concept is often used synonymously with the term 'extended producer responsibility.' However, the notion of 'product stewardship' is more encompassing. It is about shared responsibility among manufacturers, retailers, users, and disposers. Nevertheless, manufacturers take a pivotal role in this relationship because it is often the design of the product that has the most direct impact on its environmental footprint.

Product stewardship entails taking responsibility for a product's environmental impact over its entire lifespan.

Manufacturers embracing product stewardship engage in life cycle analysis in order to reduce the total lifespan environmental impact of their products. Specifically, product stewardship requires that firms take responsibility for what happens to their products after they have been sold to consumers or other firms, and in particular what happens to their products at the end of their useful life. Consumers embracing product stewardship engage in practices that reduce the environmental impact during the use and disposition of the goods they use.

The most familiar example of product stewardship involves deposit-paid cans and bottles. Beer brewers and wineries sell their cans and bottles to consumers, who pay a refundable deposit on these containers. Such deposit-paid schemes have helped improve recycling rates of these containers dramatically.

Product stewardship often involves manufacturers rethinking the design of their products. Take the billions of batteries that are used and disposed of every year in North America. Some types of batteries contain toxic materials such as mercury and cadmium. Disposing them improperly can cause harm to human health. Battery producers actually have grown to the challenge by reducing the use of mercury by over 98% since the early 1980s, and they have promoted rechargeable batteries. Nevertheless, battery technology is evolving and new materials are used increasingly, requiring novel types of responses and fresh ideas for product stewardship.

8.2.2 Product innovation and differentiation

A green company needs green products. For many existing businesses, this involves a process of product differentiation through which new environmentally friendly products are introduced, either side by side with existing products or replacing existing products. The introduction of fuel-efficient gas-electric hybrid cars was in some instances accomplished by creating a new product line (e.g., the Toyota Prius), while in other cases it involved retooling existing vehicle lines (e.g., the Ford Explorer). When technologies are relatively immature, creating a new product line (or brand) can help create a 'safe zone' for product development and fence off negative spillovers if the product development runs into problems. On the other hand, when technologies become more mature, there are economies of scale that come along with larger market share, and there are economies of scope that can be harvested by sharing platforms or components.

Developing green products can be successful only when consumers are willing to pay for the increased cost of the green attributes. Willingness to pay a green price premium is much stronger when consumers perceive goods as either truly innovative or qualitatively superior. For example, consumers may be willing to pay a premium for hybrid gas-electric cars (after allowing for fuel cost savings). They may also be willing to pay for organic produce if it is perceived to be healthier than non-organic produce.

In general, consumers have difficulty making cost-benefit calculations that involve longer time horizons. For example, certain types of lighting are more durable and reduce electricity consumption. On a cost-benefit basis with conventional discount rates, the more efficient lighting may even be less expensive. Yet, consumers may still pay more attention to the initial purchase price (the higher fixed cost) than to long-term savings (the lower variable cost). Overcoming such perception issues requires substantial educational effort, and sometimes it requires monetary incentives that lower the fixed cost. A company's salesforce needs to be trained to deal with the 'fixed-cost versus variable-cost' conundrum.

Green attributes usually do not stand on their own, but are usually just one dimension in which consumers evaluate a product. Most consumers still care more about price, quality, and service when selecting a product, and the environmental dimension is often further down the list of decision criteria. Rarely is environmental friendliness the top criterion. A 'green' product is much more likely to succeed if it can also offer other benefits.

Importantly, a green product may need to overcome an adverse perception that it is less functional in a particular dimension. When compact fluorescent light bulbs (CFLs) were first introduced, consumers were often dissatisfied that CFLs could not be dimmed like conventional light bulbs, that the temperature colour was 'too white,' or that the initial flickering was annoying. Product innovation has overcome all three obstacles.

Electric cars are suffering a similar fate at the moment. Pure plug-in electric cars are limited in range, and because of battery capacity, their motors tend to be somewhat undersized. While the battery problem remains unsolved, possible solutions are appearing on the horizon. That propulsion performance is not an obstacle per se is demonstrated by Tesla Motors, a manufacturer of premium electric vehicles with sports car characteristics based in Palo Alto, California. During 2013 Tesla Motors became the world's most valuable electric vehicle company with a valuation of US$20 billion, about a third that of General Motors. Tesla targets the luxury vehicle market, where a hefty price premium matters much less to buyers. The company's Model S sedan has impressive performance. With an 85 kWh battery it offers a range of 425 km, a top speed of 200 km/h, and an impressive acceleration. The cheapest model S retails for over US$60,000. Tesla sold about 18,000 Model S vehicles in 2013, making it the third-most popular plug-in electric vehicle after the Chevrolet Volt and the Nissan Leaf. More importantly, the Model S eclipsed the Mercedes-Benz S-Class as the best-selling full-size luxury sedan. Tesla's competitors in the EV market have a much harder time making the Volt and Leaf profitable.

Product innovation is closely linked to product differentiation. Successful green products need to aim for the right market segment. For example, it makes more sense to focus sales effort for hybrid gas-electric vehicles in urban areas rather than in rural areas. In urban areas hybrid cars may appeal to cost-conscious commuters, cars tend to be smaller, and are driven in stop-and-go conditions that are particularly suitable for hybrid vehicles. By comparison, efficient turbo diesel engines perform better on highways than in city driving, and thus it makes sense to focus marketing on a different clientele.

Developing a new product does not always guarantee success. There are important differences between international markets. What works in one country is not guaranteed to work in others. For example, Esty and Winston (2006) cite the story of Shell, which launched a diesel-blend in Thailand that reduced emissions and was apparently well received by customers who were exposed to significant levels of air pollution every day. However, when the company tried to introduce the same product in Europe, it faltered because air pollution was not a significant concern.

8.2.3 *Servicizing*

A rather different approach to delivering green products is the idea of servicizing: turning a product into a service. Xerox has developed servicizing for its printing business. One business model rests on the idea of simply selling printers. An alternative business model rests on the idea of selling the use of these printers. Faced with a commoditization of printing technology, Xerox re-invented itself as the 'document company' by delivering office services. Environmental benefits derive from the consolidation of printing devices in fewer but higher-performing multi-functional service stations. Instead of having a printer in each office, each business unit can be served centrally with faster, higher-quality printing in a convenient location that is connected through the local area network. Xerox provides installation and maintenance services, as well as parts and accessories. Servicizing provides value to the company and its customers, who can save money through centralization and consolidation.

Servicizing can also be used for air conditioning (HVAC) systems. It is not the product itself that is useful but the service that it delivers: cooled or heated air flow. Selling HVAC units is a product-oriented business model; selling the heating and cooling provided by HVAC units is a service-oriented business model. In practice this means that HVAC firms retain ownership of their HVAC units, install them, and charge for their use. An HVAC manufacturer selling HVAC units is concerned about meeting performance specifications at a low capital cost. Once a unit is sold, the energy use and cost is a burden on the owner of the HVAC unit, not the manufacturer. The owner's choices may be limited by the similarity of the designs, which do not favour energy efficiency. A servicizing HVAC firm would have an incentive to design HVAC systems that are cheap to operate rather than cheap to manufacture. They would take into account the total lifetime cost of the system in order to offer the most affordable heating or cooling service. Thus, servicizing can promote product stewardship by extending a firm's time horizon for a product.

Another example involves using cloud computing for data storage rather than using local computer systems. In addition to providing much larger scalability (and thus cost savings), the 'cloud' can be operated in locations where electricity is not only cheap but also relatively clean. Servicizing shifts the product-centric model of owning computers to the service-centric model of offering computing services.

Servicizing faces limitations. Not all products are amenable to servicizing. Nevertheless, servicizing can evolve parallel to conventional product-centric business models in pursuing novel niche markets. Thus, servicizing is catching on even in the automotive industry. Box 8.2 illustrates the case of car2go, a car-sharing service that utilizes iconic Smart cars.

8.3 Green sourcing

The notion of green sourcing entails procuring environmentally friendly goods and services. The 'greening' of the supply chain can help in important ways according to Christensen et al. (2008). First, green sourcing may not be a costly extravagance but a source of profitability for a company. Second, it can improve a company's public image and reputation with the company's stakeholders. Sourcing is mostly about meeting cost reduction goals: finding the cheapest supplier for goods and services of a particular specification.

Where green sourcing can add value is through introducing life cycle analysis and life cycle costing into procurement. The total cost of a procured product is not simply its purchase cost. It also includes the cost of using, maintaining, recycling, or disposing it. In practice this means looking at opportunities for procured products to (1) reduce electricity and energy use; (2) improve recycling or reduce waste streams; (3) reduce water consumption; (4) reduce consumption of raw materials; (5) reduce packaging; (6) reduce transportation; and (6) facilitate environmentally beneficial material substitution (switching from polluting to non-polluting ingredients). For example, suppose a production facility

Box 8.2: Servicizing Cars: The Story of car2go

Car sharing is an idea that has come of age. Originally conceived as co-operatives in which members share cars rather than rent vehicles from car-rental companies, car-sharing is increasingly turning towards servicizing cars. The idea behind servicizing is to turn a product into a service.

The prime example of servicizing cars is car2go, a subsidiary of Daimler AG of Germany, the manufacturer of Mercedes-Benz luxury cars as well as Smart microcars. Daimler pioneered the concept in the city of Ulm in Germany in 2008, and quickly expanded from Germany to 25 more cities in Europe and North America. In Canada, car2go operates in Calgary, Montreal, Toronto, and Vancouver; in the United States in Austin, Columbus, Denver, Miami, Minneapolis, Portland, San Diego, Seattle, and Washington (DC).

car2go vehicles lined up near the bus terminal at the University of British Columbia in Vancouver. Photo by author.

The concept is simple: members pay for one-way trips on a time basis (by the minute) rather than for two-way trips that require return to the origin destination (and payment on a daily basis). car2go members use their electronically readable membership card to open the doors to a vehicle wherever it may be parked, and after completing a trip leave the car in available or designated parking spots within a particular service area (usually an urban core). Often, a key benefit is that municipalities allow parking of car2go vehicles in parking spots that are otherwise restricted to residents, or provide designated parking spots in downtown cores where parking is expensive. Vehicles can also be reserved up to 30 minutes in advance, and GPS-equipped smartphones can navigate members to the nearest available vehicle using a dedicated car2go app. Voluntary refuelling of a vehicle earns a time credit.

Unlike other car-sharing companies such as Zipcar, car2go makes use of a single type of vehicle: microcars manufactured by Daimler's Smart division in France. Having a single type of car simplifies maintenance and reduces cost. Using microcars also keeps fuel costs low, which benefits car2go members through lower per-minute rates as fuel is included in the rate. car2go also introduced the plug-in electric drive version of the Smart car, which has a top speed of 100 km/h and a range of about 135 km on a full charge. The relative paucity of charging stations remains an obstacle to wider adoption of such vehicles despite the strong environmental benefits, in particular in cities where electricity is from low-emission sources.

car2go has started a trend towards selling the use of cars rather than cars themselves. The future of mobility is multi-modal, in particular in urban areas. Urbanites may combine trips that include walking, biking, using public transportation, or driving a car. The market for car-sharing services is expected to increase rapidly worldwide as young people appear to be embracing the concept.

requires fluorescent lighting in the form of 4-ft T8 bulbs. New generations of these bulbs consume 28W instead of 32W and last considerably longer. Although slightly more expensive to purchase, their life cycle cost is lower due to energy cost savings.

The companies that are best applying green sourcing are those that deploy this methodology company-wide. Environmental thinking must pervade the entire enterprise in order to be effective. Engaging internal supply chain stakeholders is necessary to gain acceptance of the green products. In practice this entails designing procurement specifications that target performance levels rather than specific product characteristics, thus giving supply chain managers more flexibility to choose environmentally friendly products as long as they meet performance requirements.

Green sourcing obviously involves engaging suppliers: understanding vendor capabilities and constraints, and developing new opportunities for product offerings through commodity substitutions or novel manufacturing technologies. This means recasting the net and looking at vendors outside the familiar scope; this often involves smaller suppliers that may be more innovative than major suppliers. However, there is a trade-off: an innovative small supplier may lack scalability and economies of scale.

Moving from strategy to implementation, what does green sourcing look like when choosing among different vendors? Compared to traditional sourcing, green sourcing captures a slew of additional data from vendors. In addition to conventional contractual terms (price, quality, quantity, warranty, service, shipment, and insurance), green sourcing requires information on supplier certifications, energy use, waste, recycling, disposal, and a variety of other environmental points of concern. When comparing two goods of identical price and quality, it is easy to choose the good that is more environmentally friendly. More often, however, there may be trade-offs among environmental performance, quality, or price. In this case, how should firms decide?

The two most widely used green procurement tools are **vendor certification** and **eco-scoring**. Vendor certification is straight forward. Vendors are required to meet a certain environmental standard—for example ISO 14001 for a manufacturer or 'USDA Organic' for an agricultural producer. The firm accepts only bids from vendors that meet the required standard. Among the qualified bidders, the firm chooses the lowest-priced bidder. Another form of qualification involves **green covenants**: legally binding contracts through which suppliers enter into an agreement to adhere to certain rules and to subject themselves to regular audits.

Eco-scoring is more demanding as it moves from qualitative criteria to a unified quantitative measure: an eco-score adjusted price. Eco-scoring involves evaluating all products along multiple dimensions of environmental concern and expressing them in dollar equivalents. This is challenging but ultimately the most compelling method. It requires putting explicit prices on environmental attributes and forces an honest assessment of the value of different attributes. In some cases it is straight forward to attach prices (e.g., electricity use, water use), but in other cases it may involve gauging the market value of an environmental attribute (e.g., organic food), or putting a price on specific emissions (e.g., mercury) for which there is no readily available market value. While greening the supply chain is a valuable element of a company's overarching green business strategy, it suffers from the same problem as virtually all the elements of a firm's green business strategy. If green sourcing adds cost, this cost must be recovered in the market place through a green price premium, or else the company loses competitiveness and market share.

A pioneer in green sourcing is Timberland, a manufacturer of shoes. The company has developed an environmental index for footwear that focuses on the carbon intensity of its products. The company has also improved its sourcing of footwear from its Asian suppliers. Conventional adhesives used to glue together shoe parts can be rather toxic. An environmentally friendly alternative is to switch to water-based adhesives, but these tend to be more expensive, primarily because their manufacture still lacks economies of scale. On the other hand, switching to water-based adhesives reduces the cost of handling hazardous materials. Advantageously, these adhesives need only one coat rather than two, which reduces production time. Application of water-based adhesives also requires less equipment cleaning, allowing for longer uninterrupted production runs.

8.4 Green marketing

Developing a product that is sustainable is one thing. Selling that product profitably is quite another. Often the most important challenge is getting the message across to consumers. It is easy to make claims that a product is 'green.' It is difficult to convince a public that has become wary of too many such claims, often with questionable credentials. Where companies succeed in getting consumers to perceive their products as environmentally friendly, they may be able to garner a green price premium: a higher price for their product than comparable products that are not perceived as 'green.' The critical point for success and failure is often the point of purchase. Consumers do not want to spend a lot of time evaluating a product for its sustainability credentials. A simple and trusted signal is needed to convey sustainability credentials effectively and convincingly. Product and company branding is one method. Another method is the use of eco-labels that confirm or certify environmental product characteristics. These methods, and the pitfalls, are explored below. Although green marketing is primarily directed at consumers, figure 8.1 emphasizes the importance of other agents: competitors (who promote their own green products), distributors (whose help is needed to reach consumers), complementors (whose products or services are needed to succeed), and a variety of stakeholders (who scrutinize green claims, certify green claims, regulate conduct, and more). These external forces constrain and inform a firm's green marketing strategy.

8.4.1 Green branding

Whereas a company may initially focus on selling green products that coexist with conventional products in its product portfolio, a much more ambitious step is to develop a green brand with an entirely green product portfolio. This is riskier than trying to balance a conventional 'gray' portfolio with a small-but-growing 'green' portfolio. Green branding is a strategy with an important trade-off: greater rewards for greater risk.

On the upside, green branding can make a company truly stand out as a green leader, allowing it to reap a green price premium in the marketplace. Also, building a strong reputation for environmental stewardship may inoculate the company against the occasional setback—for example if there are environmental problems with a supplier or distributor that may temporarily taint an otherwise 'green' product.

On the downside, a company with a strong green reputation must measure up to its own claims. A green-branded company must at all times assure its customers of its unbending commitment to its core sustainability values. Branding is a long-term strategy. The green strategy must be the core business, not an afterthought or sideline. A charge of 'greenwashing' could be the rapid undoing of the green reputation. This means that a green-branded company must have a crisis management strategy in place to deal with the almost unavoidable slip-ups that even the best-intentioned company may face. Concretely, unintentional violations of trust must have immediate consequences. For example, at one point the Body Shop discovered that one of its suppliers bought materials that were not free of animal testing. The consequence—excluding this supplier—must be swift and must be communicated effectively.

8.4.2 Eco-labelling

Eco-labelling has proliferated widely in the last decade as consumers demand more sustainable products and companies are eager to satisfy this growing consumer demand. Eco-labels—any type of symbol, image or wording describing environmental performance or sustainability attributes that are clearly visible on the packaging of a product—are meant to signal environmental superiority of a product compared to its competitors.

There are three different types of eco-labels. A seal of approval indicates that a product meets a particular product standard. This may include using a particular production technique, participation in resource conservation, sourcing from sustainable sources, and engaging in other environmental activities. A seal of approval is issued by an organization, which may include governments and their departments, environmental non-governmental organization (ENGOs), industry associations, consortia of companies, and even individual firms in what is known as own-brand eco-labels. The reputation of the issuer of the seal of approval matters significantly in this context. On one side is the government-backed or independent third-party seal of approval. On the other side is the own-brand eco-label that may lack in conformity and acceptance.

One variant of the seal of approval is the 'top of class' label. Products in a given category can be ranked by a set of environmental performance criteria, and the eco-label can be awarded to the top-performing products. For example, the international Energy Star logo marks products as the most energy efficient in their class. This eco-label covers major household appliances, heating, cooling, and ventilation equipment, lighting equipment, electronics, office equipment, and windows. Due to technical progress, the market share of Energy-Star-rated products tends to increase over time. Therefore, the specification for the Energy Star rating is revised whenever such products exceed more than 50% of market share.

The Canadian EcoLogo (also known as Environmental Choice) is constructed similarly but covers a much larger set of products. Eco-Logo standards are designed so that only the top 20% of products available on the market can achieve certification. Currently, more than 7,000 products carry this label.

Eco-labels may also come in the form of general claims. Here, a generic green term such as 'organic' or 'biodegradable' is added to the product. It is possible to back up a general claim with a seal of approval, of course. For example, the term 'organic' can be backed up with certification by the US Department of Agriculture (USDA) or other national bodies. General claims do not need to be certified, and there are few if any regulations that limit the use of generic terms such as 'green' or 'environmentally friendly.' As a result, general claims without certification are suspect in the eyes of many consumers.

Figure 8.2 shows the eco-labels for organic products in the United States, Canada, and the European Union. The USDA label is probably more widely recognized in Canada than the Canadian label, which was launched in 2009. Canadian agricultural producers selling to the United States often covet the USDA certification more than the equivalent Canadian certification, although the 2009 *Canada-US Organic Equivalence Arrangement* aims to ease export concerns by allowing Canadian-certified producers to use the US logo, and vice versa. In Europe, many competing national labels were replaced in 2010 with a new EU-wide logo without text.

Fig. 8.2 Organic Eco-labels in the United States, Canada, and the European Union

The third type of eco-label is the graded label which quantifies the environmental performance of a product. Almost by definition, it is the most informative type of eco-label, especially when it compares the performance with other products. A good example is the Canadian Ener-Guide label, which lists a product's estimated annual energy consumption and compares it to the energy performance of similar products. Thus, consumers who purchase a new washing machine can immediately compare the electricity usage (and operating cost) of competing models. Similarly, the EnerGuide label on new cars informs buyers about the typical fuel consumption under city and highway driving conditions.

The underlying problem for eco-labels is the information asymmetry between producers and consumers. Producers know the true environmental performance characteristics of their products. Consumers do not, and must assess each product before they buy it. This imposes information and transaction costs on consumers. Eco-labelling is one way of reducing consumers' information costs by using standardized signals that are easily recognizable. Firms invest in green marketing (from obtaining certification to advertisement) to reduce consumers' information cost, which could otherwise prevent them from buying the environmentally friendly product. One particularly successful strategy to overcome the information asymmetry is to use quality signalling. This means combining superior quality with superior environmental performance. Consumers who are not sure about the environmental performance are reassured that the premium they pay also covers other desirable quality characteristics. Perhaps the success of organic products can be attributed to the consumer perception that such products are also healthier rather than just better for the environment.

Eco-labels pose a number of challenges to consumers. The first problem is one of **recognition**. Once a label has been introduced, it takes considerable time to get recognized widely. Governments often rely on the mass media to popularize a particular eco-label rather than investing in direct marketing campaigns. Consumers need to educate themselves about what a label conveys, and what it does not.

The second problem is **noise**. The number of competing eco-labels has increased to the point where consumers get increasingly confused about which label means what. As standards for eco-labels are uncertain and not always independent of the producers using the eco-label, consumers are increasingly confused about which label is which. Firms that develop own-brand eco-labels actually devalue the eco-labels in that category by adding to consumer confusion.

This leads to the third problem for eco-labels: **trust**. The success of eco-labels depends crucially on the trustworthiness of the entity issuing the eco-label. Government-backed and independent issuers are typically more trusted than issuers backed by industry associations and producer consortia. Where product standards are developed with commercial backing, the trustworthiness of the label can be enhanced by seeking independent audits or endorsements from ENGOs.

Recycling labels are yet another type of consumer-oriented label. With the spread of municipal recycling programs, the universal recycling symbol that designates recyclable material is perhaps the most widely recognized logo of all environment-related symbols (leftmost in figure 8.3, three arrows that form a Möbius loop). Recyclable plastics are identified by a number (plastic identification code) that identifies the group of polymers used in its fabrication. For example, number 1 identifies polyethylene terephthalate (PET), often used in soft drink and water bottles, and number 5 identifies polypropylene (PP), often used in kitchenware and disposable take-away containers. Not all types are recycled. Many municipalities only recycle a subset, often 1, 2, 4, and 5.

Fig. 8.3 Generic and Plastic Recycling Logos

8.4.3 The greenwashing trap

Many companies make claims about the green credentials of their products. In 2007, Terrachoice Environmental Marketing embarked on a survey of 1,753 claims made on 1,018 products in six category-leading big box stores. It found that all but one of the claims were subject to one or more patterns of 'greenwashing.'

> **Greenwashing**: disinformation disseminated by an organization, etc., so as to present an environmentally responsible public image; a public image of environmental responsibility promulgated by or for an organization, etc., but perceived as being unfounded or intentionally misleading.   —*Oxford English Dictionary*

Terrachoice identified the 'six sins of greenwashing,' and this list has been updated and expanded. Box 8.3 provides a contemporary list of ten signs of greenwashing. The Terrachoice report found that the most common greenwashing strategies involved making irrelevant claims, making vague claims, or lacking proof of claims.

Making irrelevant claims involves suggesting that a product is 'green' based on a single environmental attribute (such as recycled content) or an unreasonably narrow set of attributes. Vague claims involve 'green' words that are broad but ill-defined, such as 'sustainable' or even 'eco-friendly.' An environmental claim that lacks proof is one where there is no reliable certification by an independent third party, or where the supporting information is not even accessible to consumers. For example, a product can claim to be energy efficient without any supporting evidence or certification.

What can companies do to avoid the trap of greenwashing? In a world where vague green claims abound, how can green marketing messages about genuine environmental performance succeed? There are five crucial steps:

1. **Significance**. The environmental achievement or performance advertised should be significant in scale and scope. This means that the business should have devoted a significant amount of resources (time, funds, people) to achieving this result, and is more than just superficial. How much did it cost the firm to achieve the advertised result? Did the firm spend more on the environmental achievement or more on advertising it?

2. **Consistency**. The environmental achievement or performance advertised should be consistent with other messages by the company. If an environmental message clashes with other messages, news, or actions by the firm, it is likely to be perceived as inconsistent. An oil

Box 8.3: The Ten Signs of Greenwashing

1. Fluffy language: the use of words or terms with no clear meaning. For example 'eco-friendly,' 'sustainable,' 'energy efficient,' 'ecologically safe,' 'recyclable,' or 'good for mother nature' (without further substantiation) are vague. Imprecise terms amount to obfuscation.

2. Green product versus dirty company: the environmental performance of the product itself (in terms of its use or disposition) may be in conflict with the environmental performance of the production methods (or suppliers). For example, efficient light bulbs can be manufactured in a factory that pollutes the local river.

3. Suggestive pictures: green imagery as a substitute for environmental performance. Marketing messages may involve imagery that suggests, incorrectly, that the product has a positive environmental impact or compares favourably with other products. Among the more ridiculous examples are flowers blooming from exhaust pipes. However, even putting a green colour, flowers, or trees on the packaging may suggest nonexistent green credentials.

4. Irrelevant claims: emphasizing one tiny green attribute when everything else is not green. A product's green credentials ought to involve all environmental aspects and impact areas. Focusing on one positive impact may ignore the substantially larger negative impact in other areas. The claim that a product that is free of mercury is irrelevant if instead the product contains large amounts of cadmium or other harmful substances. Or the claim that a product is free of CFCs is irrelevant because CFCs were banned years ago.

5. Best/better in class (superiority and comparative claims): declaring that a product is slightly greener than the rest, even if the rest are quite bad. The 15 mpg fuel economy of a (regular gas) sport utility vehicle may be better than that of a comparable vehicle with just 12 mpg, but this is still very poor compared to the performance of a similar type of hybrid vehicle with a fuel economy of 30 mpg.

6. Incredulity: some products are inherently environmentally unfriendly, and no amount of branding can change that. Cigarettes can never be 'eco-friendly,' and 'greening' a dangerous product does not make it safer. Turning bitumen from Albertan oil sands into 'ethical oil' does not make it cleaner.

7. Jargon: information that only a scientist could verify or understand. Businesses should not assume that customers have any expert knowledge.

8. Imaginary friends: a 'label' that looks like third-party endorsement, even though the label is an own-brand label that is specifically made up to look like an independent endorsement.

9. Lack of proof: a claim that could be correct but is not substantiated by (scientific) evidence. For example, a detergent could claim that it was not tested on animals, but this assertion is difficult for a consumer to verify unless an independent third party has verified the claim. Lack of proof is a particularly harmful practice when claims are made that involve both environmental and health benefits, and the health benefits are not established in a rigorous scientific study.

10. Lying/fibbing: entirely fabricated claims or data. This is comparatively rare, and may even constitute fraud.

Adapted from Horiuchi et al. (2009). Reprinted by permission of Futerra.

firm will always have a difficult time portraying itself as sustainable. Does the environmental message contradict the firm's image or past actions?

3. **Stakeholder engagement**. Advertising an environmental achievement is more likely to succeed if the process involves soliciting input and feedback from key stakeholders, including ENGOs. Engaging stakeholders creates transparency through participation, and this will help with the credibility of the message.

4. **Verifiability**. An environmental achievement must be verifiable by an independent third party or it is not credible. Obtaining a seal of approval from a recognized certification body enhances the credibility of the advertised message, especially if certification involves one of the more widely recognized eco-labels. To make environmental achievements verifiable, the company must keep suitable records of all relevant data, and must be prepared to share these data with the public.

5. **Simplicity**. Advertising an environmental achievement or environmental performance is useless if the targeted audience is unable to appreciate it. The targeted audience must be able to 'decode' a marketing message about an environmental achievement. This means that the company should avoid scientific jargon and instead opt for information that can be understood in seconds rather than minutes. Visual methods such as a performance point on a sliding scale are quickly understood (e.g., the annual electricity use of a clothes dryer on an Energy Star label).

8.4.4 Green price premium

The above discussions about green marketing strategies point to two roads to financial success. The first road to success runs along the familiar win-win strategy where environmental efficiency goes hand in hand with commercial efficiency, and where improving environmental performance saves cost. The other road to success involves generating environmental attributes that are valued by customers and that induce them to pay a green price premium. Generating green product attributes incurs a cost, and this cost needs to be passed on to the consumer as a higher price.

Passing on higher manufacturing costs for green product attributes is made difficult, however, by two factors. First, competitors may enter the market with lower-quality imitation products that claim the same environmental attributes, but in fact do not possess them. Where it is possible to use vague statements about environmental achievements, or where consumers face difficulties appreciating the relative magnitude of environmental achievements, such 'me-too' competition from pseudo-green competitors can make it difficult to recover the extra cost of a genuine green product attribute. Second, consumers may or may not value the green product attribute sufficiently. Only the green product attributes whose cost does not exceed the consumers' valuation of these attributes can succeed in the marketplace. This raises the question: for which green product attributes are consumers willing to pay?

Manget et al. (2009), a study carried out by the Boston Consulting Group, has looked at the reasons companies struggle with capturing green consumers. The report highlights several issues that help explain how green product attributes and consumer perceptions interact.

Perhaps the most fundamental question is: what do consumers perceive as a green product or green product attribute? The report highlights important differences across attributes as well as across survey respondents in different countries. For example, respondents in Germany were often the most skeptical about any of the offered statements. For example, only 57% of German respondents considered products as green that are made of natural or organic materials, whereas 82% of respondents thought so in China. And whereas 87% of US respondents thought that products that can be recycled or reused are green, only 76% of respondents in Germany agreed with that statement. The results from this survey highlight that perceptions of 'green' differ across countries and cultures. What is considered 'green' in Japan may not be considered green in the United States. Perhaps it also useful to understand what is considered borderline green. Products that were low on the 'green' list were those that: use innovative technology; are not tested on animals; are made under fair-trade conditions; are produced locally; or are handmade. On the other hand, products that were high on the 'green' list were those that: can be recycled or reused; generate less pollution or consume less energy in their production or use; are made of recycled materials; or involve less packaging.

So, when do consumers actually buy green products? Manget et al. (2009) find that about half of consumers already buy green products, and the other half not at all. What keeps people from buying green products? In particular, is it the green price premium? Perhaps surprisingly, the answer is no. Price appears to be less of a barrier than commonly thought. There may be two reasons for that. First, green consumers tend to be more affluent and thus less price sensitive. Second, green consumers also tend to be better informed and to appreciate green attributes more. More than the price barrier, the study found that two other problems keep people from buying green products: product awareness and product choice. Unawareness was by far the largest hurdle in the survey. Consumers were simply not familiar with the availability of greener choices. The second-largest problem was that consumers felt that the available range of green products did not offer sufficient choice. Consumers who are used to choosing among five or six leading brands often face a narrow selection among green alternatives, sometimes just one brand. The lack of variety may thus limit the appeal of green products.

The study also sheds light on the conditions under which consumers are willing to pay a green price premium. Labelling a product as 'green' is not a licence to charge more. Consumers will pay more for green products, but only if the products also offer another quality attribute such as being safer, healthier, tasting better, or helping save money. This link between additional quality attributes and green product attributes is crucial. This quality link is particularly pronounced for ingestible products. Consumers who thought that environmentally responsible fresh meats and seafood, or organic dairy products and baby food, were of higher quality than their non-green counterparts were also the most likely to pay a green price premium.

8.4.5 The credibility gap

How can businesses develop an effective green marketing strategy? Specifically, how can a company establish credibility for its green products? Without credibility, consumers will not be prepared to pay a green price premium for a product. Perhaps because consumers find it more difficult to verify claims about green product attributes than about other quality-related product attributes, green marketing relies strongly on credibility. Why should anyone believe the company's claims? The performance must match the rhetoric, or consumers will lose confidence in the claims, the brand, or the company.

Makower (2009) considers this credibility problem as a virtuous cycle. Credibility is established through product and brand differentiation, demonstrating relevance, and effective messaging. He calls it the CRED strategy. A more fundamental way to look at the credibility gap problem is through an analysis of the factors contributing to credibility and the process through which they are established. Figure 8.4 visualizes the concept.

Credibility is established through two factors: trustworthiness and experience. Trustworthiness is what consumers believe to be true based on prior own knowledge, evaluation of information from the producer and its marketing agents, and third-party information from intermediaries. Experience is what consumers know to be true from using a product or service directly. Put another way, trustworthiness is 'indirect knowledge,' and experience is 'direct knowledge.' In the diagram, these elements constitute the outer ring.

The inner ring in figure 8.4 reveals the two mechanisms through which information about a product is relayed. The first mechanism involves subjective claims, such as those made in a marketing campaign.

Fig. 8.4 Elements of Green Credibility

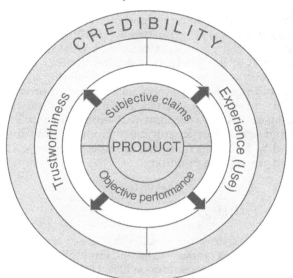

The objective performance of a product speaks for itself once observed. Subjective claims are *ex-ante* information, before a consumer purchases a product. Objective performance is *ex-post* information, after a consumer purchases a product. It is essential that these two agree. One can fool a customer for some time, but not forever. Especially for repeat purchases, a customer will learn about the actual performance and evaluate the quality of a product. In the diagram, 'experience' straddles both 'subjective claims' and 'objective performance.' Consumers will determine agreement or dissonance. On the other side, 'trustworthiness' is informed by 'subjective claims' and 'objective performance' as well. A consumer may take some subjective claims at face value. Some performance characteristics may be difficult or impossible to observe, however. Reduced material or energy use, or elimination of toxic substances in a product, cannot be observed by individual consumers but instead must be established through trust intermediaries: ENGOs, researchers, certification bodies, governments, and journalists that have the resources to carry out detailed analyses.

As pointed out in the previous section, the 'twinning of benefits' is crucial to achieve credibility. Linking environmental benefits to other quality attributes (performance, durability, style, etc.) reinforces credibility. If consumers can observe attributes such as performance and find them credible, this credibility is extended to other claims that are more difficult to observe or verify.

In many instances it is not possible to demonstrate green credentials through product attributes or observable product quality. In this case it is necessary to rely more on effective communication. As Makower (2009) points out, effective communication of environmental messages often involves translating arcane scientific facts into statements that people can understand intuitively. The starting point is often asking what people can easily relate to. For example, 'purchasing 125,000 tonnes of carbon offsets' is not readily understood because few people have an intuitive sense of a tonne of carbon emissions; is that little or much? Effective messaging requires translating this into a frame of reference that is intuitively accessible—for example, the amount of carbon dioxide emissions from an average car. Thus, 'our purchase of 125,000 tonnes of carbon offsets amounts to the same as taking 29,000 cars off the road' is much more understandable. Effective messaging does not imply, however, that companies should spend more on marketing than creating the underlying environmental achievement.

Ultimately, credibility is fragile. It is hard work to establish credibility, and it can be lost quickly if claims do not hold up to scrutiny. Companies that rely on a few products to establish green credentials and then try to benefit from the halo effect—green products shining on products that are not green—will often find that consumers will become skeptical or even cynical. Box 8.4 illustrates the challenges of the oil industry to overcome the credibility gap.

8.5 Stakeholders and the role of ENGOs

Who are the stakeholders that firms need to engage? Figure 8.5 shows a stakeholder hexagon. Consumers determine a company's ability to sell green products and charge a green price premium. In the long term, consumers also build perceptions of a company's environmental performance and its brand. A company also interacts with other companies in two dimensions. Horizontally, it interacts with competing businesses. Vertically, it interacts with suppliers through green sourcing practices, distributors, complementors, and business partners in strategic alliances to develop green standards or to co-develop innovative green technologies. Companies also face investors (and risk assessors such as rating agencies). Securities regulators may require publicly traded companies to prepare statements of their environmental risks and potential liabilities, and investors may prefer investing into companies deemed sustainable and environmentally responsible. Governments and government-mandated regulators set the institutional framework in which companies operate. This goes beyond mere com-

Box 8.4: The Oil Industry's Credibility Gap

The oil industry faces perhaps the largest credibility gap of all industries. Not only is oil contributing to air pollution and climate change, the oil industry also has had to reckon with some of the most notorious industrial disasters such as the oil spill from the Exxon Valdez tanker in 1989 and the explosion of the Deepwater Horizon platform in the Gulf of Mexico in 2010.

Some oil companies have tried to reposition themselves by including renewable energy in their portfolio and following through with rebranding themselves. For example, BP (formerly British Petroleum) launched its 'Beyond Petroleum' strategy in 2000, which among other initiatives involved replacing the old green-yellow shield logo with a new sunburst logo. Unsurprisingly, many observers criticized the company for greenwashing and the new motto became the target of much ridicule.

The tension between spin and substance has also been brought into focus by Levant (2011). He argues that oil from democratic countries is essen-tially more ethical than oil from un-democratic countries. This has been used as a justification for the expansion of the bitumen industry in Alberta. Even though synthetic oil is more energy intensive and more polluting than conventional oil, synthetic oil from western countries should be preferred over oil from undemocratic countries or countries with human rights violations. The notion of 'ethical oil' is an example of a false dichotomy. Support for energy security and human rights on one side does not preclude support for a cleaner environment. It is feasible and desirable to pursue both objectives at the same time. It is possible to develop the Alberta oil sands while significantly reducing their environmental footprint.

Consumers are wary of oil companies that promote a green image when their commitment to sustainability is less than solid. In 2008, Shell was criticized by the UK Advertising Standards Authority, an industry watchdog, for using the term 'sustainability' in conjunction with its $10 billion investment in Alberta's oil sands.

pliance with environmental regulation. Because firms often have deeper knowledge about technological processes and capabilities, they often work closely with regulators to develop new environmental standards and regulations.

Lastly, companies face a diffuse set of stakeholders that can be loosely described as 'idea generators' and 'opinion leaders.' These are public figures that can help promote new environmental solutions, set the agenda for public discourse, provide technological expertise, or otherwise engage people to think about the environment. In the United States, former vice president Al Gore's 2006 documentary *An Inconvenient Truth* educated citizens about climate change. In 2007, Gore was awarded the 2007 Nobel Peace Prize together with the Intergovern-

Fig. 8.5 Corporate Environmental Stakeholders

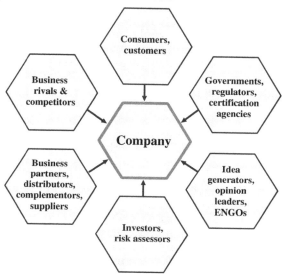

mental Panel on Climate Change (IPCC). In Canada, David Suzuki is a renowned science broadcaster and environmental activist whose work has had a significant impact on environmental awareness. The David Suzuki Foundation, which he co-founded, has become a vocal and influential ENGO in Canada. On the other hand, there also contrarian positions such as Bjørn Lomborg's book *The Skeptical Environmentalist*, which sparked intense public debate, criticism, and counter-criticism. One of the groups that took a vocal position against Lomborg's work (especially on climate change policy) is the Union of Concerned Scientists, a US-based ENGO founded in 1969, whose membership includes numerous prominent scientists and public figures. It is in this arena of competing policy positions that companies have to chart their course.

ENGOs, short for Environmental Non-Government Organizations, play an important stakeholder role. They often articulate concerns shared by the public, and they span a wide range of political preferences. Businesses often look at ENGOs as opponents that try to block proposed projects. This is particularly true in the energy sector, where proposed pipelines, oil and gas extraction projects, or nuclear power plants have long been the target of (sometimes pointed) opposition from environmental groups. Local projects such as airport extensions or new power lines often face stiff opposition from local communities.

ENGOs are often viewed as interest groups that pursue their own limited agenda. In this sense they are no different than any other group

or institution in society that articulates a particular world view or political view. Yet, ENGOs are not merely lobby groups. They also play
an important role as intermediaries that channel public opinion on environmental issues. Where ENGOs are well established and research
focused, they can make highly useful contributions to protecting the environment and sustainable economic development. For example, they
can contribute to environmental impact assessments.

Many ENGOs see their primary role as 'watchdog' over companies'
environmentally harmful behaviour. While this is unwelcome to companies with a poor environmental record, it is helpful for companies
that are environmentally proactive. Where ENGOs spot harmful behaviour, they can engage in a variety of tactics. For example, they can
make harmful behaviour public, and lobby regulators or governments
to take action against offenders. Some ENGOs may choose to use legal instruments such as class-action lawsuits to further their objectives.
In some cases ENGOs have also advocated consumer boycotts or even
tried to impede business operations.

Which firms get targeted by ENGOs? It is not necessarily the firms
that cause the most environmental harm. Lyon and Maxwell (2011) find
some interesting patterns when they investigate which firms get targeted by ENGO action. ENGOs often react very strongly to perceived
falsehoods. Where a company portrays itself as environmentally responsible and engages in acts of corporate social responsibility, it is held
to its high standards. If such a firm fails to meet its own standards and
its actions belie its actions, it often draws the most criticism for its perceived hypocrisy. Worse than the polluter is the polluter who lies about
it. Therefore, ENGOs like to attack greenwashing. They are more likely
to attack a firm with a good environmental reputation if it engages in
hypocrisy rather than a firm with a poor record that is expected to fail.
Paradoxically, firms with a poor environmental record are more eager
for disclosure than firms with a strong environmental record, as the latter have more to lose.

ENGOs are not always adversaries. They can also become allies. Environmental corporate social responsibility that improves the production process produces credence goods,[1] as the 'environmental clean-
liness' of the good is unobservable to the consumer. ENGOs can also
act as trusted parties for certifying products or auditing environmental
reports by businesses. ENGOs can provide a valuable service to busi-

---

[1] A credence good is a good whose benefit (utility) is difficult to measure before and
after consumption. Credence goods are distinguished from experience goods, where the
benefit (utility) can be observed after consumption. Examples of credence goods include
vitamin supplements, medical treatments, and various types of repair services. The seller
of the good knows more about its quality than the buyer, which constitutes an asymmetric
information problem. Because of information asymmetry, suppliers of credence goods
tend to overcharge for low-value goods and undercharge for high-value goods.

Box 8.5: Partnering with ENGOs

Partnering with ENGOs can make good business sense. Unilever, a Dutch-British multinational consumer goods company, provides a good example. Unilever produces a number of different brands of packaged frozen fish (Iglo, Birds Eye, and Findus). A serious decline in the fish stock in the 1990s threatened the supply of fish. In 1996, Unilever worked with the World Wildlife Fund (WWF) to create the Marine Stewardship Council (MSC).

The MSC has been tasked with setting standards for sustainable fishing. Products that are certified by the MSC are allowed to carry the MSC eco-label shown below. Unilever and the WWF had different motives but shared the common vision of protecting the fish stock from overexploitation. The WWF had already pioneered a similar approach with the creation of the Forest Stewardship Council. While Unilever and the WWF provided the initial funding for the MSC, in 1999 the MSC became an independent ENGO. Today, the bulk of the MSC's funding comes from charitable trusts and foundations and government agencies.

Worldwide, more than three thousand seafood products carry the blue MSC eco-label. This amounts to more than 10% of the global catch for consumption. However, the vast majority of fisheries remain uncertified and many remain subject to overfishing.

The Marine Stewardship Council eco-label

The MSC uses two standards, one for sustainable fishing and one for seafood traceability. Fishing is considered sustainable if the fishing activity operates at a level that can continue indefinitely and is not overexploiting the resource, while the fishing operation must maintain the structure, productivity, function, and diversity of the ecosystem on which the fishery depends. The second standard ensures that fish sold with the MSC eco-label indeed comes from a certified sustainable fishery. This requires that all companies in the supply chain—from boat to plate—must have MSC chain of custody certification. Chain of custody certification also helps keep illegally caught fish out of the seafood supply chain.

nesses if endorsements build trust in a brand's green credentials. Thus ENGOs can make powerful allies if they audit corporate social responsibility and back audits and certifications with their own credibility. Box 8.5 provides an example of successful partnering between a business (Unilever) and an ENGO (the World Wildlife Fund), leading to the creation of the Marine Stewardship Council.

8.6 Overcoming nimbyism

The acronym NIMBY stands for 'not in my back yard,' and nimbyism is the opposition by local residents to proposed new industrial developments. Nimbyism is pervasive, and many businesses that propose new developments face strong opposition from various groups. Opposition is rooted in the expectation of negative environmental externalities from the new development such as increases in traffic congestion, air pollution, water pollution, noise pollution, or light pollution. Occasionally, aesthetic arguments such as visual blight are added to the list.

In order to deal with nimbyism, businesses need to understand its different types, or origins. Opposition to proposed developments can be rooted in different assumptions or perceptions about the proposed developments.

First is **economic nimbyism**. This type is rooted in the assumption that a new development adversely affects property values of homeowners. For example, power lines or pipelines crossing behind one's backyard may lower property values. To the extent that such adverse effects can be captured empirically, the business proposing the new development can compensate affected parties. Economic nimbyism is essentially rational and can be dealt with effectively through monetary compensation.

Next is **environmental nimbyism**, which is more challenging to deal with because it is based on expectations of future states of the world. Various types of environmental externalities can be forecast with a degree of accuracy. For example, building a new runway for an existing airport will certainly lead to more noise pollution. On the other hand, many environmental externalities are much more difficult to predict even with sophisticated models. As a result, much environmental nimbyism is based on predictions, some of them accurate, and some of them speculative. The key to success is to take objections seriously, take them back to the scientific evidence, and tackle them point by point. The tone of such responses is vital; they have to be factual and avoid condescension.

Sometimes perceived negative environmental externalities can have adverse psychosomatic effects. For example, the noise generated by wind turbines is perceived by some local residents as an annoyance. Wind turbines are not placed within 500 m of residences, and this lowers their sound level below 40 dB(A). There is no epidemiological evidence that links noise (or infrasound below 20 Hz) from wind turbines to direct health effect.[2] However, some people indeed develop sleep

[2] See *Wind Turbine Health Impact Study: Report of Independent Expert Panel*, prepared for the Massachusetts Department of Environmental Protection and the Massachusetts Department of Health, January 2012. Health Canada launched a Wind Turbine Noise and Health Study in July 2012.

problems. The problem is not really the level of sound, but the perceived annoyance; affected people increasingly focus on just that sound, and this sound cannot be tuned out in their mind. The number of people affected in such a way is small, but often quite vocal. The appropriate way to respond is with science. In this particular instance, the numerous environmental benefits of wind turbines hugely offset limited ill effects on local residents. If needed, regulators can increase the spatial separation of wind turbines from nearby homes.

Third is **ideological nimbyism**. Some people are categorically opposed to 'big business' and their perceived intrusion into local communities. Such nimbyism is built on deep-seated mistrust. The extreme form of that is called by the acronym BANANA: build absolutely nothing anywhere near anyone. Nevertheless, it is not impossible to overcome such nimbyism. It requires trust-building through extensive stakeholder engagement. It is a large step forward if a business is not seen as an 'enemy' but at least as a partner-in-dialogue. Removing hostility from the relationship virtually always requires having representatives present in the community all the time, ready to engage at short notice, and being seen as part of the community. This approach necessarily takes time, and businesses should engage such communities well before proposing new projects.

The last type of nimbyism is **psychological nimbyism**. This type of nimbyism is rooted in a deep-seated, perhaps even irrational, fear of change. It is often diffuse (quite unlike ideological nimbyism). The upheaval brought about by new developments upsets an existing order that the opponent is trying to defend against. New developments are seen as an unwelcome intrusion (or invasion) by an unfriendly party. As fear is the crucial element in this type of opposition, assuaging such fear requires community building. The proposed new development must be seen to fit into existing community, endorsing its values and characteristics. Many projects can be modified to make them fit better into a community by helping them 'blend in' with surrounding architecture, or patterns of use. Some projects can be improved by attaching some value or form of use for local residents. On the other hand, businesses need to realize that some projects will never be able to overcome psychological nimbyism if the proposed projects change the nature or culture of the community profoundly. In that case, the last remaining option is to find a more accommodating community elsewhere.

Overcoming nimbyism is easiest when proposed new developments take place in a 'company town' where the proposing business is a major employer. The best way to compensate communities for negative environmental externalities (after reducing them as much as possible) is by providing employment. Where possible, co-ownership of assets (e.g., wind turbines) can help overcome nimbyism as well.

8.7 Managing adversity

8.7.1 Environmental risk management

Companies engage in risk management to prevent or prepare for a panoply of adverse situations and dampen their financial impact. This involves (1) preventative strategies that lessen the chance of an adverse event, (2) operational strategies that reduce the severity of an adverse event or its impact, and (3) distributing the impact of an adverse event among multiple parties (this is the essence of insurance).

Risks are either idiosyncratic or systemic. A systemic risk is common across economic agents and thus one cannot insure against it. A worldwide recession is an example of a systemic risk. One cannot escape planet Earth (yet). Idiosyncratic risk involves firms facing different types of risk. One can insure against such risk by building a risk portfolio. When it comes to the environment, climate change is a systemic risk, although it may affect different firms in different ways. The risk of environmental spills and leaks is an idiosyncratic risk for firms.

There are different sources of risk. A firm's potential environmental liabilities (e.g., spills and leaks) contribute to a firm's financial risk. Financial risk usually originates with capital markets (e.g., interest rates or exchange rates) or a firm's liquidity and cash flow.

Shifting environmental needs contribute to a firm's strategic risk. This risk originates with innovation and competitors. For example, in 2012 many North American producers of solar panels were confronted with a dual challenge. First, governments in many jurisdictions lowered or phased out incentives for installing solar panels (due to budget austerity). Second, low-cost producers based in China emerged and quickly conquered the international market. Shifting environmental needs are often triggered by external events or shifts in key prices. For example, a rise in the price of gasoline will reduce the demand for gas-guzzling SUVs and increase the demand for efficient gas-electric hybrid cars.

Tighter environmental regulations can pose an operational risk for firms. Such risk may lead to higher compliance costs, or even operational shutdown in the worst case. Operational risk can also emerge in the supply chain. Requirements that products meet a certain environmental standard can lead to costly supply chain realignments if previous suppliers are unable to meet the new specifications.

Risk management involves dealing with uncertainty—but essentially quantifiable uncertainty where one can rely on an empirical distribution. Actuaries table such distributions, and this forms the basis for insurance contracts. An entirely different class of risk is what sometimes labelled the 'unknown unknowns,' the risks for which empirical instruments are unavailable. Natural events, societal disruptions, and even firms' latent but unknown environmental hazards fall into that category. The severity of the effects of climate change is another example of a difficult-to-forecast risk.

8.7.2 Crisis management

Whenever a company is engaged in production activities with substances that could cause environmental harm, there is the risk that accidents can create leaks, spills, or other unintended environmental disasters. Companies need to prepare diligently for a variety of potential environmental emergencies through developing an environmental emergency plan (see section 7.3.2) that deals with the environmental issues. Beyond containing the emergency on a technical level, the company also needs to act swiftly to protect its brand and reputation.

> During a environmental crisis or emergency, companies need to act swiftly and boldly to protect the brand or company reputation from long-term damage. Successful crisis management involves: (a) immediate disclosure and full transparency through effective media communication; (b) taking command of the situation by forming a crisis response team at the highest executive level; (c) comprehensive containment through carrying out a tested and rehearsed environmental emergency plan in cooperation with local authorities; (d) compassion towards the victims of the incident; (e) proactive prevention of recurrence.

The gold standard of handling a crisis situation for a business is the Johnson & Johnson Tylenol tampering case.[3] Tylenol, the Johnson & Johnson brand name for acetaminophen, is one of the most successful over-the-counter products in the United States with over 100 million users and roughly a third of the market share for pain remedies (analgesics). In the fall of 1982, a murderer added cyanide to some Tylenol capsules on store shelves in the Chicago area, killing seven people, including three in one family. At first the company only learned about the incident when journalists called and asked for comment. The company had to react quickly. The company CEO, James Burd, reacted immediately by forming a seven person strategy team that was charged with two tasks: (1) how to protect the people, and (2) how to save the brand. The first step was to alert consumers through the media not to consume any type of Tylenol. Then they halted all advertising. They established a toll-free phone number for answering questions by the public. They

---

[3] The discussion of the Tylenol tampering case is loosely based on the CBC radio broadcast 'Marketing in a Crisis' on the program *Under the Influence* hosted by Terry O'Reilly.

withdrew all Tylenol bottles from shelves in the Chicago area. When more tampered products were discovered elsewhere, they recalled 31 million bottles nationwide at an estimated cost of $100 million. This decision was crucially important to reassure consumers that the company cared and was not willing to risk public safety. Johnson & Johnson had become the victim of a malicious crime, and the cyanide lacing was not the result of an accident at a plant. To reassure consumers, Johnson & Johnson introduced tamper-resistant triple-seal safety packaging. The way the company handled the crisis revealed the company's integrity, which included giving grieving families counselling and financial compensation, even though the company was not at fault. The road to regaining the full trust of consumers took a long time and involved significant marketing effort. The company issued coupons, reduced the price by 25%, and sent 2,500 representatives out to reassure the medical community. Tylenol regained 70% of its pre-incident market share within six months.

The lesson from the Tylenol case has not been widely understood. While Johnson & Johnson was the victim of a crime, companies that are responsible for an environmental incident may feel less inclined to act swiftly and boldly. Many companies struggle with the aftermath of an environmental disaster, fearing that admitting responsibility may trigger large financial liabilities that may even endanger the very existence of the company.

A few years before the Tylenol incident, during the night of December 2-3, 1984, a gas leak occurred at the Union Carbide pesticide plant in Bhopal in the Indian state of Madhya Pradesh. The leaked methyl isocyanate gas spread over the city and caused death and injury. Government estimates put the death toll at 3,787, with many more partial and permanent disabling injuries. The Union Carbide plant was owned by the company's joint venture with the government of India (which owned 49.1%). Medical staff in the area were clearly unprepared for a disaster of this magnitude. Communication between the company and local officials was slow and incomplete, and the exact composition of the leaked gas was not immediately clear. The plant was lacking an action plan to deal with an environmental emergency, and several smaller incidents in previous years were ignored. It has been alleged that many of the plant's safety systems were not functioning properly. Union Carbide denies allegations that the incident was caused by malfunctioning or non-functioning safety equipment, and maintains that the incident was an act of sabotage. Legal proceedings against Union Carbide eventually resulted in an out-of-court settlement of $470 million in 1989. The Bhopal incident illustrates the blame shifting that follows an environmental incident. It also illustrates how the lack of an environmental emergency plan, communicated widely to the local community, and the lack of a crisis management plan for dealing with the strategic fall-out from the crisis, can imperil a company's brand and reputation.

Two major oil spills have tainted the oil business. In March 1989 the oil tanker Exxon Valdez struck a reef in Prince William Sound, Alaska and spilled about a quarter million barrels of oil, roughly, 20% of the ship's load. The accident was caused by a combination of human fatigue and inoperative equipment; the ship's collision avoidance system was switched off and apparently broken. The environmental impact was quite extensive, and the response from Exxon was considered slow and inadequate by the Alaskan communities affected by the crisis. An Alaskan court assessed actual damages worth $287 million and punitive damages of $5 billion. Exxon challenged the punitive damages as excessive. In 2008 the US Supreme Court ruled that even Exxon's actions 'worse than negligent but less than malicious.' The court reduced Exxon's punitive damages to $500 million. Exxon merged with Mobil in 1999 to form ExxonMobil. As a result of the disaster, the US government required all new oil tankers built for use between US ports to be equipped with a full double hull, which is safer than (cheaper) single hull designs. Nevertheless, many single-hull ships continue to be used as oil tankers. The oil spill in 1989 damaged the corporate image of ExxonMobil for over twenty years. Perhaps held back by the aftermath of the oil spill, ExxonMobil did little to rebrand itself as more environmentally conscious, unlike BP.

As mentioned in box 8.4, BP attempted to rebrand itself as 'Beyond Petroleum.' In 2001, the company changed its name to the BP after a merger with Amoco two years earlier. It replaced its well-known 'green shield' logo with with the Helios symbol (a yellow-and-green sunflower pattern) and launched its rebranding under the 'Beyond Petroleum' slogan. In 2007, BP announced that it would spend more than $8 billion over the next ten years researching alternative energy sources. However, a change in corporate leadership seems to have slowed down the company's foray into alternative energy. In April 2010, the offshore drilling rig Deepwater Horizon in the Gulf of Mexico exploded and sank. The lives of eleven workers were lost in the accident. It took several months to cap the underwater well, and during that time just under five million barrels of oil escaped. BP moved quite quickly to create a $20 billion spill response fund; the company had to sell $10 billion in assets to contribute to the fund. In 2012 BP settled to pay $7.8 billion as compensation to parties injured by the oil spill, and prior to this the company had already spent roughly the same amount on clean-up costs and other compensation. Unlike Exxon, BP was much quicker to respond and take responsibility for the accident. While court cases remain pending, the proactive response and willingness to settle claims make it less likely that courts will award large punitive damages. In November 2012, BP also agreed to pay $4.5 billion in fines and other payments to the US government and pleaded guilty to 14 criminal charges. It is likely that BP will obtain closure on the Deepwater Horizon file much sooner than ExxonMobil did on the Exxon Valdez spill, which continued its path through the courts for over two decades.

8.8 Summary

Corporate environmental strategy unfolds in a strategy space that spans technology (innovation) and markets. Innovation drives decisions for production process and products. Process innovation occurs in four environmental areas: energy use, materials use, pollution control, and waste reduction. Product innovation is connected to feedback from markets through product differentiation and turning goods into services (servicizing). Firms can pursue process-oriented strategies to reduce costs while improving environmental performance. Firms also pursue product-oriented strategies to design and market green products whose potentially higher costs are compensated by a green price premium that consumers are willing to pay for desirable environmental performance characteristics. Green sourcing and product stewardship are two important methods through which firms extend their green strategy beyond their own boundaries.

Green marketing emphasizes green product attributes and attempts to overcome a potential credibility gap in several ways. The most prominent green marketing technique is the use of eco-labels, which involve certification of the environmental product attributes by an independent third party. Unfortunately, eco-labelling often suffers from (a) poor recognition of labels, (b) too many competing eco-labels that confuse consumers, or (c) a low level of trust in the certifying body. Green marketing sometimes deteriorates into greenwashing, a practice in which claims about the green merits of a product are dubious or spurious. Successful green marketing enables companies to charge a price premium for their green products or green product attributes. The green price premium is largest for products that combine perceptions of superior environmental performance with perceptions of superior additional quality attributes (e.g., health or safety benefits, durability, energy efficiency).

Businesses whose activities involve the risk of environmental accidents of any kind—in particular, spills and leaks, must prepare for such incidents both technologically and strategically. Technologically, companies need to put the resources into place to deal with the physical and ecological dimensions of the accident. Strategically, companies need to be prepared to deal with accidents swiftly and resolutely. This requires having an environmental emergency plan ready that can be executed promptly and effectively; it also requires sufficient financial reserves to compensate victims appropriately. Acting promptly, accepting responsibility, and responding to the lessons from the accident diligently can help restore confidence and trust; it can also help diminish long-term legal and financial repercussions.

8.9 Study questions and exercises

1. Which three key problems do consumers encounter when confronted with eco-labels on packaging?
2. Discuss the notion of 'servicizing.' Can you find further examples where products can be turned into services?
3. Environmentally friendly goods often depend on complementary goods and services. Find examples of such dependencies and discuss the 'chicken or the egg' problem of how co-dependent technologies can emerge successfully.
4. Consider the 'greenwashing' problem from the consumer's perspective:

   a. What are the signs of greenwashing that consumers can recognize?
   b. How does greenwashing harm the consumer?
   c. Is buying 'greenwashed' products necessarily bad with respect to promoting the development of more green goods?
   d. How can consumers avoid greenwashed products?

5. Consider the 'greenwashing' problem from the firm's perspective:

   a. What are tell-tale signs that firms engage in greenwashing?
   b. How can firms avoid greenwashing?

6. Which type of products are considered 'green' by consumers?
7. What are the key factors that prevent consumers from shopping more for green products?
8. What are the kinds of potential green products that consumers are willing to pay more for?
9. Should ENGOs always be considered adversarial, or can they also become allies?
10. How can firms overcome nimbyism when proposing new projects?
11. In managing the environmental business risk of a firm, which key areas of 'risk' need to be assessed?
12. How should firms respond during an environmental crisis?

Exercises

1. Explore the topic of 'greenwashing' by identifying recent examples. You can find some interesting videos on this topic on YouTube. The Canadian Broadcasting Corporation's *Marketplace* program on television has a number of examples of greenwashing (search for '10 worst household products for greenwashing'). How are consumers duped?
2. Consider the recent controversy over proposed pipeline expansions in the United States and Canada. Analyze and compare the strategies chosen by different pipeline companies to rally support for their projects. How do they deal with the concerns of opponents? How does their historic performance influence the companies' public perception?
3. On a visit to your local supermarket, inspect a section (or entire aisle) of products systematically. Take detergents, for example. How much space is devoted to 'green' products compared to conventional products? Where are the 'green' products placed, and what makes them stand out? Taking note of (unit) prices of all competing offers, what is the price premium for the 'green' products?

Chapter 9
Pollution Abatement Technology

Environmental engineering is primarily concerned with the control of water, soil, air, and noise pollution, and the proper disposal or recycling of wastewater and solid wastes. A key objective is the extraction and separation of hazardous components from benign components (such as clean air and clean water), so that the hazardous components can be dealt with appropriately while the benign components can be returned safely into the environment. From a practical perspetive, environmental engineering helps design and operate pollution control devices. This section provides an overview of some of the methods and technologies that are widely used in industry. Such knowledge is essential for environmental managers as it defines the set of available tools in the toolbox. An environmental manager needs to understand which situation requires which type of intervention and the related trade-offs between environmental benefits and economic costs.

There are several good textbooks on environmental engineering, although most of them will require a sufficient command of physics, chemistry, and engineering principles. Davis and Cornwell (2008) is very accessible because it blends scientific rigour with well-written explanations that even someone without the subject area background will be able to appreciate. This textbook also covers all relevant areas of environmental engineering comprehensively. In addition to Davis and Cornwell (2008), books that were consulted extensively in preparing this chapter included de Nevers (2000) for air pollution, Hammer and Hammer, Jr. (2012) for wastewater treatment, and Woodard & Curran, Inc. (2006) for industrial wastes of all types. A book that blends environmental engineering and pollution prevention is Bishop (2004), which is a strong reminder that avoiding pollution is better than abating pollution. Yet, the reality is that pollution abatement technologies play a major role in our industrial landscape.

9.1 Air pollution

There is a hierarchy of air pollution control strategies. The best option is the elimination of the problem source. Elimination typically involves using a completely different production method or substituting inputs. When elimination is not feasible, modification of the production process or inputs is the next best option. Another possibility is relocation of the production process to a different site with a lesser environmental impact. Obviously, this is not possible where the operation is bound to a particular location (e.g., a mine). In many instances the only remaining option is the selection and application of the appropriate abatement control technology. This section is concerned with identifying these 'end-of-pipe' control strategies.

Air pollution comes in the form of particulate matter (any finely divided liquid or solid substance) and gaseous pollutants such as sulfur oxides, nitrogen oxides, volatile organic compounds, or various types of hydrocarbons. Particulate matter can be emitted as smoke, dust, or some forms of fine mist, and is typically entrained in effluent gas streams or suspended in ambient air. Particulates less than 10 micrometers in diameter (PM_{10}) are regulated as a criteria pollutant in the United Sates and Canada. Respirable PM_{10} can bypass the body's respiratory filters and penetrate deeply into the lungs. Particulate matter is predominantly contained in sulfates, sulfites, nitrates, heavy metals, and polycyclic organic matter.

9.1.1 Dispersion

The ill effects of air pollution are due to its concentration, which often translates into adverse health outcomes through a non-linear dose-response function. It is therefore important to understand how air pollutants disperse, and which design parameters affect the dispersion process. Essentially, pollutants vented into the air will spread over a certain distance with diminishing concentration, and then either fall out or decay through chemical reactions. Some pollutants will spread out widely (some even globally such as carbon dioxide), while others (especially particulate matter) spread out only locally.

There are a variety of dispersion models for point sources of pollution (stacks). A relatively simple approach is known as the Gaussian plume model; it is named that way because the mathematical expression looks a lot like a Gaussian distribution. The key variables in the dispersion process are the flow rate of emission (usually measured in weight per time) Q, the effective stack height H (the sum of the physical stack height plus the plume rise, which in turn is a function of the stack's exit velocity), the wind speed u and the downwind distance x in the direction of the wind (Turner, 1970). The value y is the perpendicular distance to x, and z captures the height above ground. The basic Gaussian plume equation is expressed as

$$c = \frac{Q}{2\pi u \sigma_y \sigma_z} \exp\left[-\left(\frac{y^2}{2\sigma_y^2} + \frac{(z-H)^2}{2\sigma_z^2}\right)\right] \quad , \qquad (9.1)$$

where σ_y and σ_z are the horizontal and vertical dispersion coefficients (measured in metres). The term before the exponential expression is the concentration along the centreline of the plume. The dispersion coefficients increase with downwind distance and drop with wind speed; they are determined empirically and can be looked up in charts that plot $\ln(\sigma_y)$ and $\ln(\sigma_z)$ against $\ln(x)$ for various wind speeds and atmospheric conditions. The emission concentration c is usually expressed in weight per volume (e.g., $\mu g/m^3$).

The plume model generates an important insight into the importance of the stack height H. Increasing the stack height from H to H' has the following effect on emission concentrations at ground level ($z = 0$):

$$\ln \left(\frac{c(H')}{c(H)} \right)\Bigg|_{z=0} = -\frac{(H')^2 - H^2}{2\sigma_z^2} \quad . \tag{9.2}$$

For example, an increase in stack height from 50 m to 80 m can lower emission concentrations at a distance of 5km (which a lookup in the relevant chart reveals $\sigma_z = 200$ m) by $-(80^2 - 50^2)/(2 \cdot 200^2) = -0.0975$, which is a reduction by 9.3%. This effect is even stronger at closer distances. At a distance of 1 km, $\sigma_z = 75$ m, and then the reduction in emission concentrations reaches about 30%.

Keep in mind that the effective stack height H is not just the physical stack height. The effective stack height can also be increased by way of increasing the plume rise, and according to Holland's formula, the plume rise is proportional to the exit velocity and the stack diameter, and the ratio $(T_s - T_a)/T_s$ of the stack gas temperature T_s and ambient temperature T_a. Making a stack wider, increasing the gas velocity, or increasing the gas temperature will all increase the effective stack height, and thus increase dipersion.

9.1.1.1 Air quality

To measure the impact of air pollution dispersion on populations, Environment Canada and Health Canada have jointly developed an air quality health index (AQHI) that provides an estimate of the short-term health risk. This measure was developed from epidemiological health studies and assigns weights to the three major air pollutants that are most strongly associated with health risks. The AQHI is measured on an open-ended scale from 1 to 10, with the possibility that 10 may be exceeded at times. The AQHI is measured in major cities across the country, is published on an hourly basis, and takes into account which pollutants are associated with the largest health risk. Table 9.1 provides a description of the health risks.

Table 9.1 Air Quality Health Index

Health risk	Range	At-risk population	General population
Low	1–3	Enjoy your usual outdoor activities.	Ideal air quality for outdoor activities.
Moderate	4–6	Consider reducing or rescheduling strenuous activities outdoors if you are experiencing symptoms.	No need to modify your usual outdoor activities unless you experience symptoms such as coughing and throat irritation.
High	7–10	Reduce or reschedule strenuous activities outdoors. Children and the elderly should also take it easy.	Consider reducing or rescheduling strenuous activities outdoors if you experience symptoms such as coughing and throat irritation.
Very High	>10	Avoid strenuous activities outdoors. Children and the elderly should also avoid outdoor physical exertion.	Reduce or reschedule strenuous activities outdoors, especially if you experience symptoms such as coughing and throat irritation.

Source: Environment Canada. At-risk population includes people with heart or breathing problems.

The AQHI encompasses three pollutants. The levels of nitrogen dioxide (NO_2), ozone (O_3), and fine particulate matter ($PM_{2.5}$) are concentrations averaged over three consecutive hours and are expressed in parts per billion (ppb) for NO_2 and O_3 and micrograms per cubic meter for $PM_{2.5}$. Equation 9.3 below shows how the measurements of ambient concentrations are converted into a single AQHI:

$$\text{AQHI} = \frac{10000}{10.4}\left[\exp\left[\frac{871\,NO_2}{10^6}\right] + \exp\left[\frac{537\,O_3}{10^6}\right] + \exp\left[\frac{487\,PM_{2.5}}{10^6}\right] - 3\right],$$
(9.3)

Even though the AQHI is continuous, it is normally reported as an integer number through rounding. The three pollutants included in the AQHI each has direct health impacts, but nitrogen dioxide is also a proxy for other air pollutants such as metals and other toxic substances. They are often produced along with the same process that generates nitrogen dioxide. Air pollution is a significant problem, as an estimated 21,000 Canadians will die annually from its effects (Canadian Medical Association, 2008). The level of the AQHI is influenced strongly by weather conditions. Strong winds disperse pollutants. Temperature inversions—when a warmer and less dense air mass moves over a cooler and denser air mass—will trap air pollutants. Clear skies allow more sunlight and UV radiation to increase photochemical reactions that produce ground-level ozone.

Even though average AQHI levels for a location can be deceivingly low, weather conditions and industrial or commercial activities can combine to produce moderate and high AQHI levels at times. For example, during 135 days per year, AQHI levels reach 4 near the Vancouver airport (mostly due to high NO_2), and in Prince George, British Columbia, each year ten days may have a high or very high AQHI (mostly due to particulate matter).

9.1.2 Control strategies

Among the modification options are various operational changes. For example, raw materials can be pre-treated so that they generate fewer emissions during their processing. Where fuel is used, companies can choose to use cleaner alternatives (such as natural gas instead of coal). Proactive plant maintenance can also ensure operational efficiency and prevent accidental leaks and spills. The limited scope of modification strategies often leaves abatement as the primary option. There are a variety of end-of-pipe treatment options that destroy or capture gases through combustion (oxidization), adsorption (accumulation on surface of an adsorbent), absorption (diffusion into an absorbent), and condensation. Selecting pollution control equipment involves consideration of environmental, engineering, and economic factors:

- **Environmental factors**

  - equipment location;
  - available space;
  - ambient conditions;
  - availability of adequate utilities (power, water) and ancillary systems (waste treatment, disposal);
  - maximum allowable emissions (regulation);
  - aesthetic considerations (visible steam or vapor plume);
  - contribution to wastewater and solid waste; and
  - contribution to plant noise level;

- **Engineering factors**

  - contaminant characteristics (physical/chemical properties, concentration, etc.);
  - gas stream characteristics (volume flow rate, temperature, pressures, humidity, composition, viscosity, density, reactivity, combustibility, corrosivity, toxicity, etc.); and
  - design and performance characteristics (efficiency curves);

- **Economic factors**

  - capital cost (equipment, installation, engineering, etc.);
  - operating cost (utilities, fuel, materials, maintenance); and
  - expected equipment lifetime and salvage value.

The starting point of the analysis is often the need to meet regulatory requirements. Emissions have to be limited so that the firm meets the regulatory standard. This consideration puts a value on the efficiency of the pollution abatement. Next is a look at the available engineering options. The characteristics of the pollutant (particle size, type of gas, etc.) determine which processes and abatement devices are technically feasible. Lastly, the available choices are assessed in terms of their cost (purchase cost and operating cost). The total cost over the expected lifetime of the device determines which of the available options is the most cost-effective.

Table 9.2 Separation Process Matrix for Gasesous Output

Recover Pollutant from Gas	Gas	Liquid	Solid
Absorption	X	X	—
Adsorption	X	—	—
Coalesce and settle	—	X	—
Condensation	—	X	—
Cyclones	—	X	X
Electrostatic precipitation	—	X	X
Filtration (baghouses)	—	—	X
Gravity sedimentation	—	X	X
Membrane	X	—	—
Scrubbing	X	X	X

On the engineering side, the starting point for evaluating alternative devices is the phase state of the pollutant that is embedded in the gaseous output: whether it is a solid (particulate matter), a liquid (droplets), or a gas (or vapour). The matrix in table 9.2 shows which separation process can be used for what type of gaseous output: gas, liquid, or solid. Mechanical collectors (cyclones, gravity settling chambers, baghouses, and electrostatic precipitators) are mostly used for solid particles. Some methods are useful only for gases (membranes, adsorption), and some only for liquids (coalesence and settle, condensation). The most versatile device is the scrubber, which can be adapted to capture a wide range of pollutants. Because of its versatility, scrubbers will be discussed in somewhat greater detail.

9.1.3 Abatement devices: Particulates

Figure 9.1 illustrates the decision process for determining suitable abatement devices for particulate matter embedded in a gas stream. First is the question whether the particulates are sticky or wet. If they are, this limits the available choices to wet scrubbers and (less often) wet electrostatic precipitators. Wet scrubbers are also the method of choice for gases or vapours that are combustible or explosive. Mechanical collectors (cyclones in particular) can also be used in some case. Filters, even though very effective, are sometimes not suitable because the filtering material cannot withstand high temperatures or clogs too easily with sticky or wet material.

For dry particles, the two key parameters are particle size and collection efficiency. Coarse particles (larger than 5 μm) can often be captured effectively in mechanical collectors such as cyclones and gravity settling chambers. For particles in an intermediate range (about 0.5-5 μm), wet scrubbers and electrostatic precipitators are quite effective. For very fine particles (less than 0.5 μm), filtration systems offer the best choice. The different abatement devices have different efficiency curves relative to the particle size. The range of particle size diameter in which the different devices can be used overlaps a fair bit, as is shown in figure 9.2. However, their efficiency drops off markedly as particles get smaller, especially in the important micrometer range.

Figure 9.2 shows the typical range of particulate matter from a variety of sources on a logarithmic scale of particle diameter.[1] Solid particles less than 1 μm (the sub-micron range) are considered fume; coarser particles are considered dust. When particles are liquid, the terms mist ($< 10 \mu$m) and spray ($\geq 10 \mu$m) are used. The chart shows that particles from a particular source can capture a wide range. Particles follow a particle size distribution, with relatively coarse particles at one end and relatively fine particles at the other end of the distribution. The chart identifies a number of typical pollutants. Paint pigments and carbon black (used in the tire industry) are mostly in the sub-micron range, whereas cement and coal dust are in the micron range. Metallurgical particles span the widest range. They can exist in the nanometer range but can also be as coarse as 100 μm.

The chart shows that mechanical collectors are most useful for dealing with coarse particles. The simplest device, the gravity settling chamber, works for particles larger than about 75 μm. Cyclones can operate down to particle diameters of 5 μm. For particles down to about 1 μm, wet scrubbers are a useful option. Electrostatic precipitators offer a wider range and can even collect particles in the submicron range (although with decreasing efficiency). For extremely fine particles (fumes), fabric filters are the only option. Filters can be effective in the nanometer range and are rarely used in the micrometre range.

Gravity settlers

One of the simplest pollution control devices for removing particulate matter is the gravity settling chamber, or gravity settler for short.

---

[1] Note: nm, μm, mm, cm denote nanometre, micrometre (also known as micron), millimetre, and centimetre, respectively. See also appendix table A.1.

Fig. 9.1 A Decision Tree for Particulate Matter Abatement

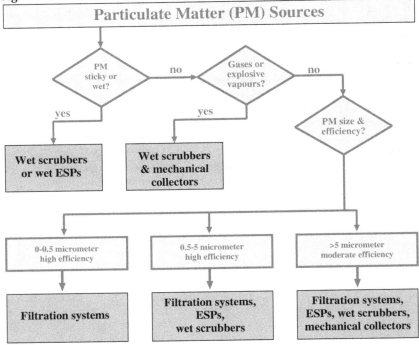

Source: United States Environmental Protection Agency

Fig. 9.2 Characteristics of Particles and Effective Range of Abatement Devices by Particle Diameter

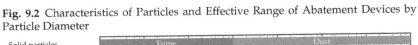

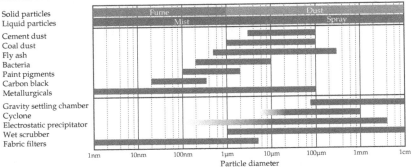

Fig. 9.3 Baghouse

Fig. 9.4 Cyclone

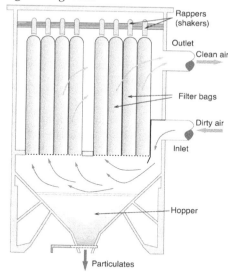

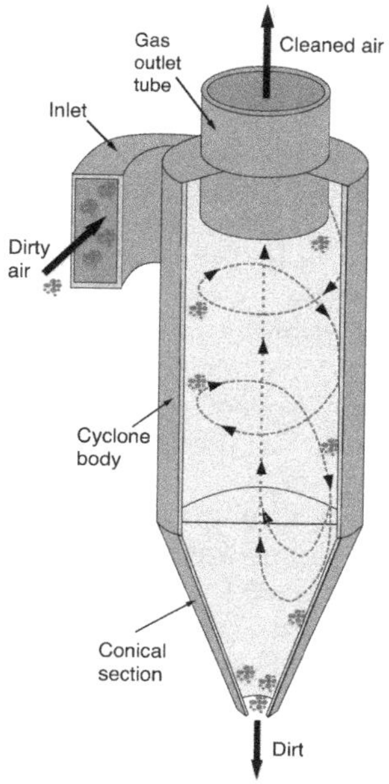

These devices are relatively cheap but offer only moderate collection efficiency. They are used only for very coarse particles (75 μm and larger) and thus are often used as a pre-treatment device in conjunction with more sophisticated devices.

The operational principle of a gravity settling chamber is quite simple. There are three forces acting on particles in the air stream. Gravity pulls particles downward. Drag force is due to air resistance and increases with particle velocity. The buoyant force (the density of the medium in which the particle is immersed) pushes particles upward like a ship on water. These three forces determine a **terminal settling velocity** at which particles of a given diameter drop out; this is known as Stokes' Law and predicts that the terminal settling velocity is proportional to the square of the diameter of the particle. This means that, as particles get smaller, settling velocities get ever smaller. Another way to put this is that the collection efficiency is proportional to the particle diameter squared.

A gravity settler works by slowing down the speed of the air flow sufficiently for the particles to drop out. This is achieved by expanding the cross-sectional flow area for a sufficient length so that the particles can drop out. The settling chamber is often rectangular in design, with a hopper below to collect the particles.

Cyclone

A cyclone, shown in figure 9.4, is used to remove particulate matter from an air stream through vortex separation. Dirty air enters a cylindrical chamber at the top and is forced into a rotation. Centrifugal forces propel the particles against the walls of the cyclone body, from where they drop to the bottom and exit through an opening through a withdrawal valve at the bottom of the conical section. Inside the cyclone body, air circulates in a helical (screw-like) pattern, and the rotational speed increases as the air is forced into the narrower conical section. The higher rotation speed helps separate out smaller particles. The cleaned air moves upward through the centre of the cyclone and escapes through an opening at the top.

Cyclones are often used in sawmills to remove sawdust. They can also be used to remove grease particles from vented air in large kitchen operations. Large diameter (30 cm to 1.8 m) cyclones are used to collect particles ranging in size from 1.5 mm to 15 cm. Small-diameter (8–30 cm) cyclones are usually arranged into arrays known as multicyclones. The small-diameter cyclones create more rapid spinning and can collect much smaller particles than large cyclones; they are effective for particles down to about 5 μm. Cyclones are most effective for coarse particles and where collection efficiency is in the low-to-moderate (50%–90%) range. They can also be used as the pre-cleaning stage in a multi-stage pollution control system.[2]

Electrostatic Precipitators

The basic principle behind an electrostatic precipitator (ESP) is that some particles can be charged electrically and then blown through an electrostatic field that drives them against collection plates. Instead of using gravity or centrifugal forces to overcome the drag force, an ESP uses an electric field force. This has one key advantage. Whereas the difficulty of separating out particles is proportional to the inverse square of the particle diameter for gravity settlers and cyclones, for ESPs this difficulty is directly inversely proportional only to the particle diameter. This allows ESPs to collect much smaller particles than these other devices.

Operationally, as shown in figure 9.5, dirty gas enters the ESP from the side and passes between two dust collection plates that are electrically grounded. Between the plates are rows of high-voltage (40,000

---

[2] Cyclones also became popular in households as bagless vacuum cleaners when the British company Dyson (founded in 1992) launched a related product line. Many other manufacturers now offer cyclone-based vacuum cleaners.

Fig. 9.5 Electrostatic Precipitator

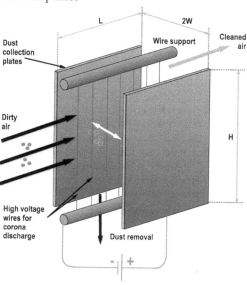

Volts) wires. The distance between wires and plates is typically 10-15cm. This combination of charged wires and grounded plates charges the particles and at the same time drives them against the plates. Once the particles bump into the plates, they lose their electrical charge and tend to stick to the plates or to each other to form what is called a 'cake.' The cleaned gas escapes on the other side of the ESP. The caked-up particles are removed periodically from the ESP through a process known as rapping. Rapping is like giving the ESP a big kick, and this helps loosen the particles from the plate and let them drop out through a hopper at the bottom of the ESP. It is common to string together multiple ESPs (usually 2–8) in an array, so that the cleaned air from the first ESP enters the second ESP for further cleaning, and so on.

The efficiency of an electrostatic precipitator with plate height H, plate length L, and wire-to-plate width W is governed by the Deutsch-Anderson equation

$$\eta = 1 - \exp\left(-\frac{wA}{Q}\right) \tag{9.4}$$

where $A = LH$ [m^2] is the collection area of a plate (see figure 9.5), $Q = HWV$ [m^3/s] is the volumetric flow through the section with average flow velocity V (typically around 1–2 m/s), and w is the particle drift velocity that captures the speed with which particles adhere to the collection walls. Drift velocity is proportional to particle diameter and approximately proportional to the ratio of wire voltage to the wire-to-plate width W. For example, assume that a $1\mu m$ particle has a drift velocity of 0.033 m/s, and that a particular ESP has an A/Q area-flow ratio of 40 s/m. Thus the ESP's efficiency is $\eta = 1 - \exp(-0.033 \cdot 40) = 73.3\%$. It is easy to use this equation in reverse. In order to obtain an efficiency of 99% with a drift velocity of 0.033 m/s, the A/Q ratio needs to be increased from 40 to 140 s/m.

As mentioned earlier, ESPs can have very high efficiencies. However, they can only be used when the gas stream does not contain droplets or other sticky material, and the gas is not combustible. Furthermore, the particles must have sufficient electric resistivity in order to be charged. ESPs are extremely effective for particle sizes above 1 μm and provide a mid-level (25%–75%) efficiency for particles around 0.1–0.5 μm.

The above eplanations are for dry ESPs. However, there are also wet ESPs whose collection plates are wetted to collect particles that are moderately sticky.

Baghouses

Baghouses are arrays of fabric filters that collect particulate matter through a combination of physical processes; see figure 9.3. In addition to the fabric layer itself, the build-up of a dust layer and electrostatic forces can also help collect particles. Fabric filters can be highly effective for collecting particles and typically operate at efficiency levels above 99%. The main challenge is cleaning the filters. Cleaning involves suspending the gas flow and shaking the filters, which are typically cylindrical and hung vertically in a baghouse. Shaking loosens the particles, which fall down into a collection hopper. Sometimes a weak reverse air flow is also used to loosen the particles.

There are two types of filters: surface filters and depth filters. Surface filters are membranes with holes smaller than the diameter of the particles to be captured. (Coffee filters are an example of a surface filter.) Making filters with tiny holes is actually quite difficult. Instead, surface filters rely on the captured dust on the edges of the hole to narrow the diameter of the hole. Thus the captured 'cake' eventually becomes the filter. Surface filters are used in the aforementioned baghouses, and their key advantage is their reusability as the capture-and-shake cycle can be repeated many times before the filters deteriorate. Baghouses typically last 3–5 years.

By comparison, depth filters collect particles through the entire filter body. Randomly oriented fibres collect the particles. Filters of this type are often used when the particles are fine drops of liquid that are not too viscous.[3] In that case the captured fine drops coalesce into larger

---

[3] Viscosity is the term for the stickiness of a fluid. A more viscous fluid moves with greater difficulty than a less viscous fluid.

drops and trickle down into a collector. The disadvantage of depth filters is that they are non-reusable and are thrown out after use. Depth filters are also known as *high-efficiency particulate air* (HEPA) filters. Beyond their industrial use, HEPA filters are also used in high-end vacuum cleaners because they capture allergens, and in biomedical applications because of their ability to capture airborne bacteria and viruses. HEPA filters capture particles greater than 0.3 μm with an efficiency of at least 99.97%.

The type of fabric used to make filters depends in part on the application. While cotton and wool fibres are cheap, they are also flammable at relatively low temperatures (82°C and 93°C, respectively). Glass fibres can be used at significantly higher temperatures up to 260°C, while synthetic fibres have intermediate temperature ranges.

Fabric filters cannot be used when the particulate matter that needs to be collected is wet, corrosive, or very hot. For such pollutants (for example, talc dust, phosphoric acid mist, foundry cupola dust, and open hearth steel furnace fumes), liquid scrubbing is a better alternative.

The fundamental design parameter for a fabric filter is the air-to-cloth ratio, the ratio of volumetric flow of the gas to be cleaned relative to the area of the filter fabric, and has the physical dimension of speed (m/s). A typical capture-and-shake baghouse has an air-to-cloth ratio of 0.010–0.017 m/s. For example, to clean a flow of 10 m³/s one needs about 1,000 m² of filter area. Filters usually have a long cylindrical shape—e.g., 15 cm in diameter and 12 m in length. Each filter thus provides $\pi(0.15\text{m})(12\text{m}) = 5.65\text{m}^2$ of surface. Cleaning 10 m³/s then requires 176.8 filters. A baghouse with twelve rows of fifteen filters will be needed.

Wet scrubbers

Wet scrubbers expose the contaminated air flow to a flow of liquid (spray), and the interaction between the particles and the liquid (known as the reagent) leads to the particles adhering to the liquid. The dirty liquid can then be collected, cleaned and recycled, and reused. The air stream will be free of the particles.

Liquid scrubbing is often used when the particulate matter is wet or sticky, corrosive, or very hot. Wet scrubbing is often used for capturing talc dust, phosphoric acid mist, dust from a foundry's cupola furnace, and fumes from open hearth steel furnaces. Liquid scrubbing is also used for treating sulfur dioxide emissions. Liquid scrubbers can vary in complexity and their capital cost varies accordingly. Operating costs depend significantly on the cost of pumping the scrubber's reagent or the cost of fans for generating a high gas velocity. While water is often used as a reagent, use of specialized reagents such as lime or limestone for the treatment of sulfur dioxide can also add to the cost.

Scrubbers can be distinguished by their flow dynamics as cross-flow, counterflow, and co-flow scrubbers. In crossflow scrubbers, the gas flows perpendicular to the liquid; the gas flows sideways and the liquid downwards. In counterflow scrubbers, the the liquid is moving downward while the gas is moving upward. In a co-flow scrubber, gas and liquid are moving in the same direction, usually both downwards. Because of the different ways of organizing the flow of gas and liquid, scrubbers come in a great many varieties. The most common types include the venturi scrubber (a co-flow scrubber), the spray tower, and the tray scrubber (both counterflow scrubbers). Crossflow scrubbers have few commercial applications.

The venturi scrubber, depicted in figure 9.6, is the most widely used system for capturing particulates. Very high gas velocities can be used in this type of scrubber, while the liquid enters at low velocities. As co-flow scrubbers, they have much higher velocity differentials between liquid and gas than counterflow scrubbers. Venturi scrubbers usually have a rectangular throat that is only about a fifth of the area of the intake. The throat accelerates the gas speed by an equivalent factor, and the conical area below the throat decelerates the gas again. Cleaning liquid is injected from the sides of the scrubber before the gas enters the throat. The operating principle is that the higher speed out of the particles relative to the droplets allows the particles to get captured by the droplets. As the particles are still suspended in the droplets and are moving with the air stream, a cyclone is typically used to separate liquid from gas.

A spray chamber (or spray tower) is a counterflow scrubber and it is used for relatively coarse particles. They are easy to build and are therefore relatively cheap. The gas stream enters near the bottom and rises upwards, while the spray liquid (water or a reactant solution) enters near the top and moves downward. The contaminated liquid is collected at the bottom, while the cleaned gas escapes through an outlet at the top.

While venturi scrubbers (or co-flow scrubbers) are more effective than spray chambers (or more generally, counterflow scrubbers), there is an economic trade-off. Because venturi scrubbers operate at high gas velocities, a fan is needed to generate pressure. The power cost of the fan is often a more important consideration than the purchase cost of the venturi.

Another design is the bubbler—a container filled with a reagent liquid as show in in figure 9.8. The gas is injected with sufficient pressure into the scrubbing liquid at the bottom of the container through many small vents. The gas then bubbles through the scrubbing liquid to the top of the container, where the cleaned gas is collected. A variation of the bubbler is the plate-type bubbler, also known as a the tray tower. Here, the scrubbing liquid is stacked in trays, and the gas rises up through the trays while the scrubbing liquid trickles down. Bubblers

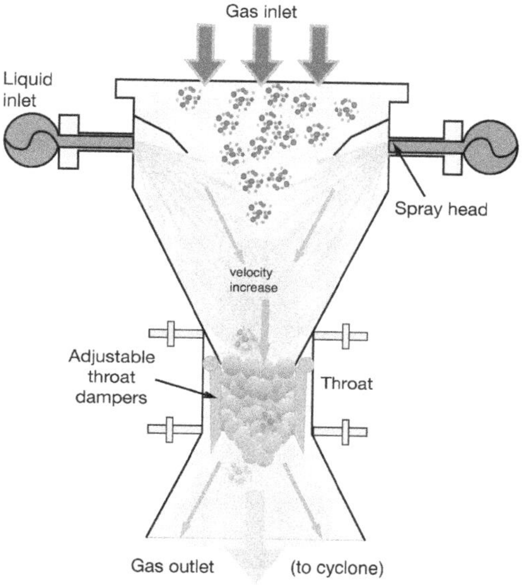

Fig. 9.6 Venturi Scrubber

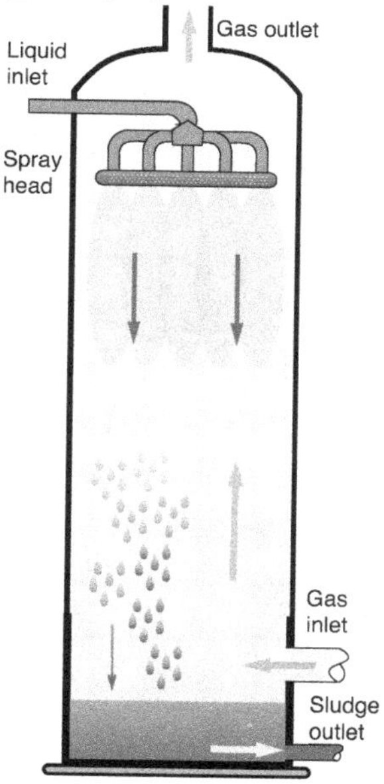

Gas inlet

Liquid inlet

Spray head

velocity increase

Adjustable throat dampers

Throat

Gas outlet   (to cyclone)

Fig. 9.7 Spray Chamber

Gas outlet

Liquid inlet

Spray head

Gas inlet

Sludge outlet

and tray towers are best used when the gas arrives at high pressure, because bubblers and tray towers have a large internal pressure drop (unlike the spray chamber).

The last wet scrubber design is the packed tower, illustrated in figure 9.9. It is similar in design to a spray tower, except that the liquid and gas are forced to interact through a column of solid material. This material allows the gas to rise upwards and the liquid to flow downwards. The liquid coats the surface of the material—which can be gravel or crushed rock as well as specially designed spheres of ceramic or plastic—and provides a much larger contact surface than in the simple spray design. Gas velocities in a packed tower are only about one-tenth of those in a spray chamber, however. Packed towers and spray towers are widely used for removing sulfur dioxide.

Dry scrubbers

A dry scrubber works very similarly to a wet scrubber, although without a cleaning liquid. One type of scrubber, known as a dry sorbent injector, injects an alkaline material such as lime into the gas stream. Chemical reactions turn the pollutant into salts that can be removed with a particulate matter control device. Another type of scrubber,

Fig. 9.8 Bubbler   **Fig. 9.9** Packed Tower

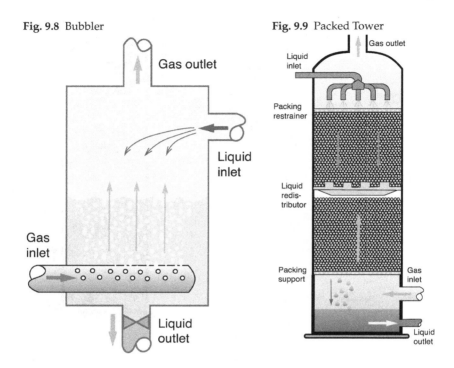

known as a spray dryer adsorber, is a hybrid: the injected material is a fine spray of akaline slurry that reacts with the pollutants to form a salt. The heat of the flue gas evaporates the moisture in the spray, leaving behind only the salts, which can be removed with particulate matter control devices. Dry scrubbers are also used to control mercury emissions.

9.1.4 Abatement devices: Gases

The key idea behind controlling pollutant gases in air is separation and concentration. The contaminant gas can be separated using a number of different techniques, which depend on the particular pollutant gas. Common pollutant gases are sulfur dioxide, nitrogen oxides and volatile organic compounds. The most widely used methods include condensation, adsorption, absorption, and combustion (oxidation). Confusingly, the names of two of these methods—adsorption and absorption—differ only by one letter. That both methods are widely used in scrubbers does not make it any easier to distinguish them. It is therefore useful to provide a concise definition to keep the two apart.

Through the process of adsorption, molecules *attach* to the surface of a solid, the adsorbent. Contrastingly, through the process of absorption, molecules *dissolve* into a liquid, the absorbent.

One of the key differences is that adsorption usually involves a solid adsorbent, whereas absorption usually involves a liquid absorbent.

Absorption

The process of absorption brings the pollutant gas into contact with a cleaning liquid, and the gas dissolves into the cleaning liquid. The contaminated liquid is collected and cleaned, while the cleaned gas escapes. A common absorption system is a spray chamber, depicted in figure 9.7, which was already encountered earlier as a useful device for collecting particulate matter as well. Instead of absorbing particulates, droplets can also act to absorb pollutant gases as long as the gases' solubility in the liquid is sufficiently high. If water is the cleaning solution, this limits the use of spray chambers to sulfur dioxide (SO_2), ammonia (NH_3), and chlorine gas (Cl_2).

Adsorption

During the process of adsorption, a gas is brought into contact with a cleaning solid in a packed tower as shown in figure 9.9. The gas clings to the surface of the adsorbent, while the cleaned air escapes. With adsorption it is typical to operate several towers in sequence, while one or more additional towers are being cleaned. The pollutant gas collected on the adsorbent can be removed through the use of steam, and the steam and pollutant can be separated in a steam condenser. The most common adsorber material is activated carbon (a cousin of charcoal) because of its truly enormous area-to-weight ratio. Activated carbon has a surface area that can reach about $1,000 \text{ m}^2/\text{g}$.

Combustion

The last option is combustion (also known as incineration). Combustion is the process of oxidizing a combustible pollutant. Pollutants that are most often treated through combustion include carbon monoxide and substances that emit unpleasant odours; this in turn includes many volatile organic compounds (VOCs) that contain sulfur. A variety of fumes with particulate matter can be destroyed through combustion, such as those generated by asphalt processing or paint manufacturing.

Burning many air pollutants generates much less harmful pollutants than the original pollutants. For example, carbon monoxide can be oxidized into carbon dioxide; hydrogen sulfide can be combusted into sulfur dioxide; and benzene can be oxidized into carbon dioxide and water. Hydrogen sulfide (H_2S) is very poisonous and emits a strong smell of rotten eggs; both its odour and its toxicity can be destroyed through incineration.

The downside of combustion is the possibility that the combustion process is either incomplete or generates undesirable byproducts. While combustion breaks down most hydrocarbon pollutants such as VOCs into carbon dioxide and water at sufficiently high temperatures, the intermediate products may include harmful substances such as dioxins and furans. Incomplete combustion can produce pollutants that are more harmful than the original pollutant. It is also possible that the incineration of a waste stream mixed with different pollutants can generate undesirable products. For example, due to the high temperatures during incineration, mercury contained in municipal garbage can be turned into dangerous mercury vapours. Incinerators must therefore deploy a number of safety measures that (a) avoid incomplete combustion and (b) avoid contaminants that generate undesirable byproducts.

To avoid incomplete combustion, it is often necessary to provide additional fuel to achieve sufficiently high temperatures. For example, ultra-toxic substances such as dioxins and furans can be destroyed through oxidization, but it requires temperatures above 850°C. Incinerators that handle chemical waste achieve temperatures in excess of 1,200°C, sometimes in so-called afterburners.

The heat from the combustion process can be recovered and used. For large-scale municipal and industrial incinerators, this process is known as waste-to-energy. For small and medium-sized industrial applications, a particularly economical device is the regenerative thermal oxidizer (RTO). RTOs use a type of heat exchange to capture the heat from the incinerator's exhaust gas to preheat the incoming contaminated gas. The heat-exchanging material is often a honeycomb ceramic, and natural gas is used as additional fuel for the burner. The combustion chamber is also well insulated, often with ceramic fibre, to prevent heat loss. To ensure efficient destruction of the pollutant, the gas that is passing through must have enough residence time in the combustion chamber (between 0.5 and 2 seconds), and sufficient oxygen must be supplied.

Figure 9.10 illustrates the basic design of an RTO. An RTO is operated in forward and backward mode. Once a ceramic bed is fully heated on the outgoing side, the airflow is reversed every few minutes so that the hot ceramic bed is now preheating the incoming gas. Because of this reversal process (facilitated by the airflow switching valves), it is customary to operate at least two units in parallel. RTOs are widely used to treat VOCs and organic particulate matter, as well as carbon monoxide.

Fig. 9.10 Regenerative Thermal Oxidizer

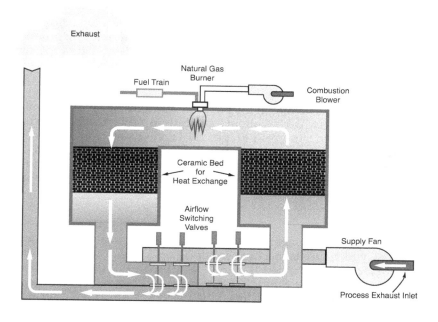

They are used in numerous industries, including coal mining, car manufacturing, paint shops, foundries, and the chemical industry. RTOs are most suitable for applications with low VOC concentrations but high flow rates. Heating the polluted gas to 850°C–900°C facilitates oxidation, and this process removes 98%–99.5% of pollutants. The back-and-forth switching of the air flow reduces the efficiency of pollutant capture, but this can be mitigated by operating multiple RTOs.

RTOs are very efficient and cost-effective, but there are some types of waste gases that cannot be processed with them. If waste gas contains droplets or particulate matter, the heat exchange media can get clogged, which leads to a drop in pressure and a loss in efficiency. If the waste gas is too combustible, the combustion process may generate too much heat. Flammability of a substance is captured by the lower explosive limit (LEL), which identifies the leanest (smallest) concentration of combustible gas in the air that sustains a flame on its own. RTOs are deemed safe if they operate below 25% LEL. For richer gas mixtures, other types of oxidation are used.

9.1.5 Specific pollutants

Nitrogen oxides

Nitrogen oxides (NO and NO_2) are generated through combustion processes, typically the burning of fuel at high temperatures. The production of nitrogen oxides can therefore be controlled by regulating the peak temperature of the combustion process. Various methods are used to achieve this, including the use of alternative fuels, lean combustion, and steam injection.

Treating nitrogen oxides at the post-combustion stage requires some form of reduction (with or without a catalyst) in which the nitrogen oxides are reduced to harmless nitrogen (N_2) and water (H_2O). The most effective process is known as selective catalytic reduction (SCR) and involves injecting ammonia (NH_3) together with the nitrogen oxides into a vanadium-titanium (or similar) catalyst bed. SCR can achieve about 70%–90% abatement efficiency.

Sulfur dioxide

Sulfur dioxide (SO_2) is generated primarily by burning fuel—particularly coal, which can have a high sulfur content. The process of removing sulfur dioxide is called **flue gas desulfurization** (FGD), and can be accomplished either through regenerative and non-regenerative systems. In non-regenerative systems, the reagent is discarded after use, while in regenerative systems, the reagent is recovered and reused. The latter are less common.

Non-regenerative FGD, based either on limestone ($CaCO_3$) or lime ($Ca(OH)_2$), converts the sulfur dioxide into carbon dioxide, water, and calcium sulfite ($CaSO_3$), which in turn is often oxidized into calcium sulfate ($CaSO_4$). The latter is marketable as gypsum, which can be used as a fertilizer in agriculture or as plaster in the construction industry. The interaction between the sulfur dioxide and the reagent occurs in a wet scrubber (venturi scrubber, packed tower, tray tower, or spray tower).

It is also possible to use a dry system. Dry alkaline particles are injected into the gas stream (and sometimes directly into the furnace) where they react with the sulfur dioxide. The dry particles can then get collected in a particulate matter collector such as an electrostatic precipitator. While a dry system avoids dealing with wet slurry and generates a waste product that is easier to deal with, the amount of collected solids is usually significantly larger, as is the use of reagent. Dry systems therefore tend to be more expensive than wet systems.

Volatile organic compounds

A class of pollutants known as **volatile organic compounds** encompasses a large number of different organic chemicals that exist in vapour form at normal temperatures (about 20°C). Substances with a high vapour pressure at normal temperatures are characterized as *volatile*. A vapour is a substance in its gas phase at a temperature where it can co-exist with its liquid phase or solid phase. The boiling point of a substance is the temperature at which its vapour pressure equals the surrounding atmospheric pressure. At lower temperatures, the vapour pressure determines the evaporation rate. VOCs evaporate (from liquid form to gas form) or sublimate (from solid form to gas form) at low temperatures even though their boiling points are between about 50°C and 250°C.

VOCs are emitted by a wide array of products (such as conventional paints) and in many industrial processes. Large contributions to total VOC emissions are from solvent use (e.g., paint thinners) and fuel use. VOCs include propane, kerosene, gasoline, and diesel. Many VOCs are also intermediate inputs in the production of plastics. VOC solvents are widely used because they evaporate quickly in the air, after which they leave behind the solids (paint, ink) they were meant to help deposit. The rate of evaporation can be controlled by the vapour pressure of the solvent.

In some cases it is possible to avoid the generation of VOCs by switching to VOC-free alternatives. For example, for indoor paints it is possible to switch from oil-based paints (with VOCs as solvents) to VOC-free water-based paints. However, for many paint applications, such as auto body finishes, VOCs are still needed.

The vapours from a liquid VOC (e.g., gasoline) can escape from a tank during its refilling as the vapours are pushed out of the tank by the entering liquid; this is known as *displacement loss*. Escaping vapours can be captured through a vapour return line into the container from which the liquid is pumped.

VOCs can be controlled through a process of concentration and recovery. Most VOCs can be removed from an air or gas stream by cooling the stream to a sufficiently low temperature at which the VOC condenses into its liquid form. The liquid can then be captured and recovered. An alternative to condensation is either adsorption or absorption. When concentration and recovery are not feasible or economical, incineration is the fourth option.

As described earlier, for adsorption it is customary to use a series of packed towers as shown in figure 9.9. When an adsorbent bed is saturated, one can switch to another packed tower while the saturated adsorbent bed is cleaned. Regeneration of an adsorbent bed involves passing steam through it, and the mixture of VOC and steam can be condensed and separated. A typical configuration includes three towers on a cycle: two towers in sequence (the first highly saturated, the second lightly saturated), and the third undergoing regeneration.

Absorption involves wet scrubbing. It is useful when the VOC is soluble in the liquid. Absorption involves feeding gas into the spray chamber, bubbler, or tray tower, where it encounters the absorbent material. Smaller absorption units may also use a packed tower design. Which material can be used as an absorbent depends on the physical properties of the VOC. Many VOCs are not soluble in water, and thus various chemicals need to be used. The absorbent cleaning liquid is passed into a stripper that is operated either at a higher temperature or a lower pressure than the scrubber. This temperature or pressure differential reverses the absorption process: the VOC is separated from the cleaning liquid, escapes as a gas, and can be captured through condensation.

The last option is combustion (or incineration)—that is oxidizing the VOC into water and carbon dioxide. This is not always straight forward if the VOC is insufficiently combustible or is not contained in air in sufficiently high concentrations. To achieve complete combustion at sufficiently high temperatures, additional (and expensive) fuel is needed. A typical solution involves the regenerative thermal oxidizer (RTO), shown in figure 9.10.

Carbon dioxide

Only in recent years has carbon dioxide been added to the list of pollutant gases. Until carbon dioxide was identified as the key culprit causing climate change, it was considered harmless. As a result, techniques for carbon capture and storage (CCS)—also referred to as carbon sequestration—remain novel and, to date, very expensive. As the name suggests, there are two technological challenges: capture (concentrating CO_2) and storage.

The method proposed for long-term storage is geo-sequestration: injecting carbon dioxide into underground geological formations. Currently, carbon dioxide is sometimes injected into declining oil fields to improve oil recovery (known as enhanced oil recovery). Other suitable geological formations include unmineable coal seams, and possibly saline formations (aquifers). The risk of storage is leakage, which depends on the quality of the geological formation. Leakage is expected to be relatively minor, although prudent risk management is needed where large quantities of carbon dioxide are involved.[4]

The key problem is developing an economical way of capturing carbon dioxide. Flue gas from a conventional coal plant contains about 20% carbon dioxide, and the remainder is mostly nitrogen mixed with sulfur dioxide, nitrogen oxides, and particulate matter. Separating the

---

[4] On August 21, 1986, Lake Nyos in Cameroon emitted a carbon dioxide cloud that suffocated an estimated 1,700 people. A magma pocket beneath the lake leaked carbon dioxide into the water, and it is believed that a landslide triggered the release of the carbon dioxide cloud. Finding geologically stable formations for carbon sequestration is important if accidental releases of carbon dioxide are to be avoided.

carbon dioxide from this mix is challenging. There are three broad approaches to carbon capture: pre-combustion capture, post-combustion capture, and the oxyfuel method.

Pre-combustion carbon capture involves gasification of coal (or other carbon fuel) into a gas consisting of carbon monoxide and hydrogen, with the carbon monoxide getting reformed into carbon dioxide that can be captured, and the hydrogen being burned with air to generate heat. Pre-combustion technology is not yet as mature as the alternative methods. It is also only useful for new plants that pursue integrated coal gasification combined cycle (IGCC). The hydrogen produced in an IGCC plant is combusted in a gas turbine, and the waste heat from that gas turbine powers a secondary steam turbine.

Post-combustion carbon capture streams flue gas through an adsorbent or absorbent in a scrubber. There is still a fair bit of experimentation with the chemistry. One popular process involves an aqueous mono-ethanolamine solution as the absorber. The problem is that these methods involve energy and costly absorbers that need to be replenished continuously. A relatively novel method involves the use of gas separation membranes, and hybrid membrane-absorbent systems.

A rather different approach has been taken at the coal-burning Schwarze Pumpe 30 MW power plant in eastern Germany. Since 2008, this power plant has operated a novel carbon capture and storage technique knowns as the oxyfuel method. Conventionally, coal is burned in air, which supplies the oxygen along with air's other gases, primarily nitrogen and a small share of argon. The oxyfuel method burns coal with (nearly) pure oxygen, and this results in only two end products: carbon dioxide and steam. These two can be separated easily. The problem with this approach is the source of pure oxygen, which has to be extracted from air. This requires energy, which reduces the overall efficiency of the power plant.

CCS systems need to prove their cost-effectiveness before becoming viable alternatives to other forms of reducing carbon dioxide emissions. The cost of current CCS technology varies greatly depending on the type of fuel and type of technology, and estimates are in the range of $100–$150 per tonne of CO_2 avoided. However, these costs may be brought down by more than 50% over time as technologies improve and become more standardized. At current prices, CSS is among the most expensive options to reduce carbon dioxide emissions. Nevertheless, the first plants are coming online in North America. In Canada, the SaskPower Boundary Dam Unit 3 coal plant is being retrofitted for post-combustion CC&S at a cost of C$1.35bn, while in the United States, a 582MW IGCC plant is being built in Kemper County, Mississippi, at a cost of $2.4bn.

Mercury

Mercury is released into the air through a number of industrial processes such as metal smelting, iron and steel production, and cement
production. The largest source of mercury is the burning of coal in
power plants and the burning of waste in incinerators. Deposited into
water or onto land, microbes can transform mercury into highly toxic
methylmercury. Through bioaccumulation in the food chain (in particular in some types of fish and shellfish), mercury poses a risk to humans.
Most at risk are unborn babies and young children whose developing
nervous system may be harmed.

A significant part of mercury emissions can be removed through particulate matter control. Nevertheless, this process is not sufficiently efficient in many instances. For municipal incinerators, it has become com-
monplace to inject activated carbon into the gas flow exiting the boiler.
The mercury particles attach to the activated carbon particles and can
then be removed more efficiently with conventional particulate matter
control devices; most effective is a combination of spray dryer adsorber
and fabric filters.

Ground-level ozone

Ground-level (tropospheric) ozone (O_3) is a major source of air pollution. As discussed earlier, it is included as one of the three major pollutants in Canada's air quality health index. Ozone is not emitted directly from industrial sources, but forms through photochemical reactions between nitrogen oxides and volatile organic compounds. These
pollutants originate with many industrial facilities and utilities, as well
as exhaust from motor vehicles. Adverse health effects are associated
even with low levels of ozone. Children are particularly at risk because
their lungs are still developing and they often spend more time outdoors than adults. Ozone can also increase asthma symptoms.

Because of the weather dependence of ozone formation, appropriate
interventions at high and very high levels may include short-term reductions of key industrial emitters combined with appeals to the public
to reduce motor vehicle traffic. In the long term, preventing the formation of ground-level ozone requires controlling nitrogen oxide and VOC
emissions.

9.2 Water pollution

9.2.1 Types and sources

Rivers, lakes, and oceans receive polluted water—effluent—from industry, households, and agriculture. Many industrial processes requires

large amounts of water, and this water may get contaminated with a variety of chemicals. Effluent from households is contaminated with a variety of organic matter. Lastly, water quality also suffers from fertilizer runoff from agriculture. Most of the nitrogen—in the form of nitrate (NO_3), nitrite (NO_2), and ammonia (NH_4)—and phosphorus released into the environment comes from these three sources. Phosphorus and nitrogen are both important nutrients in fresh water, but high concentrations can lead to eutrophication—when an excess of nutrients overstimulates plant growth and decreases oxygen supplies, making the water unusable. In Canada, eutrophication is a serious water quality issue for the Prairie provinces, southern Ontario, and Quebec.

In southern Ontario, nitrogen and phosphorus released from agriculture, municipal sewage, and industrial wastewater have hurt the water quality of the Great Lakes and other inland waters. In the Prairies, nutrient concentrations are naturally high in rivers, and intensive agriculture magnifies the problem. British Columbia has fewer eutrophication problems than other provinces, but its heavily populated lower Fraser River Basin has high levels of agricultural runoff and municipal waste-water discharge. An estimated 90% of the province's municipal wastewater is discharged into the lower Fraser River or its tributaries. The city of Victoria discharges its municipal wastewater directly into the ocean on the principle that oceanic dilution is sufficient.

Municipal waste-water discharges are one of the largest sources of pollution in Canadian waters. Municipal wastewater effluents produced by households, businesses, and industry generates over four-fifths of the water effluents reported to the *National Pollutant Release Inventory*. Municipal wastewater is composed of sanitary sewage and stormwater, and can contain grit, debris, suspended solids, disease-causing pathogens, decaying organic wastes, nutrients, and about 200 identified chemicals. What is contained in wastewater is perhaps best illustrated with actual data from treatment facilities. Table 9.3 shows the most important pollutants that are discharged by three major treatment plants in the Greater Vancouver area. Their capacity is measured in million litres per day (MLD). By weight, ammonia and phosphorus are by far the largest contributors. Important are also various discharges of metallic substances, such as copper, manganese, and zinc.

There are four broad categories of water pollution problems. First is low dissolved oxygen. A lack of oxygen in water kills fish as well as aquatic microorganisms, and can in turn change the ecosystem of rivers and lakes. A lack of oxygen can also contribute to nuisance odours. This lack of oxygen in water is captured by the biochemical oxygen demand (BOD, in milligrams per litre).[5]

---

[5] BOD usually carries a subscript that indicates the number of days for incubating the sample. The standard measure, BOD_5, uses a five-day time window.

Table 9.3 Municipal Wastewater Plants in Metro Vancouver, 2009

	Treatment plant	Lulu	Iona	Annacis
	Treatment type	Secondary	Primary	Secondary
Substance	Average capacity	80 MLD	587 MLD	497 MLD
Ammonia		831 tonnes	3,039 tonnes	5,188 tonnes
Hydrogen sulfide		—	12 tonnes	9.6 tonnes
Nitrate ion (pH≥6.0)		—	76 tonnes	3.7 tonnes
Phosphorus		93 tonnes	639 tonnes	564 tonnes
Various PAHs		—	56.3 kg	9.837 kg
Nonylphenol (for detergents)		—	—	6 tonnes
Arsenic (and its compounds)		—	291 kg	126 kg
Cadmium (and its compounds)		7.0 kg	265 kg	46 kg
Copper (and its compounds)		—	18 tonnes	8.1 tonnes
Lead (and its compounds)		20 kg	1,056 kg	182 kg
Manganese (and its compounds)		—	10 tonnes	12 tonnes
Mercury (and its compounds)		0.932 kg	17 kg	5.1 kg
Zinc (and its compounds)		—	16 tonnes	6.9 tonnes

Source: *National Pollutant Release Inventory*. MLD: million litres per day. Lulu Island and Iona are located in Richmond, BC; Annacis Island is located in Delta, BC.

The second problem is the presence of a high level of bacteria in wastewater. Bacteria transmit disease and their presence in water often contributes to gastrointestinal disturbances and eye irritation. To determine the presence of bacteria, a wastewater sample is tested first for the presence of total coliform bacteria, and tested again for the presence of fecal coliform (E. coli) bacteria, which live in the intestines of humans and warm-blooded animals. Any coliform presence in drinking water is cause for immediate action.

A further problem is eutrophication, which is related to the presence of excessive amounts of nutrients in the water. Nitrogen (nitrates, ammonia) and phosphorus in water, which are often contributed by run-off of fertilizer from agricultural land, promote the excessive growth of phytoplankton—a broad category of microorganisms that also includes algae. Algal bloom can be spotted easily as a green discolouration of water. Oceanic algal bloom can even be spotted by specialized satellites from space.

The fourth and last problem is the presence of toxic chemicals in the water. Some of these toxic chemicals are carcinogens. Others can increase the mortality or impair the reproductive ability of fish or other aquatic life. In extreme cases, the presence of toxic chemicals can lead to the closure of river or lake fisheries. The presence of such substances is often related to industrial activities in the metallurgical industry, as well as to the run-off of pesticides and herbicides from agricultural land.

9.2.1.1 Water Quality

There are a number of standardized tests to determine the quality of water. The first measure is the amount of dissolved oxygen. It is becoming increasingly common to use an oxygen meter with a probe rather than relying on field test kits with a reagent (known as the Winkler method). Oxygen meters are more expensive, but the results are quicker. Measuring biochemical oxygen demand (BOD_5) is slightly more involved and requires taking two samples five days apart. The first sample is analyzed immediately for its dissolved oxygen. The second sample is stored in darkness for five days at 20°C, and measured for dissolved oxygen at the end of the period. The BOD is the difference between the two samples. Heavily polluted water may be diluted by a given factor so that the dissolved oxygen level is not zero after the five-day period.

BOD and dissolved oxygen are easily confused. BOD captures the lack of oxygen. This means that higher numbers of BOD indicate higher pollution loads. Pristine rivers have a BOD_5 below 1 mg/l; moderately polluted rivers have a BOD_5 below 10 mg/l; and heavily polluted rivers have a BOD_5 below 100 mg/l. Untreated sewage is in the range of 200-500 mg/l. BOD also has a cousin known as chemical oxygen demand (COD), which captures the amount of organic matter in water indirectly. COD tests are typically quicker to perform (two hours rather than five days). COD measures oxygen demand from all chemical sources in water, not just biochemical. Therefore, COD measurements are typically higher than BOD measurements. BOD is the preferred measure for evaluating the efficiency of wastewater treatment plants. COD is the preferred measure when dealing with industrial wastewater that is rich in substances that are toxic to microbes.

The second measure is the pH level, which captures the acidity or alkalinity of a water body. If water becomes too acidic or too alkaline, aquatic organisms may be harmed directly (by impairing respiration, growth, and development of fish) or indirectly (by increasing the bioavailability of certain metals such as aluminum and nickel).

It is also common to test the conductivity of water—its ability to carry an electric current, which depends on the presence of ions. Increases in conductivity can lead to changes that reduce biodiversity and alter the composition of organisms in water. Water's salinity is also relatively easy to measure.

Modern multi-parameter metering equipment can capture pH, conductivity, salinity, dissolved oxygen, and total dissolved solids at the same time. Measuring nitrogen and phosphorus content is somewhat more difficult and involves chemical tests.

In Canada, a water quality index (WQI) introduced by the Canadian Council of Ministers of the Environment (CCME) is used to capture the numerous contributing variables in a convenient way that is easy to interpret. The index incorporates **scope** (the number of variables not meeting water quality objectives), **frequency** (the number of times the water quality objectives are not met), and **amplitude** (the amount by which the objectives are not met). The index is rescaled to a 0-100 range where zero indicates worst quality and 100 indicates best quality. The range is divided into five descriptive categories: excellent (95-100); good (80-94); fair (65-79); marginal (45-64); and poor (0-44). Mathematically,

$$\text{WQI} = 199 - 0.57737\sqrt{(F_1)^2 + (F_2)^2 + (F_3)^2} \quad , \qquad (9.5)$$

where F_1 is the percentage of variables that do not meet their objectives at least once during the evaluation period, F_2 is the percentage of failed tests, and F_3 is a three-step measure that captures the deviation of measurements from their objectives.

Calculating F_3 starts with defining measures for the deviation from the objective. These deviations are known as **excursions**. They are calculated differently depending on whether the objective is a minimum standard ('must not fall below') or a maximum standard ('must not exceed'). When the measured value must not exceed the objective, the test value is divided by the objective value. Alternatively, when the measured value must not fall below the objective, the objective value is divided by the test value. In both cases, the result is greater than 1, and therefore 1 is subtracted from the ratio. These excursions are added up and divided by the number of tests. This normalized sum of excursions (nse) is transformed into $F_3 = 100 \cdot \text{nee}/(\text{nse} + 1)$. The WQI is useful because different measurement stations do not always capture the same variables. The CCME objectives for dissolved oxygen are 5 mg/l and 6.5-9.0 for the pH level range.

9.2.2 Wastewater treatment

Wastewater from industrial sources is most often pre-treated and then fed into the municipal wastewater system. Some very large industrial installations maintain their own treatment plants. When industrial wastewater is pre-treated, the purpose is to make the effluent compatible with the treatment potential of the municipal wastewater system. This means that the pollutants contained in the wastewater must not pose a fire or explosion hazard, must not corrode the treatment plant, must not obstruct the flow, must not be too oxygen-demanding (as this could interfere with the biological treatment stage), must not be too hot, and must not release vapours or fumes that could pose a hazard to the workers at a treatment plant.

Table 9.4 identifies the treatment stages for wastewater. It is customary to consider the treatment stages additively: primary treatment in-

Table 9.4 Wastewater Treatment Stages

Process	Description
Pre-treatment	
Screening (bar rack)	Removal of large objects
Grit chamber	Settling of sand, silt, broken glass, pebbles, either through horizontal flow, aeration, or vortex.
Equalization basin	Regulates and equalizes the water flow through the WWTP during the daily cycle
Primary (Mechanical or Chemical-Mechanical)	
Settling tank	Settle sludge on bottom, skim scum floating on top
Parallel plate separator	Removal of fat, oil, and grease through skimmer and removal of grit through sedimentation
Secondary (Biological)	
Trickling filter	Wastewater sprayed on trickle filter; aeration provided by space between filter material
Aerated lagoon	Basin with oxygen injection through mechanical aerators floating on top or bubble diffusers below
Rotating biological contactor	Rotating discs that are partially submerged provide aeration to the biofilm on the discs' surface
Membrane bioreactor	Combination of micro-filtration and a suspended growth bioreactor
Tertiary (Advanced)	
Filtration	Removal of suspended matter or toxins through sand or activated carbon filters
Lagooning	Settlement and additional biological treatment in large ponds (lagoons)
Nutrient Removal	Removal of nitrogen through biological oxidation, and removal of phosphorus through bacteria
Disinfection	Chlorination; UV radiation; ozone
Odour control	Containment vessels; wet scrubbing; carbon adsorption

Table 9.5 Municipal Wastewater Treatment in Canada

Treatment Level	1989	1999	2009
No treatment	14%	3%	3%
Primary treatment	14%	14%	16%
Secondary treatment	29%	28%	53%
Tertiary treatment	23%	30%	15%
Septic system or haulage	29%	26%	13%

Source: Environment Canada: *Municipal Wastewater Treatment Indicator*, April 2012, based on data from the *Municipal Water and Wastewater Survey*. The percentages indicate the population covered by the indicated treatment level.

Box 9.1: Victoria's Secret

Victoria, the capital city of British Columbia, together with the surrounding municipalities that form the Capital Region District (CRD), has a badly kept secret: over 100 million litres per day (MLD) of its wastewater flows into the ocean without treatment. Two underwater outfall pipes transport the sewage about a kilometre each into the ocean water of the Strait of Juan de Fuca, where the effluent is discharged 60 metres below the surface. Coarse objects are filtered out through 6 mm screens.

Victoria is the only major city on the North American west coast without sewage treatment. On the east coast, the city of Halifax used to discharge its sewage into the ocean until it opened a new wastewater treatment plant in 2008. In 1992, several communities in the CRD conducted a referendum on the matter; a large majority opted for the status quo, albeit only a quarter of the electorate turned out to vote. A public opinion poll in 2004 found only 16% supporting the status quo, about a third favouring enhanced source control, and just under a quarter each favouring either primary treatment or secondary wastewater treatment.

In 2012, the CRD decided to build a wastewater treatment plant (WWTP) and a biosolids energy centre. The wastewater treatment plant will provide secondary treatment for wastewater. The biosolids energy centre will treat the organic solid waste from the wastewater treatment plant. Biogas generated through the process will be used to generate electricity. A signif-

icant contribution to the funding of the project is provided by the federal government, and the biogas facility will be developed through a public-private partnership. Nevertheless, the new treatment facility is expected to lead to significant increases in local property taxes.

There has been a vigorous debate about the merits of the proposed WWTP. On one side of the debate, the project has been described as an unnecessary boondoggle. Critics point to the fact that the effluent plume from the sewage pipes is dispersed and diluted widely and rarely surfaces near the coast. These critics suggest that the current method of dilution is economical and environmentally sufficient, and that the load of toxins in the wastewater could be reduced through improved source control measures.

On the other side of the debate, a 2006 report by a panel of scientists from the Society of Environmental Toxicology and Chemistry concluded that there are both health and environmental concerns, and that 'relying on dilution and natural dispersion processes of the Strait of Juan de Fuca is not a long-term answer to wastewater disposal, especially considering the growth predicted for the CRD and adjacent communities that also contribute contaminant loads to the Strait and to Puget Sound.' The provincial government sided with this view and in 2006 ordered the CRD to end the current ocean-dumping practice and start the process of building a WWTP.

cludes pre-treatment, secondary treatment includes primary treatment, and tertiary treatment includes secondary treatment.

In Canada, advanced forms of wastewater treatment have been progressing only slowly, as indicated in table 9.5. By 2009, the wastewater of a fifth of the population was treated not at all or only through primary treatment. A small fraction of the population (13%) operates its own septic systems.

Table 9.6 reveals the prevailing methods in wastewater facilities surveyed in a 2001 study of wastewater treatment plants (WWTPs). This survey included a fair number of municipal facilities with no wastewater treatment, but most of them are in small communities. Only 30 of the surveyed facilities were servicing communities with a population of more than 100,000. The most popular secondary treatment options include primary sedimentation, chemical flocculation, activated sludge, and extended aeration. Trickling filters and rotating biological contactors are used less frequently. Many smaller WWTPs use lagoons, whereas many of the larger WWTPs use disinfection through chlorine or ultraviolet light.

Table 9.6 Wastewater Treatment Methods in Canada

Treatment method (2001)	Total	Share
No treatment	263	35.6%
Primary sedimentation	179	24.3%
Chemical flocculation	104	14.1%
Activated sludge	186	25.2%
Oxidation ditch	19	2.6%
Rotating biological contactor	31	4.2%
Trickling filter	18	2.4%
Extended aeration	119	16.1%
Sequencing batch reactor	18	2.4%
Nitrogen removal	39	5.3%
Phosphorus removal	191	25.9%
Lagoons	410	55.6%
Disinfection	280	37.9%
All facilities	738	100%

Source: *National Survey of Wastewater Treatment Plants*, prepared by the Canadian Water and Wastewater Association for Environment Canada, June 2001.

The effectiveness of wastewater treatment is often measured by the WWTP's ability to reduce the biochemical oxygen demand. The log ratio of BOD_5 of the influent to the effluent is a widely used measure.

The story in box 9.1 illustrates that the appropriate level of wastewater treatment is complex. There are economic and ecological trade-offs.

Industrial wastewater

Industrial wastewater poses unique challenges due to the specific nature of industrial processes. At refineries and chemical and petrochemical plants, an oil-water separator is often used to collect oil and suspended solids from the effluent. An example of such a pre-cleaning device is the parallel plate separator shown in figure 9.11. In a parallel plate separator, tilted parallel plates provide surface area for the oil particles suspended in the water to coalesce into oil globules that will rise to the surface of the water, where they are skimmed off by an oil skimmer. Gravity helps settle grit to the bottom of the device, where the sludge is removed periodically by a scraper.

Fig. 9.11 Parallel Plate Separator

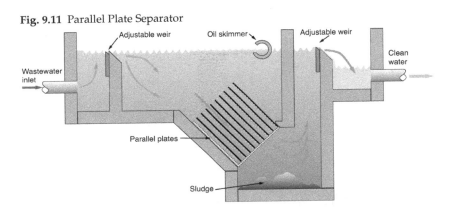

In some industries, acids and alkalis in water need to be neutralized by adding a neutralizing agent. This process results in significant amounts of solid residue. In the iron and steel industry, hydrocholoric acid and sulfuric acid are used to remove rust.

Mines and quarries produce wastewater contaminated with byproducts from the extraction process, such as unwanted metals and materials. For example, during its operation between 1948 and 2004, the Giant Mine near Yellowknife in Canada's Northwest Territories produced some 237,000 tonnes of highly toxic arsenic trioxide dust during the extraction of gold. The dust is water soluble. Originally, the dust was stored underground where it was believed to be safe because of a protecting layer of permafrost above. However, melting permafrost has allowed water to seep into the underground storage, and the contaminated water is now collected in tailing ponds and is treated later. Generally, arsenic contamination can be treated through membrane filtration with reverse osmosis as well as adsorption through alumina.

In the oil and gas extraction industry, flowback from fracking and other processes is rich in salts. Boiler water from power plants may also have high concentrations of salt. The resulting brine (salts dissolved in water) needs to be treated through suitable processes such as membrane filtration with reverse osmosis. Where industrial wastewater is rich in nutrients (phosphorus and nitrogen), pre-treatment is necessary to avoid excessive algae formation.

Primary treatment

The primary stage is intended to remove pollutants that can be separated easily through sedimentation (gravity settlement) or through flotation (surface skimming). Many older WWTPs only perform primary treatment, which removes about two-thirds of the suspended solids and about one-third of the biochemical oxygen demand.

One of the most common designs in wastewater treatment is the circular settling tank, shown in figure 9.12. Such tanks are 20–60 metres in diameter. The main purpose of the settling tank is to separate solids that drift to the slightly conical bottom of the tank, where they are scraped with a slowly rotating blade into a drainage system. The rotating sludge scraper defines the circular design of the settling tank. Attached to the scraper is a skimmer, which pushes scum (foamy material) that is floating on the top into a separate drainage system. The settled water runs over weirs on the side into a circular drainage channel from where it is piped to further treatment stages. Baffles just in front of the effluent weir prevent scum floating on the surface from flowing out into the effluent line. Circular settling tanks can be used at several stages in the wastewater treatment process. They can be used for treating raw wastewater as well as for clarification of treated wastewater.

Particles suspended in water can also be removed through a process known as chemical flocculation—the addition of a chemical (known as a flocculating agent, flocking agent, clarifying agent, or coagulant) that help the particulates stick together (flocculate) and form a floc. The process is also described as 'coagulation and flocculation,' where the term coagulation describes the rapid mixing-in of the flocculating agent in mixing tanks. Common flocculating agents are based on aluminum (e.g., aluminum sulfate, aluminum chloride) or iron (ferric sulfate, ferrous sulfate, ferric chloride). As a physical-chemical treatment process, it is usually considered part of primary treatment. A disadvantage of this treatment method is the cost of the flocculating agent and the treatment of the sludge. On the other hand, this method provides a trade-off between low (fixed) capital cost and high (variable) operating costs. Chemical flocculation is therefore often used where raising capital is more difficult for individual municipalities—for example, in developing countries. This method can also be used as an emergency measure (during seasonal high volume or storm events), and it is also frequently used as a precursor stage before biological treatment.

Fig. 9.12 Circular Settling Tank with Sludge Scraper and Scum Skimmer

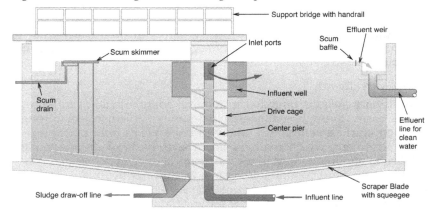

Secondary treatment

Secondary treatment involves biological rather than mechanical processes. It is intended to remove most of the organic matter that is suspended in the wastewater. Organic matter includes human waste, food waste, and soaps and detergents. In secondary treatment, microbes (bacteria) digest the organic matter. This requires a supply of oxygen and nutrients. Oxygen is supplied through aeration (circulating air through water), while the nutrients are supplied by the organic matter in the wastewater.

Secondary treatment falls into either of two categories: attached growth or suspended growth. Attached growth systems include trickling filters (depicted in figures 9.13) and rotating biological contactors. In such a system, the bacteria grow on a contact surface while the wastewater is flowing over it. In a trickling filter, the contact surface is provided by a bed of rocks, gravel, ceramic, or plastic. A layer of microbial slime develops on the contact surface. As the layer of slime (also called a biofilm) grows too thick, it breaks off in small pieces and washes out with the treated water. Therefore, the treated water passes through a clarifier (or settling tank) that removes the microbial sludge.

Suspended growth systems make use of activated sludge, where recycled sludge that contains microbes is mixed with wastewater in an aeration tank, where air is blown into the mixture (known as mixed liquor) from the bottom of the tank through a system of diffusers. The wastewater has a typical residence time of six to eight hours. The solids that are generated by the microbial digestion are separated through a clarifier (or settling tank). Much of the sludge is returned to the aeration tank, while the remainder is transported to sludge treatment. The

Fig. 9.13 Trickling Filter

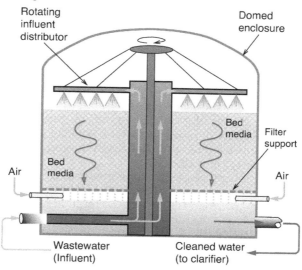

removal of sludge offsets the growth of the microbes, and this equilibrium is what gives 'suspended growth' its name. A variation of the suspended growth system is the membrane bioreactor (MBR), which combines the use of activated sludge with membrane microfiltration and ultrafiltration. MBRs are more common in smaller-scale WWTPs. A relatively inexpensive activated sludge system is the oxidation ditch, which uses long retention times for the water (1–2 days) and the sludge (12–20 days). These systems require large areas of land and are often arranged in round or oval form. One or more rotating aerators supply oxygen.

Another type of secondary treatment system involves rotating biological contactors (RBCs), which consist of a stack of narrowly spaced vertical discs that are typically about 3.0–3.5 m in diameter. These discs, which are made with lightweight plastic, are submerged up to about 40%–50% in a reservoir of wastewater and rotate slowly (about 1–2 revolutions per minute) on a horizontal shaft. The rotation provides for an aerobic environment as the water is brought into contact with air while the disc surface is not submerged in water. Microbes attach to the surface of the discs and build a biofilm that reaches about 1–4 mm in thickness. As the microbes in the biofilm pass through the reservoir of water, they also pick up other organic matter and deliver oxygen into the wastewater. Excess biofilm is stripped off in the reservoir and removed with a conveyor-like sludge scoop. RBCs are particularly useful for treating wastewater with a high biochemical oxygen demand and are often used to treat industrial wastewater from petrochemical facilities. RBCs are more effective than trickling filters, but tend to be more costly due to their more complex mechanical design. Their operation also requires careful monitoring as excessive biofilm growth can overload the system. RBCs do not work well when water temperatures drop below about 13°C.

Suspended growth systems are somewhat cheaper to build and operate, but attached growth systems are more efficient in removing organic matter. Conventional suspended growth systems often suffer from poor settling of sludge during the clarification stage, but this can be improved by the use of membrane bioreactors. Attached growth systems tend to be better able to cope with changes in the concentration of biological matter in the wastewater.

The decomposition processes that are involved in secondary treatment depend on the particular catabolism (biochemical processes for breaking down organic material) of the bacteria: aerobic, anoxic, and anaerobic decomposition. Aerobic decomposition requires the presence of oxygen. For relatively dilute wastewater with low biochemical oxygen demand (BOD_5) less than 500 mg/l, aerobic decomposition is fast and efficient. At concentrations above 1,000 mg/l, it is difficult to supply sufficient oxygen to make the process work. The denitrification of wastewater (removal of nitrogen) can be achieved with anoxic decomposition, where the microbes use nitrate ions instead of molecular oxygen. Lastly, microbes can also use sulfate ions when neither nitrate ions nor molecular oxygen are present in the water. This leads to anaerobic decomposition, which generates carbon dioxide, methane, and water as the major end products, along with ammonia, hydrogen sulfide, and other sulfur compounds (known as thiols or mercaptans). Anaerobic decomposition is used to stabilize sludge (see below) that was produced with aerobic and anoxic decomposition.

Tertiary treatment

Secondary treatment of wastewater can remove over 85% of the BOD and suspended solids, but it is not able to remove nitrogen, phosphorus, and heavy metals. Tertiary (advanced) treatment encompasses a variety of possible treatments that improve water quality by removing these other pollutants, as well as further reducing the BOD.

Removing phosphorus (phosphates) from wastewater prevents eutrophication. The conventional method of removing phosphorus involves chemical precipitation using iron salts (e.g., ferrous or ferric chloride), aluminum salts (e.g., aluminum sulfate or aluminum chloride), or lime. This process requires a reaction basin and a settling tank for removing the resulting precipitate. There are also alternatives using biological (anaerobic decomposition) processes that involve phosphorus-accumulating microbes.

The level of nitrogen (nitrates) in wastewater can be reduced either chemically (through ammonia stripping) or biologically (through a two-stage nitrification-denitrification process). Nitrogen in the form of ammonia can be removed chemically through the use of lime or caustic, typically in a packed tower. A chemical reaction turns the ammonia into gaseous form. Chemical treatment works well for low ammonia concentrations (10–100 mg/l). For higher concentrations, biological nitrogen removal is preferred.

Biological nitrogen removal involves a two-stage process. In the first stage, wastewater is treated with activated sludge, which converts nitrates into nitrite ions. In the second stage, anoxic denitrification reduces the nitrite ions into molecular nitrogen (the major constituent of air), carbon dioxide, and water. The microbes involved in the process requires aerobic conditions. Nitrification requires a long residence time.

Tertiary treatment can also involve additional filtration using either sand filters or activated carbon filters. The latter are used primarily to extract residual toxins and heavy metals. Another technique is lagooning, large settling ponds populated with aquatic plants (often tall grass-like reeds).

In some cases, WWTPs use disinfection methods to control the number of microorganisms in the water. Common disinfection methods include chlorination, ultraviolet (UV) radiation, and ozone. Chlorination is cheapest but may generate harmful byproducts. Ozone treatment remains relatively expensive. UV irradiation has become the method of choice at newer WWTPs.

Fig. 9.14 Effective Range of Water Filtration Methods

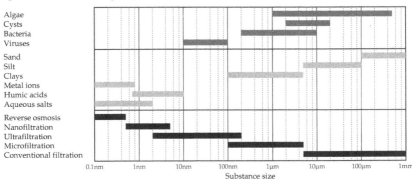

Membrane filtration is mostly considered a form of tertiary treatment, although it may also be used in a membrane bioreactor (discussed above). Figure 9.14 indicates the effective range of membrane filtration methods with respect to a variety of biological and chemical substances. The terms nanofiltration, ultrafiltration, and microfiltration indicate the size of the particles they target, and also relate to the pore size of membranes used for filtration. Filtration using membranes involves pumping contaminated water at high pressure against a semi-permeable membrane, allowing clean water to permeate through the membrane, and carrying the contaminants away with the remaining flow. The pressure needed increases with declining pore size. Microfilters that operate in the micrometer size require pressures in the 50–100 kPa range.[6] Nanofiltration, which operates in the nanometer scale, requires pressures of 500–1000 kPa. Reverse osmosis processes—commonly used to separate salts from brine, brackish water, or seawater—require pressures in the 1,000–8,000 kPa range. The difference between nanofiltration and reverse osmosis is that filtration is primarily based on straining (size exclusion) and only needs modest pressure to accelerate the process, whereas reverse osmosis is based on diffusion and high pressure is needed to reverse diffusion. The energy needed to power high-pressure pumps makes filtration and reverse osmosis very expensive. Additional costs arise from replacing the filters at regular intervals.

Sludge treatment

The process of cleaning wastewater creates residue known as sludge that must be further treated. The quantities of sludge are significant. Processing one cubic meter (1,000 litres) of wastewater generates about 2.5–3.5 litres of sludge during primary treatment and 15–20 litres of sludge during secondary treatment. Primary sludge comes from the bottom of the primary clarifier and contains about 3%–8% solids, most of which is organic matter. Sludge from secondary treatment consists of micro-organisms (about 90%) and some solids. The composition of tertiary sludge depends on the treatment process. Sludge from nitrogen removal is biological in nature, but sludge from phosphorus removal is chemical in nature and more difficult to process.

Sludge is treated in several steps. First, the sludge is thickened through gravity settlement or rotation, removing as much water as possible. The sludge can also be treated with chemicals or heat in order to remove water. Yet other forms of removing water include subjecting the sludge to a vacuum (to speed up evaporation) or to pressure (to squeeze out the moisture). Second, a digestion (biochemical oxidation) process converts the organic solids into an inert form that can be used

---

[6] Standard atmospheric pressure is 101.325 kilopascals (kPa).

Box 9.2: Shell, Dawson Creek, and Water Recycling

Oil giant Shell operates the Ground-birch complex of five natural gas processing plants and over 250 wells and gas-gathering systems near the city of Dawson Creek in British Columbia's remote Peace River region, about 1,200 km northeast of Vancouver. Dawson Creek is the centre of BC's natural gas and oil industry. The Groundbirch operation also makes use of hydraulic fracturing, or fracking for short. Fracking is a method of gas extraction that requires pumping pressurized water laced with proppants and other chemical additives into rock formations in order to open up pathways through which the gas can escape. Fracking requires large amounts of water. (More about fracking appears in section 10.2.)

The water use of fracking is a significant practical concern as surface water in northeastern British Columbia can be scarce, especially during the occasional drought conditions in this region. Shell competed with the city of Dawson Creek for fresh water from the Peace River. To resolve this conflict, Shell and the city teamed up to build an effluent treatment facility that obviated the need for river water at the Groundbirch complex. Shell invested more than $11 million and the city contributed another $1.5 million. The treated water is near potable quality. The new treatment plant has a capacity of 4,000 cubic metres per day (equivalent to providing water to about 12,000 households). Shell will not be drawing water from its 5,000 cubic metres a day licence on the Peace River. The new facility even leaves surplus water for the city.

Shell has also built a 48 km pipeline for transporting water from the treatment plant to the Groundbirch complex, where the water will be stored in ponds and later mixed with recycled production water. The pipeline eliminates the need for trucking water to the site, which helps reduce traffic, noise, and dust. Shell estimates that the pipeline eliminates 3 million km a year in truck trips.

This collaborative venture between Shell and a local community is a good example of how companies and communities can work together successfully. It helps the community, which previously did not have a wastewater treatment plant and released minimally treated effluent into a local river. It also helps industry by providing a more reliable source of water.

as a soil conditioner. One such form is composting, where the sludge is mixed with sawdust, straw, or wood chips. Another method is anaerobic decomposition in large tanks, where the sludge is held for about two weeks. This process also produces biogas, which can be used to generate electricity. Lastly, sludge can be incinerated and the resulting ash can be removed to landfills.

Industry and municipalities

The needs of industry and households for clean water can result in conflict as water resources are scarce in many places. Wastewater treatment can help recycle water and ease the strain on water supplies. Untreated wastewater from industry and households can put tremendous strain on rivers and lakes, and the problem may be aggravated by multiple users along a river. Downstream quality deteriorates increasingly. It is possible for industry and households to accommodate each other. Box 9.2 provides an example where the city of Dawson Creek in northern British Columbia and the oil company Shell found it useful to co-develop a wastewater treatment system.

9.3 Solid waste management

The term solid waste refers to a wide array of items that are discarded by households and industry—commonly referred to as garbage, rubbish, trash, and refuse. As with gaseous and liquid pollutants, a key objective of solid waste management is separation: splitting the waste stream into a reusable or recyclable materials on one side and materials for terminal disposition on the other side. The better solid waste is separated, the more effectively it can be treated.

Solid waste can be broadly classified into **organic waste** that decomposes over time and **inorganic waste** that does not decompose over time. It is also useful to distinguish solid waste that is combustible (e.g., paper) and solid waste that is not combustible at typical incineration temperatures of 700°C–1100°C (e.g., glass, ashes, metals).

Landfilling has been the conventional approach to solid waste management. However, as sites for landfills have become scarcer (and often face strong nimbyism) and costlier (due to the need for environmental protection), other alternatives have gained in importance. From a perspective of resource conservation, the amount of solid waste should be minimized through a hierarchy of waste management approaches that may be described as the four Rs: reduce, reuse, recycle, and recover.

The concept of integrated solid waste management defines a hierarchy of practices known as the four Rs: **reduce** material use so that less waste is generated, **reuse** materials by repurposing them wherever possible, **recycle** materials by separating waste streams and returning waste products into new raw materials, and lastly **recover** energy from combustion of waste or from landfill gas.

The purpose of the four Rs is to minimize the amount of solid waste for terminal disposal. First, avoid generating solid waste. Second, if waste cannot be avoided, turn it into something useful through reusing items, recycling constituent materials, or using waste to extract energy.

Conventional disposal of waste involves landfilling and combustion in incinerators. However, simple landfilling and incineration can be improved significantly by recovering energy. The combustion of waste can be used to recover energy from heat; this process is known as waste-to-energy (WTE). Similarly, landfill gas (mostly methane) can be recovered and combusted to produce energy; this process is known as landfill-gas-to-energy (LFGTE).

Households and industry need to cooperate to help reduce and recycle waste. Industry needs to design products with product stewardship in mind. Products need to be designed so that they can be disassembled rather than discarded. On the other hand, households must enable themselves to separate waste streams and facilitate recycling of materials. Influencing consumer and household behaviour, as well as promoting product stewardship among producers, requires a system of appropriate incentives and regulations. As box 9.3 illustrates with the battle over plastic or paper bags in grocery stores, making the right choices is not always easy.

Recycling of materials is driven by a combination of government-mandated programs, such as blue boxes and blue bins for recyclables or refundable container deposits, and the evolution of markets for recycled materials. Source separation of recyclable materials (glass, paper, plastics, metals) is very effective and keeps the overall cost of recycling low because it economizes on sorting. Source separation is also known as dual stream or multi-stream recycling because it involves two or more separate collection systems. Shifting the burden of sorting to households makes it less attractive for households to participate in recycling activities. Over the last number of years, capital-intensive single-stream sorting has emerged as an alternative. Recyclables are mixed together, and different types of machinery extract different components. For example, disc screens separate containers from mixed paper; aluminum is extracted with an eddy current separator (a powerful metal detector that induces an eddy current in aluminum); steel is extracted with drum magnets or other types of conventional magnets; plastics are separated through an optical sorting machine that analyzes the composition of the plastics with near-infrared technology and colour sensors; and light materials can be separated from heavy materials using air streams. What remains a challenge to recycling is the multitude of multi-component waste materials that would need to be disassembled before separation. The cost of disassembly can be significant for products that were not designed with a cradle-to-cradle approach.

Box 9.3: Plastic Bag or Paper Bag?

You reach the end of the checkout line and the cashier asks: plastic or paper? Which is the correct answer if you want to be environmentally responsible? It isn't plastic. It isn't paper either. The correct answer is: 'neither.' There has been a long-standing controversy over grocery bags. Environmental pros and cons are associated with both types of bags.

Paper bags tend to get recycled because paper recycling rates are generally very high in most communities. Paper bags are fully biodegradable. On the other hand, producing paper bags requires significant amounts of energy. It has been estimated that manufacturing a paper bag takes 2.5 times more energy, requires 25 times more water, and generates 70 times more air pollutants than producing a plastic bag.

Plastic (polyethylene) bags have numerous practical advantages; they have handles that are less prone to rip. They use less energy and water to produce, and generate fewer air pollutants. On the downside, plastic bags do not biodegrade in landfills, and like all plastics they are based on petroleum that will become scarcer in

the future. Lastly, the phenomenon of stray plastic bags is not only an eyesore but can also harm wildlife and marine life.

The pros and cons of paper and plastic bags are complex. Neither is a clear winner. The introduction of biodegradable plastics (known as OXO plastics) has not swung the pendulum to plastic bags. Even though these bags biodegrade, the additives (metal salts) that are used to manufacture them may pose environmental problems of their own.

The superior alternative to plastic bags and paper bags at the grocery store is the durable reusable bag (or crate if you use a car for your grocery shopping). If you can only remember to bring them along!

In many countries, plastic bags are only available for a small fee. Ireland passed a plastic bag tax in 2002 (at 22 euro cents), and within a week there was a 94% drop in plastic bag use. In June 2012, the Toronto city council dropped a 6-cent tax on plastic bags it had introduced three years earlier, but at the same time moved to introduce an outright ban starting in 2013.

The economics of recycling is driven by several factors. Most important is the price of virgin raw materials: as they become scarcer, their price rises, and this makes recycled materials more cost effective. As the demand for recycled materials—and thus their market share—grows, more investments in technological improvements help bring down the cost of recycling. And as recycling programs become more comprehensive, there are additional economies of scale. On the other hand, slumping demand for raw materials (as happened during the 2008–2009 recession) will shrink demand for recycled materials; it can even (temporarily) jeopardize the cost effectiveness of municipal waste programs.

9.3.1 Solid waste streams

According to Statistics Canada, 767 kg of waste was disposed and land-filled per person in 2007. There is a fair bit of variation across provinces. British Columbia averaged 630 kg, Ontario 737 kg, and Alberta 1097 kg per person. Nova Scotia had the lowest per capita waste disposal, 377 kg. In the same year, the average Canadian diverted and recycled 251 kg of waste. The Prairie provinces had the lowest waste diversion at 140–198 kg per person, while British Columbia, Quebec, Nova Scotia, and New Brunswick diverted 308–357 kg per person.

Figure 9.15 shows the composition of a typical city's waste stream (net of recycled materials collected separately). The Greater Vancouver Regional District conducted a study of the region's waste by analyzing numerous samples in 2007. It found that roughly a third of waste is compostable, and about a quarter is paper and cardboard. The next largest category is plastics, which accounted for about one-seventh of total waste.

Figure 9.16 breaks down the composition of diverted (recycled) solid waste based on a cross-Canada survey of the waste management industry. The largest amount of recycled materials by weight is newsprint, mixed paper, and cardboard; together they account for about 40% of diverted waste. Plastic materials, glass, and metals are often part of curbside municipal recycling programs. The apparent small amount attributed to plastics is due to their relatively low weight; plastic containers are often bulky and hollow, and their weight-to-volume ratio is small. What is perhaps surprising is that organic waste constitutes about 30% of diverted materials. Only a few large municipalities have comprehensive composting programs, and thus the largest contributions to organic waste come from institutional and commercial sources.

Fig. 9.15 Waste Stream Composition

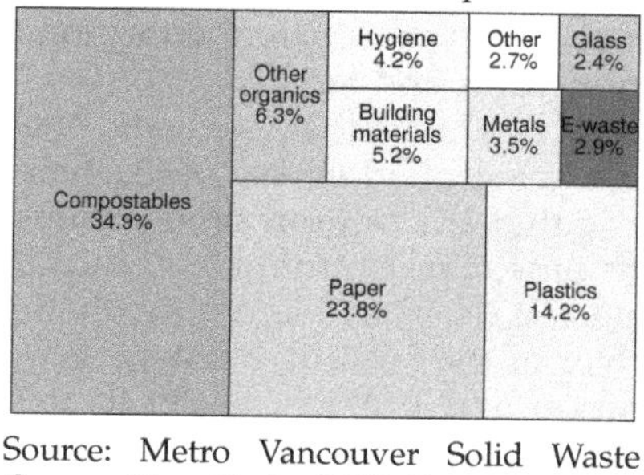

Fig. 9.16 Diverted Materials by Type

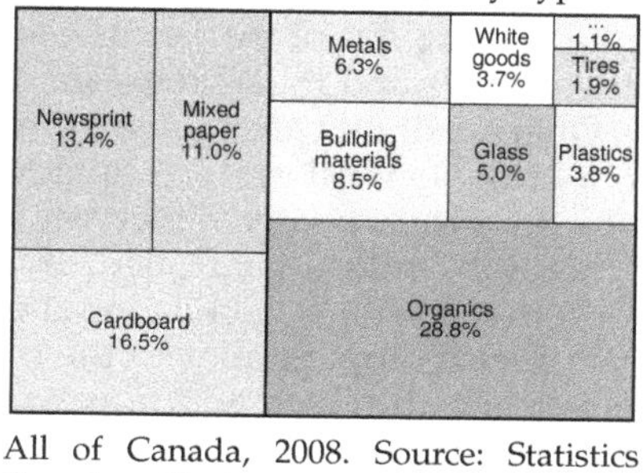

Source: Metro Vancouver Solid Waste Composition Study 2007. Composition is based on weight.

All of Canada, 2008. Source: Statistics Canada, Environment Accounts and Statistics Division, CANSIM table 153-0043, Waste Management Industry Survey.

9.3.2 Landfills

Landfills can be distinguished by the type of waste they store. Sanitary landfills are designed to accept all types of municipal solid waste. Selected waste landfills accept solid industrial wastes, bulky wastes (white goods such as appliances), derelict motor vehicles, and demolition and building materials. Hazardous waste is usually treated and processed rather than stored; see section 9.3.4 below.

When a landfill has been filled to its permitted volume or height, it is closed with a top cover that prevents water ingress. The cover is quite similar in composition to the bottom liner and typically involves multiple protective layers that include a geomembrane.

Figure 9.17 shows a cross-section of a typical landfill with a landfill gas recovery facility. Waste is added along the working surface of the landfill, often with benches along the slope of that surface. Waste that is deposited during a day is spread out and compacted into a thin layer about 60 cm thick, which at the end of a day is covered with a 15 cm layer of soil to contain odours, prevent fires and blowing litter, and keep away birds and bears. Each such daily layer is called a cell. Eventually, the top of the landfill is covered with a multi-layered top cover as shown in figure 9.18. The top cover is typically over a meter thick. A 30 cm barrier layer of surface material, composed of clay or clay liner, constitutes the bottom of the top cover. A flexible geomembrane (defined below) is placed on top of the barrier layer. A drainage net on top of the geomembrane collects rain water. This layer is covered with protective soil cover, at least half a meter thick, and often more than that. An erosion control layer of top soil (about 15 cm thick) must be able to sustain vegetation.

An important part of a landfill's bottom liner—and in many instances also the top cover—is the geomembrane, and impermeable sheet made of durable plastic, often reinforced (high-density) polyethylene. Geomembranes are commercially available at a thickness between 30 mils and 80 mils.[7] They are designed to prevent contaminated water from leaking out of the landfill, and they have to withstand enormous tensile loads and must be resistant to punctures and tears.

Of great significance is the bottom liner of a landfill, because the bottom of the landfill protects against the uncontrolled egress of leachate into the groundwater. The basic idea is that the bottom liner creates a 'bathtub' with a controlled drainage pipe. The bottom of a landfill is prepared with a thick layer of compacted (clay) soil and a synthetic clay liner on top. Similar to the top cover of the landfill, a plastic geomembrane provides additional separation and protection. On top of the geomembrane sits the leachate collection system, a system of per-

---

[7] This is about about 0.8–2.0 mm; see table A.4 for unit conversions.

Fig. 9.17 Landfill Cross-Section

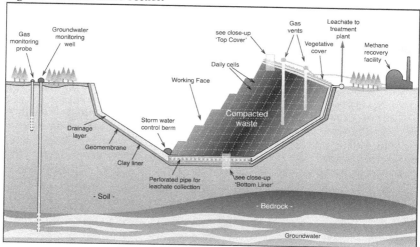

Fig. 9.18 Landfill Top Cover

Fig. 9.19 Bottom Liner

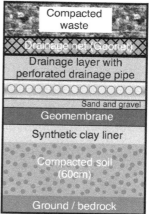

forated pipes surrounded by a bed of gravel. The pipes drain leachate into so-called sumps, and pumps located within the sumps transport the leachate to a treatment facility. This drainage layer is often separated from the compacted waste above with a filter-like drainage net or geonet. A key issue with geomembranes is the likelihood of perforation and decomposition through chemicals leaking through the landfill. Despite multiple layers of protection, a certain amount of leakage will probably occur.

The cost of landfilling depends on several factors. Municipalities pay the landfill owners a gate fee (also known as a tipping fee) upon receiving waste. The gate fee has to cover the cost of opening, operating, and closing the landfill; it may also vary by type of material received. Municipalities charge a landfill disposal fee to households and commercial clients. This fee also has to cover the cost of hauling the waste, and possibly treating the waste.

Hauling

The amount of solid waste that is landfilled every day has a weight and volume that requires collection and hauling over long distances to landfills near and far. Municipal waste is usually collected on large garbage trucks that travel from home to home and deposit their load either directly at a nearby landfill or at a transfer station from where trucks or trains transport the waste to more distant landfills. The distance that garbage trucks travel depends much on the population density, and the distance between transfer stations and landfill. In many instances, landfills near major urban areas have become scarce, and solid waste is transported over long distances. For example, until 2010 Toronto transported much of its solid waste to Carlton Farms Landfill some 50 km southwest of Detroit; a total distance of about 420 km. Toronto is currently shipping its waste to a new landfill near London, Ontario. In British Columbia, Vancouver's waste is shipped in part to a landfill near Cache Creek, 350 km northeast of Vancouver. The related traffic and the emissions from the trucks transporting waste can be considerable.

Landfill gas

Decomposing organic waste in landfills generates landfill gas, a mixture composed primarily of methane (30%–60%), some carbon dioxide (20%–50%), nitrogen (<10%), oxygen (<2%), and traces of hydrogen sulfide, mercaptans (organosulfur compounds), and volatile organic compounds. The sulfuric compounds and VOCs are responsible for the foul odours that are often associated with landfills. Methane emissions from landfills contribute significantly to greenhouse gas emissions because methane is 21 times as potent as a greenhouse gas than is carbon dioxide. Methane from landfills accounts for as much as 20% of

Canada's overall methane emissions.[8] The methane contained in landfill gas can be used to generate electricity. One can expect landfill gas generation in the range of 0.05–0.40 m^3/kg of waste (three quarters as solids and one quarter as moisture).

Waste in landfills decomposes in several stages, starting with aerobic decomposition (while oxygen is still present), followed by anoxic decomposition, and eventually transitioning to anaerobic decomposition (without oxygen present). It is during that latter stage that methane production reaches its peak, typically about 1–3 years after depositing the waste. Landfill gas will continue to be emitted for several decades, but will eventually decline. The amount of moisture that enters a landfill is one of the most important factors that determines the production of landfill gas. Moisture will speed up the generation of methane, but will shorten the time span of methane production. A key performance parameter for designing methane capture is the collection efficiency. Regulatory standards aim for at least 75% efficiency.

Leachate

There are two main sources of water in a landfill. Infiltration occurs through rain and groundwater, either while the landfill is not yet covered, or because of imperfections in the top cover. The deposited waste also contains water, and as the waste decomposes, the water leaks out slowly. Water that has percolated through the solid waste in a landfill turns into leachate that is contaminated with a wide range of pollutants, including dissolved organic matter, organic chemicals, inorganic matter, and heavy metals. Landfills require a leachate control system to prevent contamination of groundwater (aquifers) and run-off into rivers and lakes. Where leachate emerges from a leachate drainage system, it appears as a black or brown liquid with an unpleasant odour.

The composition of leachate changes over time as the landfill matures. Leachate from new landfills has a biochemical oxygen demand that often exceeds 10,000 mg/l, while the BOD for leachate from a mature landfill (older than 10 years) drops to about 100–200 mg/l.

Collected leachate is too contaminated to discharge directly into the municipal sewage system. Leachate is often subjected to physical-chemical treatment using coagulation and chemical flocculation (see section 9.2.2), as well as biological treatment. More recent landfill designs recirculate the leachate back into the landfill in order to promote growth of microbes, which in turn accelerates the decomposition of the biodegradable waste. This acceleration of decomposition is known as a bioreactor landfill design.

---

[8] The oil and gas industry accounts for about half of all methane emissions in Canada, and agriculture for about a quarter.

9.3.3 Incineration

Incineration has a vast array of applications. It can be used to deal with gaseous, liquid, and solid pollutants. Modern incinerators, especially municipal waste incinerators, also use waste-to-energy systems to generate electricity or heat.

Combustion in an incinerator oxidizes waste. With complete oxidation, the carbon and hydrogen in the waste (and additional fuel) are turned into carbon dioxide and steam. What complicates things is that oxidation may be incomplete, and that traces of other chemical elements may generate air pollutants such as sulfur dioxide and nitrogen oxides. Hazardous substances in the incinerated waste, such as mercury, may also enter the air stream and need to be filtered out before exhaust gases exit through the incinerator's stack. Scrubbers and electrostatic precipitators are often used to control emissions from incinerators. Incineration reduces the volume of waste by as much as 90%. The remaining material is made up of bottom ash, which may be reused as building material, and fly ash, which in most instances is landfilled because of hazardous contaminants.

Incinerators are categorized as **mass burn** or **refuse derived fuel** (RDF). Mass burn involves burning all combustible material in the waste, whereas RDF systems separate the combustible components and gasify them into a fuel gas that can be burned more cleanly.

Combustion depends on the amount of oxygen supplied, the residence time in the combustion chamber, the temperature, and the turbulence (mixing). As waste enters a combustion chamber, the temperature rises, and volatile organic components gasify. As the temperature increases further, remaining carbon in the waste ignites at temperatures of about 700°C. To burn the material completely with sufficient (excess) air and turbulence, the material must remain in the combustion chamber 1–2 seconds. To achieve complete combustion in a mass burn incinerator, it is usually necessary to provide additional fuel.

A challenge for incinerators is the mixture of combustible and incombustible elements in the waste. RDF incinerators process the incoming waste, which is sorted on a rotating screen, shredded into smaller pieces, and run through a magnetic separator. This sorting process helps ensure that the remaining waste has sufficient heating value for oxidation, and this reduces or eliminates the need for additional fuel.

Successful waste diversion can impede the efficiency of municipal waste incinerators. Recycling reduces the amount of combustible material, in particular paper and cardboard. Careful monitoring of the composition of waste is required to operate incinerators effectively.

There are four major designs for incinerators. Fluidized bed incinerators use a bed of sand or sand-like material that is fluidized (suspended against the force of gravity) through an air stream. The **fluidized bed** is heated to incineration temperatures, and that heat is recovered. Fluidized bed incinerators can be used for hazardous and non-hazardous waste because these systems achieve near-complete combustion. The combustion chamber of a rotary kiln incinerator is a slowly rotating inclined cylinder. The rotation mixes the materials that are combusted, and the downward inclination ensures the forward motion of the waste material. This design is often used for mass burning of waste. Rotary kiln systems produce a relatively high load of particulate matter that needs to be filtered out, which requires the use air pollution control devices such as venturi scrubbers, electrostatic precipitators, and baghouses. The hearth incinerator is a mass burn system where the waste material is spread out on a horizontal surface, and multiple such surfaces are stacked in the furnace. New waste enters on the top surface, and rakes transport it downwards from one layer to the next. This design cannot be used for hazardous waste, but it is useful when waste has a high water content. The fourth design uses pyrolysis. Here, the waste is heated to release volatile gases, and this gas is burned instead of the waste. The waste decomposes through the heat while oxygen is absent. This design is useful for processing hazardous waste because the burn conditions of the gas can be controlled precisely. Depending on the type of waste, the residence time in the gasification chamber can vary significantly, from a few minutes to a few hours.

Table 9.7 Comparison of LFGTE and WTE

Process	Landfill Gas to Energy	Waste to Energy
Electricity that can be generated from 1 tonne of waste	41–84 kWh	470–930 kWh
Emissions for 1 MWh electricity: — $CO_2(e)$ — sulfur oxides — nitrogen oxides	2.3–5.5 tonnes 0.43–0.90 kg 2.10–3.00 kg	0.5–1.5 tonnes 0.14–0.73 kg 0.81–1.80 kg

Source: Kaplan et al. (2009).

As shown in table 9.7, waste-to-energy can recover significantly more energy from a tonne of waste than landfill-gas-to-energy systems. The two approaches differ by about an order of magnitude. A typical waste-to-energy facility can be expected to generate about 500 kWh per tonne of processed waste. For example, the waste-to-energy system operated by Metro Vancouver processes 800 tonnes of garbage per day and generates 400 MWh of electricity per day. It also generates 130 tonnes of bottom ash that is used in part for building roads, and 30 tonnes of fly ash that is landfilled. The facility also recovers 25 tonnes of metal that is recycled. Furthermore, the facility generates 2,740 tonnes of steam. A fifth of that steam is sold to a nearby paper recycling facility, and the remainder drives the turbo generators that produce electricity.

9.3.4 Hazardous waste

Hazardous wastes are those types of waste that pose a hazard to human health and the ecosystem. Particular hazards are associated with the ignitability, corrosivity, reactivity, or toxicity of the substances. To control the hazard, such wastes require special handling, labelling, storage, transportation, and disposal.

Hazardous waste is the by-product of many manufacturing processes. It includes motor oil, acids, asbestos, solvents, certain metals, and many chemicals. Biomedical and radiological waste is also considered hazardous. Even laboratories in universities and hospitals generate hazardous waste. Sludge from wastewater treatment plants and fly ash from incinerators may also be considered hazardous. Hazardous waste is either processed, stored permanently in designated storage facilities on land, or stored permanently by way of underground injection into geologically stable salt dome or salt bed formations, as well as underground mines or caves. Whoever handles hazardous waste must ensure proper storage; prepare for an emergency (have an E2 plan); and train personnel in the proper handling of that waste.

A first step in treating hazardous waste is separating the hazardous material from non-hazardous material. Concentrated specific hazardous waste is more amenable to further treatment than diluted or mixed hazardous waste. Carbon adsorption, distillation, ion exchange, electrodialysis, and reverse osmosis are common methods in the extraction and concentration process.

Some types of hazardous waste can be destroyed through incineration (combustion) or through pyrolysis. A rotary kiln incinerator is often preferred for handling hazardous waste because of its versatility in processing solid and liquid wastes. Such systems often have an afterburner where additional fuel and oxygen is supplied to reach temperatures in the range of 1,000°C–1,600°C, sufficient to break up many complex molecules. With pyrolysis, hazardous waste is subjected to extremely high temperatures in an electrical arc (a plasma) under conditions that prevent combustion.

A variation of pyrolysis is known as plasma gasification. Plasco Energy Group has built a demonstration facility in Ottawa for processing 85 tonnes per day of municipal waste. At this facility, a waste converter generates crude syngas, and plasma torches refine the syngas. The clean syngas is used to generate power, and solid residue from the conversion process is landfilled. The main advantage of plasma gasification over conventional waste-to-energy systems is that the gasification results in fewer air pollutants, which economizes on pollution abatement equipment. A tonne of waste generates approximately 1 MWh of electricity, 300 litres of water, 7–15 kg of metal, and 150 kg of construction aggregate.

9.4 Summary

The appropriate method for abating pollution depends crucially on the phase state of the pollutant as a gas, liquid, or solid (particulate matter). Technological solutions exist to treat most types of pollutants, although choosing the appropriate technology involves environmental, economic, and technical trade-offs.

Air quality is measured by combining concentrations of common air contaminants, in particular ozone, nitrogen oxide, and particulate matter. There is a wide range of air pollution control devices. Gravity settling chambers, cyclones, and electrostatic precipitators operate by making the particles in the air collide against a wall, where they can be collected. Filters are most effective for collecting small particles, but single-use types have high operating cost, and can operate only in dry and relatively cool environments. Surface filters (baghouses) are used to collect gas streams heavily laden with particles, while depth filters are more often used for final cleanup of a gas. Among the wet scrubbers, the venturi co-flow design is the most effective because of the high velocity differential between particles and and cleaning liquid. The power costs for venturi designs are important.

There are three stages of wastewater treatment: primary treatment (mechanical or chemical-mechanical); secondary treatment (biological); and advanced tertiary treatment (removal of nitrogen and phosphorus, disinfection). Additional (often chemical) processes are available to treat particular types of industrial wastewater. Most modern wastewater treatment plants are at least secondary. A key metric for water quality is the biochemical oxygen demand (BOD), which can be combined with other measures into a comprehensive water quality index.

Integrated waste management emphasizes a hierarchy of approaches: reduce waste, reuse waste if possible, separate waste and recycle it, and if all else fails, recover energy from the waste materials.

The choice between landfills and incinerators involves trade-offs. Landfills produce toxic leachate that may contaminate ground or surface water. Landfills also generate landfill gas, which can be used to generate electricity. While the capital cost of landfills is low, high transportation cost can offset the cost advantage. Incineration produces a variety of air pollutants, but most of these can be removed effectively. Incineration also produces contaminated ash that must be disposed safely. Per tonne of solid waste, modern waste-to-energy facilities generate significantly more electricity than landfill-gas-to-energy systems.

As the dangers of climate change are becoming more apparent, methods for carbon capture and storage are being developed and tested. The three most important approaches include pre-combustion capture, post-combustion capture, and the oxyfuel method. Despite technological advances, they remain too expensive for widespread adoption.

9.5 Study questions and exercises

1. Which technical methods are most effective for removing particles, liquids, and gaseous contaminants from gaseous output?
2. How does the particle size (diameter) determine the choice of abatement device?
3. Characterize air pollution control devices by their fixed (capital) cost and variable (operational) cost. Which devices have disposable (single-use) elements? Which require large amounts of energy?
4. What are the options to dispose of the particle residue collected by air pollution control devices?
5. When treating gaseous emissions in gaseous output, what is the difference between adsorbers and absorbers?
6. How would you treat gaseous volatile organic compounds from a paper mill? What are the options?
7. What are the most significant water pollution problems, and what causes them?
8. How does one measure the quality of (river) water?
9. How does one measure air quality and the potential health impacts of air pollution?
10. What are the three stages of (municipal) wastewater treatment?
11. How does the treatment of industrial wastewater differ from the treatment of municipal wastewater? What additional septs or processes may need to be used?
12. How is the sludge from wastewater treatment disposed of?
13. Describe the three different approaches to carbon dioxide capture. Which approach can be used in retrofits of existing plants, and which can be used only in new plants?
14. What are the key arguments for continuation of landfills as the major waste disposal system in North America? What are the key arguments in favour of incineration?
15. What are the economic and ecological differences between waste-to-energy systems (from incineration) and methane-to-energy systems (from collecting landfill gases)?

Exercises

1. Visit the nearest local water treatment plant in your community. What type of treatment does it use? Has the treatment technology been updated over the years, or through expansions of the plant? What is the scope for improvement considering the technologies discussed in this chapter? How does the treatment plant monitor water quality?
2. If you have access to a dissolved oxygen meter, test the water quality of a nearby river or lake by taking samples. Use the oxygen meter to measure the five-day biochemical oxygen demand (BOD_5).

3. Arrange to visit a nearby cement plant. What type of cement does it produce, and through which process? What type of fuel is used in the process? How does the plant deal with its emissions into air, in particular carbon dioxide and heavy metals?

4. Arrange for a visit to a nearby paper mill. Explore the technologies used at that site. In particular, what type of delignification and bleaching processes do they use? How does the plant treat emissions, especially volatile organic compound emissions into air?

5. Investigate noise pollution in your local environment. Buy or borrow a sound meter. You can even use a smartphone app for this purpose, even though these readings will tend to be less accurate. Measure the ambient sound levels indoors (for example, in empty classrooms) and outdoors (for example, around the residential areas where you live). For indoor noise, compare your readings with guidelines developed by ASHRAE (American Society of Heading, Refrigeration, and Air Conditioning Engineers). Pay particular attention to the role of HVAC systems. Are there any classrooms at your university that do not meet ASHRAE guidelines? For outdoor noise, assemble and discuss a time profile of the noise levels. Develop ideas to reduce ambient noise levels.

Chapter 10
Energy Systems

Energy is used by every single enterprise. Energy use has an immediate environmental footprint because most forms of conventional energy production and use are associated with environmental externalities, in particular emissions. Yet few of these environmental externalities are priced correctly. Very few jurisdictions price the negative effects of carbon dioxide or sulfur dioxide emissions.

Most nations rely on a broad mix of energy supplies rather than a single source of energy. The diversity of energy types is not merely a function of production and transportation costs. Different types of energy are useful for different types of mobile or stationary applications. In a volatile political world, diversity of energy sources—both geographically as well as categorically—is also a matter of energy security. As the oil price shocks in 1973 and 1979 demonstrated, reliance on energy imports can make economies vulnerable to external political forces.

The world's energy portfolio is propelled by a mix of discovery of new sources of conventional fossil fuels as well as innovation into renewable energy sources. Overall energy use is driven by economic growth but also energy efficiency. Improving energy efficiency through energy conservation remains one of the most important challenges.

As energy is an essential input for any type of business, businesses need to make choices about their current and future supply of energy. What is driving these choices is, of course, the relative price of the competing sources of energy: oil, gas, coal, and electricity. Businesses also need to worry about possible disruptions to their energy supply. Defending against such disruptions, should they stockpile fuel and invest in back-up capacity for generating electricity? By how much will energy prices rise, and what options do businesses have to adjust? In a world of volatile energy prices, businesses need to make strategic choices about their energy use. In short, every business needs an energy plan.

There are a number of excellent books that cover both the macro and micro aspects of energy. In his book *The Quest*, Yergin (2011) looks at the history and future of energy and the intricate interplay of economics, politics, and technological advances. A key argument in his book is that the world will not run out of oil for quite some time. For a closer look at energy systems and individual energy sources, Boyle et al. (2003) provide a more technical and in-depth treatment. For those interested in a more detailed treatment of renewable energy sources, MacKay (2009) combines an in-depth look at the various options (wind, solar, etc.) with a look at how to reshape modern energy systems.

10.1 Energy supply, energy demand, and Hubbert's peak

With oil prices hovering around $100 per barrel in 2012 and having peaked at $145 in July 2008 (see figure 10.1), many argue that the world has reached the point where oil production is starting to decline. A declining supply of oil, which inevitably would be associated with rising prices of oil, would have far-reaching consequences. As oil is a fundamental input for transportation, rising oil prices imply higher transportation costs. Rubin (2009) takes this argument to its logical conclusion. Without cheap oil, the globalized economy that relies on cheap transportation is under threat. A world of high and rising oil prices is a world of deglobalization.

Oil-producing regions experience periods of expansion and contraction over time. This pattern follows a roughly bell-shaped curve that is known as the Hubbert curve, proposed in 1956 by American geophysicist M. King Hubbert. As oil is discovered in a particular region, production expands slowly at first, then more rapidly, eventually flattens, and peaks at a particular point. Afterwards, production declines as individual wells produce less and eventually are exhausted. Hubbert predicted that US oil production would peak in the late 1960s. He was not too far off the mark: as can be seen in figure 10.2, the maximum output of 3.45 billion barrels was reached in 1972, and the estimated Hubbert curve peaks a few years later in 1976. The point at which oil production reaches its historic maximum is often referred to as Hubbert's peak. Generalizing the prediction for individual regions and applying it to a world with finite oil supplies leads to the peak oil theory.

Fig. 10.1 The Rising Price of Crude Oil 1988–2013

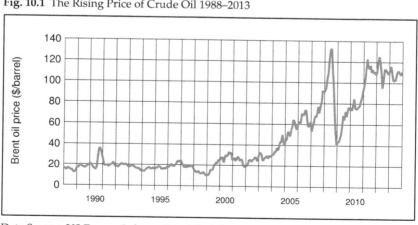

Data Source: US Energy Information Administration (www.eia.gov).

Fig. 10.2 The Hubbert Curve: U.S. Oil Production 1900–2013

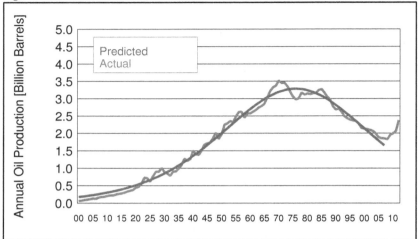

Notes: The actual annual production data (available from the US Energy Information Administration) was used to estimate a logistic function with a mean (peak year) of 1975.9, scale of 17.74 years, and total stock of 233 billion barrels. Years after 2007 were excluded from the regression to highlight the importance of recent oil discoveries.

Proponents of the peak oil theory assert that the world reached the peak in the first decade of the 21st century, but the empirical evidence for this proposition is weak. While global oil production averaged 78 million barrels per day in 2000, in 2011 it had increased to 87 million barrels per day. The main reason the world has not reached Hubbert's peak is that we continue to find new sources of oil. The proven reserves of crude oil have continuously risen. In 1980 world oil reserves were 642 billion barrels (bbls). By 1990 they had risen to 1,000 bbls, and stayed flat until 2002. In 2009, world oil reserves had risen to 1,342 bbls. At current production rates this implies over 40 years worth of remaining reserves. Canada's proven reserves for 2012 are reported as 174 bbls, the third largest in the world after Saudi Arabia and Venezuela. When new oil fields are discovered, there can be significant jumps. For example, Venezuela's oil reserves were revised from 99 to 212 bbls in 2011. Even US oil production has experienced a renaissance. As can be seen in figure 10.2, production seems to have been deviating significantly from its long-term 'Hubbert' trend since 2008.

The reserves-to-production ratio (RPR) plays an important role in the gas and oil industry. It is defined as the ratio of proved reserves to annual production (and use). The RPR can be used for individual regions or countries as well as the world overall. Discoveries of unconventional sources of oil (including in Canada and Venezuela) have pushed up the RPR ratio further. There is no indication that the world is running out of oil soon.

What is driving the expansion of oil reserves? In short, rising prices. As figure 10.1 shows, the price of crude oil has risen steadily over the last two decades. While the extraction cost of crude oil in the Middle East is typically below $20, the extraction cost of offshore oil and unconventional oil is significantly higher. Exploration of these unconventional reserves is economical only when oil prices are sufficiently high for a prolonged period.

It is important to understand that even though oil is traded globally, the world oil market is not fully integrated in the short term. While spot contracting is the norm (unlike the natural gas business, where long-term contracting is common), regional constraints in transportation capacity (pipelines, oil tankers) and processing capacity (refineries) can lead to significant price gaps. There are two benchmark prices for oil: Brent (North Sea oil) and West Texas Intermediate at Cushing, Oklahoma (North America). As figure 10.3 shows, over the last few years the cost of Brent was at a considerable premium over Cushing; the gap only closed in mid-2013. This wide price gap made domestic US and Canadian oil cheaper than their international counterparts, and it spurred numerous proposals to construct new pipeline capacity.

Fig. 10.3 The North American Oil Price Gap

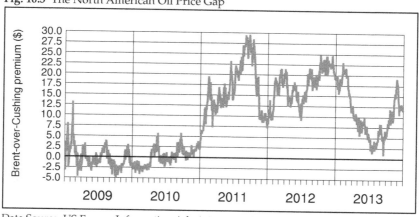

Data Source: US Energy Information Administration (www.eia.gov)

Among the more controversial projects are the Keystone XL pipeline for carrying crude oil from Alberta to Nebraska, and the Northern Gateway pipeline from Alberta to the northern coast of British Columbia.

The routing of the Keystone XL pipeline has been of particular concern, prompting the US government to change the routing to avoid a sensitive aquifer. The proposed route of the Northern Gateway pipeline crosses sensitive ecosystems and faces opposition from local First Nations communities. A proposed expansion of the existing Kinder-Morgan Trans Mountain pipeline would also carry dilbit (diluted bitumen), a blend of heavy crude or bitumen diluted with condensate because of bitumen's high viscosity and density. The dilutant is often natural gas condensate, refined naphtha, and synthetic crude oil. Dilbit spills may pose a particular environmental problem. While the condensate evaporates, the heavy bitumen may be heavier than water under some conditions, and sink to the bottom of rivers or the sea. Competing claims about the properties of dilbit exist, and require further comprehensive research.

10.2 Coal, oil and gas

Coal, oil, and natural gas will play an important and dominant role in the world's energy supply for many decades yet. The expansion of renewable energy will not be fast enough, even under optimistic scenarios, to replace fossil fuels. The main reason for the continuing dominance of fossil fuels is price. In the absence of policies that put a price on environmental externalities generated by fossil fuel use (for example, through carbon pricing), the price of fossil fuels will remain lower than that of competing alternative sources. The discovery of so-called unconventional sources of fossil fuels is contributing to keeping prices of fossil fuels low.

It is useful to compare the major characteristics of the three major types of fossil fuels. Table 10.1 shows proven reserves, annual production, and RPRs. Coal remains by far the most abundant (and cheapest) fossil fuel. On the other hand, coal is also the most carbon intensive of the three fuel types. For each Gigajoule of energy, coal is associated with 75% more carbon dioxide emissions than natural gas.

The term unconventional oil is used to describe a variety of novel production methods and sources. These methods and sources of oil have in common that they are relatively expensive compared to conventional methods.[1] Unconventional oil can refer to conventional drilling methods but also unconventional (novel) locations that used to be inaccessible. For example, drilling in the high Arctic was not feasible due

---

[1] Beyond conventional and unconventional *proven* reserves, there are also large *undiscovered* (but technically recoverable) conventional reserves. As part of the World Petroleum Assessment in 2012, the United States Geological Survey (USGS) estimated 565 bbls of undiscovered oil outside the United States. With world oil consumption around 30 bbbls per year, this yields roughly another two decades worth of oil.

Table 10.1 Fossil Fuels in Comparison

	Oil	Gas	Coal
Proved Reserves (EJ)	8,210.4	6,846.2	25,199.7
Production (EJ/year)	190.5	117.5	198.3
RPR (years)	43.1	58.3	127.1
CO_2 emission factor (kg/GJ)	68	50	88

Data Source: US Energy Information Administration. Data points are for 2009. Conversion factors used: 1 barrel of oil equivalent is 6.12 Gigajoule (GJ); 1 Megawatt-hour (MWh) is 3.6 GJ; 1 short ton of coal is 26.582 GJ; 1,000 cubic feet of natural gas is 1.088568 GJ; 1 Exajoule (EJ) equals 1 billion GJ equals 10^{18} Joules.

to the inhospitable climate. As climate change is altering conditions in the Arctic, drilling there has become possible for the first time. Technological advances have also been made with respect to offshore drilling. Drilling platforms in the North Sea operate at a water depth of a few hundred metres; they typically extend to the bottom of the sea. Deepwater drilling platforms, which have been developed in recent years, have now started to operate at much greater depths than in the North Sea. The deepest platform, operating in the Gulf of Mexico, operates in a water depth of 2.4 km. Such platforms are floating. Deepwater oil fields are now starting to be developed off the southern coast of Brazil.

Instead of drilling, production of oil from oil sands involves open-pit strip mining of bitumen. As some deposits are too deep for surface mining, other methods are being developed, but are not yet widely used. The two most important oil sands deposits are the Athabasca field in Alberta and the Orinoco field in Venezuela. While Canada has over 170 bbls of oil recoverable with today's technology, there are an estimated 2,500 bbls of bitumen that could be recovered with future technologies. Processing oil sands is very energy intensive and capital intensive and comprises three steps: extraction, separation, and upgrading. One needs about two tons of oil sands to produce one barrel of oil (less than 10% of the original weight). Excavation involves enormous excavators and trucks. The excavated oil sands are mixed with hot water and caustic soda, and the resulting slurry is piped to an extraction plant where the bitumen is skimmed off. An upgrader converts the recovered bitumen into synthetic crude oil using vacuum distillation and other distillation processes. Upgrading typically removes or reduces impurities such as sulfur, nitrogen, and heavy metals such as nickel and vanadium. This upgrading process is necessary because refineries are designed to handle lighter crude oil, and bitumen has a viscosity that is a thousand times higher.

Another unconventional source of oil is oil shale, a type of sedimentary rock that contains kerogen from which one can extract both shale oil and shale gas. The kerogen in oil shale is chemically processed through hydrous pyrolysis or steam cracking. The global deposits of such oil shales are significant. The largest known deposit occurs in the Green River formation in the United States. Overall, the United States accounts for the majority of known oil shale deposits worldwide.

Shale gas has recently become a very important source of natural gas in the United States—in particular with the exploration of the Bakken formation in Montana, North Dakota, and Saskatchewan. The development of this and other such fields through a production technique called fracking has created a gas boom in the United States. The share of shale gas in total natural gas production has risen from 4% in 2005 to 25% today. As a result, prices for natural gas have fallen dramatically.

Hydraulic fracturing, or fracking, is a recovery method for shale gas (sometimes referred to as tight gas) that involves fracturing rock layers through pressurized fluids, which opens up pathways through which trapped oil and natural gas can escape. The injected fluid is typically composed of water, proppants, and chemical additives. Proppants (often fine sand) keep a hydraulic fracture open, and the additives are used to control the viscosity of the fluid, dissolve limestone, or prevent bacteria growth (using biocides). The exact composition of fracking fluids is often a matter of fine-tuning for different shale formations. Fracking is associated with significant water use. The fracking fluid is recovered partially through the well and requires treatment.

There are important environmental concerns about fracking. There is a risk of small artificial earthquakes (sometimes called microquakes) and the possibility of aquifer (groundwater) contamination. In some countries there has been a political backlash against fracking. While most of the environmental concerns about fracking appear to be manageable, the necessary environmental regulation and oversight is perhaps slow to catch up to this booming industry.

10.3 Nuclear power

Nuclear power has held great promise ever since the first nuclear reactor started providing electricity to the grid in the Soviet Union in 1954. By 2010, the installed capacity of nuclear reactors reached almost 400 Gigawatts (GW). Yet, in its March 10, 2012, issue, *The Economist* magazine called nuclear power 'The dream that failed.' After the most recent nuclear accident in Fukushima (Japan) that followed a massive earthquake and tsunami on March 11, 2011, the world has grown wary again of the prospects for nuclear energy, which had in previous years blossomed under the prospects of a 'nuclear renaissance.' In some countries nuclear energy faces stiff opposition. In Germany, all nuclear reactors were shut down temporarily following the Fukushima disaster. Several have now been shut down permanently, and the remaining reactors are to be phased out gradually.

Despite the tragic developments in Fukushima in 2011 and in Chernobyl in 1986, nuclear energy is comparatively safe. Far more people perish or get injured in coal mine accidents than in nuclear power plant accidents. China has a particularly bleak record on coal mining safety, reporting several thousand deaths per year. Nuclear energy is not inherently less safe than other forms of energy.

Notwithstanding the widespread concerns about safety, what has really been holding back nuclear power is its relative cost. The actual construction cost of a nuclear reactor often exceeds the projected construction cost by a large margin due to delays, changes in regulation and certification procedures, and other factors. High capital cost and long construction periods make nuclear power expensive overall.

The environmental case for nuclear power hinges on the fact that nuclear power plants do not emit carbon dioxide. Nuclear power could play a significant role as a 'bridge technology' to combat climate change while renewable energy sources remain even more expensive than nuclear power. The environmental case against nuclear power rests on two key arguments: radioactive contamination due to leaks or accidents, and storing the radioactive waste safely for millennia into the future. While the environmental balance is debatable, the economic argument for nuclear energy remains weak unless the cost of new reactors can be brought down significantly. Much of the recent new nuclear capacity is being built in China, where construction has indeed been more cost effective than in North America.

What prospects remain for a nuclear renaissance after Fukushima? Much of that answer hinges on what type of nuclear fuel and what type of reactor designs will be developed in the future.

Nuclear fuel

The most common type of nuclear fuel is uranium. Uranium is mined from uranium ore, a body of rock that contains uraninite (UO_2), pitchblende (U_3O_8), or other uranium minerals in an economically mineable quantity of up to a few percent. The uranium ore is crushed and treated with leaching solutions to extract the uranium. The resulting yellowcake powder is smelted into purified uranium dioxide. Natural uranium contains over 99% of the U-238 isotope; only about 0.7% is fissile U-235. Reactor-grade uranium therefore needs to be enriched, typically in cascading gas centrifuges. Low-enriched uranium contains about 3-4% fissile uranium.[2] There remain large proven uranium reserves in Australia, Kazakhstan, Canada, and Russia. Canada is the world's leading uranium producer, accounting for 21% of global production and 9%

---

[2] The waste product of this process is depleted uranium, which has found commercial applications for radiation shielding and military applications as armour plating and for armour-piercing projectiles.

of global reserves.[3] Australia and Kazakhstan are the next largest producers, each accounting for about 19% of global production.

The second type of nuclear fuel uses plutonium (Pu-239), which is produced synthetically from uranium by extracting it from spent nuclear fuel. Mixed oxide (MOX) fuel contains a mixture of plutonium and natural uranium that has properties similar to low-enriched uranium.

There is yet another type of nuclear fuel: thorium (Th-232). Thorium is approximately three times as abundant as natural uranium in the Earth's crust due to its longer half-life; it is also often present in higher concentrations (by weight) than uranium. Thorium can be turned into a fissile material (U-233) in a nuclear reactor by capturing neutrons. However, this requires the use of fissile uranium or plutonium to initiate a nuclear reaction. A key advantage of the thorium fuel cycle is that it generates significantly less radioactive waste than the uranium fuel cycle. Nevertheless, commercialization of the thorium cycle has not made much progress over the last few decades.

Reactor designs

There are numerous competing reactor designs, with the lightwater design being the most popular because of cost considerations. What distinguishes the different designs is the type of fuel, moderator, and coolant that is used. Nuclear reactors operate a tightly controlled nuclear fission process in which one neutron from each fission should interact with exactly one other fissile nucleus to induce another fission; if the ratio is less than one, the reaction fizzles out, and if it is more than one, the fission runs out of control. The nuclear fuel is mostly enriched uranium (isotope U-235), but some use natural uranium (isotope U-238). The uranium is used in its oxide form (UO_2), and oxide pellets are typically enclosed in cylindrical casings. The casings form rods that can be inserted into or withdrawn from the reactor core to control the fission. The moderator is used to slow down the nuclear chain reaction by slowing down neutrons without absorbing them. The three most widely used moderators are light water, heavy (deuterium) water, and graphite. Heavy water is fairly expensive (over $300/kg) because it needs to be distilled from ordinary water. For the tonnes of heavy water needed for a reactor, the total cost of heavy water can easily exceed $1 billion (or about a quarter of the total capital cost). Graphite has the disadvantage of being flammable. The coolant is a fluid or gas that acts as the heat exchange medium. It can be the same as the moderator if water is used. Table 10.2 identifies the main designs as well as their percentage shares of commercial use.

---

[3] All uranium now produced in Canada comes from three mines, all in the province of Saskatchewan. Note the unusually high grade of the Canadian ore, particularly that found at McArthur River and Cigar Lake (requiring special robotic procedures for extraction). The two major uranium producers in Canada are Cameco and Cogema Resources.

Table 10.2 Current and Future Nuclear Reactor Designs

Type of Reactor	Fuel	Coolant	Moderator	Share
Pressurized water	enriched UO_2	light water	light water	61%
Boiling water	enriched UO_2	light water	light water	21%
Pressurized heavy water	natural UO_2	heavy water	heavy water	9%
Gas cooled	enriched UO_2	CO_2	graphite	5%
Advanced gas cooled	enriched UO_2	CO_2	graphite	
Fast breeder	PuO_2, UO_2	liquid sodium	none	
Liquid flouride thorium	thorium	molten salt	graphite	

The CANDU design developed by Atomic Energy of Canada is a pressurized heavy-water design and is used for all reactors in operation in Canada. The CANDU design is now in use in several other countries, including South Korea, India, and China. The CANDU design has several advantages over other types of reactors. First, it uses natural uranium. Except for the start-up, no enriched uranium is needed. This helps prevent proliferation of enriched uranium, which can be enriched further for use in nuclear weapons. Second, a CANDU reactor can be re-fuelled while in operation. No batch refuelling is needed. Third, heavy-water moderation provides greater stability of the chain reaction than light-water moderation, giving operators more time to react in an emergency. Fourth, the CANDU design contains a number of 'passive' safety features along with various 'active' safety features. Passive safety helps shut down a reactor core even without operator intervention. Shut-off rods are held up by electromagnets. When power fails completely, these rods will drop under gravity into the reactor core and stop the fission. The current advanced CANDU design, ACR-1000, produces 1200 MW of electricity, but uses low-enriched instead of natural uranium.

On the drawing board of nuclear engineers are 'fourth-generation' reactor designs. These are meant to make reactors more economically efficient while also making them safer. One such design is the very high temperature reactor (VHTR). High temperatures (over 1,000°C) enable a variety of new applications such as the production of hydrogen through the iodine-sulfur process (i.e., three chemical reactions whose main input is water and whose output is hydrogen and oxygen). Another design is the liquid flouride thorium reactor (LFTR), which makes use of the thorium fuel cycle. In an LFTR, molten salt containing flouride and thorium acts both as fissile material and coolant.

Nuclear waste

Spent nuclear fuel remains one of the most formidable challenges of nuclear energy. Spent fuel undergoes reprocessing, and the nuclear waste requires long-term storage. Most spent nuclear fuel remains at the reactor site for about five years and is then moved to a reprocessing facility. The three most important reprocessing facilities are located in the United Kingdom (Sellafield), France (LaHague, Marcoule), and Russia (Mayak). Reprocessing involves chemical separation of three components: uranium that can be re-enriched for use as new nuclear fuel; plutonium that can be used as a minor component in MOX fuel; and high-level radioactive waste that carries almost all of the radioactivity of spent fuel.

Nuclear waste requires safe storage for hundreds of thousands of years in deep underground repositories. Safe disposal of nuclear waste requires (a) stable enclosure material to protect against thermal or chemical perturbations; (b) stable geological formations to prevent leakage; and (c) stable human institutions to monitor and safeguard the storage sites. Nuclear waste can be enclosed in glass or ceramics. Underground repositories require tunnelling into geological formations where rooms or vaults are excavated. Proposed sites include Östhammar in Sweden and the Yucca Mountain in the United States.

If the thorium fuel cycle finds widespread use, the problem of managing nuclear waste would change radically. The need for long term storage would diminish significantly because the radioactivity of the waste products decreases to safe levels in a few hundred years, which compares favourably with the tens or hundreds of thousand years for the uranium and plutonium cycles.

Nuclear reality

Figure 10.4 shows the position of countries along two dimensions: the installed generation capacity of nuclear reactors (horizontal axis, logarithmic) and the percentage share of nuclear power in total electricity generation (vertical axis). The three leading nuclear power countries are the United States, France, and Japan. The United States is by far the largest generator of nuclear power, although France has the highest dependence on nuclear power, deriving about three-quarters of electricity from nuclear power plants.

While some countries continue building new nuclear reactors, other countries are preparing for an exit from nuclear power. China is currently operating 16 nuclear power reactors (at four sites) and has another 26 reactors under construction. In the United States, numerous projects have been proposed, but only two new reactors are currently being built at the Vogtle plant in Georgia, for a total of 2.4 GW of additional electricity.

After the 1979 Three Mile Island nuclear accident in the United States, a referendum was held in Sweden about the future of nuclear power in that country. Following the referendum, Sweden's parliament put a moratorium on new nuclear plants and set a phase-out target for 2010. However, in 2010 the Swedish parliament reversed the phase-out and allowed the replacement of existing reactors. In Germany, where

Fig. 10.4 Nuclear Energy around the Globe

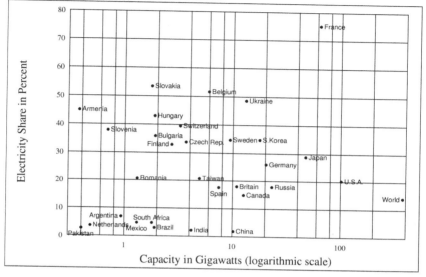

nuclear power accounts for less than a quarter of electricity generation, a phase-out of nuclear power was announced in 2011 following the Fukushima nuclear accident. Six nuclear reactors that were already shut down for maintenance were closed permanently. The remaining nine plants are scheduled to be shut down by 2022 (moved up from a previous phase-out target of 2036). It is a rather remarkable fact that France and Germany have opposing views on nuclear power, with France relying on it heavily (with 58 active plants).

10.4 Levellized energy cost

Comparing the cost of competing energy sources is unfortunately not straight forward. While it is easy to compare the prices of fossil fuels based on their energy content, comparisons with other forms of energy are made difficult by the capital cost of building installations for their use and distribution, such as power plants and transmission grids. Such installations also have a life expectancy and renewal cycle. Add to this the complexities of financing, depreciation, and taxation. A useful concept in energy economics is the *levellized energy cost* (LEC). It allows us to compare the cost of competing energy sources.

The levellized energy cost (LEC) is the life time cost of an energy project per unit of lifetime energy output. LEC is used to compare the cost of different energy sources per unit of energy output.

Consider an energy project that is assumed to have a lifetime of T years. The levellized energy cost (LEC) can then be calculated as

$$\frac{I_0 + (D_T - F_T)(1 + r)^{-T} + \sum_{t=1}^{T} [(1 - \tau)M_t - \tau\delta_t I_0] (1 + r)^{-t}}{\sum_{t=1}^{T} E_t(1 + r)^{-t}}.$$

$$(10.1)$$

The numerator in the above equation captures the lifetime cost of the project. The initial investment expenditure is I_0. At the end of life, the expression $(D_T - F_T)$ captures the cost of decommissioning minus the residual (scrap) value of the facility. This expression is discounted to the present with the discount rate r. During the operation of the project, there are annual costs for fuel and maintenance M_t. The tax regime has an impact on the cost structure as well. Assuming a corporate income tax rate of τ, operational costs generate a tax benefit and thus the after-tax maintenance cost is only $(1 - \tau)M_t$. Similarly, there is a tax benefit from capital depreciation. Let δ_t denote the fraction of the initial capital that can be depreciated in year t; then the capital cost allowance for tax purposes is $\tau\delta_t I_0$.

The denominator in the above equation captures the total energy output over the lifetime of the project. For example, E_t can capture the electricity output in kWh in year t. For certain types of power plants, this can be captured by assuming that output degrades with rate κ so that $E_t = E_0(1 - \kappa)^t$.

The LEC measure is sensitive to two key numbers. While the various cost measures, tax rates, and depreciation rates can be established with a degree of reliability, the project lifetime T is often difficult to estimate and the discount rate r is assumed (although often based on historic interest rates). Figure 10.5 (with a logarithmic scale for the project lifetime) illustrates the importance of these two numbers. Consider a hypothetical (simplified) project to build a 1 MW wind turbine for a construction cost of \$3 million and with an estimated annual output of 3 million kWh, with no maintenance cost, residual value, or tax implications. The turbine has an hypothetical output of 8,760 MWh/year. However, wind conditions at the proposed site suggest a utilization rate of 34%. This amounts to an expected annual output of only 3,000 MWh/year for the turbine. With these simplifications,

$$\text{LEC} = \frac{I_0/E}{\sum_{t=1}^{T}(1 + r)^{-t}} = \frac{I_0}{E}\left[\frac{r(1 + r)^T}{(1 + r)^T - 1}\right], \qquad (10.2)$$

where I_0/E is calculated as 100¢/kWh. This amount is amortized over the turbine's expected lifetime. For any given discount rate and project lifetime (years of amortization), the curves in figure 10.5 show the corresponding LEC. For example, at a discount rate of 5% and a projected lifetime of 30 years, the turbine's LEC is 6.5¢/kWh. As figure 10.5 shows, the LEC calculation becomes more favourable as the amortization period gets longer and the discount rate gets smaller. Note that equation 10.1 can be further refined to include the cost of financing through equity or debt, or to account for a lengthy period of construction. LEC can also be widened in scope to include the cost of transmission, which can be an important consideration for power-generating facilities (wind farms, hydro dams, solar plants) that are expensive to connect to the electricity grid.

Fig. 10.5 Levellized Energy Cost: Sample Calculation (cents per kWh)

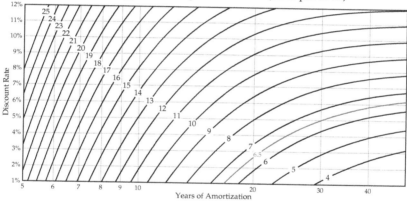

The method of financing a new power project can have significant influence on the LEC. The rate r above can be treated as a discount rate, but in practice it is the rate at which a project is financed. This in turn depends on the method of financing: debt or equity. Then the **weighted average cost of capital** (WACC) is defined as

$$r = \frac{E \cdot r_E + D \cdot r_D(1 - \tau)}{D + E} \quad , \tag{10.3}$$

where E is equity, D is debt, r_E and r_D are, respectively, the financing cost of debt and equity, and τ is the income tax rate.

In its *Annual Energy Outlook 2012*, the US Energy Information Administration presented levellized costs for generating technologies that are expected to be available in 2017. Table 10.3 shows these projections.

Among the renewable types of energy, electricity from wind is becoming increasingly competitive, although hydro remains the cheapest energy source. Among the non-renewable energy sources, advanced natural gas plants that use a combined cycle gas turbine will be the cheapest form to produce electricity after hydro. Introducing carbon capture and storage will add about $28/MWh to the LEC.

Table 10.3 Estimated Levellized Energy Cost for 2017 Plants ($/MWh)

Plant Type	Capacity Factor	Capital Cost	Fixed O&M	Variable O&M	Trans- mission	Total LEC
Conventional coal	85%	64.9	4.0	27.5	1.2	97.7
Coal with CCS	85%	91.8	9.3	36.4	1.2	138.8
Natural gas CCGT	87%	17.5	1.9	42.4	1.2	63.1
CCGT with CCS	87%	4.3	4.0	50.6	1.2	90.1
Advanced nuclear	90%	87.5	11.3	11.6	1.1	111.4
Geothermal	91%	75.1	11.9	9.6	1.5	98.2
Biomass	83%	56.0	13.8	44.3	1.3	115.4
Wind	33%	82.5	9.8	0.0	3.8	96.0
Solar photovoltaic	25%	140.7	7.7	0.0	4.3	152.7
Solar thermal	20%	195.6	40.1	0.0	6.3	242.0
Hydro	53%	76.9	4.0	6.0	2.1	88.9

Note: O&M denotes operation and maintenance cost. Source: US Energy Information Administration, *Annual Energy Outlook 2012*, June 2012, DOE/EIA-0383(2012). Note: CCS is carbon capture and storage. CCGT refers to a combined cycle gas turbine power plant. Hydro is assumed to have seasonal storage, but overall operation is limited by resources available by site and season.

10.5 Renewable energy

The case for renewable energy is simple: fossil fuels are exhaustible (although not for a long time yet), and renewable energy sources are inexhaustible. The primary source of renewable energy is the sun, regardless of whether sunlight is captured directly through photovoltaic cells and solar-thermal installations, or indirectly through wind turbines and hydroelectric dams. The secondary source of renewable energy is Earth's own heat, which is generated mostly from radioactive decay of potassium, uranium, and thorium isotopes. Together these renewable sources may suffice to eventually replace our dependence on fossil fuels. While enormous progress has been made in recent years to make renewable energy sources more competitive, they still account for only a small share of total energy production. There are four key reasons for the slow progress: (1) with the exception of hydro and wind, renewable energy sources remain relatively expensive; (2) fossil fuels are not priced to include their negative externalities (air pollution and contribution to climate change); (3) there remain formidable technical challenges introducing these energy sources into an energy system that has been optimized over decades to function with fossil fuels; and (4) some forms of renewable energy are intermittent and thus require storage. Figure 10.6 shows the world's progress of electricity generation from renewable sources over the last three decades. The diagram includes hydro-electric power, which remains the most important source of renewable energy.

Fig. 10.6 Worldwide Net Electricity Generation from Renewable Sources, 1980–2011

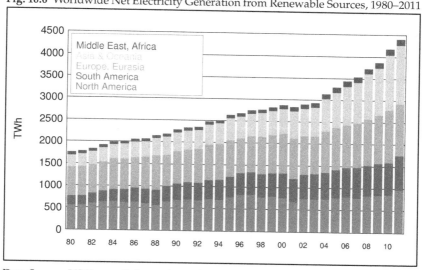

Data Source: US Energy Information Administration (www.eia.gov).

Solar energy

Perhaps the most exciting of the renewable energy sources is (direct) solar energy. Unfortunately, it remains also the most expensive form of renewable energy despite cost-reducing innovations in recent years. The promise of solar energy is huge. As the sun will keep on radiating energy for billions of years, the supply of solar energy is nearly inexhaustible given the right technology. The problem is how to harvest a sufficient amount of solar energy on the surface of Earth. The first problem is that only one side of Earth is facing the sun at any given time.

The second problem is that places close to the equator get more sunshine than those closer to the poles. The third problem is that some places have more cloud cover than others. The fourth and last problem is that many sunny places (such as the Sahara Desert) are not close to population centres. Put another way, solar energy faces problems of intermittency (and thus the need for storage) and long-distance transportation of electricity.

The two dominant technologies for direct harvesting of solar energy are photovoltaics (solar-electric power) and heliostats (solar-thermal power). Solar-electric installations can be found both at small scales (rooftop installations) and industrial scale (power plants). Heliostats are the domain of large-scale power plants. However, small rooftop solar-thermal panels are also in use in suitable locations.

Photovoltaic cells convert sunlight directly into electricity. There has been enormous progress to make these cells cheaper and more efficient, but there is a trade-off between cheap and efficient. Making solar cells more efficient makes them more complicated (by adding more layers or exotic chemicals) and thus more expensive. On the other hand, simpler types of cells can be massed produced more cheaply. As of 2012, the most advanced multijunction solar cells can reach efficiencies of over 40%. Mass-produced thin-film solar cells reach efficiencies of about 17%, and this is the most cost-effective technology at the moment. There are other emerging technologies, although they are still far from commercialization. Organic solar cells use conductive organic polymers to convert sunlight into electricity. This technology has relatively low efficiency, but eventually could be produced very cheaply.

The cost of photovoltaic installations is dropping considerably. Over the thirteen-year period from 1998 and 2010, capacity-weighted average installed cost in the United States declined from $11.0 per Watt to $6.2 per Watt (adjusted for inflation). This cost is somewhat higher for smaller systems; there are noticeable economies of scale in photovoltaic installations. In Germany, where grid-connected photovoltaic capacity is larger than in the United States, installed costs are noticeably lower ($4.2/W).

Heliostats focus sunlight through arrays of (adjustable) mirrors onto a central receiving tower, where the sunlight heats a working fluid that in turn drives a conventional steam turbine. There are a number of ways in which the mirrors are designed, or through which they track the sun over the course of the day. Heat storage is one way in which heliostats are evolving. The PS10 solar power plant in Spain, operating since 2006 with an installed capacity of 11 MW, stores pressurized steam (at 50 bar and 285°C), which works on the scale of about one hour. In July 2011, a new 19.9 MW installation in Spain that uses molten salt as heat storage was reported to generate electricity continuously during one day, achieving an important milestone for this industry. Perhaps more promising is the idea to combine a heliostat with a natural gas turbine system. The largest solar plant is the Ivanpah solar power plant in California's Mojave Desert, 64 km southwest of Las Vegas. Developed by BrigthSource Energy, the 173,500-mirror plant has a nominal capacity of 392 MW when fully completed. It opened in February 2014 and cost $2.2 billion. The project received extensive loan guarantees from the US Department of Energy to help build the plant.

In the very long run, space-based solar power may offer a better solution than earth-bound solar systems. Orbiting satellites could capture sunlight 24 hours a day, unobstructed by the atmosphere and thus receiving 1.4 times as much energy as Earth-based solar systems. The power generated in space can be beamed to a base station's rectenna as microwaves. A rectenna, or rectifying antenna, converts microwave energy into direct current electricity. Space-based solar power is not science fiction; the physics behind it is solid. It is economics that will put space-based solar systems out of reach for many decades yet. The cost of launching the required infrastructure into space is daunting. The necessary materials need to become lighter, and rocket launchers need to become much cheaper before such options could become reality.

As of 2011, most solar electricity was produced in Europe, with a large share of that in Germany, where solar electricity has been heavily subsidized by utility ratepayers. Overall electricity production, however, remains small. As shown in figure 10.7 (on page 309, in 2011 solar electricity generation (about 59 TWh) amount to just one-eight of wind electricity generation (about 446 TWh), which in turn was just about one-eight of hydroelectric generation (3,471 Twh).

Can solar energy ever produce enough electricity to satisfy world energy needs? World primary energy use comes to about 150,000 TWh per year. At current performance, a typical photovoltaic installation in mid-latitudes can generate about 1 kWh per square metre per day. Assume that future improvements in efficiency increase this to 4 kWh/m²/day, or 1.5 MWh/m²/year. Thus, we would need 100,000 km² of solar photovoltaic installations to produce world energy needs. This is roughly the size of Kentucky or Indiana. On a planetary scale, this is relatively small. This back-of-the-envelope calculation demonstrates that solar energy has the potential to be a true long-term energy alternative.

Wind energy

Next to hydroelectric power, wind energy is the most effective way of harvesting solar energy indirectly.

It is useful to understand some of the basic physics behind harvesting wind energy through wind turbines. The amount of power P transferred to a wind turbine is proportional to (a) the area πr^2 swept out by the rotor with radius r; (b) the density of the air $\rho = 1.225$ kg/m³; (c) the cube of the wind speed v^3; and (d) the efficiency of the turbine

$\alpha \leq 0.59$ According to Betz's Law, a wind turbine can extract a maximum of 59% of the energy that flows through the turbine's swept area. Good modern designs achieve $\alpha \approx 0.35$.

A point that is often not sufficiently appreciated is that the available power depends on the cube of the wind speed. Wind speed and power are not related in a simple linear fashion. In other words, a wind farm site with an average wind speed of 12 m/s is not 20% better than a site with average wind speed of 10 m/s, but 73% better!

Wind turbine design has undergone many important improvements in recent years, helped by increasing competition among manufacturers. The rotors of modern wind turbines can reach 90 m in diameter and most often have three blades. They operate at typical wind speeds between 4 m/s and 25 m/s. The blade pitch can be adjusted when wind speeds change, and gears inside the turbine adjust to keep the rotation speed in an optimal range. At very high speeds, the rotors need to cut out for safety reasons. Each wind turbine has a power curve that links wind speed to power output; this power curve is bounded by the cut-in and cut-out rotor speeds.

A wind turbine's blades make up the rotor, which causes a low-speed shaft to rotate. A gearbox translates this low-speed rotation into a high-speed rotation, which in turn generates high-voltage electricity in a generator. The sealed unit on top of a wind turbine tower is called a nacelle. A controller inside the nacelle reads data from an anemometer (a wind speed meter), which is used to rotate the tower into the wind using a yaw motor. As wind speeds vary, the pitch of the blade can be adjusted to boost power output at low winds or to protect the blades during high winds. A state-of-the-art wind turbine such as the Vestas V112 generates about 3 MW of rated capacity at a wind speed of 12–25 m/s. At a typical site, a wind turbine generates about 20% of the rated capacity. This means that a 3 MW turbine can generate about 5.2 GWh per year. To put this number into perspective, it would take about 115,000 of these 3 MW wind turbines to generate Canada's annual electricity demand. Put another way, electricity consumption averages about 17 MWh per year per person in Canada. This implies that a single 3 MW wind turbine can generate sufficient electricity for about 300 Canadians.

Building a wind farm involves numerous planning steps. A proposed site undergoes meteorological assessment. Not all good wind sites can be readily connected to a grid; many such sites are in inaccessible locations that would be too costly to connect to the grid.[4] A wind farm is designed to optimize the location of the wind turbines

---

[4] Locations are usually categorized as class A (within 50 km of a transmission line, more than one year of wind data), class B (less than one year of wind data, or not within 50 km of a transmission line), or class C (less than one year of wind data, and not within 100 km of a transmission line).

Fig. 10.7 Worldwide Net Electricy Generation from Wind Energy (left panel) and Solar, Tide, and Wave Energy (right panel), 2000–2011

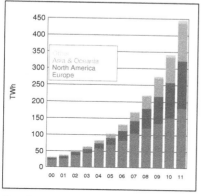
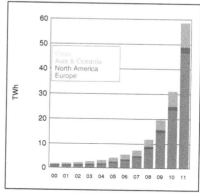

Data Source: United States Energy Information Administration (www.eia.gov).

with respect to wind flow, turbine performance, and a variety of other parameters. The proposed project is subject to an environmental impact assessment and subsequent approval. Often, land acquisition can involve complex negotiations with multiple parties, or it may involve dealing with difficult ownership rights.

The most important objection to wind energy is the intermittency of wind. Intermittency occurs at different scales. At the second/minute scale, intermittency is actually quite low. This means that power grids have time to adjust to changing wind conditions. At an hourly scale, variation is within ±1% about 70% of the time. Variability becomes larger at a scale of 4–12 hours. Winds also undergo seasonal cycles and are often stronger in the winter than in the summer. Intermittency can also be compensated on a local scale by grouping individual turbines into a wind farm. At regional scales, wind farms can be placed sufficiently far from each other so that they face different (uncorrelated) wind conditions.

One of the frontiers of wind energy is the development of offshore wind farms. Winds are usually stronger offshore than onshore. However, offshore wind farms are more expensive to construct because of higher connection costs to the grid and higher construction costs. The largest offshore wind farms are currently operating in the United Kingdom, with even larger projects under construction or in planning.

Biofuels

Biofuels are primarily derived from the conversion of biomass. The most prominent examples are bioethanol and biodiesel. Bioethanol is an alcohol produced through the fermentation of sugar and starch crops such as corn (preferred in the United States) or sugarcane (preferred in Brazil). Ethanol can be used as a fuel additive. Most gasoline engines can work with blended fuel that contains up to 10% ethanol. Biodiesel is produced primarily from vegetable oils through methanolysis and can be used in pure form or as an additive in conventional diesel fuel.

When Henry Ford started producing the Model T in 1908, it could run on any pure gasoline or pure ethanol, or any combination thereof. At the beginning of the 20th century, biofuels competed with oil-based fuels because of the limited supply of the latter. Only in recent years have car manufacturers returned to introducing vehicles capable of using a blend of ethanol and gasoline, known as E85 (a blend of 85% ethanol and 15% gasoline). Despite the introduction of E85-capable vehicles, their use in the United States remains very limited because the network of refuelling stations for E85 is not very dense; most of them are located in the 'corn belt' where ethanol is produced. Government mandates in the United States and Canada seek to increase the ethanol content of gas sold at the pump to 10%. Unmodified engines are able to handle an E10 blend.

Since the oil crisis in 1974, Brazil has turned to biofuels to reduce its dependence on oil. After the United States, Brazil is the second largest producer of biofuels. Production of ethanol from corn is significantly less efficient than producing it from sugarcane. Sugarcane is one of the most efficient photosynthesizers, but it requires a tropical or subtropical climate with sufficient rainfall. Brazilian sugarcane-derived ethanol is noticeably cheaper than US corn-derived ethanol. Using corn as feedstock also requires an additional technical step. Whereas ethanol can be produced from sugarcane through yeast fermentation, producing ethanol from corn requires upgrading the corn starch into sugar before distilling. Until the end of 2011, the United States restricted imports of Brazilian ethanol with a 54-cent per gallon tariff.

Controversy surrounds the production of fuel ethanol from corn in the United States. First, ethanol production used to be heavily subsidized. The US Congress let a production subsidy expire at the beginning of 2012, which cost taxpayers about $6 billion per year. In Canada, ethanol production continues to be subsidized at a rate of about $250 million per year. Second, corn is also used to feed livestock, and therefore diverting corn to ethanol production increases input prices for food producers. This induced substitution towards ethanol production raises food prices.

Could a country such as the United States ever replace all its energy needs with biofuel? The answer is a resounding no. Even if the United States' entire 340 million acres (1.376 million km^2) of in-use cropland (according to the US agricultural census 2002) was dedicated to ethanol production, and assuming (optimistically) a productivity of 440 gallons

Fig. 10.8 Worldwide Production of Biofuels, 2000–2010

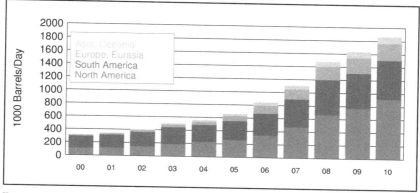

Data Source: US Energy Information Administration. Biofuels includes bioethanol and biodiesel. Net generation excludes energy consumed by generating units.

of ethanol per acre per year, total output would amount to only about 150 billion gallons (3.56 bbls) of ethanol. Because the energy density of oil is about 50% higher than ethanol, this is equivalent to about 2.4 bbls of oil per year. The United States consumes about 6.9 bbls of oil per year, so biofuel could replace only about a third of total US oil consumption even in an exaggerated scenario where cropland is used exclusively for ethanol production—and zero food production.

It would require a new type of biofuel with a much larger energy density than that offered by conventional crops to turn biofuel into a large-scale source of energy. It has been proposed to produce ethanol from algae, a process that is projected to have a productivity sixteen times higher than corn-based ethanol and seven times higher than sugarcane-based ethanol. No commercial operation exists yet, and these projections remain speculative. Even with a major breakthrough in algae-based biofuels, it is difficult to envision how this technology could be scaled up sufficiently to make a major contribution to the world's energy supply.

Propelled primarily by generous subsidies, worldwide production of biofuels has increased significantly in the last decade as shown in figure 10.8.

Geothermal energy

Our Earth contains a large storage of heat that is trapped inside its core and mantle. With increasing depth from the surface, temperatures rise along a temperature gradient. Below Earth's crust, beneath about 60 km depth, temperatures in the partially molten rock reach 700°C–1,200°C.

Heat is constantly escaping from Earth's surface, but the heat flow is concentrated in certain areas where the crust is thinner, primarily along the mid-ocean ridges and mantle plumes.

Earth's heat can be harvested as geothermal energy. However, to be economically useful, the heat has to be sufficiently close to the surface to be within drilling reach. In most parts of the world, the depth temperature gradient is insufficient to make geothermal energy economical. Therefore, the temperatures available to drive a steampower plant are relatively low, and this in turn limits the thermal efficiency of converting heat into electricity. Large-scale geothermal plants thus remain the domain of geologically favourable locations where steam occurs naturally, such as Iceland, which is on top of a mid-oceanic ridge, and along what is knowns as the 'ring of fire' of volcanic activity (along the west coast of North and South America, and in Japan and Indonesia).

There are two commonly used methods of converting geothermal heat into electricity. The flash steam process requires temperatures in excess of 180°C. Subsurface high-pressure water is brought to the surface where it 'flashes' into low-pressure steam that drives a turbine. The other method is known as the binary cycle process and is useful for lower-temperature environments. Hot geothermal water is run through a heat exchanger that transfers the heat to a liquid that boils at a low temperature, and the steam from this working fluid drives the turbine. The name 'binary cycle' derives from the use of two closed loops. In a binary cycle, the geothermal water is re-injected into the ground.

Technological advances in recent years have expanded the scope for geothermal energy use. So-called enhanced geothermal systems (EGS) allows tapping into the heat in hot dry rock formations. EGS involves hydraulic stimulation: pumping pressurized water through injection wells into the rock formations in order to fracture the rock and increase its permeability.[5] Injecting water into these dry rocks generates heat, which in turn drives a conventional turbine.

Beyond the use of geothermal energy for power generation is the potential for a so-called geothermal heat pump, also known as a geo-exchange system. These devices actually do not make use of geothermal energy. A heat pump takes advantage of the ground's heating and cooling property—namely that temperatures near but below the ground remain relatively stable while above-ground temperatures change with the weather. Heat pumps facilitate heat exchange: they cool when it's hot outside, and they heat when it's cold outside. Their use is often very cost effective. However, geo-exchange systems should not be confused with true geothermal power systems.

---

[5] Hydraulic stimulation in EGS generates hydraulic shearing, which is similar to but not identical to hydraulic fracturing. Hydraulic fracturing uses proppants, whereas hydraulic shearing does not. Hydraulic fracturing also creates much larger fractures than the hydraulic shearing involved in EGS.

Compared to the recent boom in wind and solar energy, geothermal energy production has been rising more gradually. As of 2010, the total of about 64 TWh geothermal energy production occurred in a small number of countries with favourable conditions: the United States (15.7 TWh), the Philippines (9.4), Indonesia (8.5), Mexico (6.3), New Zealand (5.6), Italy (5.1), Iceland (4.3), and Japan (2.5).

10.6 Smart power grids and super grids

Electricity transmission grids are a backbone of modern society that we easily take for granted. We only realize how dependent we are on electricity when the grid goes down. A massive ice storm in January 1988 crippled the electric grid in Ontario and Quebec. Trees and utility poles toppled, and more than 130 hydro towers collapsed. Four million people were out of power for days. In August 2003, malfunctions originating with an electric utility in Ohio tripped a cascading system failure that shut down transmission lines and power plants all across the Northeastern and Midwestern United States and Ontario. As many as 45 million people in eight US states and 10 million people in Ontario were affected. But even this blackout pales in comparison with the power outage in India in July 2012. Hundreds of millions of people were left without electricity in northern and eastern India after the power grid collapsed due to overload and coordination failures. Enter the smart grid. The box below provides a definition.

The smart grid overlays the electricity distribution grid with an information and net metering system. It includes intelligent monitoring systems and two-way communication between producers and consumers of electricity. The objective of the smart grid is to facilitate energy conservation and increase the reliability of the distribution network. A smart grid is able to self-adjust to demand and supply fluctuations.

A smart grid pursues three objectives. The first is energy conservation. One way to promote energy conservation is to price electricity differently at different times of day or during summer and winter; this is known as peak-load pricing and has a strong foundation in economics. Table 10.4 shows the pricing structure in Ontario as of May 2012. The off-peak time covers nights, weekends, and holidays. The peak period is switched between winter and summer. During the summer, the peak load is during working hours, while in the winter, peak load is during the 'shoulder' hours when most people are at home.

Table 10.4 Ontario, Residential Weekday Time-of-Use Pricing, May 2012

	Summer (May-October)	Winter (November-April)	Rate (cents/kWh)
On-peak	11:00-17:00	07:00-11:00, 17:00-19:00	11.7
Mid-peak	07:00-11:00, 17:00-19:00	11:00-17:00	10.0
Off-peak	19:00-07:00	19:00-07:00	6.5

Note: weekends and statutory holidays count as off-peak period.

The second objective of a smart grid is to facilitate the deployment of renewable energy sources, and in particular to support microgeneration (households with rooftop solar panels, for instance). More important in the long run is the third objective: building an adaptive infrastructure where demand can be adjusted by communicating with devices that use electricity. A smart appliance such as ventilation or air conditioning system could shut itself off during periods when power supply has trouble meeting demand. Such adaptive systems can prevent blackouts. A key element in a smart grid is the smart meter.

A smart meter is an advanced electrical meter that records consumption in intervals of an hour or less and communicates that information at least daily through a two-way link to the utility company for monitoring and billing purposes (telemetering). Smart meters facilitate time-of-use metering and net metering; they can also communicate with smart appliances.

Net metering is a method for small producers of electricity (typically from renewable sources) to receive credit for the net amount of electricity they feed into the distribution network. Net metering is needed to facilitate microgeneration.

Smart appliances are equipped with a control system that interfaces with the utility provider through the smart meter. If a client has agreed to participate and registered a smart appliance, the utility company can remotely control the appliance if needed. For example, an air conditioning unit's thermostat could be temporarily changed to reduce electricity use, or completely shut off for a limited time. If a utility company can do this with many such appliances, the disruptions to individual customers can be quite small. It is even conceivable (and economically sensible) to compensate customers for their participation or their incurred inconvenience. Paying off customers in this manner may be cheaper than bringing peak-load generating capacity online.

Even a smart grid will not be able to overcome a basic constraint that hampers the progress of renewable energy: interconnectedness. Today, continental Europe has the largest unified grid in the world that connects more than twenty countries. North America's power grid is divided. The western states and provinces are part of the Western interconnection, and the eastern states and provinces are part of the Eastern interconnection. Quebec and Texas have separate interconnections. In each interconnection, the alternating current (AC) in its grid is synchronized to the same 60 Hz cycle. Coupling interconnections occurs through direct current (DC), but the capacity of these interties is small. The idea to integrate these separate grids is not novel, but has become more urgent recently. The idea is to form a super grid.

A super grid is the integration of small power grids into a wide-area interconnected network of power grids. It requires connecting separate grids through interties and building long-distance transmission capacity.

Renewable energy sources—sun, wind, and hydro—are often located far away from urban centres. The transmission system needs to be expanded to reach these remote locations. In addition, when renewable energy sources are intermittent, the intermittency can be compensated for by having a higher degree of wide-area interconnectedness: the wind blows always somewhere, and the sun always shines somewhere. Building such a grid requires a lot more long-distance transmission capacity. Technologically, the best way to achieve this is through high-voltage direct-current (HVDC) lines.[6] Superconductors, although technologically superior, are not yet economical for long-distance bulk transmission.

10.7 Energy conservation and energy efficiency

Faced with rising energy costs, the most attractive option for small and large businesses alike is to explore ways to improve energy efficiency and engage in energy conservation. Often, energy efficiency measures are cost effective and environmentally beneficial: a win-win strategy. The potential for energy conservation is quite large, and the need for energy conservation is even larger if economic growth and increasing prosperity in developing countries ramp up energy demand. Rather than accommodating the planet's growing population

---

[6] HVDC lines have fewer losses and can be used as undersea cables through salt water. AC cables suffer high line losses due to high capacitance when used in salty water. On the downside, HVDC requires more costly conversion, switching and control technology. There are two types of HDVC cables: monopole and earth return, or bipole. In Canada, the Nelson River Bipole consists of three lines to connect the Nelson River Hydro Project to the Manitoba grid. A 2 GW HVDC line connects Quebec to New England.

Box 10.1: Energy Efficiency and the Rebound Effect

Promoting energy efficiency lacks the red-ribbon-cutting appeal of opening a new geothermal power plant or wind farm. Yet energy efficiency is one of the low-hanging fruits of reducing emissions and dependency on fossil fuels. In many cases, energy efficiency can go hand-in-hand with cost reductions. Cars that are more fuel efficient reduce emissions and operating costs at the same time (even though their capital cost may be somewhat higher).

The Achilles heel of promoting energy efficiency is the rebound effect. Basic economics tells us that expenditures saved from improved efficiency may in turn lead to higher demand. If your car is 25% more fuel efficient, you may decide to drive more as you can now afford to drive 25% more on the same budget. Determining the magnitude of the rebound effect is an important empirical question. The rebound effect is generally expressed as a percentage of the expected environmental benefit that is lost due to the induced increase in consumption. In principle it can even exceed 100%; a

situation where the policy backfires completely is known as the Jevons paradox. In practice, the rebound effect for better fuel efficiency is probably in the 10%–20% range. In other applications it is unlikely to exceed 30%. This means that promoting energy efficiency makes a lot of sense: the rebound effect is not ignorable, but it is small.

Why do people focus so little effort on energy efficiency? This is sometimes called the 'energy paradox.' Many people are simply unaware of the potential emission and cost reductions. This is in part a problem of product labelling. Consumers need to be able to take energy consumption into account when making purchasing decisions. Energy Star labels are a useful step in this direction. The other big challenge is political. Governments are often not interested in designing clever incentives for energy efficiency. Such bread-and-butter programs offer fewer photo-ops for presidents and prime ministers than cutting ribbons.

and wealth through a massive expansion of energy supply, investing in energy efficiency provides a more sustainable solution for future generations. Energy efficiency has already increased dramatically over the last decades. Per unit of gross domestic product, the United States uses less than half as much energy as in the 1970s. This reduction is a combination of composition and technique effects. An economy can change its industrial composition towards less energy-intensive activities (e.g., services), and innovation contributes to pure efficiency gains. Specialization through international trade is a significant determinant of an economy's sectoral composition. If a trade-induced composition effect was driving efficiency improvements in the United States, other countries would pay for this by seeing their own efficiency decrease. Estimates attribute about half or two-thirds of the efficiency gains to technique effects. This leaves some scope for benefits from a composition effect.

Companies in the industrialized world are well-prepared to pursue greater energy efficiency. What is often holding back investments in energy efficiency is a type of market failure. Companies may have locked in prices for energy (in particular electricity) through long-term contracts, or they are subsidized by utilities through preferential rates. The same is true for many developing countries that subsidize fuel prices for political reasons. Removing these subsidies and liberalizing energy markets is an important element in promoting greater efficiency. For market mechanisms to do their work, prices need to reflect scarcity.

The airline industry is a good example for effective response to changing energy prices. As fuel prices rise, airlines are eager to improve efficiency in both the short term and long term. In the short term, airlines strive to increase the capacity utilization of their planes. In the long term, airlines demand ever more efficient airplanes from aircraft manufacturers. The world's first and only commercial supersonic passenger jet, the Concorde, now retired, was massively fuel inefficient; it consumed about 17 litres per passenger per 100 km. The new Airbus A380 and Boeing's new 787 'Dreamliner' both manage about 3 litres per passenger per 100 km.

The pursuit of energy efficiency faces one potential obstacle: the rebound effect. Cost savings from greater energy efficiency have a beneficial income effect. This income gain can lead to more energy use. Box 10.1 explores this issue. Pursuing energy efficiency also requires a change in the corporate mindset: focusing on many small steps rather than few big steps. Yergin (2011) explores this question in the discussion of US-based Dow Chemical, one of the world's largest chemical companies. The company managed to reduce energy use by 25% between 1995 and 2005, spending $1 billion on this effort but reaping $9 billion in benefits. One important solution involved cogeneration: plants that provide heat and power together, which increases the overall efficiency. Box 10.2 illustrates in greater detail how energy efficiency can be pursued in an industry. As investigated by Xu et al. (2012), the pulp and paper industry in North America is in the process of adopting numerous improvements in energy efficiency to stay competitive.

10.7.1 Technology

Improvements in energy efficiency are ultimately guided by technological developments. Replacing inefficient incandescent light bulbs with efficient fluorescent or LED light bulbs is made possible by the technological innovations into the latter.

Box 10.2: Energy Efficiency in the Pulp and Paper Industry

Pulp and paper mills in North America are often decades old. Global competition has put them under intense pressure to innovate and stay competitive. Due to the industry's high energy intensity, improving energy efficiency can reduce costs as well as greenhouse gas emissions. While the industry is consolidating and the oldest and least efficient plants are shut down, the surviving plants are investing in new technologies to generate greater efficiencies. Because pulp and paper mills produce a variety of different products, their approaches can be quite different.

The first step towards greater efficiency always involves an audit of the current performance and bench-marking with respect to other plants, in particular 'best-of-class' performers. Auditing involves a systematic analysis of the separate steps in the manufacturing process. For mechanical pulp mills, this involves wood preparation (debarking and chipping), grinding and refining, screening and washing, and bleaching. For chemical pulp mills, this involves wood preparation, cooking, screening and washing, evaporation, chemical preparation, and bleaching. For paper mills, this includes forming, pressing, drying, and calendering. For each of these steps, the audit estimates the amount of energy (fuel, steam, and electricity) that is required per unit of output. This analysis reveals where energy is used the most, and where small efficiency improvements can yield large energy savings.

In the next step, potential energy gains are combined with cost estimates for achieving them. This information can be visualized in a McKinsey curve that ranks each project by increasing discounted cost (per unit of energy use). Projects whose cost is below the prevailing energy price should be adopted immediately because they save costs. Projects above the prevailing energy price should be adopted only if there are additional incentives (from utilities or governments) or cost considerations (such as carbon taxes).

Research by Xu et al. (2012) has identified several significant sources of energy efficiency in the pulp and paper industry. Some of them are at or below the prevailing energy price. The greatest energy savings by far can be achieved through increased use of recycled paper. Using fibres from recycled paper instead of virgin material can save over 40% of energy in this step, and 15%–20% overall. However, using recycled fibres does pose some challenges with de-inking and lower quality of the final paper product.

Improved maintenance can also generate significant improvements in energy efficiency. Steam traps are automatic valves that discharge condensate without loss of heat. They have a relatively high failure rate (about 10% per year). Proactive maintenance and replacement of steam traps can reduce the failure rate and resulting steam losses. Replacing steam traps is relatively inexpensive. Saving energy also improves operational efficiency through reduced downtime.

Some options are technologically feasible but are not cost effective. For example, the drying section of conventional paper mills uses steam. An alternative is the use of a condebelt, where paper is dried through contact with a continuous hot steel band. This process dries paper much faster, but has high capital cost.

Until recently, most coal-and-gas-fired power plants achieved thermal efficiencies of about 35%. This means that only about a third of the energy content of the fuel was converted into electricity, and the remaining two-thirds was wasted as heat. The development of the combined cycle gas turbine (CCGT) has improved the thermal efficiency to over 50%. The most advanced CCGT systems, such as the 561 MW Irsching power plant in Vohburg, Germany, reach 60.4% efficiency. Conventional power plants use a single cycle, where a boiler converts water into high-pressure steam, which drives a turbine, which in turn drives an electric generator. Mechanical limits of the system limit steam temperatures to about 650°C, which limits the the thermal efficiency of the cycle.

A CCGT operates two thermal cycles: a gas turbine cycle and a conventional steam cycle. The gas turbine is relatively compact and makes use of alloys that can withstand much greater heat than can a steel-based steam turbine. A gas turbine consists of a gas compressor, a burner (combustion chamber), and an expansion turbine. The intake temperature of the gas turbine can range from 900°C to 1400°C, and the exit temperature from 450°C to 650°C. This exit temperature is still sufficient to drive a secondary steam cycle by way of a heat exchanger. Typically, the gas cycle generates about twice as much electricity as the steam cycle. The higher efficiency of such plants helps reduce the cost of electricity, which adds to the benefit from the emerging sources of cheap natural gas discussed earlier. The Irsching plant in Germany emits about 330 g of CO_2 per kWh. This compares very favourably with electricity from coal (835 g/kWh for anthracite/hard coal and 940 g/kWh for lignite/soft coal) or even fuel oil (620 g/kWh).

10.7.2 Conservation measures

While large companies often face specific energy efficiency challenges due to the nature of the industry in which they operate, small and medium-sized businesses can engage in a number of activities. Such firms are well-advised to perform an energy audit to establish a baseline of their energy consumption and assess the costs and benefits of energy-saving measures. Below are suggestions for such measures.

Lighting

All commercial buildings have lighting, and especially for firms in the services sector, lighting can account for a sizable share of the electricity budget. Energy-efficient fluorescent lamps save about 15%–20% of the wattage that is used by standard fluorescent lamps, and they often last longer too. For example, standard 4-foot T8 lamps consume 32 Watts. Newer low-wattage versions of this type consume 25 or 28 Watts. The slight reduction in light output is generally not detectable by most people, and is actually compensated for by the higher colour temperature (5000 K versus 3500 K or 4100 K) that is perceived as brighter. When standard fluorescent lamps are replaced with energy-efficient lamps, it is necessary to replace the existing ballast. Electronic ballasts are much quieter than conventional ballasts. Electronics ballasts can change the power frequency of 60 Hz to 20,000 Hz or higher, which eliminates the familiar flicker and hum of older fluorescent lights. The cost savings can be substantial. Replacing lights amortizes within two or three years.

Another way to improve lighting is to focus the light by using task lighting (focused light rather than illuminating everything) and reflectors. Compact fluorescent lamps (CFLs) are also highly cost-effective replacements for ordinary incandescent light bulbs.

Often lighting is not controlled effectively. Manually controlled, it may be on when nobody is around or when daylight is providing satisfactory natural illumination. Automatic controls using motion detectors and light sensors can play an important part in reducing energy use. Areas that are less frequently used (storage rooms and conference rooms, for example) are ideal candidates for installing automatic controls.

Buildings

A popular misconception about building ventilation is that buildings need a certain amount of air flow and air leakage to bring in fresh air. Many buildings, especially older buildings, have far more air leakage than required for ventilation, thus wasting large amounts of money. Windows are a major source of leakage of air and heat. Proper insulation can prevent excessive air leakage. Newer generations of windows also experience less heat loss. Insted of using single-glazed windows, double-glazing or triple-glazing—where the panes are separated by a vacuum, air, or another gas such as argon, krypton, or xenon—can significantly reduce heat transfer.

Buildings often contain spaces that are not used or not used during certain periods of the day. Reducing space heating in areas that are not permanently occupied or during periods in which they are unoccupied can reduce energy use. In many instances a simple timer-controlled thermostat can improve the situation.

Retrofitting existing buildings faces limitations. Designing a new building as a green building offers significantly more opportunities for energy conservation. Developed by the US Green Building Council in the late 1990s and later mirrored by the Canada Green Building Council, the Leadership in Energy and Environmental Design (LEED) is a rating system for the design, construction, and operation of new buildings. In the current LEED 2009 version, a building can earn up to 100 points in five categories: site sustainability (28 points), water efficiency (10 points), energy and atmosphere (37 points), materials and resources

(13 points), and indoor environmental quality (12 points). Projects that reach at least 40 points may also qualify for 6 extra points for innovative design or for 4 extra points for regional priority. The sum of points determines the certification level: certified (40–49); silver (50–59); gold (60–79); and platinum (80+).

The single most important LEED category is energy efficiency. Because buildings have different uses (office buildings, small retail stores, large warehouses, schools, etc.) the specific design guides and baseline calculations also differ. The energy savings over the baseline determine the number of points. For example, a building with a 25% energy reduction over baseline only earns 1 point, whereas a building with an energy reduction of 56% or more earns the maximum 19 points in this category. LEED buildings can also earn points for making use of renewable energy; new constructions can earn the maximum of 7 points in this category if 13% or more of its energy is from renewable sources.

For individual homes, architectural innovation (primarily originating in Germany and Sweden) has led to the development of the passive house, also known as an ultra-low energy building. The method to accomplish the goal of limiting primary energy use to 120 kWh/m^2/year involves superinsulation, passive solar heating, reducing air leakage through airtightness, and reducing heat loss through high-performance windows. Houses that achieve the target could in principle make do without conventional heating systems, although most such buildings will include a heating system for occasional supplemental use. Because passive houses are more airtight than conventional houses and therefore have less ventilation, a heat recovery system can provide fresh air without losing heat. The heat recovery system works as an air-to-air heat exchanger: it exchanges the heat between the incoming and outgoing air so that the heat stays inside the building. In a passive house, heat is generated by its occupants. On average, a person emits heat equivalent to 100 Watts.

HVAC systems

Heating, ventilation and air conditioning (HVAC) systems often account for the largest share of energy cost in small firms. Where employee or customer comfort is paramount, or where products require storage under certain ideal temperature conditions, businesses place great demands on the performance of their HVAC systems. There are essentially two options for dealing with HVACs: reduce the need for HVACs, or run existing HVACs more efficiently. Reducing the need for HVACs is easiest at construction time. A suitable building design can reduce the required capacity of an HVAC system, and in some cases even obviate the need for an HVAC system. A geo-exchange system, a solar-thermal rooftop, and cleverly designed natural ventilation can change the energy balance of a new building significantly. As for retrofitting existing HVAC systems, often the most promising option is the use of smart control systems and sensors that operate HVACs only as much as needed and only when needed.

Computers and office machines

There is a widespread perception that keeping computers, monitors, copiers, and other office machinery on all the time prolongs their lifetime, as frequent power cycles are thought to accelerate wear and tear or lead to more frequent machine failures. Modern office equipment has become very resilient to power cycling, and shutting off equipment when not in use has little if any effect on their durability. Consequently, shutting off machinery when not in use can save considerable amounts of electricity. Some machinery can be programmed to shut itself off at night and turn back on in the morning.

Electric motors

Electric motors are used extensively throughout businesses; they are used in pumps, fans, compressors, drills, and in materials processing and handling. It is quite typical that the annual operating cost of an electric motor in terms of electricity use widely exceeds the capital cost of that motor. Replacing less efficient motors with more efficient motors can thus amortize remarkably quickly, even though energy-efficient motors can be 30% more expensive. Higher-quality motors may also have a longer operating life.

Vehicles

Many businesses maintain vehicle fleets for procurement or delivery, or a variety of other tasks. The key operating expense is fuel. Purchasing alternative energy vehicles, or retrofitting existing vehicles, can be an effective response to rising fuel prices. For passenger-size vehicles, moving towards hybrid gas-electric or diesel-electric cars often provides long-term cost savings. Plug-in electric vehicles remain relatively expensive and have limited range, which makes them less attractive for many business applications. Converting trucks from diesel fuel to (compressed) natural gas is becoming an increasingly attractive option in the presence of low prices for natural gas.

10.8 Summary

The era of cheap abundant oil has passed. The world is about to enter an era of expensive oil, increasing substitution towards alternative energies, and increasing energy conservation. The notion of peak oil correctly predicted a peak in production of oil in the United States in the 1970s. Nevertheless, worldwide oil production has slightly increased over the last few years and hovers around 80 million barrels per day; there is no indication that the global peak has been reached. It is more likely that the world has entered a plateau phase of oil production where production is shifting from conventional (cheap) oil sources to unconventional (expensive) oil sources that include oil sands, shale oil, deep sea oil, and Arctic oil. At the same time, increasing demand for oil from rapidly developing economies in Asia will squeeze available reserves and continue to keep prices near or above $100/barrel. Proven reserves continue to expand, and the high price of oil will continue to propel the development of unconventional sources.

Meanwhile, new production methods such as fracking have produced a glut in natural gas production. Prices for natural gas have fallen in the United States. Wellhead prices in early 2012 were at about $100 per thousand cubic metres ($2.89 per thousand cubic feet), well below their all-time peak price, which was three times higher in mid-2008.

Nuclear energy is marred in controversy, and the Fukushima disaster following the earthquake and tsunami in March 2011 have renewed the public's unease with this technology, which had already been tested by the Chernobyl disaster in 1986. While nuclear energy helps reduce the world's carbon footprint, many of the existing reactors are aging and use outdated technologies. Innovation shows the way to safer and more efficient designs. For example, the CANDU reactor design that uses heavy water as a coolant and moderator is inherently safer than older technologies. Even if reactors can be operated more safely, questions about storing radioactive waste safely for thousands of years remain. Less radioactive alternatives exist (based on the thorium cycle), but remain underutilized. Nuclear energy will continue to play a significant and useful role, but probably more as a transition technology than as the main energy source of the future.

Renewable energy sources are making inroads, but slowly. The oldest and best-developed source is hydroelectricity, but the potential for new dams is small. The most competitive of the newer sources is wind energy. Many countries have started deploying wind turbines and wind farms effectively. However, a key challenge for wind energy (as well as solar energy) is its intermittency. Such alternative sources require back-up supply or storage options. Large-scale storage is still costly, and thus the share of electricity that can be provided by intermittent power sources is currently limited. Other types of renewable energy such as geothermal energy are ideal for certain locations, such as Iceland, but face significant technical and economic hurdles in other regions. In the long term, the only abundant inexhaustible energy resource is solar energy. Finding the most efficient way to tap into this resource will be the key technological challenge for the future, along with novel methods for transporting and storing energy and electricity.

Last but not least, with rising energy prices, energy conservation will become more and more attractive. Investing in energy efficiency is often a win-win proposition for businesses and consumers alike. Often it involves substituting higher (up-front) capital costs for lower operating costs.

Businesses are confronted with the challenge of planning ahead and making choices about their energy systems in a world of uncertainty about future prices and energy sources. Therefore, the key strategies for businesses involve

- investing in energy efficiency to save costs;
- planning for energy flexibility where feasible, allowing for switching fuel or energy sources in response to changing prices;
- relocating to low-cost locations if the business operation can be moved (e.g., a cloud computing centre);
- long-term energy contracting to secure prices and supply; and
- developing partnerships with utilities and energy companies to facilitate energy-related R&D that generates new options and technologies for the future.

10.9 Study questions and exercises

1. What is 'peak oil,' and what are the pros and cons of the argument that the world has reached the peak of global oil production?
2. What is the difference between conventional sources and unconventional sources of oil and gas?
3. Explain the price gap for oil between the Brent and Cushing (West Texas Intermediate) benchmarks. What are potential reasons?
4. What are the major problems associated with electricity from renewable sources?
5. It has been suggested that solar-thermal power could be combined with natural gas into a hybrid power plant that uses sunlight during the day and natural gas during the nights. What are the economic merits of such a compromise?
6. What are the economic and societal conditions for and against a 'nuclear renaissance,' before an after Fukushima?
7. Explain the concept of 'passive safety' in relation to modern designs of nuclear reactors.

8. It is technologically conceivable that fossil fuels could be used cleanly without greenhouse gas emissions? What would be needed to make that happen? Is it economically feasible?
9. What are the low-hanging fruits of energy conservation? Identify examples.
10. What is the 'rebound effect'?

Exercises

1. Work through an example of levellized energy cost (LEC). Use a spreadsheet or similar numerical software application. Assume a wind turbine of 3 MW nominal capacity costs $4 million to deploy. Operating it costs $25,000/year, and the decommissioning cost (minus residual value) amounts to $250,000. Further assume a tax rate of 18%, a depreciation (capital cost allowance) rate of 30%, and a discount rate of 10%. The lifespan of the turbine is 30 years. The turbine has a load factor of 34.25% (or 3,000 hours per year). Calculate the LEC for the turbine. (Answer: $45.4/MWh)
2. Investigate the building in which you work or go to school. How much electricity and natural gas is used for lighting, cooling, and heating? Establish an energy balance and try to benchmark this building's energy intensity (kWh per square metre) against similar buildings. Is there potential to improve the energy efficiency of that building?
3. Tidal power has been proposed as a further contributor to renewable energy. Explore the available technological options and economic potential of this power source. The Bay of Fundy, bordering New Brunswick and Nova Scotia in Canada and Maine in the United States, has been identified as a key location. The first commercial tidal power system was launched in Eastport, Maine, in 2012 by Ocean Renewable Power Company; output is scheduled to expand from 180 kW to 5 MW of electricity over the next years.
4. As a classroom exercise, discuss the 2013 documentary film 'Pandora's Promise' (see pandorapromise.com for additional information). In conjunction with the discussions in this chapter, what are the economic and environmental pros and cons relating to nuclear power? How does public perception square with the scientific facts?

Chapter 11
Resource Management

The management of resources is an integral part of environmental management. Virtually always the extraction of resources is associated with environmental impact. This chapter identifies important links between resource and environmental management. To facilitate a sound understanding of resource management, it is necessary to discuss some of the underlying economic principles. The economic theory underlying resource management can be fairly complex because it often involves dynamic optimization problems. While this chapter does not eschew mathematical treatment, it tries to do so by focusing primarily on the key assumptions and outcomes of the economic models. While knowledge of optimal control theory is helpful, it is not essential. Readers unfamiliar with the mathematical approach can skip most of the related discussion and focus on the prescriptive elements.

Exhaustible resources are those that have a finite stock, even though the exact amount of that stock may not be fully known yet. The key economic question about exhaustible resources is how fast a society should draw down these resources. And furthermore, what comes after the resource is exhausted? Is there a backstop technology that takes over, or can the recovered resources be recycled and reused?

A renewable resource is characterized by its ability to regenerate itself in some form, such as through a biological growth process. Fish and forests fall into this category. The key economic question about renewable resources is: what is the rate at which the resource can be harvested sustainably?

Whereas property rights for exhaustible resources are usually well defined, the same is not true for renewable resources. Many renewable resources suffer from open access problems, which leads to the tragedy of the commons problem that was discussed in the chapter on environmental economics. Policy interventions attempt to rectify property issues by creating or enforcing property rights. This problem is particularly pronounced in the fisheries industry.

Natural renewable resources often exhibit social benefits that exceed the private benefits. For example, timber harvested in a forest is a private benefit, whereas the ecosystem functions provided by a forest are social benefits. The gap between social and private benefits—the positive externalities—justifies the use of policy interventions to protect the renewable resource.

This section is organized around major resource industries: mining, forestry, and fisheries. The beginning of each section introduces underlying economic principles for exhaustible and renewable resources. The discussion of forestry and fisheries highlights the importance of property rights, which are well defined for forests but much less so for fisheries. The discussion of exhaustible resources in this chapter is based on Slade and Thille (2009) and Gaudet (2007). Elements of this chapter are inspired by the treatment of resource economics and resource management in Field (2008) and Mitchell (2010).

11.1 Mining

Mining activities cover a wide range of natural resources. They include metals, minerals, as well as fossil fuels. Mining an exhaustible resource always has a time dimension: how fast should the resource be extracted, and what happens when the resource is exhausted? The underlying economic questions are addressed in greater detail below.

Mining activities also have an environmental footprint. Extraction activities are associated with land and water use. Geological conditions determine where the metals and minerals are found, and working within this location constraint can make extraction environmentally problematic. Processing resources through smelting and refining is often associated with considerable amounts of emissions and waste materials. There are three main approaches to mining:

- **Surface mining** or **open-pit mining** involves extraction of layers of deposits at increasing depth. Ore is transported to industrial facilities for concentrating, smelting, or refining. Open pit mining is used extensively for iron, copper, gold, and silver extraction.
- **Underground mines** require construction of a shaft to a layer of ore deep in the ground. Passages (known as drifts) are excavated from the central shaft at different depths, typically following a particular seam. The central shaft can be vertical into the ground or horizontal into a mountain. Ore is brought to the surface for further processing. Underground mines are used for a variety of metals and minerals, including coal and salt.
- **Fluid mining** entails drilling into rock and using chemical leaching solutions (usually a dilute acid) to penetrate the deposits and dissolve the ore. The solution is brought back to the surface for separating the metals from the solvent. Fluid mining is sometimes used for extracting copper.

In general, open-pit mining is more economical and safer than underground mining. The availability of large-scale earth-moving equipment has made open-pit mining more practical even though it often involves removal of much larger quantities of rock and soil because open-pit deposits tend to contain ores that are lower grade than those in underground mines. Processing of ores can involve a variety of processes:

- **Leaching** extracts a soluble metallic compound from the ore by dissolving it in water, sulfuric acid, hydrochloric acid, or a cyanide solution. The latter is called cyanidation and is used for recovering gold and silver. The so-called 'pregnant' leach solution is subjected to an electrochemical process (electrowinning) or to chemical precipitation to extract the target metal.
- **Milling** subjects the ore to crushing and grinding in order to achieve a desired particle size. Milled ore is turned into a slurry that can be pumped and treated in a further processing stage.
- **Magnetic separation** can be used to separate magnetic metals from a slurry. This is useful for iron ores.
- **Flotation** employs a number of different flotation agents (reagents) to make the metals or minerals adhere to air bubbles that allow separation in a flotation cell.
- **Gravity concentration** separates minerals based on their specific gravity (a ratio of the mineral's density with respect to water).

11.1.1 Economics of exhaustible resources

An exhaustible (or non-renewable) resource is characterized by a fixed stock that can be utilized. This stock need not all be known or have been discovered at a given time. Minerals and fossil fuels are prime examples of non-renewable resources. There are two key economic issues concerning exhaustible resources. First is the speed at which a known resource stock is depleted; this is the extraction rate. Second is the speed at which unknown stocks are discovered; this is the discovery rate. The extraction rate is primarily influenced by the market price of the resource. Extracting resources becomes increasingly expensive as locations become more remote and difficult to access and require more complex extraction processes. Marginal resource stocks will therefore be discovered and exploited only when the market price for the resource becomes sufficiently high.

There are two key questions about extracting a natural resource. The first question is about the speed of extraction: what is the optimal path of extraction until the resource is fully exhausted? The second question is about what happens when the resource is fully used up: is there a substitute for the exhausted resource (a backstop technology) or can the extracted resource stock be put into long-term circulation through recycling and reuse?

What determines resource extraction dynamics in the short run is, of course, supply and demand. When demand is high, the price of a natural resource can exceed its extraction cost by a significant margin. This has been the case for fossil fuels such as oil. Eventually, a high resource price will bring more expensive resource reserves into production, which will dampen further price increases.

Resource demand is driven my numerous factors. Population growth and economic growth are important elements. Rapid growth leads to more demand for resources, in turn driving up resource prices. Market structure also plays a significant role. Production levels can be controlled by important supplier countries (e.g., South Africa for diamonds) or international producer cartels (e.g., OPEC for oil). Resource supply reacts to market forces as well. Higher prices stimulate more resource exploration, but they also stimulate the search for suitable substitutes. In turn, resource exploration depends crucially on the heterogeneity of the resource—different levels of quality and accessibility. Suitable substitutes depend crucially on the rate of technological innovation, which is driven by investments in research and development.

What happens after a natural resource has been extracted is crucial. Resources such as fossil fuels are consumed to produce power. Once used up, they are gone. The path of resource extraction therefore depends crucially on finding a substitute technology that can replace the resource. A resource such as aluminum (produced from the mineral bauxite) can be recycled and reused. Scrap aluminum can be collected and re-melted, requiring one-twentieth of the energy it takes to refine bauxite ore into aluminum. Today, recycling rates for aluminum exceed 80% in many countries. As resources become more expensive, more efficient (and thus more expensive) forms of recycling will be used, further improving recycling rates.

How fast should mining companies get the resource out of the ground? And is that speed socially optimal? From a business perspective, a mining firm will pursue a project if its net present value (NPV) is positive. Geological considerations, along with the logistics of extraction, processing, and transportation often determine the scale of the operation. Whether a mining operation is economically viable is primarily determined by the current and expected future price path of the resource and the production cost over the lifetime of the mine.

The socially optimal path of resource extraction is governed by two efficiency rules, summarized as follows:

(1) The marginal utility of the resource should be the same in each use: extracted or remaining *in situ*. (2) The rate of return of extracting a resource unit should be the same in all periods.

The first efficiency rule concerns the optimal extraction in a given period, and the second efficiency rule concerns the optimal extraction path over time. The latter rule requires that the *discounted* price of the resource is the same in all periods. This is the same as saying that the price should increase over time at a constant rate: the social discount rate. The second rule about dynamic efficiency is known as the Hotelling rule (Hotelling, 1931). This model has evolved substantially over time to accommodate the reality of resource exploration. Modern versions of the model allow for three major effects that influence the marginal cost of resource extraction: the effect of resource depletion; the effect of technological progress over time; and the effect of resource exploration.

Fig. 11.1 Resource Price Path

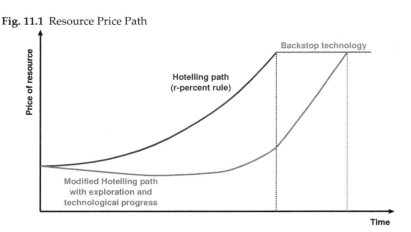

Figure 11.1 summarizes key insights of the original Hotelling model and modern modifications of this model. The main insight of the original Hotelling model is that the price path of the resource evolves according to a simple r-percent rule: the optimal path of resource extraction is along a path where the price increases continuously at the rate of interest (r), which can also be viewed as the social rate of time preference. In figure 11.1, the price increases exponentially as the resource becomes scarcer and scarcer. Ultimately, the price reaches a level where an alternative technology takes over completely. This technology is called a backstop technology and is discussed in greater detail below.

The simple r-percent rule of the Hotelling model must be modified to accommodate the empirical fact that the price of most resources has not been increasing exponentially. In many instances, the price has been falling or flat, seemingly contradicting the Hotelling model.

The first addition to the Hotelling model is that resource depletion proceeds in a particular sequence. Resources come in varying degrees of purity, concentration, and quality. Crude oil can be sweet (low in sulfur) or sour (high in sulfur); crude oil can also be light (low density) or heavy (high density). Market prices reflect this variation in quality. Resources may also differ substantially in the ease of accessing them. Oil in Saudi Arabia is relatively easy and cheap to get out of the ground. Canadian oil sands are expensive to get out of the ground and requires expensive upgrading. The sequence in which resources are extracted follows their extraction costs. This is known as the Herfindahl principle of resource extraction:

> The optimal sequence for extracting deposits of a non-renewable resource is determined by the effective unit cost of the deposits: the lowest-cost (highest-quality) deposits are extracted first, and the highest-cost (lowest-quality) deposits are extracted last.

The second addition to the Hotelling model is to allow for technological progress. It may be the case that, over time, the mining industry improves methods of resource extraction. The industry may come up with innovations such as enhanced oil recovery, discussed in the previous chapter. There may also be economies of scale as the industry gets larger over time. Technological progress will lower the price of the resource, and initially this rate of progress may be large enough to offset price increases due to increasing scarcity.

The third modification to the Hotelling model introduces resource exploration. Mining firms hunt for new deposits with increasingly advanced instrumentation. Proven reserves can increase over time, and they have in the case of many fossil fuels. The discovery of shale gas and shale oil in the United States is a good example. Mining companies take some of their profits and invest them in exploration, adding to the available resource stock. Eventually, this process will slow down as even unconventional resources are finite. Resource exploration will postpone the arrival of alternative technologies and dampen price increases for considerable periods.

Taking all modifications of the Hotelling model into consideration, a more realistic price path in figure 11.1 is the inverted-U shape curve. Prices initially may fall due to technological improvements, remain flat or increase only slowly due to new resource exploration and additional finds, and shift when a backstop technology takes over. As figure 11.1 shows, resource prices may go through a very extended *plateau phase* during which they remain stagnant.

A further important consideration is the market structure of the resource industry. If the resource is owned by a monopolist, resource extraction will proceed more slowly than when the resource is extracted by a large number of competing mining companies. Perhaps surprisingly, the monopolist acts as a resource conservationist. Of course, governments can mimic a monopolist. If a country has significant market power but not its many individual mining companies, introducing an export tax can achieve the same outcome as when the resource is managed by a single owner. Oligopolistic market power can also be exercised by resource cartels. The most notable case is the OPEC cartel that coordinates and constrains the oil production of a dozen nations.[1]

The Hotelling model seems to leave an important question unanswered: how fast should an individual deposit be drawn down? The answer is simply: as fast as the market permits. As long as the price path evolves along the r-percent rule, resource extraction is not too fast. If resource extraction happens too fast overall, the price of the resource will fall rather than rise. In practice, resource prices may sometimes follow a sawtooth path. If prices rise too far, resource exploration brings new supplies online, which lowers the price rapidly. The sawtooth movements occur due to lags in reacting to price signals. When prices are favourably high, it takes time to engage in further resource exploration and develop new production capacity.

The discussion above identifies the trajectory of resource extraction that is optimal for individual mining firms. What about the social optimum? The key variable is the discount rate. A discrepancy emerges only if the social discount rate is different from the private discount rate. A society as a whole may have a different time preference than an individual company. If a society's social discount rate is smaller than the company's private discount rate, a government would want to put restrictions on the speed of resource extraction. Government can do so by limiting resource exploration and resource extraction permits, or by charging resource extraction fees.

> A patient society (with a low social discount rate) will enjoy longer use of a finite exhaustible resource than an impatient society (with a high social discount rate). If mining firms have a higher private discount rate than society's social discount rate, excessive resource extraction will take place.

The gap between the market price of the resource and its extraction cost often leaves a considerable economic rent. This economic rent is shared between the mining firms (resource producers) and governments that license the resource use. In many instances, governments own the right to subsoil deposits and therefore grant extraction rights in exchange for licensing fees or royalties. In this context, it is noteworthy that a resource extraction tax does not affect the optimal extraction

---

[1] OPEC is the Organization of the Petroleum Exporting Countries, founded in 1961. The power of the OPEC cartel was displayed during the 1973 oil crisis, when a politically motivated embargo by key OPEC members saw the price of oil quadruple.

path because the tax dampens current and future prices equally: the Hotelling rule remains unchanged. However, taxes (or subsidies) can change the path of resource exploration by decreasing (or increasing) the expected payoff from such activities.

From a policy point of view, an important question is what governments should do with the revenue from resource extraction fees. Should such revenue be used for consumption purposes (by way of higher government expenditures or lower taxes), or should it be invested? This comes down to the question who should benefit from the resources: only the current generation, or current and all future generations equally. According to the Hartwick rule, the standard of living of a society can be maintained if the declining stock of non-renewable resources is offset perfectly by investments in physical and intellectual capital. To the extent that capital and resources are substitutable, all revenue from resource extraction should be invested in order to maintain intergenerational equity. Governments that use resource rents to finance consumptive activities for the current generation are essentially diminishing the standard of living of future generations.

> In order to maintain a constant standard of living across generations, a society needs to invest the economic rents from resource extraction in produced (physical or human) capital.

In practice, resource rents can be invested in a sovereign wealth fund. For example, Norway has set up such a fund to sequester the considerable wealth generated from the production of North Sea oil through its state-owned petroleum company Statoil. The Norwegian petroleum fund holds assets in excess of $1 trillion. For a country of about five million people, this fund will generate income for many generations into the future.

Many jurisdictions do not follow the Hartwick rule, but instead opt to consume most of the resource rents. Many developing countries with poor political governance use resource rents to subsidize the resource use. For entirely political reasons, Venezuela's fuel subsidy allows motorists to fill up their tanks at a price of 9 cents a gallon. Nevertheless, affluent countries are not immune to consuming their resource wealth. In Canada, the province of Alberta created the Heritage Savings Trust Fund in 1976 to sequester wealth generated from its oil sands production. However, the trust fund remains woefully underfunded at barely $16 billion of assets. Albertans prefer exceptionally low taxes, which prevents the provincial government from saving up most of the resource rents for future generations. The current generation of Albertans is depriving future generations of Albertans of the fruits of the resources in their ground.

11.1.2 Backstop technologies

The overarching question about any exhaustible resource is what happens once the resource has been depleted to a level where further recovery is not economical. It is unlikely that resources will be depleted fully. The technology at a given point in time limits the ability to explore resources beyond the point that is economically viable. Conventional oil wells run 'dry' when there is insufficient pressure to propel the oil to the surface. However, there is still plenty of oil left in the ground at that point, typically more than half of the reservoir's capacity. Technological advances such as enhanced oil recovery allow the recovery of additional oil from the reservoir. Enhanced oil recovery makes use of a variety of methods. The most widely used method involves injection of carbon dioxide, natural gas, or nitrogen. As the price of oil increases over time, more expensive recovery methods can be used to recover increasingly larger shares of the original reservoir.

Ultimately, the price of the natural resource may be too high to justify ever more costly recovery methods. Alternative technologies then may become more affordable. Such alternative technologies are commonly referred to as backstop technologies.

> A backstop technology produces a close substitute to an exhaustible resource, rendering the remaining resource stock obsolete, when the mining cost of the resource reaches a point where it exceeds the production cost of the backstop technology.

The classic example of a backstop technology is solar energy, which eventually can replace fossil fuels. Backstop technologies may be short-term or long-term substitutes. While solar energy is a super-abundant substitute (our sun will shine for a few more billions of years), nuclear fission may be used as a shorter-term transition technology that is used only for a limited period.

The usefulness of a backstop technology is characterized by the degree to which it is a substitute for the existing resource. For example, solar electricity may not be a perfect substitute for fossil fuels in motor vehicles. Gasoline and diesel have a very high energy density, about 46 MJ per kilogram. Rechargeable lithium-ion batteries have an energy density under 1 MJ per kilogram. This means that electric cars have a significant weight disadvantage compared to conventional cars, which translates into a shorter range for electric cars, and thus reduced usefulness. On the other hand, whether electricity in the power grid comes from gas-fired power plants or solar farms is indistinguishable to the end user. In this case solar power is indeed a perfect substitute for power from fossil fuel.

The presence or discovery of a backstop technology can have important consequences for the path of resource extraction. By shortening the planning horizon for the resource extraction, a backstop technology can accelerate extraction and dampen the market price of the resource. Backstop technologies can lead to a rush of last-minute resource exploration before the resource becomes obsolete.

The evolution of backstop technologies is endogenous to the level of resource scarcity. During the transition phase, immature backstop technologies will coexist with the continued use of the resource. Eventually, backstop technologies become more mature and will lead to obsolescence of the original resource. The ultimate question in all cases is whether a suitable substitute technology exists. Clearly, many backstop technologies that will be necessary in the future are not yet known because many resources remain plentiful. The burden is therefore on human ingenuity, guided by market forces, to develop novel backstop technologies that will solve our future resource constraints.

Unanticipated innovations in backstop technologies can have unintended consequences: they may speed up resource extraction and this may in turn lead to higher emissions associated with the use of that resource. This is known as the green paradox and is explored in box 11.1. There is a significant scientific controversy over the importance of the green paradox—and thus the policy prescriptions that follow from the opposing views.

11.1.3 Recycling

The virtue of recycling has been understood for millennia. Metal items have been recycled through melting them and forming them into new tools (and more often than not, weapons). The iron and bronze used in the Colossus of Rhodes statue—considered one of the seven wonders of the ancient world—was probably recycled for scrap some 800 years after an earthquake toppled the statue in 226 BC.

The role of recycling in solid waste management was explored in an earlier chapter in this book. The underlying economics is simple. Recycling will take place if it is cheaper to obtain the resource from used rather than from virgin material. This in turn is driven by the price path of the virgin resource and the cost of recycling. The latter is also influenced by technological progress. As a resource becomes scarcer and more expensive, new and more expensive methods of recycling may also become feasible.

Complete recycling would see the conversion of a resource stock in the ground into a resource stock in use, with no losses. With perfect recycling, a resource stock in use could be used indefinitely by generations to come. In practice, however, some materials will be lost dur-

Box 11.1: The Green Paradox

The unanticipated discovery of a new backstop technology may lead to what Sinn (2008) has coined the 'green paradox.' If resource producers believe that a backstop technology will take over as a substitute for the resource sooner than expected, then resource producers have an incentive to increase output rather than leave part of the resource in the ground unexploited. The increased production will lower prices, and this in turn will drive up consumption of the resource—and along with it emissions from consuming the resource. A backstop technology intended to reduce emissions may, paradoxically, increase emissions through the accelerated use of the resource. Similarly, government subsidies aimed at boosting the use of a backstop technology may—unintentionally—raise resource production and thus emissions.

The green paradox was first suggested in the context of fossil fuels and carbon dioxide emissions. For example, if a major innovation appeared on the horizon that would make solar power extremely cheap, oil and gas producers would find it economically optimal to accelerate fossil fuel production while it remains profitable.

If the adverse effects of the green paradox are sufficiently strong, policy makers may need to focus on the supply side rather than the demand side when trying to curb greenhouse gas emissions. Instead of curbing demand through the price mechanism, policies can be aimed at curbing the supply of fossil fuels directly. However, the level of international cooperation needed to limit fossil fuel supply is certainly as large as to implement global emission limits.

The green paradox may not be as bad as it may appear at first. A research paper by van der Ploeg and Withagen (2012) shows that the green paradox goes away if the backstop technology already exists, but as an imperfect substitute for the resource. For example, electricity from solar and wind power is an imperfect substitute for oil, which has more versatile use due to its high energy density. In this case, rising resource prices also increase the share of the backstop technology over time. A lower cost of the backstop technology (due to a subsidy or innovation) will postpone resource extraction or leave more resources in the ground permanently.

ing processing, use, or improper disposal. Most metallic minerals are amenable to recycling because their chemical properties and concentration will be preserved during use. The same is not true for many nonmetallic resources, including fossil fuels: chemical conversion makes them a single-use resource.

Public policy can impact recycling rates in several ways, illustrated in the four panels of figure 11.2. Consider the market for aluminum cans. Producing aluminum cans requires either virgin or recycled aluminum. The demand for aluminum is shown by the downward-sloping curve in panel A. The supply of virgin aluminum is considered price-elastic,

Fig. 11.2 Recycling and Government Intervention

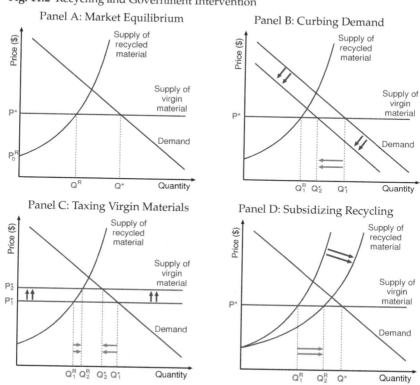

whereas the supply of recycled aluminum increases with price. At the outset, recycled aluminum is cheaper than virgin aluminum (P_0^R) because re-melting aluminum requires much less energy than refining it from bauxite. Eventually, recycled material becomes more and more expensive as collection, sorting, and processing become more difficult. A typical outcome is that the total supply of aluminum cans is a mixture of virgin and recycled materials. The total supply of cans makes use of recycled materials until it reaches the point where virgin material becomes cheaper (Q^R), and the remainder is supplied by virgin material (Q^V). In equilibrium, the market price P^* is determined by the price of virgin aluminum, and the equilibrium quantity is $Q^* = Q^R + Q^V$.

Introducing government policies can change the total supply of cans (Q^*) as well as the composition Q^R/Q^V of recycled and virgin material. Consider a policy that curbs demand for aluminum cans, illustrated in panel B of figure 11.2. The demand curve shifts downward, which depresses the total supply of aluminum cans while leaving the supply of recycled material unchanged. Q_1^* drops to Q_2^*. The entire adjustment takes place within the supply of virgin aluminum. As a result, the share of recycled material rises.

Government policy could also focus on making the supply of virgin aluminum more expensive, illustrated in panel C of figure 11.2. An increase in the price of virgin material from P_1^* to P_2^* shifts the corresponding supply curve upward. This draws in more supply of recycled materials (Q_1^R increases to Q_2^R), but also reduces overall demand (from Q_1^* to Q_2^*) so that the supply of virgin materials decreases (from $Q_1^* - Q_1^R$ to $Q_2^* - Q_2^R$).

Lastly, the government can also boost the supply of recycled materials through a direct subsidy or through indirect support (e.g., administering collection and sorting). This case is illustrated in panel D of figure 11.2. Depending on the type of intervention, the supply curve shifts downward or rotates out. The market outcome for the supply and demand of aluminum cans remains unchanged, but the share of recycled materials increases from Q_1^R to Q_2^R.

Which of these three interventions is best? Byh curbing demand for aluminum cans and taxing virgin aluminum, the regulator will change the market outcome. This is not the case for subsidizing recycling. The steepness of the recycling supply curve is a key determinant of the efficacy of the different policies. If the supply of recycled material is price-inelastic (the curve is steep), policy that targets recycling directly is relatively ineffective, and is better to focus on adjustments to the supply of virgin materials in order to boost the share of recycled materials.

In practice, governments use a variety of incentives to stimulate recycling. Many US states offer a recycling equipment income tax credit or a recycling equipment sales tax credit to boost recycling capacity. Municipalities can also build recycling infrastructure through collection systems. Nevertheless, successful recycling always needs an aftermarket for recycled materials. This often requires product innovation. Slag from blast and steel furnaces is not just a wasted by-product of metal smelting and processing. Blast furnace slag can be ground to a particulate size equivalent to cement, which can be used in poured concrete (as a partial substitute for cement) and lightweight masonry. It was used extensively in the construction of the 68-floor Scotia Plaza office tower in Toronto. Steel furnace slag can be used as an aggregate in asphalt during road construction. It can also be used in the remediation of surface areas that are subject to acid rock drainage. Finding innovative uses for recycled materials will be crucial in shaping the future of recycling.

11.1.4 Environmental challenges

Mining is associated with a number of environmental risk and challenges. The most important effects are related to water use and contamination, and to land use and remediation after a site is abandoned. Specifically, the following issues arise:

- **Mine water** can originate from precipitation, surface water inflows, or groundwater leakage. Disposal of mine water can be problematic if contaminated. Mine water can be severely contaminated through acid mine drainage (from contamination within a mine) or through acid rock drainage (from contamination in waste rock and tailings).
- **Overburden** and **waste rock** is the soil and rock that must be removed before the ore can be accessed.
- **Tailings** are the slurry discharged after processing of the ore. They are typically collected in tailing ponds, although submarine disposal is used in some instances.
- **Spent leach solutions** are similar to acid leaching, as the leach solutions are highly acidic. Environmental problems are caused by leaks and spills. Solution ponds, especially if not lined with geomembranes, may leak and contaminate groundwater and surface water.
- **Slag** is the glassy by-product of ore smelting. It is mostly chemically inert and is sometimes used in the construction industry for building roads. Traces of toxic materials contained in certain types of slag can be released into the environment through natural weathering. However, slag from iron and steel making is safe for use in many industrial applications and can be an environmentally-friendly alternative to other products.

These challenges are considerable. However, a number of useful mitigation measures can be deployed.

The volume of mine water that needs to be handled during the operation of a mine often makes it the most obvious candidate for mitigation measures. Collection and reuse of mine water in processing operations is preferable. When this is not feasible, controlling run-off through ditches and berms is the next step, allowing the water to evaporate and for the contaminants to accumulate through sedimentation. Discharge into rivers is the least favourable option. Constant monitoring of discharges and water quality is necessary. After the closure of the mining operation, appropriate water management needs to be put into place to control and mitigate acid rock drainage.

Overburden and waste rock can be used to fill parts of the mine. Overburden can be used also in the reclamation of the mine at a later point. Reactive waste rock, which is prone to acid rock drainage, should not be exposed to the surface, but it should be covered with non-reactive soil or materials. Reactive rock should never be used for construction purposes.

Appropriate treatment of tailings can also mitigate their environmental risks. Proper containment is the first objective. Tailing ponds need to be designed to resist leakage and to withstand adverse weather. Liners can be used to prevent leakage. Double-lining provides additional safety. Retaining walls can be built with sufficient height to withstand rare but heavy rain storms. Providing secondary containment in case of a (rare) rupture of a tailing pond can be crucial for preventing catastrophic damages. Furthermore, leachate detection and continuous monitoring of groundwater and surface water are necessary both during the operation and after the closure of a mine. Box 11.2 discusses some of the problems with tailings, tailing ponds, and submarine discharges of tailings.

Novel extraction technologies offer the potential of avoiding the use of toxic materials, such as those used in leaching. Non-toxic resource extraction methods such as bioleaching ores with live organisms have started to be applied more widely, particularly in copper mining. While bioleaching is usually quite inexpensive, it takes considerably more time than conventional roasting and smelting processes. An important advantage of bioleaching is the ability to use this process on low-grade ores that are not suitable for conventional leaching techniques. For example, copper ores that contain 0.5-1.0% copper can be processed with bioleaching. Bioleaching has the potential to reduce the environmental impact of mining significantly.

11.2 Forestry

Forests provide a large economic value to societies. The extractive value of a forest is generated through logging and processing trees. Harvested timber can be processed industrially, and wood material can also be used as fuel. Forests also provide a non-extractive value through various ecosystem functions: soil and water protection, maintaining biodiversity, or providing carbon sinks that mitigate climate change. Other non-extractive values are generated through the use of forests for recreational purposes. Overall, the contribution of the forest sector to gross domestic product is declining. In 2005, it was roughly 1% in the United States and 3% in Canada. Within Canada, the forest sector is particularly important in British Columbia (5.7% of gross provincial product).

Not all forests can be considered an economic resource. Quality and accessibility are key considerations that determine the economic value of a forest. Some forests are too remote and others are of insufficient quality to provide any economic use. Many forests are on public land. In the United States, publicly-owned forests are managed by the National Forest Service and the Bureau of Land Management. In Canada, provincial governments control logging. These government entities set

Box 11.2: Mining and Tailings

Mining of minerals involves the processing of ore, rocky material that contains both valuable minerals or metals as well as worthless components. The value of an ore is defined by its grade or concentration. Separating the valuable from the worthless components involves processing techniques that generate waste, which are known as tailings. These tailings often pose considerable environmental hazards due to the chemicals that are used in the process.

Processing gold ores generates large amounts of arsenic. Gold ores are found in sulfide mineral deposits that are naturally rich in arsenic. At the Giant Mine near Yellowknife in the Northwest Territories, smelting gold ore generated arsenic dust (arsenic trioxide) that was collected and stored in underground chambers. Water ingress into these chambers due to melting permafrost made it necessary to commence a remediation project.

Historically, tailings were often released directly into the environment. Eventually, tailing ponds were constructed to retain the tailings. Tailings are usually mixed with water and can be pumped through pipelines to suitable tailing ponds. As the water evaporates, sedimentation accumulates the tailings at the bottom of the ponds. Tailing ponds suffer from two problems. Most significant is the failure of the retaining dam. When a coal slurry dam burst in West Virginia in February 1982, 500,000 cubic metres of slurry buried more than 500 houses in its path. The incident, known as the Buffalo Creek Flood, left 125 people dead. A second problem is leakage, particularly in the form of acid rock drainage.

Novel approaches to tailings disposal have been pioneered in several places. Pressure filters can be used to remove the water from the slurry, and the resulting dry tailings can be stacked compactly with much less land use than for tailing ponds. Water that is recovered through this method of dry stacking can be recovered and reused.

Somewhat more controversial is the practice of submarine tailings disposal, where the tailings are pumped to the bottom of the sea, where sedimentation occurs. However, it is often difficult to find a site that is sufficiently deep to prevent spreading the tailings over a larger area. Significant damage to the seafloor may occur if submarine disposal is carried out in unsuitable locations. This disposal method involves trade-offs. While it avoids the risk of leakage or ruptures of tailings ponds, it comes at the cost of posing significant risks to marine ecosystems. Suitable locations must be at least 100 metres deep and have a slope of at least 12% to move the tailings from the end of the pipe along the sea floor. In addition to the marine life on the sea floor (known as benthic life), other risks emanate from pipe breaks, wider-than-expected dispersal of tailings, and increased water turbidity. The latter can inhibit photosynthesis. Mining companies are attracted to this disposal method because it is much cheaper to use than tailing ponds. More research is needed to establish 'best practice' approaches, and rigorous monitoring is necessary to safeguard existing sites.

stumpage prices for allowing private firms to harvest trees on public land. Stumpage rates vary by tree species and location.

Traditionally, the main objective of forest management was the maximization of forest yields. Managing forest stands and rotation cycles remains a key element. In recent years, the environmental dimension of forest management has gained increasing importance. There are several important environmental issues concerning forests. First and foremost is the risk of deforestation: the disappearance of forest land cover to make space for agricultural land use, or the encroachment of urban space onto forested land. Second is the risk that forest management practices—such as monocultures—will endanger the resilience of forests to pests and fires, or reduce biodiversity by destroying habitat for species that use forests as their natural home. Third is the environmental impact of processing facilities, in particular pulp and paper mills.

The forest industry spans a wide array of activities along the value chain. It begins with the standing timber and activities related to planting and managing commercially used forests. It continues with the harvesting of logs and their transportation to manufacturing facilities. At the end of the value chain are manufactured products that include lumber and plywood for construction purposes, paper and cardboard for printing and packaging, or furniture. The three stages of the value chain are mirrored by three benchmark prices: the stumpage price for standing timber (often set by governments), the sawlog price for harvested and sawed logs (as an intermediate product), and the lumber price for processed wood (as a finished product).

In forest economics, there is a crucial distinction between long-term and short-term supply of timber. Short-term supply is constrained by existing logging facilities and mills and by the inventory of standing timber. Producers can vary inputs only slowly over time. Consequently, supply of timber is relatively inelastic in the short run. It becomes more elastic in the long run. However, growing new forests takes decades. This means that today's investment decisions about growing new timber will not affect market conditions for many years into the future.

11.2.1 Optimal forest rotation

The material in this section makes use of a modest amount of mathematical notation and calculus. Readers unfamiliar with these mathematical methods may skip straight to the grey box below, which discusses the optimal harvest strategy, known as the Faustmann rule.

The key issue in managing a forest is determining the optimal forest rotation—deciding the age at which to harvest trees. The length of a forest rotation decides how much capital is tied up in a timber stand.

It can be readily seen that the optimal forest rotation depends on both biological and economic factors. Figure 11.3 illustrates the rotation cycle for tree stands. Logging takes place at optimal time points $1t^*$, $2t^*$, $3t^*$, and so forth when the volume (biomass) of the tree stand, $Q(t^*)$, has reached a certain level. Determining the optimal harvesting points t^* is the focus of this section.

Fig. 11.3 Forest Rotation Sequence

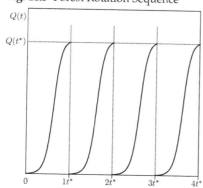

Fig. 11.4 Optimal Forest Rotation

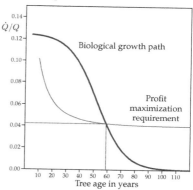

The starting point for the analysis is the biological growth function of a tree stand over time. It can be expressed as biomass or yield per hectare, depending on the circumstances. There are several bioeconomic models in use that describe forest growth. They all have in common that growth is sigmoid (S-shaped): slow at the beginning, reaching a maximum growth at a certain age, and eventually slowing down. A popular sigmoid growth function for biomass Q over time t is known as **Richard's curve**, shown below:

$$Q(t) = \frac{K}{(1 + \exp(-\delta(t - m))/\nu)^{1/\nu}} \quad , \tag{11.1}$$

The level K describes the carrying capacity of the tree stand. The biomass converges over time towards K but cannot exceed it. The parameters δ, ν, and m determine the growth path and are estimated empirically for particular tree species and locations from observed data. Incremental changes in biomass over time are obtained as the derivative with respect to time, $\dot{Q}(t) \equiv \partial Q/\partial t$. The effective biomass growth rate is therefore

$$\frac{\dot{Q}(t)}{Q(t)} = \frac{\delta}{\nu}\left[\frac{\exp(-\delta(t-m))}{\nu + \exp(-\delta(t-m))}\right]\tag{11.2}$$

When $t \to 0$ in equation (11.2), then $\dot{Q}/Q \to \delta/\nu$, and when $t \to \infty$, then $\dot{Q}/Q \to 0$. This means that the growth rate $\dot{Q}/Q$ follows an inverse-sigmoid pattern. It is relatively flat during the first decades, and then declines rapidly and approaches zero. The thick curve in figure 11.4 illustrates the path of the $\dot{Q}/Q$ curve for biological growth. Initially, forests grow rapidly, faster than the typical rate of interest. Eventually, the growth rate declines and falls below a point that is less than the returns on other uses of capital. From equation (11.2) it can be inferred that the time at which biomass growth reaches the level $g = \dot{Q}(t)/Q(t)$ is given by

$$t^* = m + \frac{1}{\delta}\ln\left[\frac{\delta/g - \nu}{\nu^2}\right]\ .\tag{11.3}$$

The time t^* is the solution to the optimal forest rotation problem for a particular value of g, determining the Faustmann rotation age.

The biological growth function also defines a maximum sustainable yield, which is identified by the age t that maximizes the average biomass $Q(t)/t$. But obtaining the maximum sustainable yield is not economically optimal. It is better to harvest a little earlier: the smaller harvest is offset by the gain from having it earlier. Economically, the optimal time to harvest is defined by the marginal cost of waiting (from delayed profits) being equal to the marginal benefit of waiting (from increased growth).

The economics of the optimal rotation problem can be expressed as a maximization of the value of a continuous rotation of a timber stand. When the trees are harvested, they have reached the yield $Q(t)$ at age t. Assume that it costs C to plant the trees, and further assume that this amount also includes any present-value discounted future costs for managing the tree stand during a given rotation period. Allowing for an economic discount rate r and a stumpage price P, the profit for the first rotation is the revenue $PQ(t)$ at time t discounted to the present, minus the cost C This present value is $V_1 = PQ(t)\exp(-rt) - C$. The value of the following rotations V_2, V_3, and so forth is discounted with $\exp(-irt)$, where i is the sequential number of the tree rotation. Summing the value of all future rotations to infinity allows us to calculate the total value,

$$V = \frac{PQ(t)\exp(-rt) - C}{1 - \exp(-rt)}\ ,\tag{11.4}$$

of a given timber stand. The first-order condition for value maximization is obtained by differentiating this equation with respect to time t and setting the solution to zero. Rearranging the expressions yields

$$\frac{\dot{Q}(t)}{Q(t)} = r \left[\frac{1}{1 - \exp(-rt)} \right] \left(1 - \frac{C}{PQ} \right) . \tag{11.5}$$

This optimal solution requires that the trees are harvested at time t^* when $\dot{Q}(t^*)/Q(t^*)$ is equal to the value on the right-hand side of (11.5). The expression in the square brackets is slightly larger than 1, and the expression in the round parentheses is slightly smaller than 1. As a simple approximation, $\dot{Q}/Q \approx r$. The discount rate r determines the optimal rotation length. The expression $1/[1 - \exp(-rt)]$ captures the effect of discounting multiple rotation periods. As t gets shorter and shorter, the number of rotations increases. This in turn increases the rate of return for fast rotations.

To provide a numerical example, assume that $\delta = 0.1$, $\nu = 0.8$, m is 50 years, and the discount rate is r is 5%. Also assume that C/PQ, the afforestation cost, is 20%. Then the trees should be logged at age $t^* = 59$ years (when the biomass growth rate reaches $g = 0.0422$). Figure 11.4 illustrates the optimal solution. The (thick) biological growth path curve shows the inverse-sigmoid decline in the biomass growth rate over time; it captures the marginal benefit of waiting. The (thin) profit maximization requirement curve shows the rate of return required to maximize profits; it captures the marginal cost of waiting. The two curves intersect at the optimal harvest time t^*. In this example, maximum sustainable yield occurs at about 70 years, 10 years later than the economically optimal harvest. The **Faustmann rule** can be summarized as follows:

It is optimal to harvest a timber stand when the marginal benefit from delaying the harvest is equal to the marginal cost of delaying harvest. This condition is reached when the relative growth rate of the forest has declined to be equal to the interest rate, adjusted for rotation cycling and reforestation costs.

The technical discussion above also leads to a few additional insightful observations:

1. The economically optimal harvest time is sooner than the harvest time for the maximum sustainable yield.
2. As the interest rate (discount rate) increases, the rotation period is shortened.
3. If the reforestation or afforestation cost increases, the rotation period is lengthened.
4. The optimal rotation period is not affected by constant annual costs for tending the forest.[2]

---

[2] This can be shown by introducing a constant maintenance fee into the equations.

It is also important to understand how taxes can affect rotation periods. A tax on the bare land value of a forest has no effect on the rotation period. However, an *ad-valorem* tax on the value of the *standing* timber has the same effect as increasing the interest rate: it shortens the rotation period. Lastly, an *ad-valorem* tax on the *harvested* timber—a yield tax— reduces the value of the harvest proportionally. The forest owner has an incentive to postpone payment of this tax, and therefore a yield tax increases the rotation period. Governments need to take into account how the choice of tax instrument affects the optimal rotation period.

The Faustmann model discussed in this section can be extended to allow for the non-extractive (non-timber) values of a forest. Incorporating these valuations into the model leads to a revised optimization model and a new optimal rotation age, known as the Hartman rotation age. The practical challenge is the quantification of these valuations. Generally, if non-timber values increase with forest age, the Hartman rotation age will be higher than the Faustmann rotation age. Furthermore, the non-timber benefits may be sufficiently large that it would not be economically sensible to harvest the forest at any time at all. Such arguments have indeed been advanced for surviving old-growth forests as well as newly established protective forests that are used to control soil erosion or maintain watersheds.

11.2.2 *Management practices*

Forests provide numerous valuable ecosystem functions. Economically, these are positive externalities. Public and private forest owners therefore ought to follow management practices that preserve these valuable functions. Following best practices is considered forest stewardship.

There has been considerable concern that clear-cutting contributes to watershed destruction, soil erosion, and habitat loss. Clear-cutting involves harvesting all trees in a particular area. Logging companies prefer clear-cutting because of its lower cost compared to selective cutting, which involves harvesting trees based on particular criteria. This is a classic externality problem because private logging firms do not internalize the negative externality of their logging practice. It is therefore important that the (public) forest owners set appropriate limits on clear-cutting.

Another problem is high-grading: selective harvesting of trees with the highest economic return, such as diameter-limit cutting and selective cutting. The first practice targets trees above a certain diameter, while selective cutting targets trees that are particularly large or valuable. This leaves behind trees that are of poor quality—those that may be physically defective or genetically damaged. High-grading diminishes diversity and may also compromise a forest's resilience with respect to disease or wildfire.

Tending a forest may sometimes involve proactive measures to protect forests from infestations and fires. Monitoring a forest can help identify insect infestations and diseased trees at an early stage. A timber harvest to salvage dead and dying trees can protect healthy stands. Increasing the diversity of tree species can help protect a forest against insects and diseases.

Management practices are crucial when it comes to protecting animal habitat. Forest owners may be unaware of the animal species living in their forests. Conducting surveys to identify the biodiversity of forests helps identify the species that need to be protected. Activities can be planned and timed in such a way to minimize disturbance of animal or plant habitat. It requires that logging firms develop management plans that identify and protect uniquely important areas and habitats. It also requires that governments develop guidelines for protecting endangered species. The dispute about the spotted owl, discussed in box 11.3, demonstrates that the conflict about preserving animal habitat may sometimes involve unexpected international repercussions.

In many US states and most Canadian provinces, government owns large swaths of forested land. On the other hand, logging companies are mostly privately owned. The public ownership of forests requires a system of access for the privately owned firms, as well as setting up a system for pricing the forest resources. A tenure system is an institutional arrangement under which logging companies operate to harvest wood. It defines rights and responsibilities with respect to the use of a forest. A tenure system establishes a process under which logging companies can apply for access to a forest, enter (competing) bids, and receive logging permits (timber licences). There are two basic forms of tenure:

- **volume-based tenure** establishes a right to harvest a specific amount of timber within a specific period and is assigned to multiple forest companies; and
- **area-based tenure** establishes a right to harvest within a specific land area and assigns this exclusive right to a single forest company.

A tenure system also establishes an annual allowable cut that constraints the total amount of timber that can be harvested in a particular region over the course of a year. There is significant variation in tenure systems across regions and jurisdictions, and individual jurisdictions often maintain a complex array of different tenures. Tenures are usually awarded to the highest bidder. Tenures can be of rather different size. Large volume or large area tenures favour large forest companies, whereas small tenures provide access to small forest companies, and communities.

Box 11.3: Logging and the Northern Spotted Owl

Image: US Fish and Wildlife Service.

The northern spotted owl lives in old growth forests on the northwest Pacific coast. It has been declared endangered in Canada, and has been listed as a threatened species in the United States. The spotted owl has been under threat from logging operations that continue to this day. In British Columbia, its population was estimated to consist of 500 breeding pairs before European settlement. In 2006 the provincial government announced that only six breeding pairs remained.

Listing the owl as endangered in the United States would restrict government agencies from selling timber from US forestland, which makes up 44% of all timberland in Washington and Oregon. This would affect the forest industry significantly. The US *Forest Resources Conservation and Shortage*

Act of 1990 called for a permanent ban on the export of raw logs harvested on federal lands and also curtailing export from state land. To placate sawmill owners who were losing raw log exports to Japan, this bill prohibited the export of logs in order to redirect log to sawmills in Oregon and Washington, keeping sawmills busy.

Japan complained that the raw log export ban violated the *General Agreement on Tariffs and Trade* (GATT), even though the US claimed a defence under GATT articles XX(b) and XX(g) (for the protection of animal life, as well as resource conservation). It is highly debatable whether the raw log export is an effective measure to protect the spotted owl. It is a rather indirect method for protecting wildlife habitat. After all, the US government continues to permit domestic sales of logs without restrictions (including the export of value-added products such as lumber). Rather than seeking a dispute settlement under the World Trade Organization, Japan is continuing to negotiate with the United States.

Conservation of spotted owls should be accomplished by restrictions on the cutting of forest rather than export restrictions of logs. However, even habitat protection may not suffice to rescue the spotted owl, and therefore Columbia's provincial government is taking extreme measures. Between 2007 and 2012, forest officials have relocated 73 and authorized shooting of 39 barred owls, the rival species that has been encroaching on the habitat of spotted owls. Only time will tell whether such last-ditch methods are successful.

Area-based tenure systems are often developed to support local communities (in particular, First Nations communities) and give local communities greater control over their local forest resources.

Forest tenure systems must be sufficiently flexible to allow for unanticipated changes. Disease and fire can ravage large swaths of forested land. The mountain pine beetle epidemic in the Pacific Northwest illustrates this challenge. Box 11.4 discusses the epidemic in greater detail.

11.2.3 Pulp and paper mills

Processing of wood in pulp and paper mills generates a variety of air and water emissions. Because effluent from pulp and paper mills can endanger fish habitat as well as downstream communities, governments have stepped in to regulate pulp and paper mills extensively. In Canada, the federal government has regulated this industry by invoking the *Fisheries Act* as well as the *Canadian Environmental Protection Act*. In the United States, the Environmental Protection Agency and individual states have also adopted effluent rules.

Effluent treatment usually consists of primary and secondary treatment. Primary treatment removes solids. Most secondary treatment involves aerated stabilization basins and activated sludge. Effluent regulations set limits for the biochemical oxygen demand and prohibit discharges that are acutely lethal to rainbow trout, a fish used as an indicator species for testing water quality. Specifically, the Canadian *Fisheries Act* requires that half the rainbow trout must survive full-strength exposure to effluent for four full days.

Pulp and paper mills typically release a side range of compounds into rivers and streams. In addition to suspended solids and fibre, organic loads and nutrients, as well as chlorinated dioxins and furans, can pose significant hazards. The latter are particularly dangerous because of bioaccumulation, especially in downstream communities with high fish consumption. Chlorine and chlorine compounds are used in the process of bleaching wood pulp in the kraft process. The use of chlorine dioxide instead of elemental chlorine has decreased the emission dioxins significantly.

At the start of the kraft process, wood chips are cooked in so-called digesters with a chemical mixture known as white liquor. The spent cooking liquor is called black liquor. If discharged as effluent it is toxic to aquatic life. Modern pulp mills can recover virtually all of the black liquor. A small part is reused, and the largest part of it is typically burnt in recovery boilers. Waste-to-energy approaches have also been tried for gasification of black liquor.

The bleaching process mostly involves chlorine dioxide, but chlorine-free bleaching processes are increasingly being adopted. Since the

Box 11.4: Mountain Pine Beetle Epidemic

Image: Ward Strong, B.C. Ministry of Forests, Lands, and Natural Resource Operations.

The mountain pine beetle has infested over 180,000 square kilometres of lodgepole pine in British Columbia. This area is about the size of Missouri or Oklahoma. The damage to forests and the forest industry is enormous. While the infestation has slowed down in British Columbia since its peak in 2005, the pine beetle epidemic continues to spread. It has moved northeast and crossed the Rocky Mountains into the neighbouring provinces. It is also starting to infect other types of pine trees. The pine beetle also lives in a number of US states: Colorado, Wyoming, Arizona, and South Dakota.

The mountain pine beetle is about the size of a grain of rice and lives one year, mostly under the bark of pine trees. They prefer mature pine trees, and the prevalence of these trees has increased over the last decades due to improved fire protection of forests. The sheer number of pine beetles overpowers the natural defences of trees. The beetle's attack proceeds in three stages. After trees have been infested initially (green attack) they turn red after about one year. They stay in this stage for another two to four years (red attack) and eventually turn grey as they lose their needles (grey attack).

Pine beetle populations are kept in check through cold winters. During mid-winter, temperatures must be below −35°C consistently for several days to kill off the beetles. Cold weather is most effective in the fall and before snow cover develops. Sustained temperatures below −25°C during the fall can kill beetles before they build up their glycerol levels for the winter. (Glycerol is nature's anti-freeze.) The increasing pine beetle populations have been linked to rising temperatures due to climate change.

Coping with the forest infestation requires short-term and long-term approaches. Large areas of dead pine stands represent a potential fire hazard. Infested trees are felled and burned in order to slow down the spread of the infestation. To preserve wildlife habitat, unharvested healthy areas need to be increased. In the long-term, extensive reforestation is needed, and more resilient species such as Douglas fir and spruce can be introduced to sustain commercial logging.

The pine beetle epidemic has highlighted the vulnerability of forest systems in North America. Climate change, acid rain, and other anthropogenic influences can affect forests severely. Protecting forests will require better management practices.

1990s, bleaching with chlorine products has been reduced significantly through the additional use of oxygen delignification. Oxygen is cheap and environmentally friendly, but the additional equipment increases capital cost. The process also requires extra heat and pressure, which makes the process slightly more expensive.

11.3 Fisheries

World fish production is dominated by ocean fisheries, which in turn are dominated by pacific ocean fisheries. Inland fisheries only account for about 10% of total capture. A third of total fish production nowadays comes from fish farming, known as aquaculture.

While total marine capture has been relatively stable over the last two decades, in the four decades between 1950 and 1990, marine capture increased about four-fold. This has led at least locally to pronounced overfishing and the collapse of individual fisheries. Some countries have responded to overfishing by suspending local fisheries or implementing quota systems.

Figure 11.5 shows how overfishing led to a collapse of fish stock. Atlantic cod stocks were severely overfished in the two decades between 1970 and 1990, leading to a virtual collapse of the cod stock in the northwest Atlantic. In 1992, Canada imposed an indefinite moratorium on fishing cod in these waters.

Fig. 11.5 Collapse of the Atlantic Cod, 1950–2009

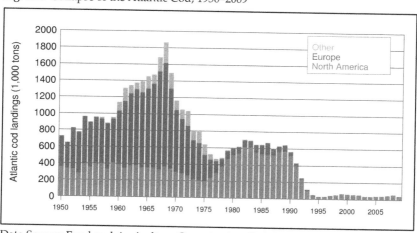

Data Source: Food and Agriculture Organization, FishStat, Global Capture Production, Northwest Atlantic, all countries.

Overfishing is a classic example of the lack of property rights or insufficient enforcement of property rights. Fishing fleets from one country may fish in the coastal waters of another country, unless property rights exist that prevent such activities. Disputes about fishing rights even led to confrontations such as the 'Cod Wars' between Iceland and Great Britain. Only in 1982 did the Third United Nations *Convention on the Law of the Sea* establish that countries can maintain an exclusive economic zone (EEZ) up to 200 nautical miles from shore, in addition to claiming sovereign rights over territorial waters up to 12 nautical miles from shore. (Territorial rights may extend even further for mineral resources found on the continental shelf.) Nevertheless, patrolling a country's EEZ may be challenging, and some migratory fish become transboundary fish stock that cross the EEZs of two or more countries.

Overfishing is mirrored by the overcapacity of fishing fleets. On one side, this leads to strong competition among the remaining fleets, and on the other side this leads to the downsizing of existing capacity. The increase in competition may push some fishing fleets into unconventional types of fish or novel territory.

Dwindling fish stock has significantly boosted fish farming. While aquaculture resolves the property right problem about fish stock, it is not without economic and environmental challenges. Economically, aquaculture is gaining in importance because of the shrinking gap between the cost of farming and catching fish. Environmentally, fish farming may exhibit problems with waste handling, side effects of feeding antibiotics, escaping stock from open (net enclosure) aquacultures that may jeopardize native fish species, and escaping parasites. Such problems can be lessened with closed aquaculture systems, but these tend to be significantly more costly. A number of technological advances for aquaculture are currently under development. Perhaps most noteworthy is the development of integrated multitrophic aquaculture, where waste from one species is recycled into input for another species. 'Multitrophic' means that fish species at different trophic levels are kept in the aquaculture. China is emerging rapidly as the dominant aquaculture producer.

11.3.1 *Fisheries economics*

Ownership of marine resources has made progress only over the last two decades. Previously, ocean fisheries could be considered a prime example of a tragedy of the commons problem. Open access, combined with technological innovations in fishing technology, led to widespread overfishing. To understand the economics of fisheries, it is useful to explore a bioeconomic model of the growth of fish populations and the harvest effort of fishing fleets. The simplest such model is known as the Gordon-Schaefer model, illustrated in figure 11.6. This model considers a single fish species in a single area. More complex versions of such models allow for multiple fish species, interactions among them, migration of fish across different zones, and other realistic features (see, for example, Clark (2006)).

The starting point of the Gordon-Schaefer model is the assumption that the growth of a fish stock follows a logistic trajectory: growth increases until it reaches a maximum level and then declines as the fish population approaches its maximum size. Growth turns negative when the fish population exceeds the sustainable size. The maximum level is determined by the carrying capacity of the marine environment.

Fig. 11.6 Efficient Yield and Maximum Sustainable Yield for a Fishery

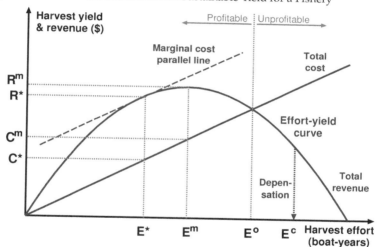

The effort-yield curve in figure 11.6 identifies the level of yield that can be sustained for any given level of effort, where effort is measured by the number of boat-hours or some other suitable metric. Yield can be thought of as tonnes of fish catch, or as the dollar revenue associated with that catch. The effort-yield curve has the shape of an inverted 'U.' At low levels of effort, the yield continues to rise until it reaches a maximum level. This level is known as the maximum sustainable yield (MSY). Applying effort level E^m continuously generates a yield (revenue) R^m. As effort is increased further, yield starts to diminish because fishing is depleting the stock quicker than it can recover. Ultimately, fishing effort could reach a level where the stock disappears completely. When fishing effort reaches the critical level E^c, depensation may occur (curtailing the effort-yield curve). Overfishing reduces the fish population density to the point where it impedes breeding success and leads to increased relative predation success. When depensation occurs, the fish population may not recover even when fishing effort ceases completely.

The effort-yield curve depicts a long-run relationship. In the short term, deviations from this curve are possible but are not sustainable. An unexpectedly high yield for a given effort will diminish the stock, which would result in an abnormally low yield in future periods for the given level of effort.

What happens when there is **open access** to the fisheries? The total cost of fishing is captured by the diagonal line. As effort (boat-hours) increases, total cost increases proportionately. As long as fishing is profitable, it will draw in more fishermen. This will continue until there are no more economic profits to be had, and total cost equals total revenue. This is the point E^o. To the left of it, revenue exceeds cost, and to the right of it, cost exceeds revenue. It is apparent that the open-access effort level exceeds the socially optimal level defined by the maximum sustainable yield (E^m).

If the fish stock were owned by a monopolist, the economic calculus suggests that effort would be expanded until marginal revenue equals marginal cost. Marginal revenue is the slope of the effort-yield curve, and marginal cost is the slope of the total cost curve. Therefore, one can find the optimal effort level E^* (with corresponding revenue R^*) by drawing a parallel line to the total cost line and see where it is tangent to the effort-yield curve. It turns out that this effort level is below the MSY effort level (E^m), and thus the total yield of a monopolist is somewhat smaller than the MSY ($R^* < R^m$). The monopolist makes a profit of ($R^* - C^*$).

11.3.2 Fisheries management and public policy

The objective of fisheries policy is to protect the fish stock and prevent overfishing. One way of doing this is to control effort. For example, government regulators often limit the number of days that boats can fish, restrict the mesh size of the fishing nets, and put limits on the size and capability of the fishing vessels. It is quite obvious that such limitations also lead to higher fishing costs because they make fishing less efficient than it could be technologically. On the other hand, effort limits favour small fishing operators over large fishing operators and are often justified because of the beneficial employment effects for coastal communities.

A common approach to regulating fisheries activities is the use of catch limits by defining a **total allowable catch** (TAC). The TAC limit can be allocated to fishing operators through a quota system. Such quotas establish property rights. Because open-access fisheries promote overfishing, creating property rights can be very effective in preventing overfishing if the property rights are fully enforced.

Setting a TAC limit may not always work as intended, as is illustrated in figure 11.7. There may be considerable scientific uncertainty about the effort-yield curve. While a regulator may design policy based on the most likely scenario (the thicker curve Y_1), natural variability of the marine environment adds considerable uncertainty about the state of the fish stock. Effort yield-curves Y_2 and Y_3 may be less likely but cannot be ruled out. When the regulator sets a TAC quota Y^* to induce an effort level E_1^*, a lesser effort level $E_2^* < E_1^*$ may be sufficient when the effort-yield curve is actually at Y_2 and the fish stock is richer than expected. When the fish stock is poorer than expected and the effort-yield curve is Y_3, the quota is too generous and may exceed the maximum sustainable yield. In other words, the TAC quota is not sustainable.

Fig. 11.7 Fisheries Policy under Uncertainty

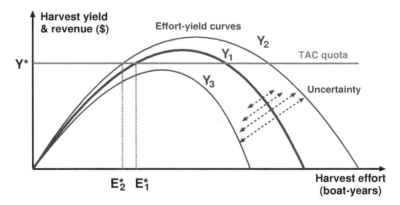

When regulators establish a total allowable catch, it becomes necessary to allocate this TAC through quotas for individual fisheries operators—companies, communities, or individual fishermen. Quotas can be used to create collective property rights as well as individual property rights. These property rights correspond to two instruments.

The policy instrument that creates collective property rights is known as territorial use rights in fisheries (TURFs)—the right to exclusive use of a fishery resource within a specific area and for a specific time. TURFs are often linked to responsibilities for stewardship of the marine resource. The concept of TURFs is usually applied to rights of a community—smaller than a country but larger than individual fishery operations. This means that TURFs involve a degree of resource sharing among members of a specific community. Defining characteristics of the use of TURFs include:

1. exclusion of outsiders through monitoring and enforcement (aided by governments);
2. control of labour and capital through constraints on vessel capacity, equipment (e.g., mesh size of nets), and eligibility for membership;
3. coordination with neighbouring TURFs and mediation and arbitration of conflicts within a TURF; and
4. flexibility to adjust to changing circumstances at the community level or due to technology.

TURFs are community-based property rights rather than individual property rights. TURFs can work well when there are strong community institutions that can support them, and they can foster the social and economic cohesion of coastal communities.

A different approach involves the use of individual property rights instead of community-based property rights. The most prominent concept is the individual transferable quota (ITQ). A regulator sets a total allowable catch, and allocates quota shares to individuals through an initial auction or a distribution formula (grandfathering), similar to the system of pollution permits discussed earlier in this book. Once allocated, ITQs can then be bought and sold among individuals. As a market-based instrument, ITQs complement the privatization of fisheries.

Fishing quotas may entice companies to engage in practices that run counter to the objective of stock conservation. The practice of highgrading involves catching more than the quota allows, selecting the most valuable fish among the catch, and dumping the less valuable fish (many of them dead or dying) back into the sea. In other words, the catch exceeds the landings.

Another problem with quotas is bycatch—the harvest of fish other than the targeted species. What happens with bycatch depends on its marketability and parallel quotas. A boat that has a quota for the main catch but no quota for the bycatch will dump the bycatch.

The choice of fishing method has important environmental consequences.

- **Trawling** is where a ship (or a pair of ships) pulls a conical fishing net behind. Bottom trawling occurs on the sea floor, whereas midwater trawling occurs through free water. Trawling has been criticized for its lack of selectivity and high volume of bycatch. Bottom trawling can also destroy marine habitat on the sea floor.
- **Trolling** involves pulling one or more baited fish lines behind a boat. Bait can be lures or bait fish that attract the fish they are meant to catch. The design of the bait can make trolling much more selective than trawling.

- **Longline fishing** is a variation of trolling where the line pulled behind the boat (the main line) is very long and short branch lines (snoods) carry hooks. Longline fishing has been associated with the incidental catching and killing of seabirds, sea turtles, and sharks.
- **Seine fishing** involves an encircling dragnet that hangs vertically in the water. With a purse seine, the bottom of the net can be closed after a school of fish has entered, and thus cannot escape. Because seine nets are much smaller than trawl nets, they can be used more selectively.
- **Gillnetting** is one of the most effective capture methods. Gillnets are typically suspended vertically in a straight line and entrap fish primarily through the mesh slipping behind the gills when they try to free themselves after slipping halfway through the mesh. Gillnets can be designed in terms of mesh size, twine strength, and deployment depth so that the incidence of bycatch can be reduced significantly. Gillnets are used quite effectively in the Pacific salmon fisheries. Unfortunately, gillnets used in tuna fishing are prone to entrapping whales and dolphins.

There are economic and environmental trade-offs involved in each of these major fishing methods. Trawling is less expensive than other methods but is associated with higher environmental damage. Fisheries regulators can ban certain practices where environmental damage is significant, and mandate alternative practices.

One of the thornier issues in fisheries management relates to the migratory behaviour of fish. Whereas property rights can be managed well within national boundaries, fish do not respect national boundaries. In open waters they swim as they please. Managing fisheries across boundaries is often a challenge even among friendly neighbours. Box 11.5 discusses the ongoing dispute about salmon fisheries in the Pacific Northwest between the United States and Canada.

Coordination among multiple countries is perhaps even more challenging than coordination between two neighbours. The European Union maintains a *Common Fisheries Policy* (CFP) that sets quotas for individual member states and different species of fish, based on the TAC and a percentage share for each country. Each member state is responsible for allocating its quota to domestic producers, and for monitoring compliance. The CFP has often been criticized for encouraging wasteful practices, such as discarding unwanted dead fish into the sea. Such wasteful discards are sometimes reckoned to account for a quarter of total catches. The European Parliament revised the CFP in 2013. Starting in 2015, the principle of maximum sustainable yield will apply to setting the TAC.

The failure of high seas fisheries management in past decades to preserve fish stock has led to a quest to identify and adopt 'best practices' that focus more on conservation of fish stock than on commer-

Box 11.5: The Canada-US Pacific Salmon Dispute

Pacific salmon freely move around the North Pacific Ocean, and do not respect international boundaries. During their migration through coastal waters, US fishermen intercept salmon of Canadian origin, and Canadian fishermen intercept salmon of US origin.

There are distinct subspecies (sockeye, chum, pink, chinook, coho) that exhibit different migratory patterns while at sea. Sockeye, chinook, and coho are the most valuable species. After spending 1–5 years at sea, Pacific salmon return to their ancestral streams in order to spawn in the summer of their last year at sea. While travelling upstream in rivers, they stop feeding and instead draw on body fat. The fish arrive at the gravel beds where they were spawned, reproduce, and die soon afterwards. Most harvesting takes place when the fish return to their ancestral streams.

Management of the Pacific salmon is a joint responsibility of Canada and the United States. The two countries signed the *Pacific Salmon Treaty* in 1985 to preserve the stock and divide the harvest between them. International maritime law attributes ownership to the country where the salmon were spawned. Therefore, the treaty's objective was for each country to 'conduct its fisheries and its salmon enhancement programs so as to: prevent overfishing and provide for optimum production; and [...] to receive benefits equivalent to the production of salmon originating in its waters.' However, disputes remain about the appropriate formula to divide the catch. The two countries augmented the 1985 treaty with the 1999 *Pacific Salmon Agreement*. Both countries agreed to set aside the dispute about an equitable division of the harvest and instead focus on implementing a new abundance-based harvesting regime that would restore and maintain a healthy salmon population. Specifically, the agreement constrained the total allowable catch; US fishermen may take no more than 16.5% of (Canadian) Fraser River sockeye.

While adopting an abundance-based management approach promotes conservation of the salmon stock, disputes may reemerge about abundance estimates. Such disputes could be mitigated if Canada and the United States relied more on independent third-party scientific research similar to arrangements between Russia and Norway about the Barents Sea fisheries. The two countries could also cooperate through the introduction of side payments to ensure an equitable balance. A model for this cooperation is Iceland's North Atlantic Salmon Fund. This endowment fund receives contributions from Icelandic fishing companies and pays fishing companies in other jurisdictions not to fish their allocated quota. If imbalances occur between accumulated catches in the United States and Canada, each country could be allowed to acquire transferable fishing quota from the other country and license them to local fishing operations.

cial production. Suggested reform of fisheries management includes ecosystem-based management (EBM) combined with the precautionary approach (PA). The starting point of EBM is the systems approach to managing fisheries: acknowledging the interdependence of different fish species and other sectors of the marine ecosystem. Therefore, fisheries activities and catch limits must be designed so that they do not compromise or harm the overall marine ecosystem. The precautionary approach supplements the EBM approach. This approach starts with acknowledging the biological uncertainties about fish populations when determining total allowable catch. The precautionary approach focuses on long-term implications of fisheries activities. Both approaches require substantially more data about ecosystem interactions and more sophisticated modelling of long-term dynamics. On a practical level, EBM/PA approaches include the following best practices:

- redefining maximum sustainable yield targets in terms of rebuilding fish spawning stock by keeping fishing effort somewhat below the MSY;
- defining trigger points for fishing bans in terms of historical minimum or average biomass of a particular species, or below a predetermined proportion of the carrying capacity;
- introducing access control systems (for fishing areas, seasonal time periods, fishing gear, etc.);
- reducing bycatch and discards by shifting fishing seasons, imposing minimum allowable fish size, imposing mesh/hook size requirements, and requiring training for safe handling techniques that reduce the mortality of discards;
- protecting habitat through regulating bottom fisheries and particularly vulnerable marine ecosystems, as well as monitoring water pollution; enforcement within territorial waters;
- reducing overcapacity of fishing fleets through fleet-capacity management schemes;
- eliminating the use of subsidies (fuel, buy-backs, etc.) that lead to overfishing;
- improving monitoring and enforcement through real-time observation, vessel monitoring systems, and catch documentation schemes that identify the origin of fish and document the legality of fish at the point where they are landed—and thus preventing or reducing illegal fishing;
- building sustainable fisheries communities by taking social equity into account when allocating fisheries rights or quotas.

Consumers are increasingly aware of the risks of overfishing and demand that their supply of fish meet standards of appropriate stewardship. To provide the certification demanded by consumers, private intermediaries such as the Marine Stewardship Council have

Box 11.6: Chilean Sea Bass

Chilean sea bass is a trade name used in North America for Patagonian toothfish, a deepwater species that lives in the cold waters of the southern oceans. (Patagonia is the southern tip of South America, shared by Chile and Argentina.) Patagonian toothfish is popular with consumers because of its texture and flavour. Illegal and unregulated overfishing around the turn of the millennium led to a near-collapse of these fisheries. The species is particularly vulnerable because it is long-lived (up to 50 years) and slow to mature (taking 10–20 years).

Established through an international convention in 1982, the Commission on the Conservation of Antarctic Marine Living Resources (CCAMLR) has been given responsibility for managing the fisheries activities in the CCAMLR convention area, which spans the Antarctic continent and southern oceans. The convention area is divided into three statistical areas: area 48 for the Atlantic sector (up to 50°S; area 58 for the Indian sector (up to 55°S and 45°S); and area 88 for the Pacific sector (up to 60°S). The CCAMLR's approach to fisheries management is based on the precautionary principle.

The magazine *Nature* reported in its 22 August 2011 edition that Chilean sea bass certified as 'green' by the Marine Stewardship Council (MSC) may not deserve this certification. The MSC maintained that some (but not all) populations of Patagonian toothfish can be harvested sustainably. The MSC certified a fishery around South Georgia and the South Sandwich Islands in 2004. But a study by marine biologists found a significant amount of mislabelling. Some of the fish sold with an MSC certification did not come from the certified fishery, while others were not even Chilean sea bass. *Seafood Watch*, a guide to sustainable seafood published by the Monterey Bay Aquarium in California, recommended that consumers avoid the fish. Some retailers followed this recommendation and removed Chilean sea bass from their shelves.

Despite the challenges, countries have made progress suppressing illegal, unregulated, and unreported catches in the CCAMLR convention area. In April 2013, *Seafood Watch* started listing Chilean sea bass sourced from the Falklands, Heard & McDonald Islands and Macquarie Island as 'best choice.' However, *Seafood Watch* also lists sea bass sourced from Argentina as 'avoid.'

Controversies about certification will continue. Environmental groups challenge certification standards, especially where the certification process relies too much on voluntary contributions by the fishing industry and too little on independent third-party auditing.

developed—and continue to develop—standards for meeting fish stock conservation goals. This process is not always easy and may sometimes be fraught with controversy, as the example of the Chilean sea bass fisheries demonstrates. Box 11.6 discusses this case.

11.4 Summary

Managing resources involves balancing economic interests with environmental consequences. Mining activities are associated with a significant local environmental footprint in terms of land and water use, as well as risks of contaminating soil, groundwater, and surface water with chemicals used in the process of mining or refining minerals and metals. Renewable resources such as forest and fisheries face the risk of excessive and unsustainable use. Overfishing and deforestation are often the result of insufficient or poorly enforced property rights.

The optimal path of extraction of a non-renewable resource follows the Hotelling rule. To maximize the value of the resource stock, resource extraction follows a path where the price of the resource increases at the rate of interest (or intertemporal discount rate). This ensures that, at the margin, a unit extracted is valued the same as a unit left in the ground for future extraction. This simple 'r-percent rule' is modified to allow for the discovery of new resources through (costly) resource exploration, technological progress in mining technology, and heterogeneity in the quality of resource deposits. The Herfindahl principle of resource extraction suggests that resource deposits are extracted in reverse order of marginal cost: the lowest-cost deposits are extracted first, and the highest-cost deposits are extracted last. According to the Hartwick rule, royalties (economic rents) from resource extraction should be saved in sovereign wealth funds for the benefit of future generations; royalties should not be used solely for the consumption benefit of the current generation.

Forest management involves optimizing forest rotation through appropriately managed tenure systems. Public policy plays a crucial role in maintaining property rights over forested land and ensuring that logging practices are in line with good stewardship and stay within sustainability limits.

Fisheries management is mostly concerned with creating and enforcing property rights because of the common access dilemma. The creation of exclusive economic zones to a 200 nautical mile limit from shore was crucial for protecting coastal fisheries. Enforcement remains a problem in remote areas and impoverished countries. Many industrialized nations have developed either individual or collective property right sharing mechanisms, such as *individual transferable quotas* and community-based *territorial use rights in fisheries*.

11.5 Study questions and exercises

1. The Hotelling rule predicts that resource prices rise continuously. However, this prediction conflicts with the empirical reality. Which improvements of the Hotelling model can explain the observed relative flatness of resource prices?
2. What is a 'backstop technology,' and how does it affect resource industries? Explain the related idea of the 'green paradox.'
3. What should societies do if they wish to follow the Hartwick rule? Compare public policy in Norway and Alberta.
4. How do different public policies influence recycling? Which approach is more effective under which conditions?
5. Which factors influence the economically-optimal rotation period of a forest according to the Faustmann rule? How is the marginal benefit of letting a forest continue to grow equated with the marginal benefit of cutting a forest now?
6. What is the difference between the Hartman rotation period and the Faustmann rotation period? Which additional issues are taken into account?
7. Which type of taxes distorts the decision about the optimal rotation period? Which type of tax should governments use?
8. Which innovations and technologies have improved the environmental performance of the pulp and paper industry?
9. What lessons have been learned from the collapse of the Atlantic cod fisheries? Which fisheries management practices have been developed to deal with overfishing?

Exercises

1. Mines are often owned by multinational corporations. What happens after they shut down an operation and leave the country? Does your province or state have rules in place to ensure that owners of mines carry out proper site remediation?
2. Research the environmental risks to the forests in your region, province, or state. Identify natural and anthropogenic factors and try to find out from statistical sources if your local forests have diminished over recent decades. Find out if your local forest companies have adopted sustainability 'best practices' and participate in forest stewardship certification.

Chapter 12
Environmental Management for the Next Thousand Centuries

This book opened with a discussion of the key environmental issues that afflict our world today, defining the notion of sustainability along the way. The book continued drilling down into the practices of environmental management, from economic and legal principles, through managerial approaches, down to the level of abatement technologies and energy system choices. It makes sense to come full circle and conclude with a perspective on how environmental management feeds into achieving sustainability and keeping our planet habitable for the generations to come. An ancient proverb of North America's native communities tells us:

> Treat the earth well:
> it was not given to you by your parents;
> it was loaned to you by your children.
> We do not inherit the earth from our ancestors;
> we borrow it from our children.

There is profound wisdom in this proverb. If our species is to survive, we need to think and plan ahead not just for our children and our grandchildren, but for all the generations that are meant to follow us.

This book would like to end on an optimistic note. The environmental problems of this planet are all intrinsically manageable. What it takes to manage them is the political will to tackle them and an economic system that propagates the correct economic incentives to limit or eliminate environmental damage. The crucial step is putting appropriate prices on negative environmental externalities, whether on water, sulfur dioxide emissions, or greenhouse gas emissions. Technology, and technological innovation, will follow these price signals.

The true test of sustainability is our civilization's ability to endure. But for how long? What exactly is the time horizon? And once we have established a reference time frame, how can we manage our resources and our energy supply for that duration? Two physicists have written an insightful book on this topic, Bonnet and Woltjer (2008). This chapter's heading pays tribute to the book's title *Surviving 1,000 Centuries*. Bonnet and Woltjer (2008) is the foundation for this chapter because it asks the right question: does our planet have sufficient resources to continue our civilization at its current size and at a high level of economic prosperity? Or are we running out of resources and doomed eventually to fall back to a level of mere subsistence? The good news is: the physical constraints on our civilization's long-term survival are not insurmountable. The bad news is: the greatest risk to humanity's endurance is—you guessed it—humanity itself. To make our civilization survive, we need to move steadily towards a higher level of planetary-scale ecological governance, and we must develop more mature and peaceful ways of resolving conflicts among nations.

12.1 The time horizon

Discussions about sustainability often diverge about the desirable end point: the steady state of society at some future point in time. Usually, little time is spent on the time horizon of the process. How long should society spend in the transition phase to the steady state, and how long is the steady state meant to last? These are both crucial questions, and the literature is remarkably silent on both.

The time horizon of policy-makers is quite short, and indeed most people do not think decades ahead either. We may worry about our children and grandchildren, but what about their children and grandchildren, and generations thereafter? The time horizon of most policy documents is in the range of a few years, and occasionally a few decades. Forecasting the state of the world even a decade into the future is tremendously error-prone. The debate about the different climate change scenarios is a good illustration. Climate change scenarios can vary greatly in outcome depending on assumptions about key parameters. Even small changes to parameters can result in large cumulative changes over a time horizon of a few decades. The difficulty of prognosticating the future is made even more complicated by the inherent non-linearities of many physical processes, which involve trigger points and abrupt state changes.

Anyone who talks about sustainability has to come clear eventually about the time horizon. Is 'sustainable' defined as keeping humanity alive and well for another hundred years, or a thousand years, or even longer? The implicit assumption is that, after a transition period, humanity can survive indefinitely. But can we?

If physical constraints are involved, what is the realistic time frame for the duration of a civilization? In evolutionary terms, homo sapiens reached its anatomical features only about 200,000 years ago, and full behavioural modernity only about 50,000 years ago. Our species turned from hunter-gatherer societies to sedentary agriculture only about 12,000 years ago by domesticating plants and animals. Recorded civilization commenced only a few thousand years ago, and modern industrial civilization is barely two centuries old. Considering evolutionary time scales, a tperiod of one hundred millennia is a reasonably long period for human civilization on this planet. If humanity manages to survive that long, perhaps the prospects are good that we (or our genetically evolved descendants) will manage to survive much longer time scales, on this planet or beyond.

12.2 Population growth

The most critical parameter in any model of our planet's future is the number of people living on it. Too few people, and economic prosperity will diminish (because larger populations allow for more economic specialization); too many people, and the strain on the biosphere leads to shortages of various kinds and potentially irreparable damage. Where is the 'sweet spot' of population size?

The 20th century witnessed unprecedented population growth: the planet's population rose from about 1.6 billion to 6 billion. World population surpassed 7 billion in 2012. The cartogram in figure 12.1 illustrates that the population on the planet is rather unevenly distributed. Population densities vary significantly across countries. The cartogram resizes the countries so that their area reflects the population size. Thus, the two most populous countries, China, and India, stand out. Sparsely populated countries such as Canada and Russia have shrunk to become nearly invisible on the cartogram.

What governs population growth is the birth rate and the death rate, shown in figure 12.2. During the 20th century, mortality declined fast along with the development of medicine and pharmaceutics (which includes the development and use of antibiotics and vaccines). This rapid decline in the death rate was not matched by a rapid fall in birth rates. Birth rates remained high, and thus there was a widening gap between birth and death rates, in particular in developing countries. This promoted rapid population growth in these countries. Only in the last three decades has population growth slowed down as birth rates trend downwards.

Fertility determines birth rates, although they are not the same. Whereas the birth rate captures the number of children born in a year as a share of the total population, the fertility rate captures the number of children an average woman is likely to have during her childbearing years (15-49). Around 2010 the world reached the point where half of humanity will be having just enough children to replace itself. The fertility rate of half the world will be below the replacement level of 2.1 at which population growth stabilizes. (This rate is slightly higher in poor countries with higher infant mortality rates.) Fertility has declined significantly in the last three decades.

Figure 12.3 shows that there is a close connection between fertility (and thus birth rates) and per capita income. Fertility drops as afflu-

Fig. 12.1 Cartogram of World Population

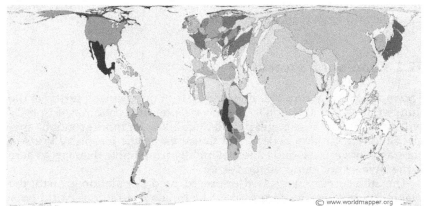

Image © SASI Group (University of Sheffield) and Mark Newman (University of Michigan). Licensed under Creative Commons conditions. The size of each territory shows the relative proportion of the world's population living there. The world map has been transformed into an equal-area cartogram, also known as a density-equalizing map.

Fig. 12.2 Trends in Birth and Death Rates of Developing and Developed Countries

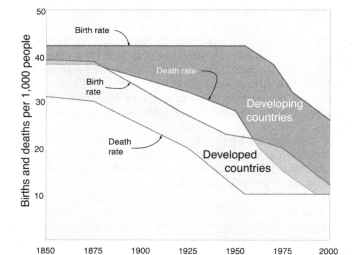

Adapted from World Bank information; stylized representation for developing and developed nations.

Fig. 12.3 Fertility Drops as Affluence Rises

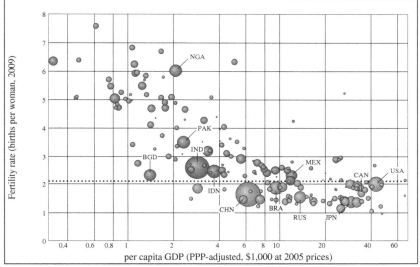

Note: Countries with a population over 100 million people are identified by their ISO 3166 country codes. The volume of the bubbles is proportional to the population of each country. The dotted line indicates the replacement rate of 2.1.

ence rises. This link makes economic sense. In agrarian societies, parents favour extra pairs of hands to help them; the benefit of an extra pair of hands outweighs the extra cost of feeding an extra mouth. And when the parents retire, more children will be better able to look after them. As income rises, however, farmers start replacing labour with capital, and the need for extra children diminishes. Higher living standards also make investment in children more attractive, as more education is linked to higher incomes. Having to pay for the education of fewer children is becoming more attractive. The state may also provide a pension, which may obviate the need to rely on children for one's retirement.

The empirics in figure 12.3 emphasizes the underlying economic logic. At a per capita income level of about $1,000–$2,000, fertility starts dropping and keeps falling until it reaches the replacement level at about $5,000–$10,000. Very affluent countries have fertility rates that are below replacement level (implying negative population growth). The income-fertility link also exists within countries where there are large income gaps.

12.3 Survival challenges

Assuming that humanity manages to stabilize its population at a sustainable level, perhaps around the 10 billion mark, our civilization still faces numerous existential challenges.

The first challenge is manmade. It may well be the most significant obstacle to our long-term survival. Can we avoid war and develop more peaceful ways to resolve conflicts? The 20th century was full of conflict all around the world, with the Second World War standing out as the most deadly episode. It has been estimated that during the second world war over 60 million people were killed, roughly 2.5% of the world population. Civilian deaths due to military activity and crimes against humanity, which includes the victims of the Holocaust, were the majority of the casualties. Considering all natural and manmade catastrophes during the 20th century, deaths due to war accounted for roughly two-thirds, epidemics for about 20%, and famines for about 10%. The possibility of large-scale military conflict in the 21st century cannot be ruled out as humanity has not freed itself of nationalistic, religious, or ideological fanaticism. A large-scale nuclear war would certainly spell the end of our civilization.

Even if humanity manages to mature and eschew warfare, can we control the risk of diseases and widespread epidemics? According to the World Health Organization, the two leading causes of death around the world are cardiovascular diseases and communicable diseases (along with nutritional deficiencies and maternal/prenatal conditions), both at about 30% of total deaths. The 20th century saw enormous progress in medicine, in particular, the development of antibiotics and vaccines. The key question is whether scientific research will be able to stay ahead of the evolution of micro-organisms that adapt to existing antibiotics or vaccines and render them ineffective. As pandemics cross borders easily, especially in a highly interconnected world, containing the outbreak of diseases has become increasingly difficult. The most devastating pandemic in human history, the Black Death that spread across Europe between 1348 and 1350, is estimated to have killed more than half of Europe's population, which took over 150 years to recover. Even in the 20th century, more than 50 million people (more than 3% of the world population at the time) fell victim to the Spanish flu pandemic

If humanity manages to keep diseases at bay, will average life expectancy continue to increase? The oldest humans on record have reached ages of around 120 years. As the human body deteriorates with age, it is unlikely that human longevity can be stretched much beyond the 100–120 mark. However, if technologies emerged that prolonged life expectancy significantly, this would have important implications for the steady-state population that the planet would be able to accommodate. If life expectancy doubled from 75 to 150 years, for example, population size would need to shrink by half in order to maintain the same ecological footprint.

Beyond war and disease lie a variety of natural dangers, both terrestrial and extraterrestrial in origin. Can we outlive catastrophes such as asteroid impacts and exceptional earthquakes? Today, scientific consensus maintains that an asteroid impact around 65 million years ago led to mass extinction of species, including the dinosaurs. The geological record of this episode is the Cretaceous-Paleogene boundary, which carries a high concentration of iridium that is abundant in asteroids and meteorites. The risk of asteroid impacts, especially from so-called Near-Earth Objects (NEOs) with orbits that cross Earth's orbit, remains real. The US space agency, NASA, has been tasked with cataloguing all NEOs that could pose a hazard to Earth. As of 2012, over 800 NEOs with a diameter larger than 1 km have been found, although none of them poses a danger over the course of the next century. Predicting the orbits of NEOs is difficult over long time horizons as orbital parameters shift due to the gravitational influence of other solar system bodies. If a NEO ever posed a real threat, technological solutions are at hand to deal with it. With years of warning, a space probe could be deployed that provides a gentle gravitational tug to correct the orbital path of the asteroid. Humanity does possess the ability to avert catastrophic asteroid impacts with global consequences, although smaller asteroids may yet slip through the net and lead to significant but locally confined damage.

Earthquakes (which may trigger tsunamis) and volcanic eruptions are a terrestrial source of risk. There is a log-linear relationship between the frequency and magnitude of earthquakes, known as the Gutenberg-Richter law. Earthquakes that reach magnitude 9.0 on the Richter scale are considered exceptional. The magnitude 9.1 earthquake in the Indian Ocean, off the west coast of northern Sumatra in Indonesia, in December 2004 triggered a massive tsunami, killing over 230,000 people in fourteen countries.

Volcanoes also pose a significant threat. The intensity of eruptions is measured on the Volcanic Explosivity Index (VEI) scale. Volcano eruptions of magnitudes 7 and 8 are known as super-colossal and mega-colossal events. Their eruption plumes can reach 40 km or even 50 km into the stratosphere, and the eject volume (which defines the VEI scale) exceeds 100 km^3 and 1,000 km^3, respectively. A magnitude 7 event is expected to occur less than once every 1,000 years, and a magnitude 8 event less than once every 10,000 years. The largest recorded volcano eruption, the explosion of Indonesia's Mount Tambora in 1815 killed over 70,000 people and caused the 'year without a summer' in 1816. The explosion of Krakatoa, another Indonesian volcano, in 1883 killed more than 36,000 people and caused a five-year volcanic winter. Mount

Tambora and Krakatoa were magnitude 7 and 6 events on the VEI scale, respectively.

The science of predicting earthquakes and volcanic eruptions is still in its infancy. The large death toll of the recent earthquakes in Indonesia and Japan bears witness to that fact. Terrestrial hazards of this type have a significant impact on local populations and in the case of volcano eruptions also affect agricultural production around the world for years thereafter. However, even in worst-case scenarios, humanity is expected to survive.

12.4 Long-term power sources

Chapter 10 on energy systems discussed the availability of energy sources over the next decades. It is also quite feasible to investigate the long-term availability of energy sources. The first question is: how much energy would we need to satisfy the demands of a steady-state population of 11 billion people? There will be two countervailing effects over the next decades. On one side, the still growing world population and the convergence of per capita incomes will lead to an increase in energy demand. On the other side, technological progress will improve energy efficiency and thus reduce energy demand. It is likely that the first effect will outweigh the second, however, if people in poorer countries are catching up to the level in developed countries. Taking 11 billion people who consume 2,000 Exajoule (EJ) per year (roughly seven times our current level) amounts to an energy flow of 63 Terawatt (TW). So every instant, the world's future energy system would need to be able to deliver 63 TW. Table 12.1 summarizes the potential of competing energy sources to contribute to this energy supply.

After the discussion in chapter 10, it is obvious that fossil fuels will be exhausted in a few centuries at most. The era of fossil fuels is a short-lived phenomenon on a 100,000-year time scale.

There are a number of energy sources that will provide minor or intermediate contributions to the total energy supply. Ocean tides and waves, hydroelectricity, and geothermal energy will have limited potential due to their overall low energy density (per surface area). These sources are concentrated in favourable locations: rivers in the case of hydroelectricity, volcanic areas for geothermal energy, and coastal regions for ocean waves and tides. Realistically, these sources will not be able to provide more than perhaps 5% or 10% of the world's energy needs.

The availability of biofuels will remain limited unless there is a major scientific breakthrough that increases production efficiency, such as the use of algae. Production of biofuels competes with the use of arable land for agricultural purposes, so increasing the supply of biofuels reduces

Table 12.1 Long-Term Potential for Energy Sources

Energy Source	Potential	Problems
Fossil fuels	exhausted	exhausted in 50-250 years
Ocean tides and waves	minor	low energy density
Geothermal	minor	low energy density except for favourable locations
Hydroelectricity	minor	limited number of useful sites
Biomass	minor	limited size of arable land; competition with agricultural use
Wind	intermediate	suitable locations; wind farm density; intermittency and storage
Nuclear (fission)	intermediate	uranium limited, thorium more plentiful; radioactive waste
Nuclear (fusion)	large	technology still hypothetical
Solar photovoltaic	large	some key materials are rare; transmission and storage
Solar thermal	large	nothing insurmountable (transmission and storage)
Space solar	unlimited	cost

the supply of food. This is an inescapable trade-off, and the production of food should obviously take precedence.

Wind energy has a much larger potential, especially if offshore locations are taken into account. A key problem for wind energy is the remoteness of favourable locations. This in turn requires effective long-distance transportation. Conversion of electricity into transportable and storable (liquid) hydrogen is a suitable form of intermediation. Another key problem with wind energy is its intermittency. On a global scale this matters less because the wind always blows somewhere. Overall, wind energy could perhaps contribute 10% to 20% of the world's energy need.

Nuclear fission has significant potential as an energy source during the transition phase to a long-term steady state. The current reactor designs, which are based on a uranium cycle, produce radioactive waste that requires secure storage for millennia. Dealing with this waste is one challenge. Another challenge is the limited supply of uranium. Conventional reserves of uranium would suffice for only a tiny fraction of the 100,000-year period. Even mining uranium from unconventional sources such as seawater would increase this period to a few thousand years at best. Thorium, another radioactive material, provides a much better option. It is more abundant, and the radioactive waste is less than for uranium due to a shorter half-life. Thorium-based nuclear fission could potentially last for a significant part of the 100 millennia.

Nuclear fusion offers even more potential, but at this point is an unproven technology. It is likely that science will overcome the technological hurdles in the decades or centuries to come. The key ingredients in nuclear fusion are deuterium and tritium. Deuterium, the heavier cousin of hydrogen, is abundant; heavy water makes up 0.01% of ocean water. Tritium is a radioactive isotope of helium that does not occur naturally; it has a half-life of only 12 years. However, tritium can be produced by striking lithium with neutrons. Known reserves of lithium only suffice for about 12,000 years, but it is conceivable to extract lithium from ocean water. Nuclear fusion could therefore provide a significant part of the world's energy supply if it could be fully developed.

Solar energy provides the largest potential for the world's energy supply. As our Sun will last for a few billion more years, there is no shortage of primary energy. It is merely a matter of converting solar radiation into useful energy on planet Earth. Solar thermal installations convert solar radiation into heat, which in turn drives conventional turbines. This is a proven technology that can be readily deployed on a large scale. The remaining challenge is to make this process more efficient and cost effective, and deal with the intermittency problem. Photovoltaic cells offer the potential for higher efficiency than thermal installations, but they require rare materials such as gallium and indium. Unless more common materials can be employed, the large-scale use of photovoltaics may remain limited. Nevertheless, both types of solar energy taken together have the potential of satisfying all the energy needs of the planet for an indefinite period. As with wind energy, the intermittency and transportation problems can be overcome through the use of hydrogen as an intermediary.

The last step would be to take solar energy from space, where the available capture area is practically unlimited and solar irradiation is stronger as well as uninterrupted. Transporting the energy back to Earth can be accomplished through microwave beams. This option is conceivable, but current rocket technology is not able to lift the required loads into space at a reasonable cost. It would require significant innovations in space-lifting technology to make this option commercially viable. Nevertheless, such advances are entirely plausible during the 21st century. SpaceX, an entrepreneurial company founded in 2002 and headquartered in California, is developing reusable launch vehicles that will reduce the cost of accessing space considerably.

12.5 Long-term mineral resources

What is truly finite on our planet is the availability of mineral resources. We have to live within the means provided, even if futuristic exercises such as mining asteroids may eventually supplement our terrestrial stock. But expanding the sphere of resource exploration beyond our solar system remains the realm of science fiction.

The proven resources only capture what is commercially viable at current resource prices. Rising resource prices will help discover and explore yet unknown resources. The good news is that, over the course of the 21st century, it is highly unlikely that the world is going to run into any major resource constraints. Nevertheless, temporary shortages or local shortages may arise along with price spikes. The question arises how the picture changes over the course of a hundred millennia. The starting point for the analysis is to assess the relative abundance of elements in the air, sea water, and the Earth's crust. On the demand side, it is difficult to forecast the composition of materials that may be used in the millennia to come, and thus a useful starting point is current use of these substances multiplied by an appropriate scalar factor (7) that allows for the rest of the world's population to catch up to the current use in industrialized countries.

Technologically, extracting basic elements from sea water is possible but energy intensive. As large-scale desalination of sea water may be needed in future centuries anyhow, the resulting brine could be harvested for about ten different basic minerals. It is also technologically feasible to extract the main and trace gases that occur in our atmosphere.

Iron and aluminum are the most essential elements for industrial society. Fortunately, iron accounts for about 4% of the Earth's crust, and in basalt (volcanic rock) it is about twice as abundant. Aluminum is slightly less abundant. A planetary annual demand of 4,000 Megatonnes (Mt) of iron would require processing 50,000 Mt of crustal rock at 8% abundance. In 100,000 years, this amounts to 15% of the Earth's land surface to a depth of 1 km, an enormous amount, but not inconceivable. Taking the baseline of 50,000 Mt of rock per year, what else is abundant, and what is not? Bonnet and Woltjer (2008) draw several conclusions:

1. The principal elements needed in fertilizers for agriculture (potassium, phosphorus, and nitrogen) are sufficiently abundant. Nitrogen can be obtained from the atmosphere. The ingredients needed for life are readily available; life would not have evolved if such elements were rare.
2. While iron itself is plentiful, its industrial use combines iron with other materials to produce alloys (e.g., steel) that have a variety of desirable properties (e.g., strength, corrosion resistance). The main elements needed for such alloys (manganese, cobalt, chrome, vanadium, and nickel) are available in sufficient quantities, but tungsten, zinc, and tin are not.
3. Copper is a basic element in the electrical industry, but its availability falls short by an order of magnitude (a factor of 10). The electron-

ics industry also utilizes a variety of heavy elements such as gold, silver, and antimony; these would also be in short supply.

4. The elements known as 'rare earths,' which include lanthanum and cerium, belie their name and are actually relatively abundant in the Earth's crust. They are used in catalysts, electrical motors and magnets, glass manufacture, and other applications. (Current shortages are mostly driven by economic factors, not resource constraints.)

5. Several heavy elements are used to catalyze chemical reactions in industry and in pollution control. The platinum group of elements, rhenium, and others, would be in short supply.

Table 12.2 summarizes the key findings and provides an overview of the abundance or scarcity of basic chemical elements over a 100,000-year period.

Table 12.2 Long-Term Resource Abundance and Scarcity

Mineral/Material	Abundance	Source
Magnesium, calcium, potassium, natrium, chlorine, sulfur	abundant	sea water
Nitrogen, oxygen, argon, neon, krypton, xenon	abundant	air
Silicon, calcium, aluminum, gallium	abundant	earth's crust
Iron, chromium, cobalt, platinum-group elements, mercury, arsenic, rhenium, selenium, tellurium, uranium	intermediate	basaltic rock
Copper, zinc, molybdenum, gold, silver, tin, lead, bismuth, cadmium	scarce	Earth's crust

The above scenario does not consider the potential for recycling. Materials are not really lost; most of them can be recycled. For example, the above calculations were based on processing 50,000 Mt of rock per year. If 80% of materials were recycled, the need for processing would drop to 10,000 Mt of rock per year. With 90% recycling, it drops to 5,000 Mt, and so forth. Even under more favourable assumptions about recycling, some materials will remain scarce. The need to promote material efficiency and recycling is paramount for time horizons of millennia.

12.6 The sustainability agenda

The ultimate test of sustainability on a planetary scale is our civilization's ability to survive a length of time that is on an evolutionary scale. The 100,000-year time scale proposed by Bonnet and Woltjer (2008) is entirely plausible, although one may hope that our civilization will endure for longer. Perhaps by then we will have also learned if we are alone in the universe. This is perhaps one of the most fascinating unanswered questions in human history. The fact that we haven't heard anything from other civilizations in the galaxy yet raises important questions about humanity's place in the universe. The Fermi paradox is the apparent contradiction between estimates of a high probability that other extraterrestrial civilizations exist and the lack of evidence of their existence. As the Italian nuclear physicist put it: 'If the universe is teeming with aliens, where is everybody?' Scientists are divided about the answer. A book by another physicist, Webb (2002), examines the competing hypotheses about the Fermi paradox.

What does the existence of alien civilizations tell us about our own planet's ability to endure? If we happen to find extraterrestrial civilizations in the future, chances are that we can learn from their experience and technologies, which should help us on our course to prolong our own species' survival. However, if we do not find any other civilizations, it makes our own planet even more special, and should bolster our desire to keep our civilization going. Our failure would not be assuaged by the success of other civilizations across the galaxy. Our own civilization's failure would spell the end of all knowledge.

Philosophical contemplations about our place in the universe do not necessarily help us with our challenges today. Our own time horizon is measured in decades, not millennia. What is in our power to do today? What are the crucial steps to set us on the right track to our civilization's long-term endurance?

Limiting population growth

Perhaps the most important number in any model of civilization and sustainability is the size of our population. Unprecedented population growth during the 20th century increased the world's population in 2012 to about 7 billion. Current projections suggest that the world population will continue to increase for some time, but that a gradual decline in the birth rate will stabilize world population at a level of about 10-11 billion by the middle of the 21st century.

What is the optimal population level for our planet? Is 10 billion sustainable? If yes, could our planet sustain even more people indefinitely? If no, what population is sustainable in the long term? Agricultural production is likely to be able to sustain 10 billion people indefinitely on our planet. However, there is an upper limit for the number of people due to the constraint on land that can be put to agricultural use. Stabilizing our planet's population requires a continuing drop in birth rates, and empirical evidence tells us that birth rates drop as per capita income rises. Lifting poor nations out of poverty may well be the most effective route to stabilizing the planet's population.

Stabilizing global warming

Climate change due to the emission of greenhouse gases from burning hydrocarbons, as well as the contribution from indirect effects, may have drastic consequences for the habitability of various regions onf our planet. The processes underlying climate change are complex, and the inherent non-linearities and trigger point effects make forecasts difficult. The emerging scientific consensus points to the dangers from climate change, as rising temperatures eventually will melt the Arctic and the ice sheets on Greenland and Antarctica. The problem is that these processes may be practically irreversible if the planet's climate is locked into a warmer state. Whereas getting to a tipping point may only take a hundred years, reversal of the effects may take centuries or even millennia.

If we take climate change seriously, we need to act swiftly to limit greenhouse gas emissions. This requires going after the low-hanging fruit first: replacing coal with natural gas and pursuing energy conservation aggressively. For some time, we may need to rely on transition technologies such as nuclear energy, particularly as newer generations of nuclear technology promise to be safer and cheaper than their predecessors. Even after Fukushima, nuclear energy will have a role to play if we want to limit greenhouse gas emissions quickly.

In the long term, our civilization needs to cut its dependence on fossil fuels and move into renewable energy. There are only two viable inexhaustible supplies of energy: solar and geothermal. The accessibility of geothermal energy may remain limited due to low overall energy density across the planet, but in those places where it is feasible, it can make significant contributions. Solar energy—and this includes second-order sources such as wind, tidal, and hydro power, as well as biofuels—has a truly unlimited potential. While the second-order solar energy sources such as hydro and wind all face natural limitations, they are among the first that are commercially viable. Solar energy is virtually inexhaustible. The potential for solar-thermal and photovoltaic installations is enormous, and the ultimate prospect of space-based solar power opens an entire new frontier that is virtually limitless.

Management of finite resources

Earth is a (nearly) closed system. The exception is the solar irradiation that we receive, which provides the energy supply for renewable resources. However, most resources are exhaustible. There is only a finite supply of them on Earth. As flawed as the 1972 report of the Club of Rome on the *Limits to Growth* was (it ignored economics and technological progress), the fact remains that certain types of resources are ultimately limited. Eventually, we will run down our stock of fossil fuels.

The ultimate question is what happens with finite, exhaustible resources in a closed system. Where do they go? In the case of fossil fuels, they get transformed through combustion into useful energy and greenhouse gases. Many other resources get used and discarded, but they remain potentially accessible. The key to managing the existing inventory of finite resources is to keep them circulating. This requires a high level of recycling, and ultimately near-perfect recycling. It also requires a gradually increasing level of material efficiency: doing the same with less finite resources.

Do finite resources limit economic growth? Economic growth does not only measure increases in material output. It captures goods and services, and services do not necessarily need a growing supply of finite resources as an input. More fundamentally, what does it take to produce goods and services? From a production function perspective, the answer is physical and human capital, energy, resources, and—last but not least—people (labour). Some of these production factors are derived from more basic inputs. The most basic inputs are renewable energy, exhaustible resources, and information (knowledge). Only one of these three inputs is finite. There are no physical bounds to energy or knowledge. So while the world economy will have to make do with a shrinking supply (or fixed inventory) of exhaustible resources, there are no physical constraints on the growth of knowledge and energy use. As long as knowledge and energy can be used as substitutes for finite resources, economic growth is not limited. The notion that economic growth is incompatible with sustainability is false. The choice is not between zero (non-positive) and positive economic growth; it is about the right kind of positive economic growth. 'Good' economic growth is one that reduces our use of unrecycled finite resources; i.e., growth that promotes material efficiency and energy efficiency. 'Bad' economic growth rests on an expansion of exhaustible resources. If our society can come to terms with the notion of what is exhaustible, what is renewable, and what is potentially limitless (knowledge, energy), the prospects for continued economic growth are strong. Environmentalism that advocates a return to pre-industrial society is misguided. Do we really want to return to a living standard with high levels of illnesses and make do without the amenities of modern life? The *reductio ad absurdum* of misguided environmentalism writes humankind out of existence: no humankind means no human-made environmental damage. Positive environmentalism seeks ecological governance that protects our biosphere and our exhaustible resources from unsustainable use.

Towards global ecological governance

Natural resources and the biosphere can be viewed as global public goods, goods that are non-rivalrous and non-excludable. Civilization has struggled with protecting public goods. The lack of ownership plays an important role. For example, overfishing is often the result of poorly defined or poorly enforced ownership rights. It is the tragedy of the commons. Coordination of environmental policies among countries remains slow and ineffective. This governance deficit calls for a new form of ecological governance. Ecological governance is not merely about the role of governments; rather, it emphasizes the systems approach to environmental management that involves all elements and activities of society. One way to define it is as follows:

Ecological governance is a set of policies and institutions that achieves sustainability: the long-term survival of our civilization and our biosphere. Ecological governance implies close coordination of environmental policies on a global scale.

Global ecological governance requires both governments and markets. In some ideological circles on the political left and the political right, it is fashionable to promote a false dichotomy. One side argues that governance requires only governments because of the apparent failure of markets to price environmental externalities and prevent environmental degradation. This side sees no or little role for markets. The opposing side argues that markets will solve all environmental issues as long as property rights are allocated correctly, and that the myopia of governments makes them unsuitable to be left dealing with environmental issues that require a long-term planning horizon. The truth lies in between. We need governments to establish and implement environmental policies, standards, and property rights. We also need functioning markets to propagate appropriate price signals throughout the economy and help achieve efficient outcomes. It would be naïve to assume that governments or markets alone suffice to deal with the problems ahead.

The example of climate change is a key example that demonstrates that the world is facing an ecological governance deficit. The difficulty of organizing a planetary-scale response to climate change is evident. Countries and their governments cannot agree on reduction targets or the path to achieve them. The resulting response may be too little too late, and as the window of opportunity for climate change mitigation policy is closing, it leaves the burden of coping with the effects of climate change to adaptation policy.

Ecological governance on a planetary scale requires an unprecedented level of cooperation among countries and governments because many—and the most important—of our environmental issues are on a planetary scale. Most governments deal with local issues, and their time horizon is limited due to electoral cycles or other political processes. Supranational institutions such as the United Nations have limited authority and must build broad consensus. There is no easy solution to the ecological governance deficit. Strengthening supranational institutions means relinquishing national sovereignty to some extent, and this takes much time and effort and trust-building. Building the 28-nation European Union took many decades, and despite economic hiccups and political setbacks, Europe is a better place for the cooperation that the European Union has fostered in many policy areas—particularly those concerning the environment. On a global scale, the road to cooperation remains bumpy and progress will be slow, but the alternative is irreversible damage to our ecosystem and our biosphere.

On the path to a higher level of cooperation—and ultimately global ecological governance—science and education will play a key role. Science delivers the understanding of how our planet works and what we need to do to live successfully within the physical constraints of our planet and its biosphere. Education turns scientific knowledge into broad awareness, which lays the foundation for the political choices of societies and their governments.

The environmental challenges that we face in the 21st century are daunting but not insurmountable. Environmental management—a system of tools and approaches to achieve desirable environmental outcomes—combined with the necessary environmental governance that guides the deployment of these tools and approaches can overcome the challenges and help us achieve economic prosperity while preserving our environment for future generations. The future is bright—if individuals, businesses, and governments live up to their responsibilities towards future generations. For businesses, environmental management is not a luxury, but a necessity and a social responsibility.

12.7 Study questions

1. Which economic processes drive birth and death rates? Why are they different for developed and developing countries? What are the implications for population growth in the 21st century?
2. Is economic growth limited?
3. What are the major (natural and manmade) challenges for the long-term survival of our species?
4. Which energy sources can we rely on in the long term?
5. How can we deal with the physical limitations of natural resources?
6. Explain the concept of 'ecological governance.' What are the obstacles to achieving it?

Appendix A
Reference Tables

Table A.1 Orders of Magnitude

Symbol	Prefix	Factor	Textual Form	Symbol	Prefix	Factor	Textual Form
da	deca-	10^1	ten	d	deci-	10^{-1}	one tenth
h	hecto-	10^2	one hundred	c	centi-	10^{-2}	one hundreth
k	kilo-	10^3	one thousand	m	milli-	10^{-3}	one thousandth
M	mega-	10^6	one million	μ	micro-	10^{-6}	one millionth
G	giga-	10^9	one billion	n	nano-	10^{-9}	one billionth
T	tera-	10^{12}	one trillion	p	pico-	10^{-12}	one trillionth
P	peta-	10^{15}	one quadrillion	f	femto-	10^{-15}	one quadrillonth
E	exa-	10^{18}	one quintillion	a	atto-	10^{-18}	one quintillionth
Z	zetta-	10^{21}	one sextillion	z	zepto-	10^{-21}	one sextillionth
Y	yotta-	10^{24}	one septillion	y	yocto-	10^{-24}	one septillionth

Table A.2 Metric System

Dimension	Unit	Symbol	Equivalence
Length	metre	m	
Area	square metre	m^2	
Volume	cubic metre	m^3	
	litre	l	$1{,}000l = 1m^3$
Weight	gram	g	$1{,}000g = 1kg$
Time	second	s	
	hour	h	$3{,}600s = 1h$
	day	d	$1d = 24h = 86{,}400s$
Velocity	metres per second	m/s	$1km/h = 3.6m/s$
Flow rate	cubic metres per second	m^3/s	
	million litres per day	MLD	$1m^3/s = 86.4$ MLD
Pressure	pascal	Pa	$1{,}000Pa = 1kPa$
Energy	joule	J	$10^6J = 1MJ$
Power	watt	W	$1{,}000W = 1kW$
Temperature	kelvin	K	
	degrees Celsius	°C	$[K] = [°C] + 273.15$
Current	ampere	A	
Voltage	volt	V	

Table A.3 Energy Units and Their Conversion

	MJ	GJ	kWh	Btu
1 MJ =	1	0.001	0.2778	947.78
1 GJ =	1000	1	277.8	947,777
1 kWh =	3.60	0.0036	1	3,412.1
1,000 Btu =	1.0551	0.00105	0.292	1,000

Table A.4 Common Metric and Imperial Units and Their Conversion

	barrels	gallons	litres
1 barrel (oil) =	1	42	158.9873
1 US gallon =	0.02381	1	3.78541
1 litre =	0.00629	0.264172	1

	metres	km	feet	miles
1 metre	1	0.001	3.2808	0.0006214
1 kilometre (km)	1,000	1	3280.8	0.6214
1 foot	0.3048	0.003048	1	0.000189
1 mile	1,609.344	1.609344	5280	1

	cm	mm	inches	mils
1 centimetre (cm)	1	10	0.3937	393.7
1 millimetre (mm)	0.1	1	0.03937	39.37
1 inch	2.54	25.4	1	1,000
1 mil	0.00254	0.0254	0.001	1

Bibliography

Alberini A, Kahn JR (eds.) (2009) Handbook on Contingent Valuation. Edward Elgar

Benidickson J (2008) Environmental Law, 3rd ed. Irwin Law

Berthelot S, McGraw E, Coulmont M, Morrill J (2003) ISO 14000: Added value for Canadian business? Environmental Quality Management 13(2): 47–57

Bishop PL (2004) Pollution Prevention: Fundamentals and Practice. Waveland Press

Boardman A, Greenberg D, Vining A, Weimer D (2010a) Cost-Benefit Analysis, 4th ed. Prentice Hall

Boardman AE, Moore MA, Vining AR (2010b) The social discount rate for canada based on future growth in consumption. Canadian Public Policy 36(3): 323–341

Bonnet RM, Woltjer L (2008) Surviving 1,000 Centuries: Can We Do It? Springer-Praxis

Boustead I (1993) Ecoprofiles of the european plastics industry, reports 1-4. Tech. rep., PWMI, European Centre for Plastics in the Environment, Brussels

Boyle G, Everett B, Ramage J (eds.) (2003) Energy Systems and Sustainability. Oxford University Press

BP (2011) BP energy outlook 2030. Tech. rep., British Petroleum (BP), London, published online, updated annually

Brander JA, Taylor MS (1998) The simple economics of Easter Island: A Ricardo-Malthus model of renewable resource use. American Economic Review 88(1): 119–138

Cameron TA (2010) Euthanizing the value of a statistical life. Review of Environmental Economics and Policy 4(2): 161–178

Canadian Medical Association (2008) No breathing room: National illness costs of air pollution. Tech. rep., Canadian Medical Association

Christensen J, Park C, Sun E, Goralnick M, Iyengar J (2008) A practical guide to green sourcing. Supply Chain Management Review 12(8): 1521–9747

Clark CW (2006) The Worldwide Crisis in Fisheries: Economic Models and Human Behaviour. Cambridge University Press

Davis ML, Cornwell DA (2008) Introduction to Environmental Engineering, 4th ed. McGraw-Hill

Esty DC, Winston A (2006) Green to Gold: How Smart Companies Use Environmental Strategy to Innovate, Create Value, and Build Competitive Advantage. Yale University Press

Field BC (2008) Natural Resource Economics: An Introduction, 2nd ed. Waveland Press

Field BC, Olewiler N (2011) Environmental Economics, 3rd ed. McGraw-Hill

Gaudet G (2007) Natural resource economics under the rule of hotelling. Canadian Journal of Economics 40(4): 1033–1059

Goodstein ES (2010) Economics and the Environment, 6th ed. Wiley

Goulder LH, Parry IWH (2008) Instrument choice in environmental policy. Review of Environmental Economics and Policy 2(2): 152–174

Hammer MJ, Hammer, Jr MJ (2012) Water and Wastewater Technology, 7th ed. Prentice-Hall, Boston, MA

Hanna KS (ed.) (2009) Environmental Impact Assessment: Practice and Participation, 2nd ed. Oxford University Press

Hart SL (2007) Beyond greening: Strategies for a sustainable world. In: Harvard Business Review on Green Business Strategy, Havard Business School Press, pp 99–123

Harvard Business Review (ed.) (2007) Harvard Business Review on Green Business Strategy. Havard Business School Press

Head G (2012) Defining and measuring sustainability. Review of Environmental Economics and Policy 6(1): 147–163

Horiuchi R, Schuchard R, Shea L, Townsend S (2009) Understanding and preventing greenwash: A business guide. Tech. rep., BSR and Futerra

Hotelling H (1931) The economics of exhaustible resources. Journal of Political Economy 39(2): 137–175

Kaplan PO, DeCarolis J, Thorneloe S (2009) Is it better to burn or bury waste for clen electricity generation? Environmental Science & Technology 43(6): 1711–1717

Kitzmueller M (2008) Economics and corporate social responsibility, eUI Working Papers ECO 2008/37

Levant E (2011) Ethical Oil: The Case for Canada's Oil Sands. McClelland and Stewart

Lyon TP, Maxwell JW (2011) Greenwash: Corporate environmental disclosure under threat of audit. Journal of Environmental Economics and Management 20(1): 3–41

MacKay DJ (2009) Sustainable Energy—Without the Hot Air. UIT Cambridge

Makower J (2009) Strategies for the Green Economy: Opportunities and Challenges in the New World of Business. McGraw-Hill

Manget J, Roche C, Münnich F (2009) Capturing the green advantage for consumer companies. Tech. rep., Boston Consulting Group

Margolis JD, Elfenbein HA, Walsh JP (2009) Does it pay to be good ... and does it matter? A meta-analysis of the relationship between corporate social and financial performance, social Science Research Network Paper No. 1866371

McKinsey (2009) Pathways to a low-carbon economy: Version 2 of the global greenhouse gas abatement curve. Tech. rep., McKinsey & Company

McKitrick RR (2011) Economic Analysis of Environmental Policy. University of Toronto Press

McWilliams A, Siegel D (2000) Corporate social responsibility and financial performance: correlation or misspecification? Strategic Management Journal 21: 603–609

Mendelsohn RO, Hellerstein D, Unsworth R, Brazee R (1992) Measuring hazardous waste damages with panel models. Journal of Environmental Economics and Management 22: 259–271

Mitchell B (ed.) (2010) Resource and Environmental Management in Canada: Addressing Conflict and Uncertainty, 4th ed. Oxford University Press

Mogren A (2007) The climate threat: Can humanity rise to the greatest challenge of our times? (conclusions from vattenfall's climate survey). Tech. rep., Vattenfall

Moore MA, Boardman AE, Vining AR (2013) More appropriate discounting: the rate of social time preference and the value of the social discount rate. Journal of Benefit-Cost Analysis 4(1): 1–16

de Nevers N (2000) Air Pollution Control Engineering, 2nd ed. Waveland Press

Noble BF (2006) Introduction to Environmental Impact Assessment: A Guide to Principles and Practice. Oxford University Press

Nordhaus WD (2007) A review of the Stern Review on the economics of climate. Journal of Economic Literature 45(3): 668–702

Nordhaus WD (2012) Why the global warming skeptics are wrong. The New York Review of Books

Nordhaus WD (2013) The Climate Casino: Risk, Uncertainty, and Economics for a Warming World. Yale University Press, New Haven, CT

Perman R, Ma Y, McGilvray J, Common M (2003) Natural Resource and Environmental Economics, 3rd ed. Addison Wesley

Pindyck RS (2013) The climate policy dilemma. Review of Environmental Economics and Policy 7(2): 219–237

Prakash A, Potoski M (2006) The Voluntary Environmentalists: Green Clubs, ISO 14001, and Voluntary Environmental Regulations. Cambridge University Press

Rees WE, Wackernagel M (1994) Ecological footprints and appropriated carrying capacity: Measuring the natural capital requirements of the human economy. In: Jansson AM, Hammer M, Folke C, Costanza R (eds.) Investing in Natural Capital: The Ecological Economics Approach to Sustainability, Island Press, Washington, pp 362–390

Roberts MJ, Spence M (1976) Effluent charges and licenses under uncertainty. Journal of Public Economics 5: 193–208

Rubin J (2009) Why your world is about to get a whole lot smaller: Oil and the end of globalization. Random House

Saaty TL (1980) Analytic Hierarchy Process: Planning, Priority Setting, Resource Allocation. McGraw-Hill, New York and London

Salzman J, Thompson BH Jr (2010) Environmental Law and Policy, 3rd ed. Foundation Press

Sinn HW (2008) Public policies against global warming. International Tax and Public Finance 15(4): 360–394

Slade ME, Thille H (2009) Whither Hotelling: Tests of the theory of exhaustible resources. Annual Review of Resource Economics 1: 239–260

Small A, Graff Zivin J (2004) A modigliani-miller theory of altruistic corporate social responsibility. BE Journals in Economic Analysis and Policy: topics in Economic Analysis and Policy 5: 1–19

Solomon S, Qin D, Manning M, Marquis M, Averyt K, Tignor MM, Miller Jr HL, Chen Z (eds.) (2007) Climate Change 2007 – The Physical Sciences Basis. Cambridge University Press

Stern N (2006) Stern Review on the Economics of Climate Change: Executive Summary. Her Majesty's Treasury, London

Stern N (2007) The Economics of Climate Change. Cambridge University Press, Cambridge and New York

Tietenberg TH (2006) Emissions Trading: Principles and Practice, 2nd ed. Resources For the Future Press, Washington, DC

Tietenberg TH (2013) Carbon pricing in practice. Review of Environmental Economics and Policy 7(2): 313–329

Turner D (1970) Workbook of atmospheric dispersion estimates. Tech. rep., United States Environmental Protection Agency, Washington, DC, report AP-26

United Nations Environment Programme (1991) Caring for the Earth: A Strategy for Sustainable Living. Earthscan Publications

van der Ploeg F, Withagen C (2012) Is there really a green paradox? Journal of Environmental Economics and Management 64(3): 342–363

Viscusi WK (1996) Economic foundations of the current regulatory reform efforts. Journal of Economic Perspectives 10(3): 119–134

Vogel D, Toffler M, Post D, Aragon NZU (2010) Environmental federalism in the european union and the united states. Tech. rep., Harvard Business School, working Paper 10-085

Webb S (2002) If the Universe Is Teeming with Aliens—Where Is Everybody? Fifty Solutions to the Fermi Paradox and the Problem of Extraterrestrial Life. Springer-Praxis

Woodard & Curran, Inc (2006) Industrial Waste Treatment Handbook, 2nd ed. Butterworth-Heinemann, Burlington, MA

Xu TT, Sathaye JA, Kramer KJ (2012) Bottom-up representation of industrial energy efficiency technologies in integrated assessment models of the u.s. pulp and paper sector. Tech. rep., Environmental Energy Technologies Division, Lawrence Berkeley National Laboratory

Yergin D (2011) The Quest: Energy, Security, and the Remaking of the Modern World. Penguin Press

Index

33/50 program, 65

abatement, 237, 238
abatement ladder, 72
absorption, 241, 242, 253
accident prevention, 187
accountability, 143
acid mine drainage, 339
acid rain, 136, 149
Acid Rain Program, 86
acid rock drainage, 185, 338, 339, 341
activated carbon, 253, 260
activated sludge, 267, 270, 349
adaptation policy, 47, 378
additionality, 87
adjusted net savings, 12
administrative agreements, 127
adsorption, 241, 242, 253, 257
adverse effects, 117, 164, 177
aeration, 270
aerobic decomposition, 272
affluence, 367
afforestation, 89
air bubble curtain, 44
Air Canada, 88
air leakage, 321
air pollution
    abatement technologies, 241
    ambient concentration, 58
    control, 241
    dispersion, 238
    health impact, 239
    hot spots, 38
    overview, 237
air quality control regions, 134
air quality health index, 239, 260
air sparging, 178
air-to-cloth ratio, 249
Airbus A380, 317
algae, 262, 311, 370
allergenicity, 119
allowance reserve, 78
alternating current, 315
aluminum, 329, 336, 373
Amazon forest, 92
amicus curiae, 154, 156, 157

ammonia, 253, 256, 261, 262, 272, 273
    stripping, 273
amortization, 303, 320
Anaconda Mining, 185
anaerobic decomposition, 272, 273, 275
analytic hierarchy process, 175
animal habitat, 347
annual allowable cut, 347
annual environmental statement, 143
anoxic decomposition, 272
anthracite, 33, 319
antimony, 374
Apple, 204
AQHI, *see* air quality health index
aquaculture, 351, 352
aquifer, 36, 294
    contamination, 296
Arctic
    melting, 48, 376
    oil exploration, 294
    permafrost, 48
ARET program, 65
arsenic, 179
asbestos, 139
assessment boundaries, 169
assimilative capacity, 56
asymmetric information, 226
attached growth, 270

backstop resources, 8
backstop technology, 8, 328, 330, 334,
    336
bacteria, 262
baghouse, 248
Bakken formation, 296
ballasts (electrical), 320
bankruptcy, 147
basalt, 373
Base-Level Industrial Emissions
    Requirements, 128
Basel Convention, 149
baseline scenario, 107
batteries, 206
bauxite, 329, 337
bedrock principle, 146
benchmarking, 318

benthic life, 341
benzene, 126, 254
Betz's Law, 308
Bhopal disaster, 232
BHP Billiton, 185
binary cycle, 312
bioaccumulation, 57, 58, 260, 349
biocapacity, 10
biochemical oxygen demand, 138, 261,
    269, 272, 283, 349
biodiesel, 309
biodiversity, 13, 148, 184, 342
bioethanol, 309
biofilm, 271
biofuels, 309, 310
    ethanol, 310
    from algae, 311, 370
    potential, 310
    trends, 311
bioleaching, 340
biomagnification, 57, 58
bioreactor landfill, 283
bioremediation, 178
biosphere, 378, 379
birth rate, 365
bitumen, 129, 295
Black Death, 368
black liquor, 349
blackwater, 37
BLIER, see Base-Level Industrial
    Emissions Requirements
BOD, see biochemical oxygen demand
Body Shop, 213
Boeing 787, 317
bottom ash, 284
bottom liner, 280
BP, 233
brand exposure, 16
branding, 213
Brazil, 310
BrigthSource Energy, 307
brine, 269
Brittania copper mine, 185
brownfield, 148
Brundtland Report, 5, 6, 12
BSI Management Systems, 193
bubbler, 250
buffer zones, 177
building design, 321
bulk water exports, 126

Bureau of Land Management, 340
Bureau of Land Reclamation, 95
business ethics, 183
bycatch, 356

CAAQS, see Canadian Ambient Air
    Quality Standards
cadmium, 179, 206
CAFE, see Corporate Average Fuel
    Economy
California Environmental Quality Act, 163
Canada-United States Air Quality
    Agreement, 149
Canada-US Organic Equivalence
    Arrangement, 215
Canadian Ambient Air Quality
    Standards, 127
Canadian Council of Ministers of the
    Environment, 126, 263
Canadian Environmental Assessment Act,
    121, 123, 127, 130, 163, 166
Canadian Environmental Assessment
    Agency, 121, 124, 130, 163, 166
Canadian Environmental Protection Act,
    121, 349
Canadian General Standards Board, 193
CANDU, 299
cap-and-trade, 49, 70, 73, 78, 79, 87
capital cost allowance, 86
carbon border adjustment, 159
carbon capture and storage, 50, 258, 304
carbon content, 159
carbon dioxide, 41, 45, 254, 258, 282,
    294, 297, 334, 336
carbon fertilization, 48
carbon leakage, 99
carbon monoxide, 38, 41, 80, 253, 254,
    259
carbon neutrality, 89
carbon offsets, 87–89, 191
    criteria, 87
    criticism, 89
    voluntary, 88
carbon pricing, 294
carbon sequestration, 87, 258
carbon sinks, 340
carbon tariff, 159
carbon tax, 49, 65, 80
carrying capacity, 5, 353
catalytic converter, 135

catch limits, 354
CCME, *see* Canadian Council of
    Ministers of the Environment
CCS, *see* carbon capture and storage
CEAA, *see* Canadian Environmental
    Assessment Act
CEPA, *see* Canadian Environmental
    Protection Act
CERCLA, *see* Comprehensive Environ-
    mental Response, Compensation,
    and Liability Act
certification, 155
CFC, *see* chlorofluorocarbons
chain of custody certification, 227
characterization, 108
chemical flocculation, 267, 269, 283
chemical oxygen demand, 263
Chicago Climate Exchange, 88
chief sustainability officer, 1, 182
chlorination, 273
chlorine, 106, 178
chlorine dioxide, 106
chlorofluorocarbons, 39
chrome, 373
citizen suit, 132
civil liability, 141
class action, 142
classification, 107
Clean Air Act, 86, 130, 131, 133–136, 165
Clean Water Act, 130, 132, 137–139
clear-cutting, 346
climate change, 32, 39, 44, 133, 258, 295,
    364, 376
  business responses, 51
  effects, 47, 295
  evidence, 45
  policies, 50, 376
  sources, 45
cloud computing, 209
coagulation, 269
coal, 294
Coase theorem, 60, 61, 75
cobalt, 373
COD, *see* chemical oxygen demand
code of conduct, 143, 182, 183, 190
cogeneration, 317
collective liability, 142
combined cycle gas turbine, 304, 319
combustion, 241, 253, 258

command-and-control, 65, 81, 131, 133,
    136
commerce clause, 130
Commission for Environmental
    Cooperation, 155
Common Fisheries Policy, 357
comparative advantage, 99
compensation, 177
complementors, 201
compliance, 194
compliance audit, 190, 193
compliance order, 147
composition effect, 99, 316
*Comprehensive Environmental Response,
    Compensation, and Liability Act*,
    130, 139, 145
Comprehensive Study List Regulations, 168
Concorde, 317
condebelt, 318
condensation, 241, 257
conductivity, 263
consistency index, 176
Constitution Act, 118, 120, 121, 124, 129
consumer surplus, 93
continental shelf, 149, 352
contingent valuation, 92–94, 147
continuous monitoring, 53
contractual terms, 211
*Convention on Lon-Range Transboundary
    Air Pollution*, 149
Convention on the Law of the Sea, 149, 151,
    352
conviction by indictment, 123
coolant, 298
copper, 185, 374
corn, 310
Corporate Average Fuel Economy, 69,
    81, 86, 135
corporate environmental strategy, 2, 200
corporate governance, 28
corporate social responsibility, 18, 226
  strategic, 23
corrosivity, 286
cost-benefit analysis, 90, 94, 187
Council on Environmental Quality, 165
cradle-to-cradle, 103, 277
cradle-to-grave, 103, 106
credence goods, 23, 226
credibility, 221
criminal law, 120

crisis management, 205
criteria pollutants, 133, 134
critical dilution volume, 108
CSO, *see* Chief Sustainability Officer
CSR, *see* corporate social responsibility
customs union, 153
cyanide, 232
cyclone, 242, 243, 246

DDT, 57
death rate, 365
decibels, 44
Deepwater Horizon, 224, 233
defendant, 141
deforestation, 342
deglobalization, 291
dehalogenation, 178
Delphi method, 170, 174
denitrification, 272, 273
Department of Agriculture, 214
Department of Energy, 307
Department of Fisheries and Oceans, 117
depensation, 353
depreciation, 301
depth filters, 248
derivative suit, 146
desalination, 37, 373
dilbit, 129, 294
dilution, 261
dioxins, 126, 128, 178, 254, 349
direct current, 315
direct measurement, 53
disc screens, 277
discount rate, 6, 8, 110, 302, 303, 332
    quasi-hyperbolic, 7
    social, 6, 7
discovery rate, 328
diseases, 368
disinfection, 273
dispersion model, 173
distribution
    empirical, 107
diversity index, 13
dose-response, 58, 64, 77, 238
double dividend, 18, 19, 67, 72
Dow Chemical, 317
Dow Jones Sustainability Index, 20
downwind distance, 238
dry sorbent injector, 251

dry stacking, 341
dry tailings, 341
due diligence, 143, 145, 194
dust, 243
duty to consult and accommodate, 129
dynamic efficiency, 77

e-waste, 40
E. coli, 262
E10, 310
E2 plan, 122, 188, 194, 231
E85, 310
earthquake, 369, 370
Easter Island, 9
eco-label, 21, 212, 214, 219
    graded, 215
    organic, 214
eco-scoring, 211
ecological capacity, 117
ecological deficit, 10
ecological footprint, 6, 9
ecological governance, 364, 377, 378
ecological reserve, 10
economic growth, 377
economies of scale, 125, 126, 206, 211, 278, 306, 331
economies of scope, 206
ecopoints, 109
ecoscoring, 109
ecosystem, 3, 4, 13, 14, 379
ecosystem-based management, 359
eddy current separator, 277
education, 367, 379
EEZ, *see* exclusive economic zone
efficiency, 60, 61, 67
    cost-benefit analysis, 96
    dynamic, 66, 81
    energy, 184, 290, 315–317
    fleet, 42
    material, 184
    operational, 42
    static, 66
effluent, 260
effort-yield curve, 353, 355
elasticity, 113
electric car, 334
electrostatic precipitator, 64, 242, 243, 246
elimination, 237
embedding bias, 94

emission concentration, 38, 239
emission factors, 53
emission intensity, 69
emission permit
    auction, 65, 75, 78
    banking, 76, 77
    borrowing, 76, 77
    grandfathering, 75
    trading, 77, 133
emission standard, 65, 69
emission tax, 65
Emissions Reduction Market System, 87
employment, 76
encapsulation, 178
end-of-pipe treatment, 118, 138, 241
Endangered Species Act, 156
energy
    audit, 319
    conservation, 34, 199, 313, 315
    efficiency, 85, 184, 290, 315–317
    geothermal, 312
    renewable, 304
    security, 290
    solar, 305
    storage, 33
    wind, 307
energy efficiency, 318
Energy Independence and Security Act, 136
Energy Policy and Conservation Act, 135
Energy Star, 86, 214, 316
Energy Tax Act, 136
engineering estimates, 53
ENGO, 132, 154, 214, 216, 219, 225
enhanced oil recovery, 33, 258, 331, 334
entropy, 13
Environment Canada, 121, 148, 188, 189, 239
environmental assessment, 165
environmental audit, 143, 190
environmental baseline, 170
Environmental Damages Fund, 148
environmental economics, 55
environmental emergency, 188
    recovery, 189
environmental emergency plan, 122, 188, 231, 234
environmental impact, 16
environmental impact assessment, 107, 109, 127, 129, 163, 164, 226, 309
environmental impact report, 163

environmental impact statement, 163, 165
environmental input-output analysis, 110
environmental justice, 62
environmental law, 116
    aboriginal rights, 129
    Canada, 118
    international trade, 153
    international treaties, 148, 150
    liability, 142
    litigation, 132
    polluter pays principle, 118
    principles, 116
    standards, 127, 133
    United States, 130
environmental load units, 109, 112
environmental management, 379
    definition, 2
    systems approach, 2, 3, 378
environmental management plan, 182, 184
environmental management system, 2, 51, 103, 143, 181, 190, 193
environmental policy
    hybrid, 68, 73, 77
    incentive, 65
    mandated, 65
    voluntary, 65
Environmental Protection Agency, 38, 91, 108, 131, 133, 165, 349
EPA, *see* Environmental Protection Agency
EPEAT, 204
equality, 61
equivalency agreement, 127
equivalency model, 108
error ellipse, 96
escalation ladder, 189
ethanol, 310
ethical oil, 224
Ethyl Corporation, 157
EU Emission Trading System, 87
European Climate Exchange, 87
eutrophication, 36, 172, 261, 262, 272
excavation, 179
excess emissions, 72
Exclusion List Regulations, 168
exclusive economic zone, 149, 352
excursions (WQI), 264

existence value, 91
export tax, 332
extraction rate, 328
Exxon, 233
Exxon Valdez, 224, 233, 234

fabric filters, 243, 248, 249
factor endowment effect, 99
fairness, 61, 67
Faustmann rotation age, 344, 346
Faustmann rule, 345
federal implementation plan, 134
federal state clause, 152
federalism, 125
feebate, 79, 81
feed-in tariff, 86
Fermi paradox, 375
fertility, 365, 367
FGD, *see* flue gas desulfurization
fiduciary duty of care, 146
filtration, 242
financial audit, 190
financial risk, 230
financing, 301
First Nations, 129
first-best approaches, 80
Fisher information index, 15
fisheries, 351
    bycatch, 356
    highgrading, 356
    management, 354
    maximum sustainable yield, 353
    overfishing, 56, 351
    techniques, 356
    total allowable catch, 354
    transboundary, 357
    under uncertainty, 355
Fisheries Act, 117, 120, 349
Fisheries and Oceans Canada, 121, 166
fixed-point scoring, 174
flash steam, 312
floc, 269
flocculation, *see* chemical flocculation
flue gas desulfurization, 256
fluidized bed, 284
fly ash, 284
foodweb, 57
*Forest Resources Conservation and
    Shortage Act*, 348
forest rotation, 342

forest stewardship, 346
Forest Stewardship Council, 205, 227
forestry, 340
    high-grading, 347
    management, 346
    optimal rotation, 342
    pulp mills, 349
    tenure systems, 347
fracking, 157, 275, 296, 323
Framework Convention on Climate Change,
    149
free riding, 59, 89, 94
free trade area, 153
freshwater, 34
FTA, *see* free trade area
FTSE4Good Index, 21
fuel consumption, 79
fuel economy, 218
fuel efficiency, 50, 64, 69, 81, 86, 110
fuel switching, 33, 34
fuel tax, 80
fume, 243
furans, 126, 128, 254, 349

gas guzzler tax, 136
gaseous pollutants, 238
gate fee, 282
Gaussian plume model, 238
General Agreement on Tariffs and Trade,
    149, 153, 348
genetically modified organisms, 119,
    174
genetically-modified organisms, 118
geo-exchange system, 312, 321
geo-sequestration, 258
geomembrane, 280, 339
geonet, 282
geothermal energy, 312
    enhanced (EGS), 312
Germany, 86
Giant Mine, 268, 341
Glen Canyon dam, 95
Global Footprint Network, 10
GMO, *see* genetically-modified
    organisms
gold, 374
Gordon-Schaefer model, 353
Grand Canyon, 95
grandfathering, 75
gravity settling chamber, 243

Great Bear Rainforest, 30
green branding, 213
green building, 320
green consumerism, 23, 65, 195, 359
green covenants, 211
Green Electronics Council, 204
green paradox, 335, 336
green price premium, 65, 206, 212, 213,
     219–221, 223
green products, 223
Green River formation, 296
green sourcing, 17, 195, 203, 209, 211,
     223
green tax reform, 72
green-tech sector, 86
greenhouse gases, 39, 282
greenwashing, 213, 226
     definition, 217
greywater, 37
Gros Morne National Park, 196
gross domestic product, 12
groundwater, 35, 178
gypsum, 256

halo effect, 223
harm, 117, 118
Hartwick rule, 333, 361
hauling, 282
hazard ranking system, 140
hazardous waste, 286
Health Canada, 228, 239
hearth incinerator, 285
heat exchanger, 319
heat pump, 312
heat recovery system, 321
hedonic regressions, 90
heliostats, 306
HEPA filter, 249
Herfindahl principle, 331, 361
high-grading, 346, 356
high-speed rail, 43
Holland's formula, 239
homo sapiens, 364
hot mix asphalt concrete, 44
hot spots, 38, 58
Hotelling rule, 330, 333, 361
Hubbert curve, 291
Hubbert's peak, 33, 291
Human Development Index, 12
hybrid cars, 80, 136, 206

hybrid regime, 68, 73, 77, 79
hydraulic fracturing, 312
hydraulic shearing, 312
hydraulic stimulation, 312
hydrocarbons, 41, 80
hydrogen sulfide, 254
hydrous pyrolysis, 295

ICE Futures Europe, 87
ice storm, 313
ignitability, 286
Ikea, 205
impact, 171
impact analysis, 104, 107, 109
impact indicators, 170
impact matrix, 170
impact prediction, 170
impact valuation, 108
improvement analysis, 104, 109
incineration, 253, 258, 277
incinerator
     designs, 284
     mass burn, 284
     refuse derived fuel, 284
     regenerative, 254
Inclusion List Regulations, 168
incomplete information, 60
incubators, 203
indemnity, 142, 148
Indian Act, 129
individual transferable quota, 60, 356
information asymmetry, 27, 65, 69, 70,
     85, 215
infrasound, 228
initial allocation, 75
injunction, 122
innovation, 81, 201, 202
     abatement, 82
     process, 203
     products, 206
innovation incentive, 78, 82, 83
input taxes, 66
input-output matrix, 111
insulation, 320
integrated coal gasification combined
     cycle, 259
integrated solid waste management,
     276
Intergovernmental Panel on Climate
     Change, 46, 225

intermittency, 33, 306, 309, 315, 323
internal rate of return, 98
International Boundary and Water
    Commission, 37
International Energy Agency, 85
International Institute for Sustainable
    Development, 157
International Joint Commission, 37, 152
International Organization for
    Standardization, 20, 103, 191
international trade, 99, 316
international trade law, 149
international treaties, 120, 148
    implementation, 150, 151
    ratification, 150, 151
International Tribunal for the Law of
    the Sea, 149, 152
Intertek Systems Certification, 193
interties (electric), 315
inventory analysis, 104, 107, 109
iron, 373
irreversibility, 4, 118, 147, 173
irrigation, 35
Island Copper Mine, 185
ISO 14000, 191
ISO 14001, 103, 181, 190, 191, 193, 195,
    197, 198, 211
    adoption decision, 194
    certification, 193, 194
    effectiveness, 197
    registrar, 193
ISO 14040, 103
ISO 14064, 88
ISO 26000, 20
Ivanpah solar power plant, 307

Jantzi Social Index, 20
Jevons paradox, 316
Johnson & Johnson, 231
joint review panel, 166, 167
jurisdiction
    federal, 120
    municipal, 125
    provincial, 124

kerogen, 295
KPMG Quality Registrar, 193
kraft process, 349
Kyoto Protocol, 149–151

La Jolla Agreement, 154

lagooning, 273
landfill bioreactor, 283
landfill gas, 282
landfill-gas-to-energy, 277, 285
landfilling, 277
leachate, 280, 283
lead, 179
Leadership in Energy and Environmen-
    tal Design, 320, 321
leakage, 88, 159
leaks, 16, 76, 145, 186, 339
LEED, see Leadership in Energy and
    Environmental Design
Leontief inverse matrix, 111
LEV, see low-emission vehicle
levellized energy cost, 302
liability, 145
    collective, 142, 190
    personal, 142
    strict, 140, 141
life cycle analysis, 103, 191, 209
    examples, 105, 110
    impact analysis, 107
    impact valuation, 108
    improvement analysis, 109
    inventory analysis, 106
    scoping, 106
life cycle costing, 109
life expectancy, 368
lifetime, 302, 303
light bulbs, 105
    compact fluorescent, 105
    fluorescent T8, 320
    incandescent, 105
lignite, 33, 319
lime slurry, 185
litigation, 132
    risk, 194
loading technique, 108
loss aversion, 93
low-emission vehicle, 135
lower explosive limit, 255

Malthusian limits, 9
manganese, 373
marginal abatement cost, 63–65, 69, 72,
    73, 85
marginal cost, 59
marginal damage, 64, 85
Marine Mammal Protection Act, 154

Marine Spill Response Corporation, 145
Marine Stewardship Council, 227, 359, 360
market failure, 56
mass balance, 53
mass burn, 284
material efficiency, 184, 374
maximum sustainable yield, 344, 353, 357, 359
McKinsey curve, 50, 318
membrane, 242
membrane bioreactor, 271, 274
mercury, 105, 126, 128, 206, 252, 254, 260
messaging, 223
methane, 39, 48, 49, 53, 272, 277, 282, 283
Methanex, 157
methanolysis, 310
methylmercury, 260
MFN, *see* most favoured nation
microfiltration, 274
microgeneration, 314
micropollutants, 123
microquakes, 296
mine water, 339
mining, 327
ministerial order, 122
mist, 243
mitigation policy, 47, 378
mixed liquor, 270
moderator (nuclear), 298
modification, 237
molten salt, 306
Montreal Protocol, 39, 149
moral hazard, 75
moratorium, 122
most favoured nation, 153, 159
multicyclones, 246
multinational enterprise, 27
municipal bylaws, 125
municipalities, 125

NAAQS, *see* National Ambient Air Quality Standards
nacelle, 308
NAFTA, *see* North American Free Trade Agreement
nanofiltration, 274
National Ambient Air Quality Standards, 133
national concern doctrine, 121

National Energy Board, 121, 123, 127, 166, 167
National Environmental Policy Act, 163, 164
National Forest Service, 340
National Highway Traffic Safety Administration, 136
National Park Service, 95
National Pollutant Discharge Elimination System, 137
National Pollutant Release Inventory, 65, 123, 261, 262
National Priorities List, 140
National Round Table on the Environment and Economy, 126
national treatment, 153, 160
natural gas, 294
    compressed (CNG), 43
    liquefied (LNG), 43
Natural Resources Canada, 121
negative externality, 56, 63
negligence, 140, 141
    criminal, 145
net metering, 314
net present value, 109, 329
net social benefit, 96
new source performance standards, 135
nickel, 373
nimbyism, 228, 229, 276
nitric oxide, 41
nitrogen, 258, 259, 261, 263, 269, 272, 273, 334, 373
nitrogen dioxide, 41, 240
nitrogen oxides, 38, 149, 238, 252, 256, 258, 260, 284
nitrous oxides, 80
noise pollution, 43, 289
non-attainment, 134
non-excludability, 59
non-rivalry, 59
North American Agreement on Environmental Cooperation, 155
North American Free Trade Agreement, 116, 149, 155
Northern Gateway pipeline, 129
NT, *see* national treatment
nuclear energy, 296, 371
    reactor designs, 298
    use, 300
nuclear fuel, 297–299

Nuclear Industry Indemnity Act, 148
nuclear waste, 299
nuisance, 141

Ocean Renewable Power Company, 325
oil, 290, 291
    enhanced recovery, 33
    pricing, 293
    reserves, 292, 293
    unconventional, 294
Oil Pollution Act, 145
oil price shocks, 290
oil sands, 37, 218, 295
oil shale, 295
old-growth forests, 346
Ontario Environmental Review
        Tribunal, 144
Ontario Power Authority, 86
OPEC, 329, 332
open access, 56, 354
operational risk, 230
optical sorting, 277
option value, 91
overburden, 339
overcompliance, 194
overfishing, 56, 227, 351
overshooting, 70
oxidation ditch, 271
oxyfuel method, 259
oxygen delignification, 351
ozone, 38, 41, 106, 149
    ground-level, 38, 240, 260
    water treatment, 273

P2 plan, 122, 186, 194
Pacific Carbon Trust, 89
Pacific Salmon Agreement, 358
Pacific Salmon Treaty, 358
packed tower, 251, 253
pandemics, 368
parallel plate separator, 268
Pareto efficiency, 61
Parks Canada, 196, 197
particulate matter, 38, 126, 238, 240
passive house, 321
passive solar heating, 321
PCBs, 178
peak oil, 291, 323
peak-load pricing, 313
per capita income, 365
performance audit, 190

permafrost, 48
permanence, 87
permit banking, 76, 77
permit borrowing, 76, 77
personal liability, 142
pH level, 185, 263, 264
phosphates, 172, 272
phosphorus, 261–263, 269, 272, 274, 287,
        373
photovoltaics, 306
phytoplankton, 262
phytoremediation, 178
Pigouvian principle, 64
Pigouvian tax, 64, 65
pine beetle, 349
pipeline, 169
    Keystone XL, 293
    Northern Gateway, 293
plaintiff, 141
Plasco Energy Group, 286
plasma gasification, 286
platinum, 374
plutonium, 298
point of purchase, 212
policy instruments, 63, 67
policy myopia, 378
political feasibility, 67
pollutants
    flow, 56, 172
    global, 58, 100
    local, 58
    regional, 58
    stock, 56, 172
    toxic, 286
    transboundary, 58, 126
polluter pays principle, 62, 117, 118,
        140, 144, 146–148
pollution abatement, 63, 64, 69
pollution haven effect, 99, 133
pollution prevention, 118, 121
    control measures, 187
    preventative measures, 187
pollution prevention plan, 122, 143, 186
polyethylene, 280
polyethylene terephthalate, 216
polymer, 185
polypropylene, 216
population growth, 9, 365, 367
potassium, 373
potentially responsible parties, 140

power curve, 308
precautionary approach, 359
precautionary principle, 118
preferences
    revealed, 88, 147
    stated, 90, 147
present bias, 7
price ceiling, 77, 78
price floor, 77
principal eigenvector, 176
priority substance list, 122
private information, 27
procurement, 209
product differentiation, 195, 201, 206
product stewardship, 103, 184, 202, 205,
    277
productivity, 52
project alternatives, 169, 174, 177
project lifetime, 110, 302, 303
property clause, 131
property rights, 56, 59, 61, 355
proppants, 312
prospect theory, 93
protectionism, 157, 158
protest answers, 93
PS10 solar power plant, 306
public goods, 59, 377
pyrolysis, 285, 286

QMI/SAI Global, 193
quality signalling, 216

r-percent rule, 330
radioactivity, 300
Ramsey equation, 7
rapping, 247
rare earths, 374
reactivity, 286
reagent, 249
rebound effect, 316, 317
recession, 78
reclamation, 173, 185, 339
record of decision, 165
rectenna, 307
recycling, 199, 276, 335, 374
    deposit-paid, 206
    economics, 278, 336
    household behaviour, 277
    industrial, 205
    labels, 216
    rates, 329

technology, 277
reforestation, 89
refuse derived fuel, 284
regenerative thermal oxidizer, 254, 258
Regional Environmental Emergencies
    Teams, 189
Regional Greenhouse Gas Initiative, 87
registration (ISO 14001), 193
regulatory exposure, 16
regulatory threat, 17, 24
relocation, 237
remediation, 140, 173
reputation, 17, 213
reserve price, 78
reserves-to-production ratio, 292
reshuffling, 100
resource
    conservation, 117
    depletion, 330
    exploration, 331
    stocks, 117
response bias, 94
restoration, 173, 189
revealed preference, 88
revenue neutrality, 80
reverse osmosis, 274
rhenium, 374
Richard's curve, 343
riparian rights, 142
risk, 230
    management, 230
risk assessment, 173
Risk-Screening Environmental Indicators,
    108
rotary kiln, 285, 286
rotating biological contactors, 271
RTO, *see* regenerative thermal oxidizer

salinity, 263
scalability, 211
scale effect, 72, 79
scarcity, 317
Schwarze Pumpe, 259
scoping, 106, 169
scrubber, 64, 242, 243, 249
seal of approval, 214
search goods, 24
second-best approaches, 80
self selection, 198
sensitivity mapping, 188

servicizing, 208, 210
settling tank, 269
shale gas, 33, 296
Shannon-Wiener diversity index, 13
Shell, 208, 224, 275
silver, 374
slag, 339
slippery slope, 81
sludge, 128, 274
smart appliances, 314
smart grid, 313
smart meter, 314
smog, 38, 41, 149
Society of Environmental Toxicology
    and Chemistry, 103
soil erosion, 8, 177
soil vapour extraction, 178
soil washing, 178
solar energy, 305
    photovoltaic, 306
    space-based, 307, 372
    thermal, 306
    trends, 309
solid waste, 276
    four Rs, 277
    hauling, 282
    hazardous, 286
    incineration, 284
    landfills, 280
    management, 39, 199, 276
    reduction, 276
    reusing, 276
    streams, 279
sovereign wealth fund, 333
sovereignty, 379
SpaceX, 372
Spanish flu, 368
spatial clustering, 58
spills, 76
spotted owl, 347, 348
spray, 243
spray chamber, 250, 253
spray dryer adsorber, 252
spray tower, 250
stabilization, 178
stack height, 238
stakeholders, 223
standard (legal), 58, 116
standard deviation, 107, 174
standard of living, 5

Standards Council of Canada, 193
state implementation plan, 133
stated preference, 90
steady state, 364
steam cracking, 295
Stern Review, 6, 7
Stokes' Law, 245
strategic bias, 94
strategic risk, 230
strategy space, 200
stressors, 108
strict, joint, and several liability, 145
stripper, 258
stumpage prices, 342
submarine tailings disposal, 341
subsidiarity principle, 125, 126
subsidies, 79, 317
    biofuel, 310
subsistence, 364
substitutability, 93
sugarcane, 310
sulfur dioxide, 38, 99, 136, 149, 249,
    251–254, 256, 284
summary conviction, 123
super grid, 315
superfund, 130, 139, 148
superinsulation, 321
supply chain, 209, 227
supranational institutions, 379
surface filters, 248
suspended growth, 270
sustainability, 4, 117, 364, 374
    definition, 6
    entropy-based, 15
sustainability portfolio, 201
synthetic crude oil, 295
systems approach, 2, 359

tailing ponds, 268, 341
tailings, 339, 341
take-back programs, 17, 40, 202
talc dust, 249
tariff, 310
taxation, 301
technique effect, 72, 79, 99, 316
technology standard, 65, 68
Teck, 183
temperature inversion, 38
temporal clustering, 58, 77
tenure system, 347

terminal settling velocity, 245
Terrachoice, 217
territorial use rights in fisheries, 355
territorial waters, 149
Tesla Motors, 43, 207
thermal desorption, 178
thermohaline current, 48
thorium, 298–300
thorium cycle, 323
threat of litigation, 194
tidal power, 325
tight gas, 296
Timberland, 212
time horizon, 363, 364
time-of-use metering, 314
tin, 373
tipping fee, 282
tort, 141
total allowable catch, 354, 356–358
toxic waste, 40
toxicity, 122, 286
Toxics Release Inventory, 65, 123
tradeable emission permits, 60, 65
trading volume, 76
traffic congestion, 80
tragedy of the commons, 56, 326, 352,
    378
Trans Mountain pipeline, 294
transaction costs, 60, 76
transboundary pollution, 58, 120
travel-cost approach, 90
tray scrubber, 250
tray tower, 250
treatment effect, 198
treatment walls, 178
trespass, 142
trophic level, 57
trust intermediaries, 222
tsunami, 369
tungsten, 373

ultrafiltration, 274
uncertainty, 65, 78, 85, 173, 230, 355
    price, 71, 78
    quantity, 70, 78
unconventional oil, 294
Unilever, 227
Union Carbide, 232
Union of Concerned Scientists, 225
United Nations, 148, 378

United Nations Development Program,
    12
United Nations Environment Program,
    103
unknown unknowns, 230
upgrader, 295
uranium, 297
use value, 91
utility, 93
utilization rate, 302

valuation
    revealed preference, 88, 147
    stated preference, 90, 147
value chain, 106
value of a statistical life, 91, 139
vanadium, 373
vapour, 257
Vattenfall, 50
vendor certification, 211
venturi scrubber, 250
verifiability, 88
Vienna Convention, 149
vintage effects, 203
virtual elimination, 122
viscosity, 248, 294
VOC, *see* volatile organic compounds
volatile organic compounds, 38, 41, 87,
    178, 252, 254, 256, 260, 282
volcano eruption, 369, 370

wage premium, 17, 91
war, 368
warning, 122
waste-to-energy, 205, 254, 277, 284, 285
wastewater treatment, 37, 264, 265
    primary, 269
    secondary, 270
    sludge, 274
    tertiary, 272
wastewater treatment plant, 137, 263,
    266, 287
water
    conservation, 37
    desalination, 37
    pollution, 260
        industrial, 268
        measurement, 263
        treatment, 264
        types, 261
    potable, 37

quality, 35
  index, 263
quantity, 35
stress index, 36
Water Quality Act, 130
weighted average cost of capital, 303
Westport Innovations, 43
white liquor, 349
willingness to accept, 92, 93
willingness to pay, 92, 93
win-win strategy, 203, 219, 315
wind energy, 307, 309, 323, 371
  trends, 309
wind farm, 309
World Bank, 12, 31
world economy, 32

World Health Organization, 368
world population, 32
World Trade Organization, 119, 149,
  152, 153
World Wildlife Fund, 227
WQI, *see* water quality index
WWTP, *see* wastewater treatment plant

Xerox, 208

Yemen, 35

zero-emission vehicle, 135
Zerofootprint, 88
ZEV, *see* zero-emission vehicle
zinc, 373

CPSIA information can be obtained
at www.ICGtesting.com
Printed in the USA
BVHW071326040221
599126BV00001B/1